beyond borders
web globalization strategies

John Yunker

New Riders

201 West 103rd Street, Indianapolis, Indiana 46290
An Imprint of Pearson Education
Boston ■ Indianapolis ■ London ■ New York ■ San Francisco

BEYOND BORDERS: WEB GLOBALIZATION STRATEGIES

International Standard Book Number: 0-7357-1208-5

Library of Congress Catalog Card Number: 2001094886

Printed in the United States of America

First Printing: August 2002

06 05 04 03 02   7 6 5 4 3 2 1

Interpretation of the printing code: The rightmost double-digit number is the year of the book's printing; the rightmost single-digit number is the number of the book's printing. For example, the printing code 02-1 shows that the first printing of the book occurred in 2002.

Trademarks

Warning and Disclaimer

Publisher
David Dwyer

Associate Publisher
Stephanie Wall

Executive Editor
Steve Weiss

Production Manager
Gina Kanouse

Managing Editor
Sarah Kearns

Development Editor
Lisa M. Lord

Project Editor
Michael Thurston

Product Marketing Manager
Tammy Detrich

Publicity Manager
Susan Nixon

Manufacturing Coordinator
Jim Conway

Cover Designer
Aren Howell

Interior Designers
Will Cruz
Suzanne Pettypiece

Compositor
Gloria Schurick

Proofreader
Linda Seifert

Indexer
Cheryl Lemmens

CONTENTS AT A GLANCE

TABLE OF CONTENTS

ABOUT THE AUTHOR

John Yunker

Over the past decade, John Yunker has worked as a writer, marketer, and web developer for such organizations as Pyramid Research, Harvard University, Foreign Exchange, and the Association for Computing Machinery (**www.acm.org**). It was his time at ACM that got him hooked on web globalization. Since then, he has developed web sites for a number of clients in a number of languages. He is a co-founder of Byte Level (**www.bytelevel.com**), a global intelligence company. He has a journalism degree from the University of Missouri and a master's degree in communication from Boston University. He can be reached at **jyunker@bytelevel.com**.

ABOUT THE TECHNICAL EDITORS

Ben Sargent

With 20 years in information technology, Ben Sargent has held executive positions and worked as a senior consultant in multilingual content management and e-business globalization; he is currently with Lionbridge. Ben has led publishing, technology, and strategy teams serving such companies as GE, Microsoft, Intel, Sun, Bloomberg, and many other Internet and IT companies. He has published, led workshops, addressed technology conferences in Europe and the U.S., and helped numerous Internet and Fortune 500 companies implement global web strategies, and has served as producer and executive producer for a number of award-winning web sites. Ben can be contacted at **Ben_Sargent@lionbridge.com**.

Eileen Sheridan

Eileen Sheridan is the Managing Director of the Web of Culture (**www.webofculture.com**), the leading Internet resource for web globalization. She is the former Web Globalization Manager for Siebel Systems and Novell, Inc., and has also worked in sales and marketing for Borland International and Xerox Corporation as well as program management for the Los Angeles World Affairs Council. Eileen is fluent in English and Spanish and has studied German, Italian, and Japanese. She currently teaches a course on web globalization management at UC Santa Cruz in Silicon Valley. Eileen can be contacted at **webmaven@webofculture.com**.

To Midge

ACKNOWLEDGMENTS

Web globalization is a team effort, and so too is this book. Thanks to all of you who contributed time, advice, and support over the years, and particularly those of you who were interviewed for this book. I also want to thank the many experts at the IETF, W3C, IANA, and the Unicode Consortium for creating a more globally friendly Internet.

I want especially to thank the technical reviewers, Ben Sargent and Eileen Sheridan. They devoted an enormous amount of time and energy to this project, and I am grateful for their wisdom and their very high standards.

At New Riders, I'd like to thank Karen Whitehouse, for getting everything started, and Jennifer Eberhardt and Victoria Elzey for their vision and for guiding me patiently through the process. And I owe a great deal of thanks to Lisa Lord for her amazing attention to detail, tireless enthusiasm, and for asking all the right questions.

Finally, I wish to thank my family for their support and patience as I spent the past year chained to my computer. Thank you Mom, Dad, Chris, Sarah, Lana, Dave, Jack, Caroline, Beck, and, of course, Midge.

A MESSAGE FROM NEW RIDERS

As the reader of this book, you are our most important critic and commentator. We value your opinion and want to know what we're doing right, what we could do better, in what areas you'd like to see us publish, and any other words of wisdom you're willing to pass our way.

As the Associate Publisher at New Riders, I welcome your comments. You can fax, email, or write me directly to let me know what you did or didn't like about this book—as well as what we can do to make our books better. When you write, please be sure to include this book's title, ISBN, and author, as well as your name and phone or fax number. I will carefully review your comments and share them with the authors and editors who worked on the book.

Please note that I cannot help you with technical problems related to the topic of this book, and that due to the high volume of email I receive, I might not be able to reply to every message. Thanks.

Fax: 317-581-4663
Email: stephanie.wall@newriders.com
Mail: Stephanie Wall
            Associate Publisher
            New Riders Publishing
            201 West 103rd Street
            Indianapolis, IN 46290 USA

Visit Our Web Site: www.newriders.com

On our web site, you'll find information about our other books, the authors we partner with, book updates and file downloads, promotions, discussion boards for online interaction with other users and with technology experts, and a calendar of trade shows and other professional events with which we'll be involved. We hope to see you around.

Email Us from Our Web Site

Go to **www.newriders.com** and click on the Contact Us link if you

- Have comments or questions about this book.

- Want to report errors that you have found in this book.

- Have a book proposal or are interested in writing for New Riders.

- Would like us to send you one of our author kits.

- Are an expert in a computer topic or technology and are interested in being a reviewer or technical editor.

- Want to find a distributor for our titles in your area.

- Are an educator/instructor who wants to preview New Riders books for classroom use. In the body/comments area, include your name, school, department, address, phone number, office days/hours, text currently in use, and enrollment in your department, along with your request for either desk/examination copies or additional information.

INTRODUCTION

ENGLISH HAS ITS LIMITS

We live in a world of many languages, many cultures, and many countries, yet we all share one Internet. Initially, English dominated the Internet because English speakers dominated the Internet. Today, more than half of all Internet users are not native-English speakers.

Want to increase your potential online audience by 200 million people? Create French, Italian, German, and Spanish web sites. Add Japanese and Chinese, and you'll gain another 200 million—without opening a single international office. Web globalization will open your organization to virtually unlimited opportunities, but also many risks. This book offers guidelines and suggestions for bridging the borders between languages, cultures, countries, and, ultimately, people.

Many people want to reach a global market but don't know the best way to get there. Web globalization is complex and constantly evolving, and the languages themselves can be highly intimidating. Although a few mistakes are unavoidable, they need not be inevitable. The field of web globalization is still very much in its infancy. There are few books on the subject, and fewer still that combine high-level thinking with hands-on strategies. This book will save you countless hours of trial and error and help you build sites that put you ahead of your competition.

WHO THIS BOOK IS FOR

This book is for the people who create global business strategies and the people who implement those strategies:

- **Web developers** who want hands-on techniques for taking their sites global

- **Marketers** who want high-level strategies, from taking brands global to multilingual domain names to maximizing global search engines

- **Translators** who want to upgrade their skills to include web pages

- **Designers** who want to know what cultural and technical issues are involved when designing for new countries and languages

- **Writers** who want to create text that's easily translatable and globally effective

- **Executives** who may want to outsource everything but need to know what's involved and how much it will cost

HOW TO USE THIS BOOK

This book covers a lot of ground—literally. From Japanese web site development to European customer support, the book covers a wide spectrum of web globalization issues. This book is divided into seven parts, encompassing 17 chapters and 6 appendixes that take you through the entire process of developing a multilingual, multi-country web site—from research and strategy to implementation and support. Along the way, you'll hear from many of the leading experts in the field.

- **Part I, "Thinking Globally."** Are you ready to go global? You'll learn the basics of web globalization—the lingo and key concepts—and get a taste for navigating the multilingual Internet.

- **Part II, "Preparation."** Before you begin globalization, you'll see some of the common mistakes that companies make when taking their web sites global. You'll assess your organization's global readiness so that you can avoid repeating these mistakes.

- **Part III, "Implementation."** It's time to get started. You'll learn the web globalization workflow, the key participants, and the costs (and hidden costs) as well as the foundations of globalization: internationalization and localization.

- **Part IV, "Text and Translation."** Managing translation is an art as well as a science. You'll learn how to select and manage translators or a translation agency and how to maintain quality throughout the process. Copywriters will learn how to tailor and edit text for a global audience.

- **Part V, "Design, Development, and Management."** Designing for one country is a lot easier than designing for many countries. You'll learn the many details of creating and managing multilingual content and see how cultural and technical obstacles affect web design.

- **Part VI, "Beyond the Web Site."** To ensure the success of your global web site, you need to promote it one country at a time. You'll learn all about multilingual search engines, portals, and domain names.

- **Part VII, "Appendixes."** Finally, this book includes an in-depth glossary and reference section. Comprehensive listings of country codes, language codes, and character sets are included. Also included is a chart that lists the significance of colors around the world.

Throughout the book, you'll also find the following elements for trying out localization techniques and examining case studies of companies with global web sites:

- **Six "Hands-On"** chapters show you, step by step, how to translate a web site from English into eight different languages. Files are also available for download so that you can follow along on your own. By the end of the book, you will have created a web page with a potential reach of more than two billion people.

- **Seven "Spotlights"** present real-world case studies of organizations both large and small. You'll learn how organizations such as FedEx, L.L. Bean, Monster.com, and the World Cup developed their web sites and the challenges they faced along the way.

5

Conventions Used in This Book

A couple of typographic conventions have been used in this book:

- A **bold** font is used for computer terms and code, such as HTML markup text.

- *Italics* are used to introduce new terms or for emphasis.

You'll also notice several sidebar elements that have been used in various ways:

FYI

"FYI" tips are Included throughout the chapters to suggest additional resources or to point you to web sites for more in-depth information.

Note

Note boxes have been used to highlight interesting background information or to offer brief explanations of terms and concepts you may not be familiar with.

Sidebar

Sidebars offer real-world examples as well as explanations on how to use some of the techniques and tools mentioned in the text.

PREREQUISITES

Don't speak a dozen languages? Don't worry. Although proficiency in other languages is a plus, it's not a necessity. You don't need to be multilingual to build a multilingual web site. Web globalization is a team effort. This book will show you how to build and manage teams of translators, editors, web developers, and marketers.

You don't need to be a technical genius, either. Some chapters do require a basic understanding of HTML and web development, but this book assumes that you have no previous web globalization experience. The following software tools are used for the Hands-On chapters: Macromedia Dreamweaver, Microsoft FrontPage, Adobe Photoshop, and Adobe Illustrator. Although it will help to have a familiarity with

these tools, you should have no trouble following along without it. Finally, because
most global corporations rely on Windows operating systems, so too does much of
this book. The Macintosh operating system and software is addressed when possible, although the Hands-On chapters are entirely Windows based. Nevertheless,
virtually all techniques demonstrated on Windows software can be duplicated on
Macintosh software.

THE WORLD AWAITS

Languages, cultures, countries, and currencies: They are what separate local web
sites from becoming global web sites. This book will help you and your organization
develop a web site that embraces the world and allows the world to embrace your
organization. A world of people is out there, waiting. All you have to do is meet
them halfway. Web globalization is the final step toward creating an Internet without borders.

7

Stay in Touch
I will be posting corrections, feedback, and additional resources at **www.bytelevel.com/beyondborders**. Also, please
contact me with any questions or feedback at **jyunker@bytelevel.com**.

1

ONE INTERNET; MANY VOICES

The Internet connects computers, but it is language that connects people. If you want your web site to connect with the world, you need to create a web site that speaks to the world. This chapter introduces you to web globalization—the history, the terminology, and the reasons that web globalization is, for many organizations, inevitable.

IN THE BEGINNING, THERE WAS ENGLISH

The Internet was designed to be global, but not necessarily multilingual. Funded by the U.S. Department of Defense, its primary purpose was to enable English speakers to communicate with other English speakers; yet a funny thing happened to this American phenomenon—it became a global phenomenon. Increasingly, non-English speakers began using the Internet to communicate in their own languages. There were many obstacles, many of which are with us even today, but the trend was clear and accelerating. Just a few years ago, nearly two thirds of all Internet users were native English speakers Today, less than half speak English as their native language. And as shown in Figure 1.1, English is on its way from being the primary language of the Internet to just another language of the Internet.

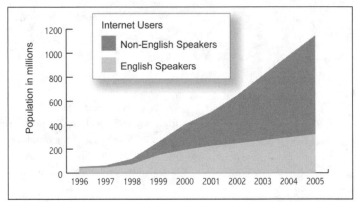

Figure 1.1   Non-English speakers are becoming the dominant force on the Internet.
*Source: Global Reach, 2001 (**www.glreach.com**)*

As more and more of the world embraces the Internet, inevitably, less and less of the world will embrace English-only web sites. The research firm IDC projects that by 2003, 36% of all Internet users will prefer to use a language other than English, up from 26% in 1999. IDC goes on to note that people are four times more likely to shop and purchase online from web sites that speak their native language.* A multilingual web site is, increasingly, not just a luxury, but a necessity.

The term "World Wide Web" has always been a bit of a fallacy. What's the good of having millions of people visit your site if only a fraction can understand what it says? Would you buy from a company that didn't speak your language? In the early days of the Internet, web users had to adapt to English-language sites because there were few alternatives. Today, web sites must adapt to the languages of their web users.

*Source: Web Site Globalization: The Next Imperative for the Internet 2.0 Era, IDC, 2001

Imagine a World Without English

Perhaps the best way to understand how challenging the Internet can be if you don't speak English is to pretend that you *don't* speak English. To someone who knows no English, Figure 1.2 might be a more accurate picture of what the Dell global home page looks like: nice pictures, but undecipherable text.

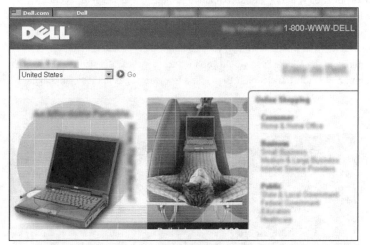

Figure 1.2   The English-language Dell home page, as someone who doesn't speak English views it.

11

Dell does, in fact, offer web sites in different languages, but if you arrive at the global home page, you must use the pull-down menu to get to those sites (see Figure 1.3). Although much of the world does recognize some English words, do you really want to assume your site visitors understand the words "Choose a Country"? This minor detail, the global gateway, is not so minor when you're building a web site for the world. Success at web globalization demands high attention to detail and the ability to look at your web site through the eyes of someone else.

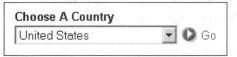

Figure 1.3   The Dell "global gateway." Before you can get to the web site in another language, you have to know what "Choose a Country" means.

For more information on global gateways, see Chapter 11, "World Wide Design."

Global Web Sites for Global Companies

Nike sells its products in 140 countries; last year it made more money outside the U.S. than it did within the U.S. However, in Nike's 2001 annual report, Philip Knight, CEO, set two priorities for the years ahead, one of which was to "become a truly global company."

Is Nike not already a truly global company? Perhaps not as much as it could be. The Nike web site could use a bit of improvement (see Figure 1.4). For a company that does business in 140 countries, its site offers only 13 languages—a great start, but far from what's needed. If your company sells products in Russia, Sweden, and the Middle East, would you neglect to include Russian, Swedish, Hebrew, and Arabic translations? Even just a few web pages in those languages would be better than nothing.

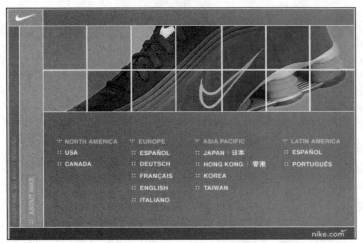

Figure 1.4 Nike sells its products in 140 countries, but its web site is only available in 13 languages.

A global web site is your link with customers around the world, a link that can strengthen relationships or damage them. And as more and more companies expand globally, they cannot afford to damage relationships.

Nike is not alone in its dependence on the world. Many major companies now owe a significant percentage of their revenues to the world outside their native countries, as shown in Table 1.1.

Table 1.1 American Companies in Search of Growth Need the World More Than Ever

Company (Reach)	Percentage of Sales from Outside U.S.
Symantec (37 countries)	43%
McDonald's (120 countries)	51%
Ralph Lauren (65 countries)	24%
Dell (12% global market share)	30%
Wal-Mart (9 countries)	17%
Coca-Cola	70%

Source: Statistics compiled from company annual reports.

Ralph Lauren was one of the first American fashion houses to go global, expanding into Japan as early as 1978, long before it had a web site. In 1982, it entered Europe, well ahead of its American competitors. Today, it does business in 65 countries, and its 2001 annual report made clear its continued global aspirations:

> *"Polo Ralph Lauren is a brand that knows no boundaries. It has universal appeal because it understands cultures and what it means to be a part of them."*

Globalization Is Inevitable

Any company that seeks long-term growth is bound to go global. Domestically, Coca-Cola has a 15% lead over its competitors, but outside the U.S., it enjoys a 4:1 market share advantage, and growth prospects are seemingly unlimited. In Nigeria alone, Coke products are enjoying a 39% growth rate. McDonald's is another global success story, operating in 120 countries. Although it might seem that McDonald's is in danger of running out of room to expand, it claims to feed less than 1% of the world's population on any given day. In fact, most multinational companies have only just begun to realize the potential of globalization. Consider Wal-Mart, in which 25% of its stores are located outside the U.S., yet in only nine countries. Wal-Mart, like most major companies, is just getting started (see sidebar "Wal-Mart Adapts to the World, One Country at a Time").

13

Wal-Mart Adapts to the World, One Country at a Time

"Wal-Mart began operations in the world's most populous nation in 1996, opening a Wal-Mart Supercenter and a SAM'S CLUB. China is an ideal example of how Wal-Mart synthesizes practices to adapt to the communities it serves. Wal-Mart modified its shopping bags to fit the needs of Chinese customers who usually shop daily for products and often arrive on a motorcycle or bicycle. During fiscal 2001, Wal-Mart opened a new underground store in Dalian beneath a new soccer stadium. The subterranean format was chosen to accommodate local needs and to address citizens' aesthetic concerns."

Source: Wal-Mart 2001 Annual Report

As Wal-Mart takes its company global, it also takes its web site global (see Figure 1.5). In a global economy, a global web site becomes a core channel for communication, sales, and support. Whether you are a multinational or simply want to function like one, you'll need a multilingual, multinational web site.

Figure 1.5   Wal-Mart, already the largest retailer in Mexico, also has a Mexico web site (***www.walmartmexico.com.mx***).

Globalization Gone Bad

Thinking globally and acting globally are two different things. Time and again, companies make the mistake of assuming that what works domestically will work internationally. And time and again, they learn the hard way that every country and every culture is, in its own way, a new world.

David Ricks writes about many of the road bumps companies encounter when selling around the globe. In his book, *Blunders in International Business*, he documents some of the more humorous examples of globalization gone bad:

- General Motors ran into trouble trying to sell the Chevy Nova in Latin America. *No va* means "no go" in Spanish. When Ricks spoke to General Motors about the incident, they told him that consumers found the name so silly that they were forced to change the name to Caribe (meaning "horse").

- Ford had an equally embarrassing problem when it tried to sell the Pinto in Brazil. *Pinto* is apparently slang for "tiny male genitals."

- Pepsodent tried to sell its teeth-whitening toothpaste in parts of Asia where culturally one gains social prestige by having darkly stained teeth.

- Procter & Gamble marketed its Cheer laundry detergent in Japan under the familiar "all-temperature" slogan, yet the Japanese wash clothes in cold water, almost exclusively.

- The Budweiser slogan "King of Beers" was translated into Spanish as "Queen of Beers."

- An American firm in India used a symbol of an owl in its marketing efforts only to find out that in India, an owl signifies bad luck.

Source: Blunders in International Business, David A. Ricks, Cambridge, MA: Blackwell Business, 1997.

15

Whether you use a web site or a billboard, the risks of going global are enormous. With the Internet, the pace of globalization increases rapidly. You no longer need the resources of a multinational company to have multinational reach, but you can also make the same mistakes multinationals make, and the consequences can be just as painful.

Chapter 4, "Are You Ready to Go Global?," will help you conduct an internal audit of your company's global readiness. And Chapter 16, "Promoting Your Site Globally," will help you effectively promote your site and products in new markets.

THE LANGUAGE OF GLOBALIZATION

There are a lot of specialized terms in the web globalization field, many of them inherited from the software industry (collected in Appendix A, "Glossary," of this book). Years ago, software developers realized the profit potential of global markets and set about "localizing" their products for various markets. The terms and processes these companies pioneered carried over to web development. As the lines between software and web sites have blurred, the terms are now more relevant than ever.

Keep in mind that definitions vary widely in this industry. Don't worry if you don't grasp them at first; they'll become much more clear as you go through the process yourself. Even if you don't find yourself using these terms, they're important to know, as your vendors most certainly will use them.

Think "Locale"

A locale is a confusing concept because its definition varies depending on how it's used. On an operating system, a locale can refer to a specific combination of language, geographic region, keyboard layout, and date/time display format, to name a few. On a web site, a locale might be as simple as "Spanish."

For our purposes, a *locale* is a specific combination of language and country, such as Portuguese Brazil or English U.K. It's important not to confuse language with country or vice versa. A country such as Canada can have more than one language (French Canada and English Canada), and a language (such as Spanish or English) is often spoken in more than one country.

Of course, a locale is often linked to much more than a language and country. Many web sites offer a high degree of personalization, which requires "localization" of functionality. When developing a site for each locale, ask the following questions:

- How are dates displayed?
- How are numbers displayed?
- What currency is used?
- What are the sorting and collating rules? For example, there is no such concept as "alphabetization" in Chinese.
- How should searches work? Once again, Asian languages don't sort like alphabetic languages; they are sorted by a host of factors, such as stroke count.
- What's the text direction (left to right, right to left, horizontal, or vertical)? Arabic is a bi-directional language; text flows from right to left and numbers flow from left to right.
- What is the default paper size? Will your web pages print properly in countries where paper sizes are not 8$\frac{1}{2}$×11 inches? If you supply PDF files for download, will they print correctly?

- Do you ask users to enter any characters that aren't available in that given language? Keep in mind that keyboards and operating systems vary by locale.

For more information on localization, see Chapter 7, "Internationalization and Localization."

- What is the user's technical environment? Do users have slow or fast connections? What is the typical screen resolution and processor speed? And what sort of devices do they use? In Japan, for example, people are much more likely to connect to the Internet by mobile phone, not PC.

Habla Español?

Spanish is the official language of more than 20 countries; English is the official language in only 7 countries.

In general, companies tend to approach the world by "language markets" or "country markets." For example, a company translates its site into Spanish, assuming that all Spanish speakers in Spain, Mexico, Latin America, and the U.S. will be happy with it. This is rarely the case, however. Spanish varies widely in its usage from country to country and region to region. There are even clear differences between the Spanish spoken in Miami and the Spanish spoken in Los Angeles.

Taking a purely geographic approach is also prone to error. What language do you offer when you localize your web site for Switzerland, a country with four official languages? For that matter, English falls far short of fully addressing the U.S. population, in which 32 million people speak Spanish. Which brings us back to locale—part language, part country. It's not the best system, but it's good enough for most companies as they begin going global.

For more information about Spanish localization, see "Hands On: Spanish."

Localization (L10n)

Localization is the process of modifying a product for a specific locale. This includes making technical, visual, and textual modifications to your site. All those questions you had to answer when thinking about the locale are applied during this process. The changes you'll need to make to your site include

- Rewriting text
- Translating text
- Modifying graphics
- Creating new graphics

17

- Changing colors
- Changing layout
- Modifying tables, forms, data fields, databases

Why L10n?

Blame software developers for the pseudo-acronym L10n. The number 10 refers to the number of letters between L and n. Similar abbreviations are used for internationalization (i18n) and globalization (g10n). These abbreviations might not be any easier to use, but be prepared to see vendors using them from time to time. Note that the L in L10n is uppercase to prevent being mistaken for the numeral 1.

Only in Basston

Localization applies to more than web sites. In Boston, several popular ads make light of the Boston accent, in which the *r* is silent and the *a* sounds more like "ah." For example, an ad for a local car wash uses the headline: "It's like a spa for your cah," and a billboard for Bass Ale reads "Basston." A question you'll often ask as you localize your web site is "How local do you want to go; how local should you go?"

Some say a perfectly localized web site should appear to the end user as though it were created by a local company, but this isn't always a good idea. Sometimes you want a consumer to know you're a foreign company. French winemakers, for example, aren't about to start pretending they're from Ohio. The goal of localization isn't to trick users into thinking your company is local, but to let users know that you understand their specific needs and wants. A successfully localized web site provides a consistent user experience, regardless of location or language.

┌─Yahoo! Gets Local ───

Yahoo! has perfected the art of localization, regardless of whether its users are in St. Louis or Singapore (see Figure 1.16). Yahoo!, in its early days, focused its localization efforts on the U.S. It launched a Yahoo! New York, Boston, and LA, and today Yahoo! offers more than 200 Metro sites. Yahoo! also expanded across borders. Today, it has portals in 23 territories in 16 languages.

Local Yahoo!s

Europe : Denmark - France - Germany - Italy - Norway - Spain - Sweden - UK & Ireland
Asia Pacific : Asia - Australia & NZ - China - HK - India - Japan - Korea - Singapore - Taiwan
Americas : Argentina - Brazil - Canada - Chinese - Mexico - Spanish
U.S. Cities : Atlanta - Boston - Chicago - Dallas/FW - LA - NYC - SF Bay - Wash. DC - **more...**

Figure 1.6   The Yahoo! local section.

For each region, Yahoo! hires a local team that manages content. This decentralized structure allows each Yahoo! portal to more easily and quickly customize content to the needs of its audience.

Internationalization (i18N)

Internationalization is the process of building (or rebuilding) a site so that it can be easily localized. To understand internationalization, think about how car companies operate. To minimize costs and maximize customer returns, a car manufacturer, such as Honda, develops a modular design that can be customized to the needs of its various consumers and the countries they live in. Just as a web site is often built on a global template, the core design of the Honda Accord also functions as a template. The internationalized version of the Honda Accord is the template of the car, the frame on which all the DXs and LXs and EXs can be assembled. Because Honda focused first on creating an internationalized template of a car, it can more easily spin off hundreds of variations, each suited to a specific audience.

If you're planning on localizing your site for multiple languages, internationalization can save you a lot of time and money because it forces you to create a template that can then be more easily localized, instead of just localizing as you go and running into expensive problems along the way.

13

The i18n and L1on of Lands' End

Notice how the Lands' End U.S. and Deutschland home pages share similar navigation systems, but feature different promotions (see Figure 1.7). The internationalization stage of the development process would have entailed developing a master design that remains consistent across locales, yet remains flexible enough to allow for the necessary localization.

Internationalized components

Localized content

Figure 1.7   On both sites, navigation systems remain consistent, but on the German site, the featured Internet access promotion is unique to the German market.

continues

The i18n and L10n of Lands' End, continued

If you look closely at the German site, you'll see that Lands' End elected to continue using its trademark slogan "Guaranteed. Period." without translating it. This type of decision—deciding what to translate and what *not* to translate—is typically made in the internationalization stage. Sometimes, internationalization decisions have localized repercussions. Lands' End had to go to court to defend its use of "Guaranteed. Period." because German law prohibited advertising unconditional guarantees. Lands' End felt that this slogan, its guiding principle, was worth fighting for. Its fight paid off, as the law was repealed in 2001.

During the localization stage, the product selections, promotions, toll-free German phone number, prices, and support options are addressed. Although the two home pages might look quite similar initially, the differences are significant. Companies are increasingly designing web sites to function as "global templates" that can easily be localized for just about any country and any language. Just as Honda develops automotive bodies that can accommodate steering wheels on the left or the right, depending on the target market, web developers must create sites that can accommodate all types of text, regardless of whether it moves from right to left or left to right.

Globalization (g11n)

Globalization is commonly used as the all-encompassing term for both internationalizing *and* localizing a web site. In reality, however, the term is much broader still. Regardless of whether you're adding one language or 20 languages, localizing or internationalizing, you are participating in the globalization process.

In fact, you're participating in the globalization process even if you have nothing to do with the web site. Customer support people must understand how to answer emails and calls in different languages; accounting must create prices in different currencies and then accept those currencies; salespeople must understand the nuances of the countries and cultures; and product developers and marketers must understand competition and the distribution channels. In other words, globalization is a companywide process. You can't do it alone.

Because of globalization's companywide nature, certain chapters of this book are devoted to areas that aren't necessarily web-centric: customer support (Chapter 15, "Supporting International Customers"), marketing (Chapter 16, "Promoting Your Site Globally"), and copywriting (Chapter 10, "Writing for a Global Audience").

FYI

Some localization vendors now use the term "glocalization" because it better conveys the dual nature of the globalization process. Perhaps glocalization is the term of the future. For this book, however, I will use globalization.

Languages Come in Pairs: Source and Target Languages

A translator typically specializes in one *source language* (such as English) and one *target language* (such as German). Rarely will you see translators manage more than one pair. Although this book largely assumes that your source language is English, this is often not the case in the real world. As sites become increasingly globalized, you might find yourself translating a French web page for an American site or a Japanese page for a German site.

Now that you're thinking like a localization expert, let's review some of the reasons your company needs to begin talking to the world in more than one language.

NUMBERS SPEAK LOUDER THAN WORDS

According to Global Reach (**www.glreach.com**), the year 2000 saw the number of non-native English speakers outnumber the number of native English speakers on the Internet. Although the number of English speakers on the Internet continues to grow, the pace is slowing. Meanwhile, the number of non-English speakers continues to grown unabated.

English is hardly endangered; it is the *lingua franca* of international business and will remain so for years to come. But on the Internet, English is clearly not on the verge of becoming a *universal* language, at least not according to the analysts.

The Analysts Have Spoken

You can tell that a trend has reached critical mass when analysts in competing firms actually start agreeing with one another. For example, IDC reports several predictions for 2003, shown in Figure 1.8.

- The United States will account for less than one-third of the worldwide Internet user base of 602 million.
- Western Europe and Japan will represent 47% of all e-commerce revenue ($764 billion).
- At least 36% of Internet users will prefer to use a language other than English, up from 28% in 1999.

Source: Web Site Globalization: The Next Imperative for the Internet 2.0 Era, IDC, 2001

Latin America
16.45 million

Middle East
2.4 million

Asia-Pacific
104.88 million

Canada & U.S.
167.12 million

Europe
113.14 million

Africa
3.11 million

Figure 1.8 Who's online?
Source: Data compiled from multiple sources by Nua Internet Surveys,
November 2000

The Aberdeen Group followed with a few predictions of its own, also for 2003:

- By 2003, 68% of web users will be non-English speakers.
- By 2003, 66% of all e-commerce spending will originate outside the U.S.
- More than 20% of web traffic on U.S.-based sites originates from outside the U.S.

Additionally, Aberdeen broke down the growth in Internet usage by region, as shown in Figure 1.9.

Region	Internet Users	Growth Rate	% of Total Population
North America	171,000,000	14%	34.3%
Latin America	37,600,000	48%	7.6%
Western Europe	24,100,000	24%	22.5%
Eastern Europe	6,100,000	51%	4.8%
Africa	6,100,000	48%	1.2%
Middle East	8,500,000	61%	1.7%
Asia/Pacific	138,800,00	39%	27.9%

Figure 1.9 Projected Internet usage through 2003.
Source: Web Globalization: Write Once, Deploy Worldwide, Boston: Aberdeen Group, May 2001.

What do all these numbers add up to? A pretty strong case for web localization. American companies in search of e-commerce growth have little choice but to look outside the U.S. Compare the 14% growth rate domestically with the 39% growth rate in Asia.

Currently, English is still a dominant language on the Internet, but every day, other languages grow more popular. The issue isn't that English is growing less popular, but that more and more of the world is going online, and more often than not, they don't speak English (see Figure 1.10).

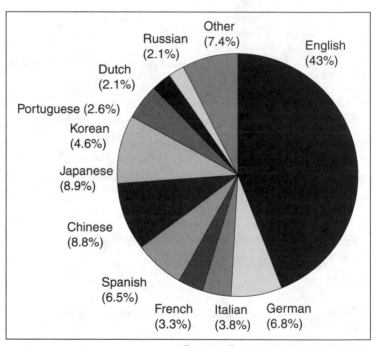

Figure 1.10   The most popular languages of web users.
*Source: Global Reach (**www.glreach.com**)*

So what language will dominate the Internet in the future? According to the World Intellectual Property Organization (WIPO) and the International Telecommunications Union (ITU), Chinese will outrank English as the most-used language on the Internet by 2007.

Not All Languages Are Localized Equally

Just because Chinese is destined to dominate the Internet doesn't mean you should rush off and hire Chinese translators. Chinese is a very difficult language to localize for. Many organizations select target languages with little thought to how challenging or expensive those languages might be. If your organization is new to localization, you probably don't want to pick the most challenging language as your first target language.

The chart in Figure 1.11 rates the relative difficulty of localizing an English U.S. web site into various languages. Each ranking, on a scale of 1 to 10, takes a number of factors into account: complexity of language and culture, talent pool, costs, readily available tools. As you can see, Chinese is a lot more challenging than Spanish.

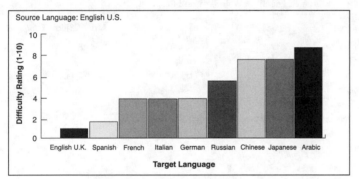

Figure 1.11   Some languages are tougher than others.

The Hands-On chapters in this book will demonstrate how to localize for eight of the nine languages on this chart. You'll begin with Spanish and work your way up the difficulty ranking until you reach Arabic.

WHO'S GOING GLOBAL?

Roughly half the Fortune 500 companies have developed localized web sites, but less than half of these efforts can be considered anywhere near comprehensive. Most companies have yet to fully embrace web globalization, which is good news for companies that have yet to begin.

Going global doesn't necessitate localizing a web site into every written language; it just means localizing into the necessary languages. The following two examples illustrate how diverse your needs may be. In one example, a multinational built 36 localized web sites; in the other, a nonprofit organization built just two sites. There's no right or wrong solution—only the solution that works best for your organization and your audience.

The Big: Mazda

Mazda's home page is an extensive global gateway that leads to 36 localized web sites (see Figure 1.12). Table 1.2 illustrates the full extent of Mazda's web globalization efforts.

Table 1.2   Mazda: 36 Localized Web Sites and Growing...

Americas	Europe	Asia	Africa/Middle East
Argentina	Austria	Australia	Kuwait
Canada	Belgium	Hong Kong	Oman
Columbia	Croatia	Japan	South Africa
El Salvador	Czech Republic	New Zealand	
Honduras	Denmark	Taiwan	
Puerto Rico	Finland	Thailand	
U.S.	France		
	Germany		
	Greece		
	Hungary		
	Italy		
	Netherlands		
	Poland		
	Portugal		
	Slovakia		
	Slovenia		
	Spain		
	Switzerland		
	Sweden		
	U.K.		

Figure 1.12   The Mazda English-language home page.

Managing all these sites requires enormous resources, and the list is sure to grow.
Mazda, after all, is just one brand in the Ford family. If you were to include the number of localized web sites for each Ford brand, the total quickly exceeds 100 localized
web sites.

And the Not So Big: The Software Human Resource Council

You don't have to be a multinational to have a multilingual web site. The Software
Human Resource Council (SHRC) is a nonprofit organization based in Canada, serving both French and English speakers (see Figure 1.13). Canada requires that organizations offer both French- and English-language web sites.

Figure 1.13   The SHRC gateway.

The site's home page is a simple and effective gateway; both localized versions, shown in Figures 1.14 and 1.15, are fully translated. Even the acronym is translated, from CHRC in English to CRHL (Conseil des ressources humaines du logiciel) in French.

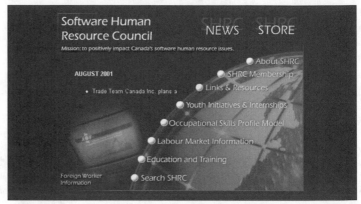

Figure 1.14   The SHRC English-language home page.

Figure 1.15   The SHRC French-language home page.

You don't have to localize your web site into a dozen languages to be successful, and you don't need to be a multinational. You just need to get started.

MOVING FORWARD: MANY INTERNETS, MANY VOICES

In the end, web globalization isn't just about translating one site; it's about creating entirely new web sites. The challenges extend well beyond language and require the support of your entire organization. Yet despite the obstacles, globalization is hard to resist—if not just to expand market share but to prevent others from taking your market share. In a global economy, if your company (and your web site) ignores the world, the world will ignore you. In the next chapter, you'll learn how so many languages coexist on the Internet and how you can effectively navigate around them.

2

NAVIGATING THE MULTILINGUAL INTERNET

Regardless of whether you want to build a multilingual web site or simply navigate around one, you'll need a basic understanding of the world's many languages and how the Internet accommodates them.

LANGUAGES 101

There are more than 6,000 languages in use today, but I'm going to focus on only the most popular, shown in Table 2.1. If you were to localize your web site to include these languages, your site would be able to communicate with well over half of the world's population—and more than 90% of all web users.

Table 2.1 Major Languages of the World

Language	Primary Regions Spoken	Estimated Number of Native Speakers (in Millions)
Chinese (Mandarin)	China	874
Hindi-Urdu	India, Pakistan	366
English	North America, Great Britain, Australia, South Africa	341
Spanish	Latin America, Spain	341
Arabic	North Africa, Middle East	183
Portuguese	Brazil, Portugal, Angola, Mozambique	176
Russian	Former Soviet Union	167
Bengali	Bangladesh, India	162
Japanese	Japan	125
German	Germany, Austria, Switzerland	100
Korean	Korea	78
French	France, Canada, Belgium, Switzerland, Black Africa	77
Chinese (Wu)	China (Shanghai)	77
Javanese	Indonesia (Java)	75
Chinese (Yue)	China (Guangdong)	71
Telugu	South India	69
Vietnamese	Viet Nam	68
Marathi	South India	68
Tamil	South India, Sri Lanka	66
Italian	Italy	62
Urdu	Pakistan	60
Ukrainian	Ukraine	50

Source: Ethnologues, *14th Edition, 2000* (***www.ethnologue.com***).

Of these 22 languages, there are even fewer writing systems, which makes web globalization a little more manageable. If you understand how one writing system works, you'll have an easier time with any language that shares that writing system. For example, the Russian language relies on the Cyrillic alphabet, but so do more than a dozen other languages, such as Ukrainian and Serbian. The Latin alphabet, with minor variances, is shared by most Western European languages, and the Chinese (traditional) language, although it features many distinct dialects, shares a common writing system. Writing systems generally fall into two categories: ideographic and phonetic.

Ideographic

The *ideographic writing system*, the world's oldest writing system, relies on symbols, or ideographs, to communicate meaning. Some of these symbols look a lot like the objects they represent. For example, the Chinese character for *fire* conveys the visual impression of a fire, as shown in Figure 2.1. Over the centuries, the Chinese language has included as many as 80,000 ideographs, although the average speaker uses only between 3,000 and 5,000.

33

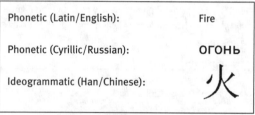

Phonetic (Latin/English):	Fire
Phonetic (Cyrillic/Russian):	ОГОНЬ
Ideogrammatic (Han/Chinese):	火

Figure 2.1 "Fire," by any other writing system.

Phonetic

The *phonetic writing system* is more abstract than the ideographic system; each character represents a sound rather than a concept. There are two major phonetic systems: alphabetic and syllabic.

- **Alphabetic:** Each character represents a vowel or consonant. Examples include Latin, Arabic, Cyrillic, and Greek. For native-English speakers, the alphabetic system is well known, but not all alphabetic systems follow the same rules as English. For example, in Arabic, text is written from right to left rather than left to right. In addition, the 28 letters that make up the Arabic alphabet change shape according to their position within a word and the letters that surround them.

■ **Syllabic:** Each character represents a combination of consonants and/or vowels. A collection of syllables is called a *syllabary*. Examples include Hangul (Korean), Katakana and Hiragana (Japanese), and Tagalog (Philippines).

Although rare, some languages incorporate more than one writing system; the Japanese language relies on two syllabaries and more than 1,000 ideographs, known as Kanji.

For more information about specific languages, refer to the Hands-On chapters located throughout the book.

DON'T LET THE LANGUAGES SCARE YOU

Foreign languages can be intimidating; the more unfamiliar they are, the more intimidating they seem. But even if all you understand is English, you'll be able to manage web globalization just fine, because HTML, XML, Perl, Java, and all those other programming languages, standards, and protocols are written in English.

No matter what language web site you want to create, you can rest assured (for now, at least) that you'll be able to navigate the HTML markup code. Not convinced? Go to any localized web site, and in your browser, select the option to view the page source. Try the eBay Deutschland page at **www.ebay.de** (see Figures 2.2 and 2.3), and look at the HTML tags. The content between the tags may be in German, but the HTML and JavaScript are in English.

Figure 2.2   The eBay German page.

```
<!-- page type 0 -->
<!-- secondary page type 0 -->
<html>
<head>
<title>eBay Deutschland - Der weltweite Online-Marktplatz</title>
<!-- Main 3 -->
<meta name="description" content="Der weltweite Online-Marktplatz!">
<meta name="keywords" content="Auktionen, Auktion, Computer, Bieten, Gebot, Verkaufen, Bücher,
Münzen, Briefmarken, trading cards, Memorabilia, Sportartikel, Musik, Puppen, Comics,
Antiquitäten, Schmuck, ebay">
<meta name="Classification" content="Auktionen, Auktion, Computer, Bieten, Gebot, Verkaufen,
Bücher, Münzen, Briefmarken, trading cards, Memorabilia, Sportartikel, Musik, Puppen, Comics,
Antiquitäten, Schmuck, ebay">
<script language="JavaScript">
<!--
function Certify(URL) {
  popupWin = window.open(URL, 'Participant', 'location,scrollbars,width=450,height=300');
  window.top.name = 'opener';
}
// -->
</script>
<SCRIPT TYPE="text/javascript" LANGUAGE="JavaScript">
<!--
var is = new Is()
function Is()
{
var agt = navigator.userAgent.toLowerCase();
this.major = parseInt(navigator.appVersion);
this.nav  = ((agt.indexOf('mozilla')!=-1) && ((agt.indexOf('spoofer')==-1) &&
(agt.indexOf('compatible') == -1)));
this.nav4up = this.nav && (this.major >= 4);
this.ie   = (agt.indexOf("msie") != -1);
this.ie3up  = this.ie  && (this.major >= 3);
this.eBayJSnotN3 = (this.nav4up || this.ie3up);
}
```

Figure 2.3   The source HTML for the eBay German page.

So from here on out, don't be intimidated by all those unfamiliar languages. To be successful at web globalization, all you really need to understand is how computers and browsers manage those unfamiliar languages.

COMPUTERS AND CHARACTERS

Every language, no matter how complex, relies on characters. A *character* is defined as the smallest component of a written language that has semantic value. Characters are typically grouped by language into *character sets*.

A character is an abstract concept. "Capital letter A" is a character. So is "Hangul letter rieul-tikeut" and "Ethiopic syllable lu." A character can be used in one language or many languages. It might even be a dollar sign or a mathematical symbol.

You cannot see a character or print a character. What you see on your computer screen is known as a *glyph*, as shown here for the character *A*. A font is a collection of glyphs.

One Character, Many Glyphs

The character: The capital letter A

And its many glyphs: A 𝒜 A **A**

The key to successful web globalization is knowing how characters in an HTML document end up as glyphs on a web browser.

Computers Speak in Numbers

When you press the "capital letter A" key on your keyboard, your computer doesn't see a letter; it sees a number—a binary number, to be precise. A binary number is represented by a combination of ones and zeros, or bits (eight bits equals one byte), as shown in the following chart of selected ASCII.

Character	Binary Value	Decimal Value
A	1000001	65
B	1000010	66
C	1000011	67
D	1000100	68

The mapping of characters to numbers is known as *encoding*, which is a critical, and often confusing, concept in web globalization. Each character must be assigned a number for it to be useful to a computer. Until a character set is encoded, it is just an abstract set of characters.

After a character set is encoded, it's often called a "coded character set," "code-page," or "character encoding system." Because a character set is largely useless to web globalization if it isn't encoded in some way, assume that when I use the term "character set," I'm implying an encoding of some sort. In fact, some character sets are encoded by default, a few of which I'll get to in a moment.

The distinction between character sets and their encodings is important when you're working with a language such as Japanese, in which one character set can have more than one encoding. If you're a little confused at this point, don't worry; the best way to learn about character sets and encodings is through using them; in fact, let's try one right now.

How do you make the "capital letter A" character appear on a web page without

actually inputting the character? Simple—you enter its code point, as shown in Figure 2.4. This example features a "character entity," which is explored more in Chapter 12, "Creating Multilingual Content." For now, all you need to know is that the code point for "capital letter A" is 65 when using the ISO-8859-1 character set.

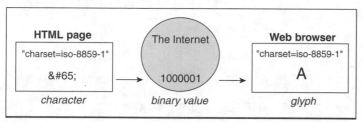

Figure 2.4   How a character becomes a glyph.

Once the web browser sees that the HTML page is using the 8859-1 character set, it simply pulls the glyph from code point 65 using a font that's aligned with this character set. This is a lot to digest all at once, but be patient. The more you work with character sets, particularly during the Hands-On chapters, the better you'll understand them, and you probably already know a lot about the following character set.

37

Once Upon a Time, There Was ASCII

ASCII (pronounced AS-key), the American Standard Code for Information Interchange, has been with us since the 1960s. As a 7-bit character set, ASCII allows for 128 characters, many of which are non-printing control characters (see Figure 2.5).

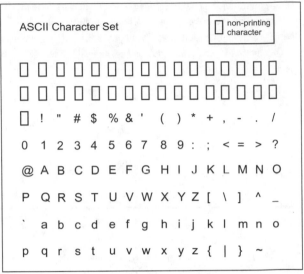

Figure 2.5 The ASCII character set.

Take a close look at ASCII. Imagine you wanted to write to your friend in Paris and needed to use some of those fancy French letters, like á or î. Don't see them anywhere in ASCII? That's because ASCII, as a 7-bit character set, doesn't have any room for those additional characters. ASCII is a uniquely American character set and a source of frustration for the rest of the world.

ASCII Lives

If you want to see where ASCII still exists, take a look at a URL (see Figure 2.6). Although there's a growing movement toward multilingual domain names, the official standard for URLs currently allows only a limited number of ASCII characters.

Figure 2.6 Notice how the name Citroën in the logo doesn't match its URL.

For more information on international domain names, see Chapter 14, "Mastering Your (Country) Domain."

A Few New Characters

Although ASCII was used on early web pages, HTML 2.0 specified the larger 8-bit character set, ISO-8859-1, popularly known as Latin 1 (see Figure 2.7). That eighth bit allows for an extra 128 characters, many of which are characters used in Western European languages.

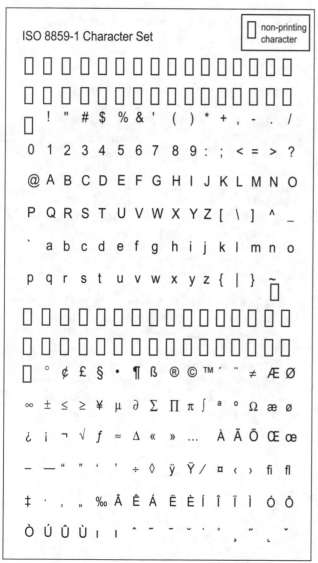

Figure 2.7 The Latin 1 (ISO 8859-1) character set.

What in the World Is ISO?

ISO is the International Organization for Standardization, a large body of experts who set global standards for just about everything, including character sets. Standards are absolutely critical for developing globally accessible and readable web sites, although vendors often promote their own standards. Microsoft, for example, has developed a number of character sets that rival ISO in global usage. For more information, visit **www.iso.org**.

See Appendix E, "Encodings," for a more in-depth list of character sets.

Using Latin 1, you can create a web page with a mixture of Spanish, French, and German. A great improvement, but what about Arabic and Cyrillic characters?

Here's where other character sets come into play. Because many languages share English characters to some degree, other ISO character sets have been developed, each with a different array of characters in those upper 128-character spaces. The following chart shows a sampling of character sets and their target languages.

Character Set	Target Language
ASCII	English (U.S.)
ISO-8859-1 (Latin 1)	Western European
Microsoft 1252	Western European
ISO-8859-2	Eastern European
ISO-8859-3	Southern European
ISO-8859-4	Northern European
ISO-8859-5	Cyrillic
ISO-8859-7	Modern Greek
ISO-8859-8	Hebrew
ISO-8859-9	Turkish

There is more than one character set for Western European languages: Latin 1 and Microsoft 1252. Microsoft developed its own character sets over the years, known as Codepages. You might already be familiar with Codepage 1252, as it was used by early versions of Microsoft Word. Microsoft created 1252 to include characters such as smart quotes and the Euro symbol (see Figure 2.8). Microsoft's Codepages illustrate the challenges of squeezing additional characters into a finite space. In the end, one byte just isn't enough room for the characters in Western European languages, let alone Asian languages.

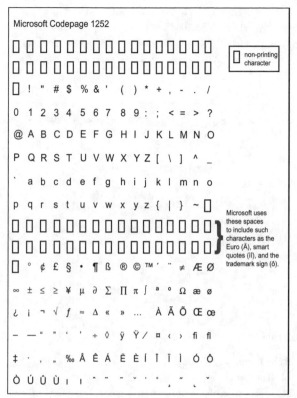

Figure 2.8   Microsoft Codepage 1252.

41

Asian languages use so many characters (more than 40,000) that they require two bytes (16 bits) to represent every character—hence the term *double-byte character set*. The following chart shows some double-byte character sets and their target languages:

Double-Byte Character Set	Target Language
ISO-2022-JP	Japanese
GB 2312-80	Chinese Simplified
Big 5	Chinese Traditional
ISO-2022-KR	Korean

There are hundreds of coded character sets in use today, but they don't all get along. Character sets are typically created to communicate a language or multiple languages. Notice in Figure 2.9 how ASCII is included within 8859-1 and both are included within Unicode. So while ASCII supports only English, Unicode supports multiple languages.

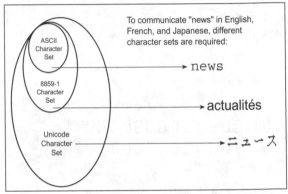

Figure 2.9   How character sets represent languages.

When Encodings Collide

When you view a web page, your browser does its best to deduce the encoding of the web page it's displaying, but sometimes it needs a little help. Fortunately, HTML includes a **<META>** tag just for this purpose. You're probably familiar with this one:

<META http-equiv="content-type" content="text/html; charset=ISO-8859-1">

When the user's browser sees the **charset** attribute, it knows to display a font that aligns with that character set. In this case, it pulls a glyph from a font that matches the Latin 1 character set. If the **<META>** tag is missing, the browser can detect encoding in other ways, but assuming that it guesses incorrectly, you might witness a problem known as *character set conflicts*.

When Is a Charset Not a Charset?

The **charset** actually refers to the encoding, not the character set. Usually, the character set and the encoding are one and the same, as is the case with ASCII and ISO-8859-1. With Japanese, however, this isn't always the case. The two most popular Japanese encodings are Shift-JIS and JP-EUC, and you need to be sure you specify the correct one. When you specify the charset attribute, think **encoding**.

For example, suppose you build a web page that uses Russian text, including the Cyrillic character **3**. According to ISo-Windows Codepage 1252, this character is located at code point 231. However, if a web user in the U.S. views this page, and the web browser cannot detect the character set, it may default to the Latin 1 character set and display the Ç character, which is also located at code point 231.

Character set conflicts are a major obstacle to displaying multiple languages on one web page. In this example, it's impossible to display all French and Cyrillic characters on the same web page, given the existing character sets. Not long ago, computer and linguistic experts set out to alleviate such character set conflicts once and for all with a "universal" character set known as Unicode.

GET TO KNOW UNICODE

Unicode (**www.unicode.org**) is the mother of all character sets. Unicode version 3.1 includes 94,140 characters—enough to represent the world's major languages. In Unicode, each character is represented by one number and one number only, so there's zero chance for character conflicts among or between various languages.

43

> **─ Unicode Has Arrived ─────────────────────────────────────**
>
> Unicode is the underlying character set used in Windows 2000, Oracle, Java, Sun, IBM, and numerous other platforms and applications. More important, Internet Explorer 5.x, Netscape Navigator 6.x, and Opera 6 all support Unicode.

Unicode is not without its faults or detractors, but because it has received enormous industry support and does such a good job of representing so many languages, it has been adopted by the HTML 4.0 specification. It's also the default character set of eXtensible Markup Language (XML), the underlying markup language for most web globalization software on the market today. For an excellent resource on XML, read *XML Internationalization and Localization*, by Yves Savourel (Sams Publishing, 2001).

Unicode is one character set, but it can be encoded in a number of different ways. The default encoding of Unicode is 16-bit, but this can cause problems on the Internet because many older servers and routers support only single-byte data. As a result, a more popular Internet encoding is UTF-8, a "multibyte" encoding. The UTF-8 encoding uses one to four octets, or bytes of data, to indicate each character, and hence is known as *multibyte encoding* rather than double-byte. Non-internationalized applications read and write UTF-8 as though it were a single-byte encoding, which means files with UTF-8 encoding pass through gateways and mail servers without being corrupted. For this reason, UTF-8 is a popular encoding for email and is increasingly used for web pages. However, use of UTF-8 is limited because older browsers don't recognize it.

Currently, the most common use for Unicode is in databases, allowing multiple languages to be stored. After the data is sent to a browser, it's converted to locale-specific character sets so that the browser properly displays it.

Unicode has already made a huge impact on global software development and is only just beginning to affect global web development. For the first time, you will be able to input, transmit, and display Chinese, Arabic, Russian, and English characters on one web page without having to worry about the technical limitations of the past. The only obstacle left will be learning to read all those languages.

MANAGING THE MULTILINGUAL BROWSER

Current versions of Netscape Navigator 6.x, Internet Explorer 5.x, and Opera 6 support viewing all major character sets, with minor adjustments. For the process to work, however, your computer must have the necessary fonts installed. For starters, let's focus on Japanese.

Open your browser and visit the IBM Japan site at **www.ibm.co.jp**. Does the site look more like Figure 2.10 or more like one of the examples in Figure 2.11? If the bulk of the text looks scrambled, as in Figure 2.11, your computer probably does not have a Japanese font installed. As for the Japanese characters that do appear correctly, they have been embedded into graphics, so they don't rely on your system's fonts. In the early days of the multilingual Internet, many companies had no choice but to create entire pages with all embedded text to compensate for systems without the necessary fonts. Today, however, if your computer doesn't have the necessary font, you can easily download it. In fact, you might have already been prompted by your web browser to download the Japanese font, which I'll explain shortly.

Figure 2.10   IBM Japan with fonts installed.

Figure 2.11   IBM Japan without fonts installed.

Microsoft, to its credit, offers significant multilingual support in its Windows XP and 2000 operating systems. Both operating systems are Unicode based and include fonts to display the major languages. The Macintosh OS 9.1 and OS X operating systems also have multilingual support built in. For those of you with older operating systems, you can download the fonts you need free from Microsoft and Netscape. Mac users with older systems are better off upgrading, as Apple no longer sells separate language kits.

First, Find the Font

Assuming that you're using Windows and you need a Japanese font, there are two ways to get the font. If you're using Internet Explorer, you were most likely already prompted to download the language support by a pop-up alert (see Figure 2.12). As you encounter web pages that require fonts your system doesn't have, Internet Explorer will alert you. Netscape isn't always so helpful.

45

Figure 2.12   If you don't have the font you need, Internet Explorer will help you download it.

If you aren't fortunate enough to have the font download automatically, visit the Microsoft site at **http://windowsupdate.microsoft.com** and select "Product Updates." After running a query of your system, the web site will display a list of software available for download. Scroll down until you find a list of "International Language Support" packs. Download the languages you want, and they will install on your system automatically.

Netscape provides a free Bitstream font for Asian languages that you can download at **http://home.netscape.com/eng/intl** (see Figure 2.13), but you still might need to configure Netscape so that the font is displayed when needed.

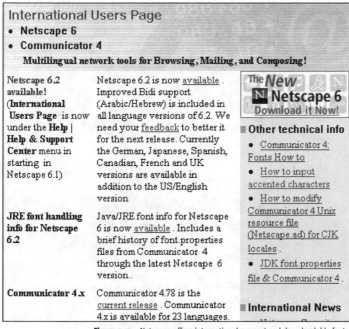

Figure 2.13 Netscape offers international support and downloadable fonts.

FYI

For additional Windows fonts, visit Dr. Berlin's Foreign Font Archive: **http://user.dtcc.edu/~berlin/fonts.html**

If you encounter a non-Latin language using Navigator 4.8, it won't automatically display a matching non-Latin font, even though you might already have one installed. To avoid this, choose Edit, Preferences on the menu, and double-click Appearances. Then select Fonts, and pair the language with the appropriate font. For Japanese, you would select MS Mincho, assuming you downloaded the font from Microsoft. Finally, select the Use My Default Fonts, Overriding Document-Specified Fonts option to ensure that this font is always used for pages that display Japanese text. Netscape 6.2 should not need any help displaying the correct font, but if any problems arise, you can adjust the preferences similarly, as shown in Figure 2.14.

47

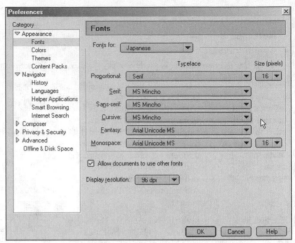

Figure 2.14   How to change language preferences in Netscape 6.x.

Now return to the IBM Japan site and refresh your web page. Internet Explorer should display the text properly; Navigator sometimes needs a nudge. If so, choose View, Character Coding, Auto-Detect, Japanese on the menu. And keep in mind that even if you do have initial problems getting a Japanese web page to display properly, web users in Japan are likely to have no problems because their computers already have Japanese fonts installed.

Sometimes Your Browser Needs a Little Help

Take a look at how Internet Explorer displays a web page by choosing View, Encoding on the menu. You'll see a black dot next to the encoding that the browser believes the web page to represent. Try visiting IBM Japan again and see what the home page looks like. The black dot should be next to the encoding option **Japanese (Shift-JIS)**.

If you're viewing a web page that's not being displayed correctly, IE might need to be told what to do (see Figure 2.15). This mistake occurs sometimes when web pages aren't correctly tagged with the **<META>** tag, as shown here for IBM Japan:

```
<meta http-equiv="content-type" content="text/html; charset=shift_jis">
```

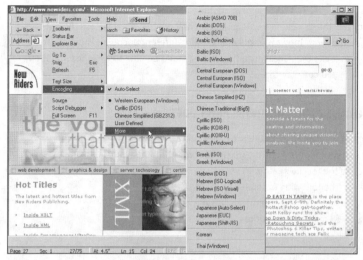

Figure 2.15 Selecting encoding options in Internet Explorer 5.5.

If you are using Netscape Navigator, the process is similar. Choose View, Character Coding on the menu (see Figure 2.16). Note that in Navigator 4.8, you would select View, Encoding. In version 4.8 and earlier, Navigator incorrectly used the term "Character Set" instead of "Encoding."

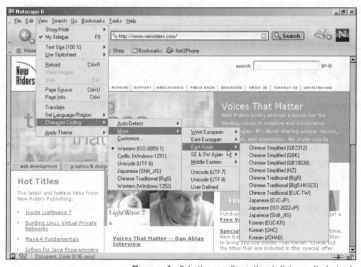

Figure 2.16 Selecting encoding options in Netscape Navigator 6.

If you ever come to a web page in another language and the text looks scrambled, one of two things could be wrong: Either you don't have the necessary font installed, or your browser is assuming that a different encoding is being used. After you make the necessary adjustments, you'll be able to view just about any language you come across.

LANGUAGES AND COUNTRIES AND CODES—OH, MY!

Now that you can successfully view most of the world's languages in your web browser, you need to know how to keep track of all the world's languages. ISO comes to the rescue again with standards for labeling languages and countries, shown in the following examples:

ISO-639-1 Language Identifiers

EN	English
FR	French
JA	Japanese
ZH	Chinese

ISO-3166 Country Codes

FR	France
DE	Germany
ZA	South Africa
SE	Sweden

For the complete lists, refer to Appendix D, "Language and Country Codes."

Language and country codes play many important roles in web globalization:

- Defining language
- Defining locale
- Organizing content

As you'll see, however, language codes and country codes are not without their flaws.

What's Your Language?

As you begin working with new languages in HTML, it's important that you label them correctly. According to HTML 4.0, the **lang** attribute allows you to label text in your web page by using a language tag. (You can read the details in RFC 1766, at **www.ietf.org/rfc/rfc1766.txt**.) This language tag can include a language identifier, a country code, or both, as shown in the following chart:

Language/Country Code	Language
en-US	English (U.S.)
en-UK	English (U.K.)
de-DE	German
it-IT	Italian
fr-CA	French (Canada)
fr-FR	French (France)
es-ES	Spanish (Spain)
es-MX	Spanish (Mexico)

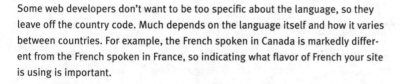

Some web developers don't want to be too specific about the language, so they leave off the country code. Much depends on the language itself and how it varies between countries. For example, the French spoken in Canada is markedly differ-ent from the French spoken in France, so indicating what flavor of French your site is using is important.

The language tag is case insensitive, although by convention, the language code is written in lowercase and the country code written in uppercase. No spaces are allowed. Many web developers don't even use language tags on their source-langauge web sites. But as the Internet grows increasingly multilingual, correctly labeling content grows increasingly important. Used correctly, language tags do the following:

- Help search engines index your pages by language. For example, Google allows you to search by language.

- Assist speech synthesizers.

- Help web browsers display text properly.

- Help web browsers display the text according to langauge-specific hyphen-ation and spacing rules.

- Assist spell checkers and grammar checkers.

51

If the entire page includes text in just one language, you can label the entire document by using, for example, **<HTML lang="ja-JP">** for Japanese. If a page consists of a mixture of languages, you can use the appropriate **lang** attribute in individual **<SPAN>** segments.

Language tags are not perfect, however. There are thousands of spoken languages and dialects in the world, but only a few hundred language codes. Furthermore, there's an inherent flaw in associating the language code with the country code because it implies that the language is spoken only in a given region, when that is rarely the case.

In 1988, ISO introduced 639-2, a three-digit language code that expands the total number of languages included to 433, still far short of what's needed. The linguistic organization SIL International is advocating an even more comprehensive coding system. For the time being, however, the working standard is the two-digit codes from 639-1. For the needs of most web developers, it works just fine, particularly because few web sites have localized for more than a few dozen languages.

What's Your Locale?

Many software applications and operating systems require a locale definition to help them customize features to their users. Often, this definition relies on pairing language code and country code. The locale code might look similar to the language tag shown previously, but it's much broader in scope. A locale code can also trigger a wide array of variables and functions, such as:

- Date/time format
- Sorting algorithm
- Currency
- Telephone number format
- Name and address formats

Unix and Java make use of the ISO codes, but Microsoft relies on its own set of locale codes. Just like language tags, however, locale tags are not without limitations. What's the locale of a web user who lives in the U.S. but speaks Russian? And what if that person is shopping on a German web site? This is an extreme example, but it's not completely far-fetched in a global economy. There is no easy answer to how you define locale. Just be aware of the codes you have to work with and their inherent limitations.

What's Your URL?

Country codes also play a major role in URLs. Want to find the IBM Japan site? Try
www.ibm.co.jp. Or Amazon France? Try **www.amazon.fr**. The better you know the
country codes, the more luck you'll have jumping from localized site to localized
site. The Internet Assigned Numbers Authority (IANA) is responsible for managing
country codes as they apply to domains.

Country code domain names are covered in
much more detail in Chapter 14.

Country and language codes also play a role in how companies organize their web
sites internally. To see these codes in use, visit **www.symantec.com** and select a
country. If you select China, you're directed to **symantec.com/region/cn**; selecting
Russia takes you to **symantec.com/region/ru**. Note that Symantec uses **cn** and **ru** to
differentiate between localized web sites.

53

THE SHIFTING SANDS OF WEB GLOBALIZATION

Given the dynamic nature of the Internet in general, and web globalization in particular, you'll need to keep an eye on the Internet standards groups and where
they're headed. Fortunately, everything you need is within easy reach. Here are a
few key organizations:

Unicode Consortium: **www.unicode.org**

World Wide Web Consortium: **www.w3c.org/international**

Internet Assigned Numbers Authority: **www.iana.org**

Internet Engineering Task Force: **www.ietf.org**

Although everything is changing quickly, now that you have a solid grounding in the
concepts, you can adapt to the changes just as quickly. Using what you now know
about language codes and character sets, take some time to explore the localized
pages on these sites:

www.yahoo.com

www.ups.com

www.symantec.com

www.lycos.com

Notice how your browser adapts to different languages. Observe how different companies organize their localized sites, and begin thinking about how you see your web site developing.

SWITCHING BACK TO ENGLISH

This chapter wasn't easy. There were a lot of foreign terms, technobabble, and complex issues, many of which will take a while to sink in. Don't assume that you need to understand everything immediately. Many of these concepts have to be experienced to be learned, and as you work through the chapters ahead, particularly the Hands-On elements, the technical issues will become clearer.

Now that you have a feel for the inner workings of the multilingual Internet, you'll better understand the outer workings of localized web sites. In the next chapter, you'll see how real companies tackle the real-world problems of web globalization.

Figure 1   The Monster global home page.

MONSTER.COM

Launched in 1994 as the Monster Board, Monster.com today serves 21 countries as part of TMP Worldwide, a global recruitment company. With more than 24 million visitors each month, Monster is the most popular career portal in the world.

www.monster.com

Localized web sites:

■ Australia	■ Hong Kong	■ Norway
■ Belgium	■ India	■ Singapore
■ Canada	■ Ireland	■ Spain
■ Denmark	■ Italy	■ Sweden
■ Finland	■ Luxembourg	■ Switzerland
■ France	■ Netherlands	■ United Kingdom
■ Germany	■ New Zealand	■ United States

ANALYSIS

Local content is not the same thing as localized content; Monster.com illustrates the value of both. Local content is content created specifically for that market, such as promotions, press releases, and the job ads themselves. Localized content is anything that was created outside that market and now must be adapted (and often translated) for that market.

Each Monster site is managed in country, so the content itself—the job ads—is supplied by local clients in the target language. All Monster must do is supply a localized web template for each country office to build on. The balance of local and localized content results in a web site that looks pretty much the same, country to country, but acts like a local job site within each country.

On the Use (and Misuse) of Flags

Monster.com features a global gateway that relies on flags, breaking one of the cardinal rules of web globalization (see Figure 2).

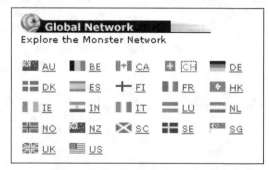

Figure 2   The Monster global gateway: a rare case when flags are acceptable.

Flags are problematic because they do not represent languages; they represent countries. You can run into trouble if you assume that one country equals one language. Switzerland, for example, has four official languages. Even a country with one official language, such as the U.S., has more than 30 million Spanish speakers. Often a flag is too limiting. Assume you translate your site into Spanish. Which flag do you use to specify Spanish?

That said, Monster.com proves the exception to the rule. Monster relies on flags because its country sites are designed to serve *only* those countries. For obvious reasons, someone who clicks the Canada button isn't looking for a job in Brazil. There are legal reasons as well; some countries have strict rules about job recruitment that require Monster to draw clear geographic boundaries.

For the flags representing countries with more than one official language, Monster includes a language selection splash page, as shown in Figure 3. The combination of flag selection and language selection ensures that users find what they need, in the language they need.

Figure 3   When users click the Swiss flag, they arrive at this language selection page. Not all official languages are included, but it's a start.

Q&A WITH MONSTER.COM

Steve Pogorzelski, President,
North America office
Monster.com

Describe your globalization strategy.

We are owned by TMP Worldwide, a human capital company that owns the largest recruitment advertising agency in the world. Our web globalization strategy was to play off the strength of the local recruitment advertising agency offices.

What countries did you begin with?

We began with the Netherlands and the U.K. because we have a very strong Dutch agency and have the largest recruitment advertising agency market share in the U.K. They enabled us to migrate their recruitment efforts to the web quickly.

Your site says "more countries coming soon"?

Japan is coming soon. We're also looking at Latin America, but we're waiting for the economy to improve somewhat before moving forward.

Who manages the content?

Each of the local Monster offices is in charge of content. All recruiting is done locally due to local regulations. The templates are managed here at headquarters in Maynard, Massachusetts. Most of the content is hosted locally.

How successfully has this decentralized management structure worked?

It's been very successful. We believe in hiring local entrepreneurs to run the Monster businesses, but give them the structure, the brand, and the financial support to help them build industry-leading businesses.

How do you prepare for launching into a new market?

We do extensive brand testing. We hire a local agency that develops a message that includes the basic tenets of our worldwide message. The slogan will change according to the market, though the Monster brand name and message remains consistent globally.

Any cultural issues you've had to deal with—say, with your name?

No. The name has traveled well globally. We did have issues in securing domain names. (The Italy URL was already taken, so Monster ended up with www.monsteritalia.it..)

What trends do you see developing?

We see a global labor market developing, one that is highly fluid, much more so than today. Borders will become less and less of an obstacle and talent will flow more rapidly between countries.

What advice would you give to other companies with tight budgets that want to add localized portions of their site?

Partner with the best-of-breed local content providers.

61

3

FIRST STEPS—AND MISSTEPS

You're bound to make a few mistakes when you begin web globalization. Although some mistakes are inevitable, and even necessary, you can avoid a lot of frustration (and costs) simply by avoiding the mistakes of those who went before.

A lot of companies have launched global web sites in the past few years, but most of these sites are far from perfect. For instance, many web sites are not fully translated, others are badly translated, and still others don't make it easy for international users to find their localized sites.

This chapter highlights a few of the more common mistakes that companies make when localizing web sites, and the rest of this book will show you how to avoid repeating them.

MULTIPLE PERSONALITY SITES

Because there are no borders on the Internet, there's little you can do to ensure that your German audience visits only your German web site and your American audience visits only your U.S. web site. Therefore, it's important to convey a consistent image globally, not just for branding but for usability—internally and externally.

Eli Lilly: Before and After

A year ago, Eli Lilly relied on a highly decentralized approach to web management; the branch office of each country managed its own web site, as shown in Figure 3.1. The result was inconsistent, as each office designed a unique site with little relation to its parent site. If it weren't for the Eli Lilly logo on each web site, it would have been difficult to know that the sites were even related.

65

Figure 3.1   Eli Lilly before: locally customized; globally inconsistent.

Recently, Eli Lilly embarked on a global redesign that enforced a consistent template across all localized sites. This arrangement left each country free to manage local content, but within global constraints. For example, the color palette and navigation system remains the same across all locales, as shown in Figure 3.2.

Answers That Matter.

health info   alliances   news   careers   about us   global   contact

welcome

Eli Lilly and Company creates and
delivers innovative medicines that
enable people to live longer, healthier
and more active lives.

Lilly products treat depressio
schizophrenia, diabetes, can
osteoporosis and many other
They create value for patients
healthcare providers and pay
reduce the cost of disease.

Lilly online is your link to info
about our products, our peop
company. We are committed

Highlights and Features

• Head-to-head study to compare

Answers That Matter.

医療情報   最新情報   採用情報   会社概要   海外情報   お問い合わせ

日本イーライリリーのホームページへようこそ

日本イーライリリー株式会社は、米国インディアナ州に本社
を置く製薬企業、イーライリリー・アンド・カンパニーの日
本法人です。イーライリリー社は革新的な医薬品を全世界の
人々に提供することを通じて、人々の健康で活動的な生活に
貢献しています。

日本イーライリリーは、インスリン製剤、成長ホルモン、抗
精神病薬、パーキンソン病治療薬、抗癌剤、急性循環不全改
善剤をはじめとする、内分泌系、中枢神経系、癌、循環器系
の治療領域における治療法を提供しています。

1975年に日本法人として設立されてから25年。全世界ですで
に高く評価されている大型新薬を日本でも次々と発売し、日
本で新たな展開を迎えようとしています。患者さんが待ち望

Lilly France

Des réponses qui comptent.

lilly en bref   maladies et traitements   lilly recrute   institut lilly

bienvenue

actualités

Engagé dans une priorité de sant
publique, Institut Lilly a lancé une
grande enquête, appelée "Villene
Santé". Son objet était de précise
facteurs socio-culturels des inég
d'accès aux soins.
Autres actualités...

qui sommes nous ?

Lilly, présent dans 160 pays, est
laboratoire pharmaceutique mond
axé sur la recherche, et dont la

Answers That Matter.

Bedriften   Terapiområder   Produkter   Karriere   Forskning   Linker

velkommen til Eli Lilly Norge A.S

Eli Lilly and Company er et forskningsbasert
amerikansk legemiddelselskap som utvikler og
markedsfører innovative legemidler over hele verden.
Hver dag bruker Lilly rundt 42 millioner kroner til
forskning. Dette tilsvarer nesten 20 % av vår globale
omsetning. Lilly har som målsetning å bidra til at
mennesker over hele verden lever lengre, sunnere og
mer aktive liv. Et annet mål er at vi ikke bare skal
levere legemidlet, men også den informasjon den
enkelte trenger for å ta bedre vare på seg selv.

Dette er et av utgangspunktene for disse sidene. Som
første terapiområde har vi valgt endokrinologi - og i
praksis betyr dette diabetes. I tiden som kommer skal

Lilly
ønsker deg
god
sommer!

Figure 3.2   Eli Lilly after: locally customized; globally consistent.

─Choose Colors Carefully ─────────────────────────────────

Colors mean different things to different cultures, so select your global palette carefully. I'll talk more about colors and how to choose and use them effectively in Chapters 4, "Are You Ready to Go Global?," 7, "Internationalization and Localization," and 11, "World Wide Design."

By instituting a degree of consistency across all sites, Eli Lilly conveys a more professional global image. Someone who skips over to the Norway site from the U.S. site will know immediately from the consistent layout and prominent logo placement that these two sites are indeed related. In addition, the global site architecture makes it easier for people who jump from site to site to quickly find what they're looking for.

The global web team also benefits from a consistent site architecture. Should a new product category need to be added to all country sites, the team can simply update the shared navigation bar and then localize it for each country. The process is much easier to implement than asking each local team to make the change and being unsure of what it would look like or when it would happen.

For more information on creating globally consistent web sites, see Chapters 7, "Internationalization and Localization," and 13, "Global Content Management."

OVERWEIGHT SITES

Nobody likes to wait for a web page to display, yet most of us do just that, day after day, because companies have built "overweight" web sites. An *overweight web site* is one that uses too many graphics or too much complex scripting (or both). Put simply, the greater the weight, the greater the *wait*.

And although overweight web sites can be a mild frustration for users in the U.S., they are a major obstacle to users outside the U.S., where high-speed Internet connections are often few and far between.

Have a Coke and Some Patience

The Coca-Cola U.S. web site, shown in Figure 3.3, is a bandwidth hog. It makes extensive use of Macromedia Flash, a software development tool used to create animated sites. The home page looks more like a commercial—with music and animation—than a static web page. Although Flash can be used to create highly engaging web sites, animation does not come without a price.

Figure 3.3   The Coca-Cola U.S. home page relies on extensive animation, putting a drain on even high-speed Internet connections.

The Weight and the Waiting

Based on the measurements of more than 300 home pages of the most popular web sites, the average web page weighs 89KB, but this number is just the average. Web pages run the gamut from Yahoo!, at 36KB, to General Motors, at 547KB. Using a dial-up modem, an 89KB web page takes roughly 14 seconds to display—a long time to expect people to wait.

You should strive to keep your web pages well below 89KB so that your users don't perceive your site as loading more slowly than average. If you compete against Yahoo!, you need to keep your site a great deal lighter than average.

The Coca-Cola U.S. home page weighs 198KB, more than twice the average. Had Coke not included animation and music, it could easily have saved 100KB in weight. Losing weight does not imply losing all entertainment value, however. Animation can still be included on a web page, but it should be used selectively. The problem with the Coca-Cola page isn't just the animation, but that so much animation was used. And when you localize a page of this weight for other countries, the problem gets that much worse.

The Coca-Cola Japan home page weighs 268KB, even more then the U.S. home page. Ironically, Japanese web users have slower Internet connections, on average, than American web users. You should never build a web strategy that relies on the patience of your audience.

Figure 3.4   The Coca-Cola Japan page also relies on animation, but most Japanese web users do not have high-speed connections.

At the other end of the spectrum, the Yahoo! Japan page weighs in at only 37KB—a much more user-friendly page weight (see Figure 3.5). Not surprisingly, according to Nielsen/NetRatings (**www.netratings.com**), Yahoo! Japan is consistently the most visited Japanese web site.

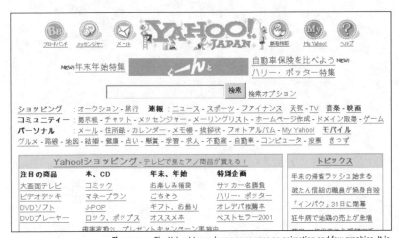

Figure 3.5   The Yahoo! Japan home page uses no animation and few graphics. It is just as lightweight in Japan as it is in the U.S.

For more information on creating web sites that load quickly—globally—refer to Chapters 7, "Internationalization and Localitation," 11, "World Wide Design," and 12, "Creating Multilingual Content."

Creating an overweight site for an audience who can't enjoy it is like inviting people to a party and not letting them near the bar. Not only is it frustrating, it's alienating—the last thing an American company wants to do to the world.

SITES THAT PLAY HARD TO GET

Navigation can make or break a web site, particularly when you are trying to help users who don't speak English find their localized web pages. Many companies simply don't plan ahead when building localized sites and then find themselves inserting a link to the localized sites at or near the bottom of the English site. This link, often called a *global gateway* or *language gateway*, is a critical component of generating traffic to your localized sites.

See if you can find the global gateway on the General Electric home page, shown in Figure 3.6. It's not easy to find if you don't speak English. Even if you do find it, a pull-down menu is not the ideal gateway, as the languages and countries are hidden from plain view.

Taking Your URL Global

Every country has its own domain address, like .jp for Japan or .no for Norway. Have you registered your country domains? And are you aware of multilingual domain names? I'll cover this topic in Chapter 14, " Mastering Your (Country) Domain."

71

Figure 3.6   The global gateway on the GE home page is located near the bottom of the left-hand column—not easy for non-English speakers to find.

People who manage web globalization projects want to see positive and measurable results from their localized web sites. But if you haven't taken the necessary steps to help users find these sites, you probably won't get the results you expected.

The Search for Sears

The U.S. Sears site is easy enough to find; just type in **www.sears.com**. Getting to the Spanish and French-Canadian Sears sites is a little more challenging, though (see Figure 3.7).

Figure 3.7 The Sears home page, with the Spanish and Canadian links circled.

The links to the localized sites are oddly set apart from one another. To further complicate matters, the link to the Spanish site is labeled "Todo para ti" ("Everything for you"). A simple "Español" would have sufficed. The phrase is the slogan for the Spanish Sears site, shown in Figure 3.8; it's also the URL: **www.searstodoparati.com**. Using your slogan as a URL prevents you from easily changing your slogan in the future.

Figure 3.8 The address of the Sears Spanish home page is
www.searstodoparati.com—hardly an intuitive address.

How would someone find the Spanish site if he or she doesn't know the slogan and
doesn't see the link on the home page? A language that is not country specific,
such as Spanish, is more challenging to find because you can't simply use a
country-specific address, such as **www.sears.com.mx**. Many sites follow a more
standardized directory structure, such as adding the language code to the end of
the URL: **www.hrblock.com/es** or **www.oracle.com/es**, for example. Although this
system isn't foolproof, it's much more predictable for users than the Sears
approach.

The Sears Canada site is much easier to manage because it's located under the
country domain **www.sears.ca**. In Canada, companies are required by law to offer
both English and French translations on their sites. In Figure 3.9, note the location
of the French link on the site—this one is easy to find.

Figure 3.9 The Sears Canada page, unlike the U.S. page, makes language selection easy to find.

The random organization of the localized Sears sites suggests that Sears did not have a clear localization strategy from the beginning. As a new localized site was added, the link to it was squeezed into the home page wherever there was room— a common problem with localization projects. Companies need to place a priority on their global gateways from both a design and usability standpoint; the navigation must be simple and consistent across all locales.

For more information on creating web sites that international users can easily find, see Chapters 11, "World Wide Design," and 14, "Mastering Your (Country) Domain."

SLOPPY SITES

Badly written sentences, mistranslations, oversights, and inconsistencies are all too common in localized web sites. Because many web developers don't speak the languages of the sites they're developing, mistakes are bound to occur. Examples of common mistakes include the following:

■ **Using the wrong icons.** For example, the U.S.-style mailbox icon is not a globally recognized icon, nor is the shopping cart.

■ **Using the wrong models.** Many sites translate every word of text, but fail to use models that reflect the target market. Some cultures are more sensitive to the models a company uses in its advertising and web sites. For example, on a Japanese web site, you'll want to use Japanese models, not the same American models you used for your U.S. site.

- **Using dated content.** Localized sites often are not kept up to date because the initial translation budget is depleted, and no one was ever given the responsibility of keeping the content current.

- **Using untranslated content.** A lot of companies don't go far enough when localizing their site, leaving some of the pages in the source language. Perhaps the obstacle was the budget or design, but in the end, the site looks unfinished. Unless your target audience consists of only bilinguals, this approach is bound to leave people feeling left out.

Novell France: Errors of Omission

On the Novell France page, the navigation buttons on the left side of the page have been translated, but the buttons at the top of the page remain in English. The design of Novell's global site, shown in Figure 3.10, is such that these top navigation buttons always remain in English because they always link to English-language pages.

Figure 3.10 Nearly half the text on the Novell France home page is in English.

Nevertheless, the visitor who doesn't understand what these buttons mean should at least be told somewhere that they refer only to English content. Better yet, the buttons could just be removed to free up space for localized content. A simple "English" link in the upper-right corner would have sufficed for users in need of English-language content.

Finally, the search engine is apparently designed only for English speakers because both the pull-down menu and "Advanced Search" options remain in English. Once again, it might have made more sense to leave this feature off the page altogether if a fully localized search engine wasn't going to be made available. At the least, the search engine should warn users of its limitation.

Even if you speak only English, you can successfully localize web sites—but you can't do it alone. You need experts who can proof your work and you need a dependable, repeatable workflow.

WEB GLOBALIZATION IS RELATIVE

The majority of companies are in the early stages of web globalization, so missteps are inevitable and quite common. And because most companies are doing a poor-to-average job at localization, you can gain a competitive edge by simply *not* repeating their mistakes.

Your competitive edge is relative, however. After you localize your site for a new market, you need to do as good a job, or better, than others in that market. If someone in France can choose between your web site and the sites of several local competitors, your site is going to have to be much more culturally relevant to stand apart. Web globalization is a long journey, but the following chapters will help you get off to a good start, one step at a time.

4

ARE YOU READY TO GO GLOBAL?

Globalization isn't as much about having a global presence as it is about thinking globally (and locally). With the Internet, you no longer need international offices to have a global presence, but you do need to assess your company's global readiness before localizing your web site. This chapter poses some of the key questions you and your organization need to answer before getting started.

Thinking Like a Multinational

General Electric has made globalization a priority and it shows. Nearly half of its revenues come from outside the United States and its more than 60 country-specific web sites help make this growth possible (see Figure 4.1).

But you don't need to be a multinational to think and act like a multinational. The Internet is the great equalizer. By localizing your web site for the world, you can capitalize on markets that years ago would have been unthinkable without foreign offices. But before you dive in, you need to do a little corporate soul searching. A global web site alone won't make you a global company. One of the keys to General Electric's success is that its employees no longer view themselves as part of an American company with foreign markets; they see themselves as a global company with local markets.

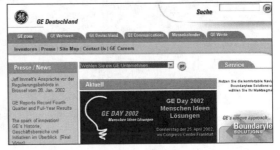

Figure 4.1 With more than 60 localized web sites, GE embraces the world, one country at a time.

Reality Checklist

Too many companies rush off and hire translators without first assessing whether they are ready to go global. Before your company begins web globalization, ask these three preliminary questions:

- Is your company ready to go global?

- Are your products or services ready to go global?

- Are your brand names ready to go global?

Just as a company's English-language web site can open a new world of opportunities domestically, so too does each localized web site. However, localization will succeed only if the entire organization supports it, from the executive suite to the factory floor to the customer support line.

Localization requires keeping an open mind about foreign languages, cultures, and traditions. Never assume that what works in one country will work everywhere else; you must be prepared to take your treasured brands and products and rename them, reposition them, or scrap them altogether when entering a new market. In today's knowledge economy, the companies and employees that are most "globally aware" are the best positioned to succeed.

81

PREMATURE GLOBALIZATION

Launching a global web site does not necessarily make a company globally aware. In fact, a global web site could create more problems than it solves. After all, the web site is just the front end of the company. To be successful, companies must also globalize the back end. For example, customer support departments can't answer questions in languages they don't understand. If your web site creates the impression that your company offers multilingual support, you must have a staff that can truly support all the languages on the web site.

Be Careful What You Wish For

True story: The marketing director of a professional society wanted to expand the subscriber base in other countries. The society already had many international members, but because none of the publications had been translated, members needed at least a moderate grasp of English to reap the benefits of joining. So the marketing director decided to translate the society's membership form into Chinese, in the hopes that it would make joining the society much easier for Chinese speakers and increase membership.

Within a few weeks, the society received its first completed Chinese form by fax. The membership director, unaware of what the marketing director had been up to, looked at this form, filled out in Chinese, and said, "What the hell am I supposed to do with this?" The membership director didn't understand Chinese. No one on her staff understood Chinese. Even if someone on her staff did understand Chinese, their membership database didn't accept Chinese characters.

So this person in China completed the membership form and subscribed to a couple of publications and the organization could do nothing about it. The professional society didn't even know what publications were selected because the publication names were translated into Chinese—and they had no English template to compare it against. It may seem obvious that you shouldn't create marketing materials in a language your company can't support, yet companies that jump into global markets too fast frequently repeat this scenario.

So much of web globalization has nothing to do with a web site: employee training, product localization, international trademarks. Before your company takes that fateful leap into web globalization, make sure you can support not only a global web site, but also the many complications and questions that will arise after the site goes live.

So Many Countries; So Many Questions

Imagine that your company has just launched localized web sites for four countries: France, Germany, Japan, and Spain. Suddenly, you and the departments in your company face a range of challenges and questions:

Customer Service
- "We just received a dozen emails in Japanese; at least, I *think* it's Japanese. Who here speaks Japanese?"
- "Someone in Germany says the order form isn't working correctly."
- "How can I help this person in France navigate the site when I can't read the site?"

Marketing

- "I need a dozen banner ads in German, French, and Spanish by Friday."
- "We just rewrote the English pages and we're tweaking the design; can you make these changes to the rest of the languages by Friday?"
- "Actually, Friday is too late. Can you have it done by 5 p.m. today?"

Legal

- "Because of privacy laws, the personal information you collect from European customers cannot be managed the same way you manage the domestic customer list."
- "We may be violating a German law on this promotion."
- "Are you collecting taxes properly?"
- "If this instructions page isn't translated correctly, we could be held liable if something goes wrong."

HR

- "Can you post these new job listings in all those languages?"

Sales

83

- "We're not allowed to sell that product in Germany, only France, or our distributor will go ballistic."
- "The web site is great, but now I need a brochure in Japanese for our sales reps. Can you have it done by Friday?"

IT

- "This globalization effort just tripled the size of the web site, and we're going to have to pay more in hosting fees. Whose budget is it coming out of?"
- "Who's going to pay for all these new international domain names you want registered?"

And let's not forget the CEO...

- "Great job on those new sites! The feedback I'm getting is fantastic. Now when are you launching sites for China, Brazil, and Israel?"

CHOOSING A MARKET

Once you're ready to go global, you must decide exactly where to go. You can't cover every country and language at once, so it's best to set priorities. Keep in mind that borders don't always define a market. Some companies may choose to target a certain country, but others might pick a language, such as Spanish, knowing full well they'll be communicating with people across many countries, including the U.S.

For more information on Spanish-language localization, see "Hands-On: Spanish."

No matter what languages you select, you'll gain the added benefit of reaching U.S. residents who also speak the languages. According to the most recent U.S. Census, more than 30 million U.S. residents don't speak English at home (see Figure 4.2). Increasingly, companies can justify their localization efforts without even planning on selling outside the U.S.

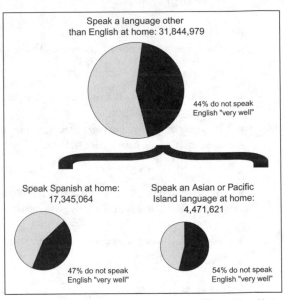

Speak a language other than English at home: 31,844,979

44% do not speak English "very well"

Speak Spanish at home: 17,345,064

47% do not speak English "very well"

Speak an Asian or Pacific Island language at home: 4,471,621

54% do not speak English "very well"

Figure 4.2 Languages spoken by U.S. residents.

Source: U.S. Census 2000.

For the purposes of this book, however, assume that you want to begin with a foreign market and that you don't have an international presence to build on. Now you must decide what that first market should be.

Listen to the Logs

Every time someone visits your web site, a log entry is recorded on the server. Often, the log includes the country code domain where that web user is located, such as **.ru** for Russia or **.kr** for Korea (see Figure 4.3).

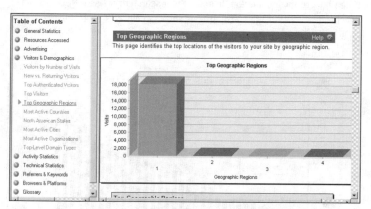

Figure 4.3 The WebTrends Log Analyzer (**www.webtrends.com**) can tell you where many of your web visitors are based.

You'll find the complete list of country code domains in Appendix D, "Language and Country Codes."

Logs are by no means a definite precursor to web localization success in a given country, but they do indicate global traffic patterns on which you can base certain assumptions. Perhaps you've noticed a lot of activity originating from Asia, as opposed to Latin America. Perhaps users from a certain region tend to visit specific sections of your site more frequently than visitors from other regions.

Look Beneath the Logs

You might notice that users outside the U.S. seem to spend more time on your web site, on average, than your domestic users, but don't mistake length of usage with interest level. Users outside the U.S. generally have slower Internet connections, which means they *must* spend more time on your site to view the same number of pages as your U.S. users.

Log analysis can help you decide which countries to localize for first and which portions of your site to localize first. For example, if you're a software developer, you might notice that users in other countries tend to spend more time on the software support pages; this data could indicate that you need to invest more time and resources into localizing this section of your site.

Listen to the World

When you compare your company's traffic patterns with global Internet usage patterns, you may discover some valuable opportunities. If many users visit your site from a country with relatively low Internet usage or access, you might have discovered a potentially promising market. In 2001, the research firm Taylor Nelson Sofres (TNS) measured Internet usage by country, as shown in Figure 4.4. As you can see, there is a wide variance in Internet usage among countries.

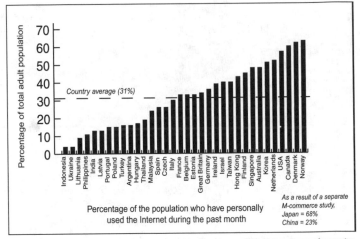

Figure 4.4   Global Internet usage by country.

*Source: Taylor Nelson Sofres Interactive (**www.tnsofres.com**), July 2001.*

Keep in mind that Internet usage does not always equate with Internet commerce. The Japanese, for example, are more likely than Brazilians to purchase over the Internet. The TNS study also found that

- The U.S. has the highest proportion of online shoppers at 33%, compared to the global average of 15%.

- In India, the Philippines, Thailand, and Turkey, 2% or less of the online population shop on the Internet.

- Germany is the most reluctant nation to supply credit card details, and was surpassed only by the Czech Republic when it came to general security concerns.

In addition, not all people are predisposed to shop for the same things online. TNS discovered that online purchasing habits vary widely by country:

■ Israel leads the pack in purchasing business travel online, while Australians are most likely to purchase leisure travel online.

■ Koreans are more than twice as likely as people from other countries to buy cosmetics online.

■ The U.S. is fourth on the list in purchasing PC hardware online, behind Denmark, Israel, and Germany.

Just as there is no such thing as an "average web user," there is no such thing as an average country. Each country and culture is going to use the Internet in a slightly different—or widely different—manner. The successful companies will be those that notice the subtleties and respond to them.

87

CALCULATE RETURN ON INVESTMENT (ROI)

The markets that offer the greatest financial rewards are the most difficult to resist. Japan, with its high Internet penetration and affinity for online purchasing, exerts a strong pull on American companies, despite the technical and cultural challenges of reaching this market (discussed in "Hands-On: Chinese and Japanese").

The best way to justify going into a new market is to weigh your investment against the potential return, typically expressed in revenue. ROI is often a tough number to come by, particularly with new markets in which you have little data to work with. Even if it's just a best guess, you should have a revenue goal in mind, as it will help determine how much to invest in the localization process. You don't want to spend a million dollars localizing a site for a country that, at best, is going to spend only $20,000 a year from your company.

Questions you should ask to determine ROI:
- Does this market need our products and services?
- If so, can they afford our products and services?
- How will consumers pay us? (Some countries are more averse than others to using credit cards.)
- How quickly is the market growing, and what's the total revenue potential?

- Can we deliver the products quickly and affordably?
- Can we effectively support our products and services?
- How expensive will it be to localize the web site?
- How expensive will it be to maintain the web site?
- Will we have to do anything special to our back-end computer systems, such as databases?
- Are there liability and regulatory issues to navigate?

BUILDING BRANDS THAT TRAVEL

You've selected a market, possibly several, and now you're ready to get started on that web site. Not so fast. First, take a hard look at what you're trying to sell. Some products travel more easily than others. For example, a washing machine that uses both hot and cold water is irrelevant in a country such as Japan, where clothes are washed exclusively in cold water. And a toaster that offers extra-wide slots for bagels might not be of much use in a country that doesn't consume many bagels. Before you invest in localizing your web site, you need to invest in localizing your products and services.

As a general rule, the first products to consider taking global are those that require the least amount of localization. Even if you have plans to create a global brand, one that needs little if any localization, your brand could still require local modification. McDonald's is one of the most visible brand names in the world, yet McDonald's in France is not the same McDonald's in Russia. Localization explains why you can buy a beer and a pork burger from the McDonald's in Germany, but you can't order a Bacon Egg & Cheese Biscuit from a McDonald's in Australia (*biscuit* is a cookie in Australia). These are relatively minor changes, but they can make all the difference in your company's success.

Increasingly, companies view their products and services as more than just products and services. They are brands. Starbucks, for instance, is much more than just coffee; it is a logo, it is packaging, it is the atmosphere of the stores. All the elements that define your brand must be modified, if necessary, as you extend your brand into new markets. Although every company faces unique challenges when taking brands into new markets, one of the most common challenges is the brand name itself.

Even Hollywood Thinks Local

Hollywood is no stranger to localization. For years, it has created "localized remakes" of foreign movies for American audiences. It first struck gold when it released *The Magnificent Seven*, a remake of *The Seven Samurai*, Akira Kurosawa's landmark film. Since then we've seen quite a few localized remakes from film and television:

- *Three Men and a Baby* (remake of the French film *Trois Hommes et un Couffin*)

- *Point of No Return* (remake of *La Femme Nikita*)

- *All in the Family* (a remake of the British series *Till Death Us Do Part*)

Most recently, *The Weakest Link* was imported from Britain. Departing from convention, the American version used the same hostess as the British version, but the set and questions were localized for American audiences.

The Name Game

Companies often develop brand names without first considering whether the names will one day be used outside the native market. As a result, the names they create are often ill-suited for globalization. For example, America Online shortened its name to AOL as it expanded its focus outside U.S. borders. With the Internet, all brand names are global names from day one, so you need to get it right the first time. With so much to worry about when taking a brand global, companies increasingly turn to outside consultants. Christiane Bernier founded the global identity practice of Lionbridge, a web and software localization company. Her group works closely with companies that need help selecting a name that will travel globally or testing an existing name before the company enters new markets.

89

When testing a name, Lionbridge relies on experts in the target markets. These people are generally chosen for their knowledge of a particular field and expertise in translating for that market. Identity testing generally breaks down into two stages:

1. **A "thumbs up or down" analysis**

    This brief evaluation is useful when a company is considering a number of new brand names and needs some quick feedback to help narrow down its list. For example, Lionbridge recently worked with a consultancy that was renaming itself and wanted to be sure the new name would travel well globally. The client hired an identity firm that had come up with several dozen possible names. Lionbridge then provided a thumbs up or down analysis, looking only at macro issues, such as negative connotations or obvious infringements on competitive names.

2. **In-depth analysis**

    After Lionbridge helped the client narrow the list to a few candidates, it conducted a full-scale review of how each name would be perceived in all potential markets. Typically, the following questions are included in the review:

    ■ Is the name aesthetically pleasing?

    ■ Is the name easy to read and pronounce?

    ■ Does the name sound too similar to other established brand names in the market?

    ■ Is the name competitively better than other brand names?

¿Tienes una pregunta?

The Internet portal Ask.com presents a more extreme example of how far a company might have to go to localize itself for new locales. At Ask.com, users can conduct searches by entering questions, instead of just keywords (see Figure 4.5). The word *ask* conveys the key value of this portal for English speakers, but means little to non-English speakers.

So when Ask.com developed a Spanish version of its site, it kept its logo largely intact (see Figure 4.6), but changed its name and URL to **www.Pregunta.com**. It then underwent a massive effort to localize its search engine to accept Spanish-language queries.

Executives at Ask.com realized that the strength of their brand *globally* wasn't the name, but the technology behind the name.

Figure 4.5   The Ask.com English-language home page

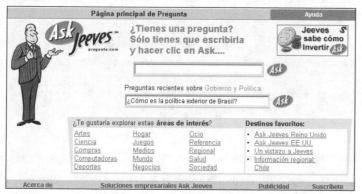

Figure 4.6   When localized into Spanish, "Ask.com" becomes "Pregunta.com," but Jeeves remains.

Each review is customized to the needs of the client and target audience. For example, a client in a business or technology field may feel less of an urgency to fully localize brand names, as global audiences in these fields generally are more proficient in English.

Clients who target consumers, particularly with products for the home, must pay close attention to cultural issues. Trust is a key factor in consumer purchases, and consumers have difficulty trusting product names that range from mildly amusing to mildly offensive. In-depth analysis can be expensive and time consuming, but Bernier notes that it costs a company far less time and money to develop a name that succeeds globally than it costs to make up for lost sales and embarrassing public relations disasters. Finally, keep in mind that brand identity analysis does not and should not take the place of international trademark reviews.

If you have the benefit of creating a brand name from scratch, Bernier offers the following advice:

- Avoid puns and word play.

- Avoid abbreviations. For example, "B2B" may make sense in the U.S. but it doesn't abroad.

- Avoid names based on abbreviations. Take IBM: Although this name is already well known globally, it does present pronunciation challenges. Sounding out letters in other languages isn't always so elegant and can often lead to unintended mispronunciations.

- Avoid metaphors or names based on images. A bull might make be a good visual reference to the "bull market" in the U.S. but be meaningless elsewhere.

- Avoid humor or anything you may see as cute. As a rule, Bernier says, "the cuter the name, the less likely it is to carry over well."

Go Global Before Leaving Home

Increasingly, companies begin testing brands globally before they launch them domestically. According to Ron Recobs, managing director of the New York office of the Brand Institute, 90% of all pharmaceutical companies test their brand names globally from the start. Testing and surveillance are also critical because language rules and culture are in a constant state of evolution. For example, the Brand Institute tested the brand name for the flu medicine Tamiflu. Americans refer to influenza as "flu," but it isn't typically the term used in other English-speaking countries, such as England or Ireland.

Therefore, a product like Tamiflu could have easily failed abroad. However, research found that usage of this term was slowly spreading throughout Europe; Tamiflu was introduced and has since been very successful in Europe.

Lost In the Translation

If you decide to translate your brand names or slogans, don't skimp on translators. Literal translations can be risky, particularly with brand names; a minor oversight can result in rather embarrassing results. The following are well-known examples of translation gone awry:

- The Clairol "Mist Stick" (a curling iron) was sold in Germany under its English name. In German, "mist" means "manure."

- The Perdue Chicken slogan "It takes a tough man to make a tender chicken" was translated into Spanish as "It takes an aroused man to make a chicken affectionate."

- The Coors slogan "Turn it loose" was translated into Spanish as "Suffer from diarrhea."

- The Kentucky Fried Chicken slogan "finger-lickin' good" was translated into Chinese "eat your fingers off."

- In Taiwan, the translation of the Pepsi slogan "Come alive with the Pepsi Generation" became "Pepsi will bring your ancestors back from the dead."

Finally, don't overlook the packaging. Gerber's famous label, with pictures of babies, was exported to African store shelves. Unfortunately for Gerber, in African countries, where there is a high rate of illiteracy, companies routinely place pictures on the labels of what the packages contain. People assumed the Gerber jars contained babies, not baby food.

A Coke and a Smile

When Coca-Cola was first exported to China, merchants transliterated the name into Chinese characters. *Transliteration* is the process of creating a new name in the target language that sounds similar to the name in the source language. Unfortunately, even though the result sounded like "Coca-Cola" in Chinese, it actually meant "Bite the wax tadpole." Coca-Cola ended up adopting a name that was not so literal.

93

Don't Offend, But Don't Blend In

The first goal of developing a global brand name is to make sure it won't offend. The second goal is to make sure it sells.

Let's say you're an automobile manufacturer that intends to enter the U.S. market. You could name yourself "Car Company" with confidence that no one will be offended, but you might find that no one buys your cars. The difference between an inoffensive brand name and a successful brand name is the difference between Car Company and Mercedes-Benz.

Currently, companies seem more concerned with not offending the crowd than with standing apart from the crowd. However, as markets grow more competitive and competitors grow more savvy, the "name game" will play a more pivotal role in your company's success.

Moving Beyond Words

The name of your brand presents the most obvious challenge to going global, but it's not the only challenge. Numbers, pictures, colors, and icons are all loaded with different meanings in different cultures. Because these elements also play a critical role in global web design, they are covered in Chapter 11, "World Wide Design." For now, just be aware that a successful global brand depends on much more than just a name.

Imagine that you're in the vacuum cleaner business. Your products have done very well globally, especially your previous model, the CleanWizard 3. However, your new model, the CleanWizard 4, is selling well in all your markets except Asia. It's almost as though Asian customers were avoiding it. So you conduct some research:

Is it the price?
No, the price is competitive.
Is it the quality?
No, the quality is excellent.
Then what is it?
The number 4.
The number 4?

The Cantonese pronunciation of 4 sounds similar to the pronunciation of "to die" in Chinese. Just as the number 13 is considered unlucky in America, in Asian countries the number 4 is considered unlucky. Using the number 4 on your products, in your products, or even in your pricing is likely to result in an unlucky downturn in sales.

Conversely, the pronunciation of the number 8 in Cantonese sounds like "getting rich," so people pay extra to have phone numbers with this number in them.

The Color of Money

The successful translation of the brand name is important in globalization, but do not underestimate the power of color to hurt or help your global branding and web design efforts. Coca-Cola may have had difficulties with its name in China, but its packaging was well received, primarily because red is a positively perceived color in China. In fact, Chinese brides customarily wear red instead of white because white signifies death. For more information on colors and their significance around the world, see Chapter 11 and Appendix B, "Global Color Chart."

WHEN "FOREIGN" IS A GOOD THING

Sometimes companies gain an advantage by being viewed as foreign. In the U.S., for example, people value watches that are Swiss, cars that are German and Japanese, wines that are French (and Australian), and clothing that is Italian.

Christiane Bernier notes that America has become more interested in other cultures, but still has a relatively naïve understanding of other cultures. Companies that market to Americans take full advantage of this fact. For example, "French vanilla" means nothing in France. Fortune cookies are an American invention and are virtually nonexistent in Asia.

The key question to ask when entering a new market is, "Am I serving a uniquely local need or am I selling a uniquely foreign product?" The answer will be the key to how you translate your brand and your product.

95

YOU'RE READY, NOW WHAT?

You've selected your target markets; you've selected and localized your products; you've tested the brand names and slogans; and you've registered the necessary trademarks and Internet domains. Now you're ready to take on that web site. The rest of this book focuses on the implementation, management, and promotion of localized web sites. In addition, you'll soon begin the first Hands-On chapter, in which you'll learn to localize a web page into one of many languages.

Figure 1 The L.L. Bean home page.

L.L. BEAN

L.L. Bean was founded in 1912 by Leon Leonwood Bean as a one-man direct mail operation. Last year, the company made a billion dollars in sales, shipping more than 12 million packages around the world. L.L. Bean has a very strong business in Japan through direct mail and more than nine retail outlets.

However, L.L. Bean has only recently begun testing the globalization waters. It initially launched help sections in four languages; however, the Japanese section proved so popular that the company decided to undergo a full-scale Japanese localization. In June 2002, L.L. Bean launched its Japanese site, as shown in Figure 2.

---

www.llbean.com

Localized web sites: In addition to its Japanese web site, L.L. Bean offers localized help sections in:

- French
- German
- Spanish

Figure 2   The L.L. Bean Japan home page.

ANALYSIS

L.L. Bean is taking an incremental approach to globalization, one that limits its upfront investment and risk, yet provides measurable user feedback on which languages are in the greatest demand. Recently, there wasn't much for non-English speakers to view—just an international help section that displayed four languages, as shown in Figure 3.

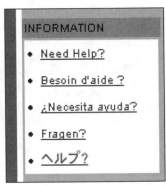

Figure 3   The L.L. Bean international help page is not very sophisticated, but it's a start.

If someone speaks no English, the L.L. Bean site isn't going to be much help at all. Even finding this international help page is going to be a challenge, as the International Help button is at the bottom of the home page and is in English (see Figure 4).

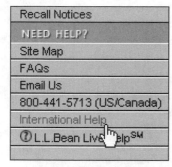

Figure 4 The link to the international help page isn't very helpful.

Despite the inherent limitations of the web site, offering some language support is much better than no support. These pages will come in particularly handy for web users who do have some understanding of English, but might still be unsure about the ordering process. These few pages could very well make the difference between completed sales and abandoned shopping carts.

99

A company can gain vital global feedback by spending no more than a few thousand dollars on localization. Victoria's Secret also implemented an incremental strategy when it launched an "International Information" section, shown in Figure 5. The incremental approach to globalization proves that you can learn a lot from a little.

Figure 5 Victoria's Secret also offers multilingual customer support. Once again, it's not much, but it's better than nothing.

Q&A WITH L.L. BEAN

Shawn Gorman, Marketing Manager, e-Commerce

How popular are the translated pages?

With the international FAQ pages, the first few months of their being published saw the greatest traffic. Page views for the FAQs are much lower now, probably due to a more savvy online audience.

Why did you choose Japan for your first full-scale localization?

After the United States, Japan is the world's second largest e-commerce market. We chose to launch there first because the Japanese market is our greatest source of overseas demand. LLB International operates nine stores and circulates six million Japanese-language catalogs annually. LLB has developed a very successful multi-channel operating model in the United States, offering Bean products through retail stores, catalogs, and the web. Our objective is to replicate this successful model in Japan.

Will you set up an overseas office for fulfillment or will you subcontract?

Our existing in-country catalog fulfillment model will support both catalog and web orders.

How do you manage your Japanese site?

Our site is built on IBM's WebSphere Commerce Suite. Our Japanese catalog team and the LLB Information Services department contribute extensively to the production of the Japanese site as well as our online catalog in Japanese. Internationalization also allows the team to perform regular maintenance on the site.

Have you had to deal with any cultural obstacles abroad, say, with your name?

Our name and high brand recognition is an advantage rather than an obstacle. However, avoiding cultural gaffes is a critical factor in gaining local acceptance for any business operating overseas. Such blunders contribute to failure more commonly than companies realize—and the vast majority of these problems are not unique to the web.

In the mail-order catalog business, for example, adding local toll-free numbers, converting to metric measurements, and offering payment and delivery options tailored to local customer preferences are just a few issues to consider. Because the requirements differ for each market, it's important to work with someone who's got the experience necessary to steer clear of any serious mistakes or omissions. Catalogs and the web are adapted, not merely translated. Copy cannot be translated literally. It must be carefully adapted, using clear guidelines, to ensure that the proper voice is maintained.

What advice would you give to executives with tight budgets who want to begin adding localized portions of their site?

The smartest decision executives can make is to begin by building a global platform, thus leveraging their current technology investment and enabling their companies to gain operational efficiencies when entering new markets. By minimizing the impact to back-end systems during the localization process, these companies will achieve smooth, cost-effective solutions, in addition to improving time-to-market and saving themselves a lot of frustration.

Are there any international web sites that you admire?

Amazon.com is a perfect example of a successful global site. A single global technology platform allows Amazon to launch operations in any market, while giving them the flexibility to quickly adapt their system to the linguistic and cultural requirements of each locale. After launching in Japan, Amazon.co.jp became the top online retailer for books there within just months.

HANDS-ON: SPANISH

Introduction

This is the first of six Hands-On chapters. Collectively, they demonstrate the process (and challenges) of localizing an English language web page into multiple languages. After completing all the Hands-On chapters, you will have localized one web page into eight languages—the languages spoken by more than 80% of the world's population. If you'd like to try your hand at these exercises, all files used in these chapters are available for download; go to **www.bytelevel.com/beyondborders**.

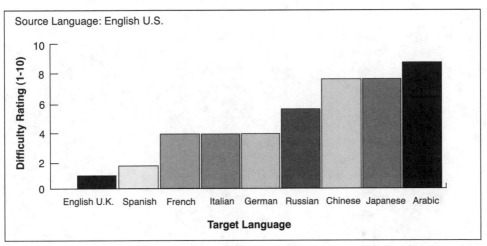

Figure 1   The difficulty ratings used in Chapter 1, "In the Beginning, There Was English."

Speakers worldwide: 322 million (28 million in Spain)
(source: *Ethnologue*, 14th edition, 2000
www.Ethnologue.com)

ISO country code: ES

Difficulty rating: 2 (see Figure 1)

Spanish is a national language of:

Country	Language Code
Argentina	es-AR
Bolivia	es-BO
Chile	es-CL
Colombia	es-CO
Costa Rica	es-CR
Cuba	es-CU
Dominican Republic	es-DO
Ecuador	es-EC
El Salvador	es-SV
Guatemala	es-GT
Honduras	es-HN
Mexico	es-MX
Nicaragua	es-NI
Panama	es-PA
Paraguay	es-PY
Peru	es-PE
Puerto Rico	es-PR
Spain	es-ES
Uruguay	es-UY
Venezuela	es-VE

FIRST THOUGHTS

Sometimes the best way to learn how to do something is to jump right in and try it yourself. The Hands-On chapters in this book are designed to ease you into web localization, beginning with Spanish and graduating to increasingly challenging languages. The focus of these chapters is on the technical and logistical challenges of web localization.

The source web page (see Figure 2) is about as simple as a web page can get. There is no functionality and only one graphic (used for the navigation bar). The text of the web page is the "Tower of Babel" passage from the Bible. Although there's a certain irony to translating this passage into multiple languages, it was chosen for practical reasons. Because the Bible is one of the most translated works in the world, you'll have little trouble locating this passage in practically any language; this will save you the trouble (and expense) of actually hiring a translator or editor if you want to try these exercises on your own. The text for most of the Hands-On chapters has been taken from the Bible Gateway at **http://bible.gospelcom.net.** Although this method bypasses the need for a translator, I've still gone through the process of hiring a translator and editor.

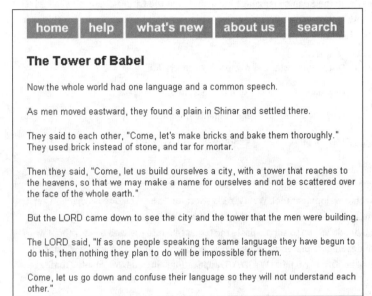

Figure 2 The source-language web page.

Spanish was chosen as the first language not just because it's one of the most popular languages that companies begin with, but also because it's one of the easiest. You'll run into fewer technical challenges localizing English into Spanish than you'll find when localizing English into Japanese. There are still a number of challenges ahead, however. Before jumping into the project, ask the following questions:

- **¿Which Spanish?** There is more than one type of Spanish in the world; you need to make sure you're speaking to the right audience in the way they want to be spoken to.

- **What to do with the embedded text?** The one graphic on the web page contains text that will require translation. Inserting and editing text within images can be painstaking (and sometimes expensive) work. Before beginning a localization project, always try to reduce the number of images with embedded text.

- **How will the Spanish site be organized?** Although the new site will consist of only one web page, you should develop an organization and naming system that works as well with one web page as it will with a thousand pages.

TOOLS

The tools used for this project are not cutting edge, nor do they need to be. The characters in the Spanish language are included in the Latin 1 character set, so just about any software application created in the past eight years will do. For this exercise, the following applications will be used:

Operating system:	Microsoft Windows ME
Graphics:	Adobe Illustrator 9
HTML:	Macromedia Dreamweaver 3
Word count:	WebBudget (free version)

Dreamweaver Basics

Dreamweaver is a popular WYSIWYG web development tool. WYSIWYG is short for "what you see is what you get," which means that the software presents the web page as it should look when finished (as opposed to raw HTML code). As shown in Figure 3, Dreamweaver allows you to simply paste the target text into the web page without worrying about the underlying code. Many developers prefer text editors over WYSIWYG editors, which we will demonstrate in subsequent Hands-On chapters. Other popular WYSIWYG applications include Microsoft FrontPage, HoTMetaL PRO, and Adobe GoLive.

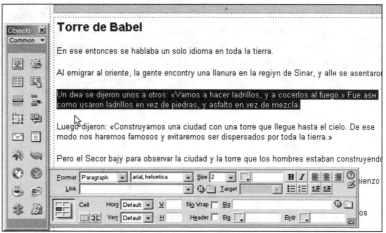

Figure 3   Dreamweaver lets you paste the target text directly into the web page.

¿WHICH SPANISH?

Spanish is a lot like English in that it's spoken in numerous countries, but rarely spoken consistently among countries. The most pronounced differences in Spanish are found between the Spanish spoken in Spain (often called Castilian or Iberian Spanish) and the Spanish spoken in Mexico, the U.S., and parts of Latin America. Castilian Spanish is more formal than Mexican Spanish. The general line of thinking is that the closer you get to the U.S., the more informal the Spanish becomes. Within the U.S., there is a growing use of "Spanglish," a mix, or fusion, of Spanish and English. The phrase *tiempo is money* is an example of how Spanish and English are now used interchangeably in many parts of the U.S.; entirely new words have also been created. Some people view Spanglish as a language all its own; others view it as a bastardization of English and Spanish. Although you probably won't localize your web site with Spanglish in mind, it's important to be aware that this trend exists.

FYI

Although Castilian (Spanish) is the official language of Spain, it's not the only language used in Spain. Other distinct languages spoken in Spain include Catalan, Galician, and Euskera (the Basque language).

Patrice Martin, business development manager of the Brazilian localization firm Ushuaia Solutions (**www.ushuaiasolutions.com**), typically sees two types of localization requests: general Latin American Spanish and Iberian Spanish. But Martin stresses that companies need to let the audience dictate what translators they hire. "If you are selling a product mainly in the south cone of the Latin American continent (Chile, Argentina), you will probably ask your translation partners to use Chilean and Argentine translators."

Spanish Within the U.S.

American companies with no plans to sell outside the U.S. are still likely to find themselves localizing for Spanish speakers because the U.S. is home to more than 30 million Spanish speakers. For example, H&R Block localized its web site for the Spanish U.S. market, as shown in Figure 4. For the U.S. market, Martin recommends using a neutral variety of Spanish with simple grammatical structures. "And avoid Spanglish by all means. Although Spanglish is tempting when translating into Spanish for the U.S., it is more a variety of English than of Spanish and could be offensive to some Spanish cultures."

Figure 4 H&R Block localized its web site primarily for U.S. Spanish speakers.

The Search for "Universal Spanish"

Given the expense of translation, it's only natural to search for one Spanish that fits all, which explains the popularity of universal Spanish. "Universal Spanish as such does not exist," says Martin. "Although universal Spanish is a growing need for American and European companies, it shouldn't be taken literally. It is a kind of compromise solution between all participants, where everyone will contribute the most neutral word instead of trying to impose the regional term."

To give you an idea of the challenges in creating universal Spanish, consider how difficult it would be for two offices—one in New York and one in London—to develop a universal English. Imagine the heated arguments that would ensue over whether to use "color" or "colour," "parking lot" or "carpark," and "elevator" or "lift." In the end, some words and spellings must win out over others, and you may find the resulting language more political than universal. To arrive at a universal glossary of language, it helps to create a table, as shown in Table 1.

Table 1 Differences Among Regional Varieties of Spanish

English	Spanish (Argentina)	Spanish (Colombia)	Spanish (Mexico)	Universal*
Order (noun)	Pedido	Orden	Orden	Orden
Order (verb)	Pedir	Ordenar	Ordenar	Ordenar
List	Listado	Lista	Listado	Lista
Slip	Boleta		Talón	Boleta
Batch	Lote	Tanda	Control	Batch
Report	Informe		Reporte	Reporte
Assembly	Equipo	Ensamblaje	Montaje	Montaje
Part	Pieza	Parte	Parte	Parte

English	Spanish (Argentina)	Spanish (Colombia)	Spanish (Mexico)	Universal*
Goods	Mercadería	Mercancía	Artículo	Productos (in this case, a completely different word that could be understood without doubt in all countries involved as chosen)
Planning	Planificación	Planeación		Planificación
Requirement	Requisito	Requerimiento		Requisito
Balance Forward	Traspaso de saldos		Acarreo de saldos	Traspaso de saldos

*This terminology was developed for a particular project. It should not be be taken as correct in all cases, in all circumstances.
Source: Patrice Martin, Ushuaia Solutions (**www.ushuaiasolutions.com**).

—Is It Spanish or Portuguese? —

Non-Spanish speakers often confuse Spanish and Brazilian Portuguese. A quick way to tell the difference is to look at the accents on the letters. Although Spanish and Brazilian Portuguese are similar, these subtle differences make it easy to identify which is which:

- Spanish uses a tilde over the *n* (ñ), but Portuguese does not.
- In Portuguese, you see a tilde over *a* and *o* (ã, õ), but these characters are never used in Spanish.
- Spanish does not use a double *s*, but Portuguese does.
- In Portuguese, you also see the cedilla (ç), but not in Spanish.
- Portuguese does not use the letter *y* unless it is incorporating a word from another language.

Source: Omnilingua (**www.omnilingua.com**).

109

Selecting the type and style of Spanish you use on your web site will be influenced by your audience, your goals, and your corporate style. For this exercise, you'll be working with a more formal style of Spanish. An unscientific method of telling the difference between formal Spanish and informal Spanish are the quotation marks. In Spain, you'll see the more traditional angular quotation marks (« »), known as *comillas*. In most of Latin America, it's more common to see the quotation marks used in English ("").

PREPARATION

Before you can budget your project, you need to know how many words are to be translated. Don't rely on your word processor for counting words, as it will count everything, including HTML tags. Instead, use a software application that counts only the text between the tags. One widely used tool is WebBudget (you can download a free version at **www.webbudget.com**). WebBudget analyzes the HTML page by parsing out only the text to be translated, and then counting that text.

WebBudget Basics

Although nearly any word processing application can give you a word count, WebBudget is designed specifically for the requirements of translators and translation vendors. It parses out all the words in HTML documents that do not need translating—such as **META**, **BODY**, **TABLE**, and **FONT**—and counts just the words that do need to be translated. Using the free trial version downloaded from **www.webbudget.com,** you simply open the web page and the HTML code appears on the left side of the screen, as shown in Figure 7. You then click the Process button, and the parsed text appears on the right side of the page, as shown in Figure 8.

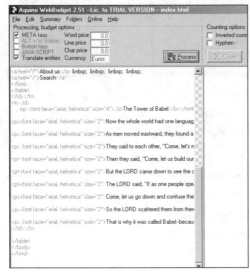

Figure 7   First, open the web page on which you want to do a word count.

Figure 8   Then click Process, and all non-translatable text is parsed out. This is the text that is counted.

For example, Microsoft Word counted 350 words in the sample source page, but WebBudget counted 225 words (see Figure 5); when you're paying 22 cents per word, accurate word counts can add up to significant savings.

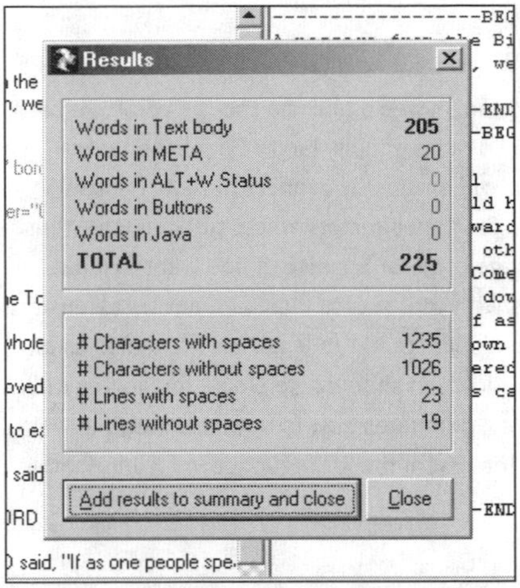

Figure 5   WebBudget found 225 translatable words
on the page.

Next, create a glossary (see Figure 6) that contains any text embedded in graphics
and any key phrases or words that you want used consistently throughout the site.
The glossary is created with Microsoft Excel, but you could use any word processing
application. You simply need to create a table that lists the source and target terms.
For this exercise, the glossary is quite short, but for large web sites, a glossary
could grow so long that it requires the support of specialized applications. For more
information on which words should be included in the glossary, see Chapter 8,
"Translation Management." Specialized applications for glossaries are covered in
Chapter 9, "Computer-Aided Translation."

	A	B
1	**Glossary**	
2		
3	**EN**	**ES**
4		
5	Home	Principal
6	Help	Ayuda
7	What's new	Novedades
8	About us	Sobre nosotros
9	Search	Buscar
10	Privacy Policy	Centro de privacidad
11	Contact	Contactar
12	Tower of Babel	Torre de Babel
13		

Figure 6   The glossary contains text used in embedded
graphics and additional words or phrases used
consistently throughout the site

Next, decide how to organize the new Spanish web site. Even though you have only one Spanish page, it is designed as part of a potentially larger Spanish site; for example, the links in the navigation bar will eventually connect to new Spanish pages. To keep things simple, create an "es" subdirectory where all Spanish pages will reside. The "es" name is the language code for Spanish. If you want to make sure you don't confuse your target files with your source files, add an **_es** extension to all Spanish filenames; many web developers prefer to leave the filenames as is, however. If you're using numerous graphics, you should also create an images directory within the "es" subdirectory. Figure 9 illustrates how to organize multiple web sites using Dreamweaver. You'll get to the rest of those languages in future Hands-On chapters.

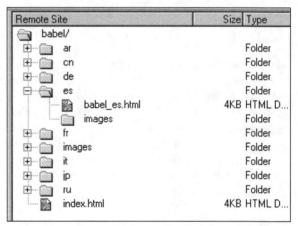

Figure 9 Using Dreamweaver, directories are created for each language site as well as subdirectories for images.

TRANSLATION

For translation, you'll need to select a translator/editor team or outsource the work to a translation vendor. Few translators or vendors will be thrilled to work on a job this small, so expect some minimum charges to apply. As a rule, always try to quote localization projects in their entirety as opposed to piecemeal; this allows you to leverage lower per-word rates and also saves you the added hassle of constantly soliciting new quotes. To get a quick idea on price, try the BerlitzIT web-based translation service (see Figure 10) at **www.berlitzit.com**. Based on 225 words, BertlitzIT quotes $54 (a bit more than its $50 minimum charge).

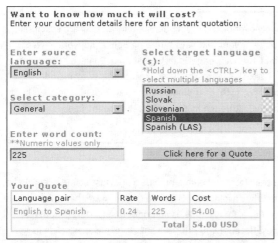

Figure 10   BerlitzIT quoted $54 for the translation.

This little page costs $54? That's right. But keep in mind that the cost includes the selection and management of both a translator and an editor. Nevertheless, you might decide to select and manage a translator and editor team yourself to save a few dollars. The best place to begin is the American Translators Association (ATA) web site (**www.atanet.org**); it offers the Online Translation Service Directory, with more than 4,000 translators listed. The ATA also provides a measure of quality control through its accreditation program. For this project, look for translators with Bible translation experience. Although you might not always find translators with subject-matter expertise, you should always make this a first step. You'll also look for translators based in the country you're targeting. In addition, look for translators with technical expertise. Not everyone understands how to navigate through HTML tags. Finally, before making any decisions, ask your translators to translate a sample HTML page. Granted, a job this small doesn't really count, but for larger projects, insist on testing your translators and editors before moving ahead.

Chapter 8 includes detailed instructions on selecting and managing translators and editors.

Don't Forget the <META> Tags

The page title, keywords, and page description are commonly overlooked during translation, yet they are essential for ensuring that search engines correctly index the web page. If your text says "Torre de Babel" but your **<TITLE>** says "Tower of Babel," a search engine might assume that the web page is in English, not Spanish. The most important way to ensure that search engines properly index the language of your web site is to include the **<html lang="es">** tag. If you're targeting a specific country, such as Colombia, the tag would need to be **<html lang="es-CO">**. The language codes are not case sensitive, although by convention the country code is upper-case and the language code is lowercase.

After you've selected your translator and editor, prepare a brief instruction sheet. To be absolutely safe, specify that they avoid using HTML-editing software that will modify existing markup code. FrontPage, for example, is notorious for inserting proprietary HTML markup on web pages. Because you just have one page, it makes sense to instruct the team to translate the page using a basic text editor, such as Notepad. They can preview their work in a web browser. Additional instructions include:

- **Deadline.** Be realistic. A translator can manage roughly 1,500 to 2,000 words per day, so plan accordingly.

- **Workflow.** Should the translator send the files back for you to forward along to the editor (recommended), or should the translator forward the files directly to the editor?

- **Glossary.** The glossary is typically the first document translated. To ensure that terminology is used consistently throughout the web pages, you should approve the glossary translation before translation of the rest of the text begins.

- **Background information.** Include a brief description of the source text and the audience.

- **Style guide.** Create a style guide that sets standards for formatting, abbreviations, and so forth. Also, indicate how literally and formally to translate the text.

- **Contact information.** All participants should have your contact information. Be prepared for frequent questions at the beginning of a project as all the participants get acquainted with the subject matter and style of translation.

You're now ready to email the instructions sheet, style guide, glossary, and HTML file to the translator.

GRAPHICS LOCALIZATION

After you receive the translated glossary from the editor, you're ready to localize the navigation bar. Although you're using Adobe Illustrator, you could just as easily have used Photoshop or Macromedia Freehand, as these tools all support layers. The Layers feature, shown in Figure 11, is important in localization, as it allows you to separate the text from the image and then edit the text into different languages. To create the Spanish buttons, simply duplicate the English text layer and edit the text.

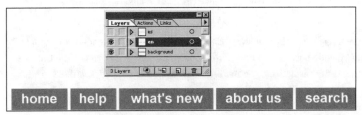

Figure 11   The navigation bar was created in Illustrator. Notice how the text is kept in language-specific layers for easy editing.

115

Unfortunately, text expansion makes the localization process a bit more challenging (see Figure 12). To accommodate the expanded text, the margins of the buttons must be moved and the text reduced in size. Fortunately, the text was quite large to begin with, so legibility doesn't suffer too much; many web designers do not plan ahead and often cannot reduce text size any further.

For more information on managing text expansion, see Chapter 7, "Localization and Internationalization."

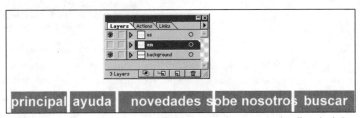

Figure 12   Notice how text expansion affects the design.

HTML LOCALIZATION

Now it's time to make final changes to the HTML page. First, preview the page in a web browser to make sure the text is fully translated and that no HTML tags have been accidentally altered. Next, make sure the content within the **<META>** tags— such as keywords and descriptions—has been translated. Also make sure a **<LANG>** tag is included at the top of the page, and you have the correct **charset** attribute indicated, as follows:

<meta http-equiv="Content-Type" content="text/html; charset=iso-8859-1">

Many web pages specify **windows-1252,** but this is not recommended. You could also specify Unicode because it aligns perfectly with ISO 8859-1. However, the Unicode encoding is not recognized by older browsers, so you should stick with 8859-1 for now. You'll learn more about Unicode in the final Hands-On chapter.

With the navigation bar localized, you'll need to resize the hyperlinked image maps to accommodate the changes in button sizes (see Figure 13).

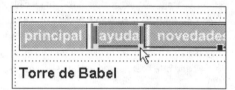

Figure 13 Resizing the image maps in Dreamweaver to align with the resized buttons.

Next, modify the hyperlinks within the navigation bar buttons so that they link to Spanish web pages instead of English web pages. Even though the Spanish web pages don't yet exist, getting in the habit of managing hyperlinks is important. All you need to do is add an **_es** extension to the filenames within the links; when the web pages *are* eventually localized, you just need to be sure to change the file- names to match.

Page Not Found

A commonly overlooked page (or script) that you'll need to localize is the "page not found" page. Be on the look-out for these error pages, as they often get overlooked during the localization process. As shown in Figure 14, the Terra web site, even though it's a Spanish site, has an English-language error page.

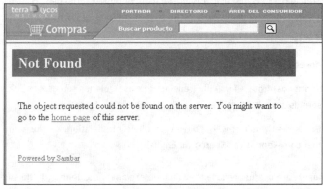

Figure 14   The error message for the Terra Chile site is in English.

117

REVIEW

Finally, preview the target web page in both Netscape and Explorer browsers (see Figure 15). You might also want to include a preview in the Opera browser. To be absolutely safe, you should hire one more editor to conduct a round of "live" proofing (or ask your existing editor to take one more look). Place the web page on a staging server, and have the editor proof it via a browser and email any comments to you.

Figure 15   The target page in Spanish, ready for one final round of review.

For this web page, the editor, Soledad Alvarez, had several comments about the text in the navigation buttons. The translations weren't necessarily wrong, but she felt they could be better. Here were her comments:

Principal → I would use "Home" instead. Although "Principal" is correct, it's standard in Spanish to use the English term.

Ayuda → OK

Novedades → OK

Sobre nosotros → I usually translate this as "Quienes somos." I think it sounds more "natural" in Spanish than the first alternative.

Buscar → I would say "Búsqueda" is a better translation. It's the noun that corresponds to "Search" in English.

These comments are useful because they include explanations along with the suggested alternative translations. When working with editors, you won't always get right or wrong answers. You'll need to exercise best judgment based on the feedback the editors provide. Just as a great editor can turn good writing into great writing, the same philosophy applies to translation. I find the editing stage particularly interesting because you can learn a great deal about a language and its subtleties. For example, in addition to the buttons, the editor offered the following general comment about the text:

"The only interesting thing I noticed is that this version of the story refers to the LORD as "Señor", instead of "Jehová," which is the name used to establish the distinction between the wrathful God of the Old Testament (Jehovah) and the all-forgiving God of the New Testament (the Lord, God)."

After you've made (or not made) any final changes based on your editor's suggestions, you're ready to take the web page live.

¡FELICITACIONES!

Congratulations—you've now expanded your audience to include more than 20 countries and more than 300 million people. Now that you have a feel for the localization workflow, in subsequent Hands-On chapters, you'll focus less on logistics and more on the technical and linguistic challenges each language presents. You're now well on your way to building a web site that will reach more than two billion people.

Credit: Soledad Alvarez assisted with editing this web page. She is an ATA-accredited translator and can be contacted through **www.thelanguagecorner.com.**

5

WEB GLOBALIZATION WORKFLOW

Web globalization is a journey that requires a detailed roadmap, otherwise known as a workflow. The workflow outlines the tasks involved in executing your company's web globalization strategy. These tasks vary depending on whether you manage localization yourself, the extent to which you localize your web site, and how you plan to manage localized web sites after they're developed.

This chapter introduces the fundamental strategies organizations use to develop and manage global web sites, along with recommendations to help you select the right strategy for your organization. You'll also see how the strategies are reflected in the resulting workflows.

BUILDING A WORKFLOW THAT WORKS FOR YOU

First, it's important to understand the major stages of web globalization. As shown in Figure 5.1, the globalization workflow can be broken down into three steps: internationalization, localization, and content management. Should you continue to expand and improve your site, the workflow repeats as many times as needed. Each of these stages has a workflow of its own, which is described in detail in subsequent chapters. Translation, which plays a role in both localization and content management, even has its own workflow. The more complex your site, the more complex the workflow becomes. Rarely are all localized web sites at the same stage in the development cycle; you may even find yourself juggling separate and simultaneous workflows.

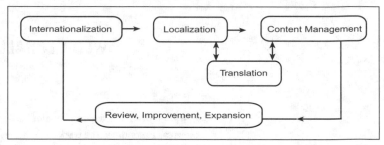

Figure 5.1 Web globalization includes three stages, each with its own workflow.

If you already manage a web site, you probably have some sort of workflow you follow. If this system is successful, don't throw it out just because you need to develop a new localized web site; you may find it easier to integrate new tasks into your existing system. Web globalization can be disruptive enough to an organization without having to force all participants to learn entirely new systems.

The challenge with integrating new tasks into existing systems is that so few companies have dependable workflow systems to build on. Take quality control. If your site is only in English, anyone on your web or marketing teams can detect a typo or odd-sounding sentence. Yet who will catch errors on your site when it expands into half a dozen languages? No one person can or should be expected to proofread every language, so you'll need a reliable and repeatable system in place to ensure consistency across all languages.

WEB GLOBALIZATION CHECKLIST

The *globalization workflow*, when put to paper, is fundamentally a "to do" list. Some of the tasks are one-time projects, such as registering a country-specific domain name. Other tasks are highly repetitive, such as ongoing translation and editing.

The following checklist is a master list of everything that might need to be accomplished to localize a web site. The list isn't concerned with who does what, just with what needs to be done. If you don't recognize all the terms, don't worry; all the tasks are covered later in this book. For now, it's important to get an idea of just how long this "to do" list can be.

Preparation

- ☐ Assess your company's global readiness.

- ☐ Select target markets/locales.

- ☐ Test company/brand names, or create new names.

- ☐ Register country-specific domain names.

- ☐ Register multilingual domain names.

- ☐ Estimate project scope, including number of words and images requiring localization.

- ☐ Designate (or hire) a project leader.

- ☐ Estimate and allocate budget.

- ☐ Set a schedule.

Internationalization

- ☐ Isolate and modify any software functionality that will require localization.

- ☐ Modify payment systems to display and accept different currencies.

- ☐ Provide language- and culture-specific search engines.

- ☐ Modify calendars, measurements, dates, and times.

- ☐ Support new collation methods.

- ☐ Modify database to support new characters and different string lengths.

- ☐ Redesign the interface so that it's both globally friendly and easily localized.

- ☐ Remove unnecessary graphics and anything that could impede download time for international users.

123

☐ Isolate all text strings in web scripts and functions that require translation, and move all strings to one resource file.

☐ Rewrite source text so it can be more efficiently and consistently translated.

☐ Develop style guide.

☐ Build terminology glossary.

☐ Plan a naming system for the localized web files and an organization system for the new localized directories.

☐ Prep source files: text, graphics, and scripts.

Localization

☐ Translation
- ■ Test prospective translators.
- ■ Create translation workflow.
- ■ Implement any computer-aided translation tools.
- ■ Create detailed instructions for translators to follow.

☐ Editing
- ■ Test prospective editors.
- ■ Create detailed instructions for editors to follow.

☐ Graphics/design localization
- ■ Text design for cultural appropriateness and effectiveness.
- ■ Develop global gateway.
- ■ Test usability of localized site.

☐ In-country review of translation.

☐ Assembly of target web pages and staging of finished web pages for testing.

☐ Functionality and usability testing of staged web site (both in-house and in-country testing).

Content Management

☐ Develop content management system:

- ■ Establish workflow that all participants must follow.

- ■ Purchase software, if possible, to automate many of these tasks.

☐ Implement translation memory software:

- ■ Store all previous translations (source and target pairs) in memory.

- ■ Make sure memory can be reused for new or modified source text.

☐ Train staff to support localized web sites and international customers.

☐ Begin ongoing localization maintenance:

- ■ Localize all new source content.

- ■ Leverage translation memory.

- ■ Translation.

- ■ Editing.

- ■ Graphics.

- ■ Staging and testing.

- ■ Reflect changes to existing content on all or selected localized sites.

- ■ Make sure translation memory can be shared if multiple vendors are used.

☐ Support customers (phone, email, fax).

☐ Promote localized web sites:

- ■ Register on local and international search engines.

- ■ Place local advertising.

- ■ Send press announcements to local media.

Review

☐ Analyze sales by market.

☐ Test brand awareness.

☐ Test usability of site.

☐ Analyze web traffic logs by country.

125

☐ Calculate return on investment (ROI).

☐ Review competitive web sites.

☐ Conduct quality audits of translation.

☐ Plan improvements to product/service selection for each locale.

☐ Plan new products or improved products.

☐ Prepare for the next-generation web site.

WEB GLOBALIZATION WORKFLOW, ONE GENERATION AT A TIME

Web sites typically evolve in generations. Amazon.com, when it first went live, did not offer "1-Click" ordering or personalized stores. These functions were added many generations later. Web globalization also evolves in generations. A company might begin with one localized site and limited functionality and then build from there, gradually adding languages and layers of sophistication. Today, it's not uncommon to see a company on its tenth-generation web site, but still on its first-generation localized web site.

Approaching your localization process in generations helps you manage expectations, logistics, and budget. A company's *generational strategy* could look something like this:

First-Generation Site

☐ Objectives:

■ Localize for three markets: Spain, Germany, and France.

■ Offer a subset of products/services.

■ Offer limited customer support: Develop localized product support pages, and notify users that email and phone support is currently available only in English.

☐ Players:

■ Web team manages implementation and testing.

■ Marketing team manages source text, translation, editing, and selection of products/services to be offered.

■ All translating, editing, and reviewing is outsourced to freelancers.

Second-Generation Site

☐ Objectives:

- ■ Add Japanese and Korean locales.

- ■ Enhance site functionality with a localized search engine.

- ■ Upgrade database to support double-byte characters.

- ■ Offer email customer support in target languages.

☐ Players:

- ■ Web developers and programmers manage double-byte enabling and testing.

- ■ Web designer manages any necessary redesign to support new locales.

- ■ Marketing team outsources text and images to a localization firm.

- ■ Customer support hires multilingual personnel to answer email in all five languages.

Third-Generation Site

☐ Objectives:

- ■ Integrate multilingual content management system.

- ■ Offer a real-time currency conversion feature and additional payment options.

- ■ Support customers via email and phone.

☐ Players:

- ■ Web developers and programmers install software.

- ■ Web designer creates global templates that work with the new content management system.

- ■ Marketing team learns to input text and images into content management system.

- ■ Localization firm works with client to manage ongoing localization of text and graphics.

- ■ Customer support hires full-time multilingual staff to provide phone support in target languages.

127

Notice how the more complex and expensive goals are delayed for future generations, such as real-time currency conversion and multilingual phone support. Give your localized web sites time to evolve, and give yourself manageable, reachable goals.

Workflow should be customized to the needs of your customers and your long-term strategy. If you're going after the German market, where credit card usage is lower than in the U.S., you'll want to build in support for money orders. If you see Japanese localization on the horizon, you should begin thinking about managing double-byte text from the onset so that your company can localize more swiftly and at less expense.

FYI

Roughly 75% of all U.S. web sites do not support non-U.S. addresses or cannot calculate international shipping costs.

Source: Forrester Research, **www.forrester.com**.

THERE'S MORE THAN ONE WAY TO GO GLOBAL

It's often assumed that when you localize a web site, you must localize the *entire* site, yet companies rarely localize their entire sites. Is it really necessary to translate all press releases if they are directed only at the U.S. media? And to what extent should the careers section of a web site be localized for markets outside the U.S if the human resources department is recruiting only within the U.S.? You'll learn early on that the fewer pages of content you localize, the lower the bill. Of course, there are tradeoffs to holding back on the amount of localization you do; customers may feel left out, or they might not get the same level of customer support as customers in other locales. Companies need to find an effective balance; to do that, they can choose from three general localization strategies, each with its own advantages and disadvantages.

Comprehensive Localization

Comprehensive localization is what most companies strive for and most users crave. After all, nobody likes to feel as though they're missing out on something. A comprehensive localization doesn't necessarily have to include everything the source site includes, but it should create an equivalent user experience.

Yahoo! creates a similar user experience across its localized sites. Although there are variations in what is offered, the majority of features remain consistent. As shown in the Mexico and Denmark sites (see Figure 5.2), most of the icons remain exactly the same.

Figure 5.2   Yahoo! Mexico and Yahoo! Denmark: Different locales, equally localized.

The advantages and disadvantages of comprehensive localization are outlined in this chart:

Advantages	Disadvantages
Gives users a complete view of your company, products, and services.	The more of your site you localize, the higher the localization cost.
Offers greater revenue potential: The more products you offer, the more you can sell.	If your site changes frequently, maintenance costs could also be prohibitive.

Comprehensive localization may be "too much, too soon" for your co-workers to effectively manage.

Incremental Localization

Although companies aspire to comprehensive localization, few actually take the leap. Instead, most companies take a more incremental approach. Not only does *incremental localization* cost less than the full-scale approach, it also allows companies to "test the waters" of new markets without making a large initial investment in localization.

Compare the advantages and disadvantages of incremental localization:

Advantages	**Disadvantages**
Produces a low-cost, low-risk, localized web site.	You might miss sales opportunities by starting slowly.
For the user, incremental localization is better than nothing at all.	Your users in localized markets could feel slighted.
For your co-workers, the process is less taxing.	Your web site is more vulnerable to competitors that *do* localize comprehensively.

Customized Localization

Sometimes a globalization project affects the design of the source-language site to such a degree that a company decides to redesign everything. The *customized localization* approach is gaining popularity as companies realize just how "globally unfriendly" their web sites are.

For example, many American sites are graphics-intensive, trying the patience of international users with slow Internet connections. Instead of trying to duplicate this graphics-intensive design across localized sites, a company might decide to simply redesign the site, stripping out the unnecessary graphics. The added benefit of this approach is that companies often save money on localization costs in the process; graphics localization can be very expensive.

To learn more about graphics localization, see Chapter 11, "World Wide Design."

The advantages and disadvantages of customized localization are shown in the following chart:

Advantages	**Disadvantages**
By building a more globally aware web site, a company avoids many internationalization costs.	You face high upfront costs. In addition to localization, you have to pay for a full redesign.
The site may be more user-friendly to global users. For example, the global gateway can be integrated into the design instead of squeezed in as an afterthought.	You face large upfront risks. What if the new design doesn't work as well as the previous design?

WHO'S DOING THE WORK?

If you think it takes a lot of people to build a web site, just wait until you see how many people it takes to build a multilingual web site. A small, four-language web site could easily require 15 people, as shown in Figure 5.3. A larger, more complex site could require twice that many.

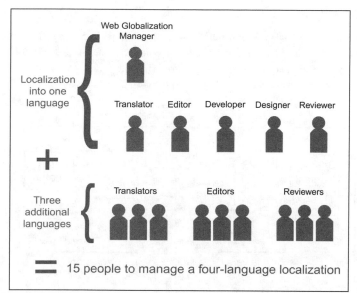

Figure 5.3   Localization is a team effort: The more languages, the larger the team.

Many of the participants are little more than bit players: They translate a specific language, and then they're done. Others, like you, have a lot more work to do. The key issue is, who's going to manage all these people? Is it going to be you, or are you going to hire a vendor to do the work?

Introducing the Web Globalization Manager

Perhaps you are the globalization evangelist in your company, the one who's been campaigning for a web globalization budget. One of these days you're going to get the budget you've been longing for. Then what? If you're the marketing manager, do you become the global marketing manager? Or, if you're the webmaster, do you become the global web manager? No matter who takes charge of web globalization, his or her day-to-day responsibilities shift dramatically from that moment on. The amount of work involved might require creating a new position entirely: the *web globalization manager*. The web globalization manager takes the lead on all web internationalization, localization, and management, regardless of whether the work is managed in house or outsourced.

Working In House

A lot of companies begin web globalization internally. Perhaps someone on the staff speaks the target language and volunteers to help, and the rest just sort of grows from there. Soon you have someone playing the role of the web globalization manager as well as a loosely knit group of freelance translators and editors, as shown in Figure 5.4.

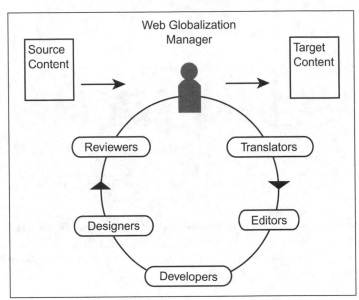

Figure 5.4   The in-house solution: Managing globalization in house requires managing workflow, deadlines, and many contributors.

The main advantage to this approach is that it's often less expensive upfront than using an outside vendor because existing employees are simply taking on additional responsibilities. The main disadvantage is that it's a heck of a lot of work. Just look at all the people who report to the web globalization manager. It's easy to see why many companies turn to outsourcing.

Outsourcing

When you hire a localization or translation vendor, you're looking for a project manager, shown in Figure 5.5, who can take away the headaches and increase the level of quality and timeliness. But a vendor can't save you from *all* headaches.

—**Localization Vendor or Translation Vendor?** —————————————

Traditionally, a translation vendor managed text translation, and a localization vendor managed the entire localization process, of which translation is just one component. However, the distinction between the two has blurred as translation vendors acquire web localization tools and skills. For more information on translation management and workflow, see Chapter 8, "Translation Management."

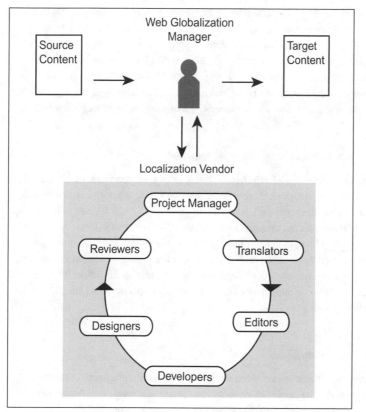

133

Figure 5.5 The outsource solution: Outsourcing saves you, the client, from managing translators, editors, and workflow.

Your company will still need a lead person to manage the vendor, and your web team will need to work closely with the vendor to cleanly integrate the target sites with the source site. You might also want to have your international offices assist with the review process. Nevertheless, many companies are more than happy to outsource the hiring and day-to-day management of all those translators, editors, and developers.

WHO'S IN CHARGE?

Nothing ensures consistency across locales more than managing them all from one location, yet many companies have numerous locations and more than one web team. For multinational companies, the struggle between home offices and foreign offices springs eternal. Home offices want more control, and foreign offices want more independence. This struggle becomes readily apparent when applied to web globalization. Will each localized site be managed by an in-country office, by headquarters, or by a combination of both? If headquarters retains all control, there's a risk that it will miss out on opportunities that only the in-country offices can see. If local offices aren't empowered to capitalize on these opportunities, sales are lost. If local offices *are* empowered, however, there's the risk that the localized sites will be haphazardly maintained or not maintained at all. And there is the ongoing issue of delivering a global message, something that needs to be managed centrally.

Centralized Versus Decentralized Management

The management model you choose should reflect your company's organizational structure and management style. A decentralized company, with independent international offices, should have little trouble managing a decentralized web site. Nor should the offices have trouble keeping content current and sufficiently localized because they more than likely manage their own budgets and marketing promotions. A centrally managed company, however, will probably have better luck managing its many web sites centrally; even if it has international offices, those offices might not have the budgetary freedom or the skilled personnel to effectively manage a local web site.

The Best of Both Worlds

A more recent web management model is a hybrid form of control, called the *distributed model*. The central office hosts the content management software, but each local office has access to its localized site to make necessary changes. This model gives local offices a higher level of autonomy, but also keeps the central office firmly in control of global design and management. The central office can also be alerted when changes are made locally, so it can ensure that everything adheres to corporate style. The drawback to the distributed model is its complexity and potential costs. Making this model work requires sophisticated content management software, which often comes with a hefty price tag.

For more information on content management, see Chapter 13, "Global Content Management."

WEB GLOBALIZATION STRATEGIES: THREE SCENARIOS

Which localization strategy is right for you? It all depends on your organization, budget, needs, and plans—short term and long term. There is no "one" strategy that all companies should adopt. What follows are three scenarios that illustrate the different localization strategies companies can use and how these strategies affect workflow.

Scenario One

Small U.S. company; small web site

Localization strategy:	Incremental
Production:	All outsourced
Management:	Centralized

In the first scenario, a small U.S. company with no international offices wants to localize its web site for several new markets. Because the web site is small and changes infrequently, there's little urgency or cost benefit to hiring a full-time web globalization manager. Instead, the marketing manager and webmaster work together to outsource the project to a localization vendor. After the localized web sites are launched, the vendor can be retained periodically to update content. The company decides to localize incrementally to keep upfront costs even lower. Should the web sites be a success, the company can expand the depth and number of localized sites. Eventually, the company might reach a point where the cost of outsourcing forces them to consider bringing management in house, which leads to the next scenario.

135

Scenario Two

Large U.S. company; large web site

Localization strategy:	Comprehensive
Production:	In-house
Management:	Centralized

Next is a large U.S. company with a much larger, more dynamic web site. This company has international offices, but not the resources or management structure to justify decentralizing web management. However, the company does want a comprehensive localization to fully support customers in the markets where it has offices. Because of the project's size and the site's dynamic nature, the company allocates a budget that allows hiring a full-time web globalization manager, who will function as an in-house localization agency, hiring freelance translators and editors to supply the necessary content.

In this scenario, the workflow is much more complex than in scenario one. The manager trains the internal web team to develop web pages and graphics in different languages. International offices assist with reviewing web pages and testing, and because the site's content changes frequently, the manager is managing numerous workflows—one for each language web site. If the workload grows too quickly, the manager will need to outsource work to a localization vendor, which leads to scenario three.

Scenario Three

Multinational company; large web site

Localization strategy:	Customized
Production:	In-house and outsourced
Management:	Distributed

Finally, there's a large multinational with a very large and dynamic web site. This company already has a number of localized web sites, all developed and managed by their respective offices. But there's a lack of consistency between the many sites, so the company allocates a budget to purchase and install a content and globalization management system and to hire a web globalization department. The department will manage the software centrally, but allow each office the freedom to continue developing its local content. A global template is designed to ensure a consistent image across all locales. The web globalization department is not large enough to manage all ongoing translation, so a combination of freelance, in-country translators, and translation vendors are retained. This scenario presents a complex workflow because of the workload as well as the distributed management structure. Fortunately, content management software automates many of the tasks involved in managing the complexity.

IMMIGRATION OFFICER
(4121)
2 5 202 2050
HEATHROW (4)

Workflow Is Relative

The three major stages of globalization—internationalization, localization, and content management—vary in relative importance as a company's web site evolves. And as the stages change, so too will your workflow. For example, a company embarking on its first localized web site might require a lengthy stage of internationalization, but a company that has already developed several localized sites might devote the bulk of its time and resources to content management. Figure 5.6 illustrates how changes in globalization needs and strategies affect workflows.

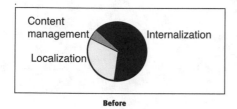

Before   **After**

Figure 5.6   When a web site is first globalized, internationalization often requires the greatest percentage of resources; after launching the localized sites, however, content management and ongoing localization take up the bulk of resources.

137

A WORKFLOW IN PROGRESS

Now that you have an understanding of the many workflows, or roadmaps, available, you face the challenging task of drawing your own roadmap. Take your time. The more thorough your planning, the fewer surprises you'll face later in the process.

The next chapter introduces you one of the cruel realities of localization: the costs. After that, you'll begin to see the workflow implemented in subsequent chapters, through internationalization and localization.

6

LET'S TALK BUDGET

Web globalization can be expensive—so expensive that executives with dreams of localizing web sites into dozens of languages often hit that budgetary brick wall right around language number two (some don't even make it that far). That's not to say that your company can't afford localization. If you want to localize a few web pages into four or five languages—and you manage the project yourself—you could do it for less than a few thousand dollars. However, most companies want to localize much more than a few web pages. This chapter provides an overview of where localization costs come from and how to keep them to a minimum.

THE SPIRIT IS WILLING, BUT THE BUDGET IS WEAK

Companies often view localization as a simple matter of photocopying a source-language web site. And, the thinking goes, because photocopying is inexpensive, so too should localization be. Furthermore, many people assume that computers manage the localization process, bringing costs down even further. As a result, budgets are often set unrealistically low, and web globalization managers are placed in the awkward position of trying to get more money or making do with what they have.

The average localization project can run anywhere from $20,000 to $100,000, but large corporations spend more than a million dollars annually on localization. Also, web localization is not just a one-time expense because localized web sites must be maintained to reflect ongoing changes to the source-language site. Sometimes the changes are so significant that maintenance expenses eclipse the one-time expenses.

Why So Expensive?

Internationalization and localization are fundamentally manual jobs. Although computers do play a vital role, the process of translation, web development, engineering, testing, and editing is largely managed by human beings—very skilled and sometimes expensive human beings.

If you think of each localized web site as a completely new web site, you can more accurately estimate costs. Just as your English-language site requires the skills of a wide range of specialists, so too does each localized site. Localization relies on many specialists:

- Project managers
- Translators (for each language)
- Editors (for each language)
- Web developers
- Graphics designers
- Programmers/engineers

WHERE THE COSTS COME FROM

Web globalization costs can be roughly divided into five major "slices":

- **Project Management**: Ongoing management of all participants and flow of content; also includes project management tools

- **Translation**: Translators, editors, and support tools

- **Testing**: Functionality, usability, and linguistic testing

- **Design and multimedia**: The initial design localization and ongoing localization of new images and multimedia files

- **Development and tools**: Assembly of localized web pages

As a percentage of the total budget, text translation typically makes up the largest slice, as shown in Figure 6.1.

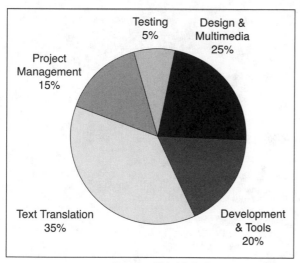

Figure 6.1 Web globalization costs: Text translation typically takes up the largest slice.

This breakdown of costs is a loose approximation. The actual distribution of costs for your company will almost certainly be different. For example, if your company purchases a content management software package as part of its globalization efforts, your initial development and tools costs could easily exceed graphics and possibly even translation costs. As your site evolves, the relative sizes of these slices will ebb and flow. Each slice is covered in detail in subsequent chapters.

Upfront Expenses

Localization costs vary widely, depending on whether you are managing the initial localization or managing updates to existing localized sites. As you develop your first localized sites, your upfront translation and development costs are necessarily higher because you're starting from scratch. All text must be translated and your site must undergo internationalization. Upfront expenses include the following:

Development and Tools

- Database integration and upgrades
- Internationalization engineering
- Assembly of localized web pages

Design and Multimedia

- Web interface redesign
- Graphics localization
- Audiovisual localization

Text Translation

- Translation
- Editing
- Terminology glossary

Testing

- Web site functionality and usability testing
- Translation quality testing

Project Management

- Globalization planning
- Strategic consultation

Ongoing Expenses

After the localized sites are launched, your development, project management, and tools costs should drop. The major ongoing expenses will be translating and localizing new or modified content.

Where the Costs Come From

If your site rarely changes, these expenses will be minimal. If you're a company like Amazon, however, adding new promotions every day with accompanying graphics, the maintenance costs could be significant. Ongoing expenses typically include the following:

Development and Tools

■   As needed for new web pages, features, and functionality

Design and Multimedia

■   Localization of new multimedia files

Text Translation

■   Translating and editing new content

■   Development and management of translation memory

Testing

■   Testing of new features added to site

■   Testing of new designs and terminology for cultural appropriateness

Project Management

■   Ongoing maintenance of site—tracking changes to the source-language site so that they're reflected in target-language sites

Related Expenses

There are also related costs that, although they typically don't affect the web team's budget, affect other departments within the company. These related expenses include the following:

■   Promotion of localized web sites

■   Customer support and fulfillment costs

■   International legal costs

■   Trademark filings

■   Sales training

When a web site is localized, all affected departments should be included in the process, such as customer support, public relations, and sales. In addition, budgets must be allocated to these departments so that they can fully support the localized web sites. If they don't support the sites, customers might be frustrated by customer support personnel who don't speak their language or sales departments that don't accept their currencies and methods of payment.

WHERE VENDORS FIT IN

Rarely does a company manage an entire localization project in house. At the least, a company hires freelance translators and editors to manage text translation. At the most, a company hires a localization firm to manage the entire project from start to finish, as well as ongoing maintenance.

This book makes frequent use of the terms "client" and "vendor." For our purposes, the *client* is the company that's localizing its web site. Although a localization or translation firm often functions like a client when it hires translators and editors, it's considered a *vendor*. A vendor can be a translation firm, a localization firm, a translator, an editor, or all of the above. One of the harder decisions to make during localization is to what extent you want to rely on vendors. There's no perfect answer, and your needs will change as your web site changes. For example, it's not unusual for a company to rely on a mixture of in-house and out-of-house talent. The key is to find a mixture that works well for your needs and your budget. The following scenarios illustrate two different client/vendor models and their relative advantages and disadvantages.

Scenario One: Outsourcing Translation Only

In this scenario, one (or more) web globalization managers are hired to manage localization. The manager outsources the text translation but typically manages everything else in-house.

Advantages	Disadvantages
Consistency—Having someone in house dedicated to localization can aid in quality control and consistency.	Potentially more expensive—If there's a spike in the workload, the globalization manager might not be able to manage the work effectively and be forced to outsource projects to localization vendors, which could end up costing more than if you had followed scenario two.
Develop in-house expertise—Having an in-house globalization expert is valuable. This person can train other personnel and departments to manage various aspects of localization.	Lack of companywide support—It's important to gauge your internal "global readiness" before you bring in someone to lead the process. Many employees resist the changes in mindset and workload that web globalization often requires. Putting a person in a position where he or she is bound to encounter resistance at every turn might not be the best idea for an organization just embarking on localization.

Scenario Two: Outsourcing Everything

In the second scenario, a company outsources most, if not all, of the localization work to a localization or translation agency. This scenario is common with small companies, who don't have the expertise, and large companies, who don't want the headaches of managing localization projects.

Advantages	Disadvantages
Potentially better quality—An outside vendor can provide the more objective quality control that a company needs. Because a vendor is removed from the company, it's more likely to ask the tough questions that an internal manager might questions that an internal manager might be reluctant to raise, and sometimes it just helps to have an outside opinion.	Over-reliance on outsiders—If your vendor starts to get sloppy, who in your company is going to notice? And how quickly will you be able to fix the problem or hire a new agency? Don't put too much faith in your vendors, as they can't be expected to never make mistakes.
Possibly less expensive—A company has to pay for localization only as needed. Outsourcing is ideal if localization projects are more sporadic than steady.	Potentially more expensive—Managing a localization vendor inevitably requires a commitment in time from someone within the company. Just keeping change orders to a minimum requires significant effort. As the localization workload increases, that person's workload could increase to the point that he or she is functioning like an in-house globalization manager, which puts you back in scenario one.

Chapter 8, "Translation Management," will take you through the many details of hiring vendors.

THE HIDDEN COSTS OF LOCALIZATION

Regardless of whether you hire freelance translators or a localization agency, you need to know where hidden costs lurk and how to avoid them.

Keep It Simple; Keep It Affordable

The most expensive mistake a company can make is to localize a web site without first deciding whether it *should* be localized. Some web sites are so complex that comprehensive localization could prove prohibitively expensive. Some companies are far better off simplifying their source-language web sites *before* they begin localization.

For example, the SBC Communications home page (see Figure 6.2) is more challenging to localize than the AltaVista home page (see Figure 6.3) primarily because it relies too heavily on "embedded text" images. An embedded text image is simply an image with text. Designers often embed text within images to ensure that the text appears exactly as intended in a web browser. Editing text embedded in images, however, takes a lot longer than just editing plain text in an HTML file. For starters, you need the image source file, then you need a graphics application, and you might need to resize the graphic if the text changes in length.

Figure 6.2   The SBC Communications page relies mostly on graphics with embedded text.

Now look at the AltaVista home page. This web page is 95% plain text. The SBC page relies on 45 embedded text images, but the AltaVista page relies on just 2 of those images.

For more information on embedded text images, see Chapter 11, "World Wide Design."

Figure 6.3   The AltaVista page, however, relies mostly on text.

How can you tell the difference between plain text and embedded text? In a web browser, try to select the text on a web page using your cursor. If you can select a few characters of a word, the text is plain text. If all you can select is the image that contains the word, you're looking at embedded text.

Graphics are not the only complex aspect of the SBC home page. SBC also uses a scrolling "news ticker" on the home page that displays the latest company news. This is a nifty feature for a web site, but is costly to maintain across a number of localized sites because the text changes frequently and thus requires frequent translation.

If SBC were to redesign its home page before attempting to localize it, it could reduce the number of images with embedded text and remove the news ticker. SBC might even find that the redesign costs would be offset by the savings generated from reduced localization costs. Interestingly, SBC Communications recently did just that—redesigning its home page to remove the news ticker and converting the majority of the embedded text images to just plain text (see Figure 6.4). By making its web site simpler, it ensures that localization will also be simple and a lot less costly.

Figure 6.4 The SBC home page, after redesign: Now with only eight embedded text images.

Graphics Aren't Pretty

Graphics with embedded text are not only time-consuming to localize, but expensive. Localization vendors may charge up to $50 per graphic, depending on the language and complexity. If you must use graphics, try to keep text out of them.

Keeping embedded text to a minimum does not mean sacrificing an attractive web page design, however. For example, compare the navigation bars of Nordstrom and the Gap in Figure 6.5.

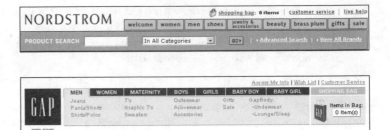

Figure 6.5   The Nordstrom navigation bar uses 21 embedded text images, but the Gap navigation bar uses just 8.

Both navigation bars share similar design goals and challenges and both are equally effective from a design perspective. However, the Gap bar uses only 8 embedded text images, and the Nordstrom bar uses 21. Nordstrom uses *rollover* or "mouseover" *images*, which are images that change appearance when a cursor "rolls over" them. Rollovers with embedded text can be twice as expensive to localize because each rollover consists of at least two graphics—one layered on top of the other—both of which must be localized.

Assuming that a localization firm charges $25 per image per language (which is on the low end), the Gap would pay $200 per language and Nordstrom would pay $525. Given that it's not unusual to find home pages with upward of 40 images with embedded text, a simple change of design can mean huge savings for your company. Furthermore, fewer images typically mean faster download times, which is a critical issue for many users around the world.

Brevity Is the Soul of Savings

Translation is typically charged by the number of words to be translated. Some languages are more expensive to translate than others, based on the number of translators available and the complexity of the language.

Spanish, one of the least expensive languages to translate, costs anywhere between 18 and 25 cents per word. Asian and Middle Eastern languages, on the other hand, can cost up to 38 cents per word. Assuming you follow the Berlitz price chart (see Table 6.1), translating 100 words (roughly two paragraphs) into Finnish costs $28 to translate. If your web site has 200 pages with roughly 200 words per page (which is not a lot), you're looking at more than $10,000 for just one language.

Table 6.1 Selected Per Word Translation Costs

Language Pair	Rate ($U.S.)
English → Chinese (Traditional)	0.29
English → Finnish	0.28
English → French	0.24
English → German	0.24
English → Italian	0.24
English → Japanese	0.38
English → Korean	0.28
English → Russian	0.24
English → Spanish	0.24

Source: Berlitz (**www.berlitzit.com**)

The subject matter of the text also plays a factor in costs. Highly technical material is generally more expensive to translate because it requires skilled and specialized translators. For example, you wouldn't want to trust the translation of catheter usage instructions to a translator who doesn't know what a catheter is.

When writing for a global market, *shorter is better.* Print marketers have long understood that more text often leads to higher costs. A four-page brochure, for example, has limitations to what it can contain. Adding another paragraph or two might require an additional page for the brochure, which leads to a jump in print costs.

Localization places a financial imperative on intelligent editing. To save money, approach the text of your web site with the same degree of scrutiny as a brochure or any other printed material. As you expand the number of languages you localize into, you may find that simply editing out a few unnecessary paragraphs could save your company hundreds or thousands of dollars.

Word Counts (and Miscounts)

If your budget is based on the number of words in your HTML web pages, you had better have a clear understanding with your vendors as to what constitutes a word. For example, count the number of words in the following sentence. Note that the HTML markup is included because this is what vendors see when they receive the web page for translation (the text to be translated is in bold).

```
<font face="arial" size="2"><br>Theo is 2 years old and
➥<a href="http://www.midge.com">Midge</a> is 32 years old.</br></font>
```

According to the Microsoft Word word count tool, there are 14 words. But if you do your own count, you'll see that there are really only 11 words, of which two are numbers and two are proper names. The additional three words that Word counted are the HTML tags, such as **</br></font>**; spaces between the tags only add to the word count. HTML tags don't need to be translated, however, so you shouldn't have to pay for those extra three words. In this one example, you would end up paying 20% extra if you assumed that Microsoft Word was correct in its word count.

There are a number of tools that you and your vendors can use to estimate a more accurate word count. Rarely do these tools agree, however. In fact, there are no universal standards for word counting. To make sure you're not being overcharged, always conduct word counts of test HTML pages with your vendor so that you both agree on what you're being charged for.

You'll find more information on word counts and tools in Chapter 8, and the "Hands-On: Spanish" chapter.

Translating the Same Word Twice

Once you pay to have a sentence translated, you shouldn't have to pay to have it translated again if that sentence is repeated on another web page. Your company's slogan, for example, might be repeated two dozen times on your web site, but you should have to pay for its translation only once. Translation memory tools allow you to reuse, or leverage, previous translations.

Translation memory tools are explained in Chapter 9, "Computer-Aided Translation (CAT)."

Translation memory can cut your translation costs by 10% to 30%, depending on the level of repetition involved and the number of updates to the site. Yet some companies aren't aware of its benefits or don't hire localization vendors who use translation memory tools properly. If you see a lot of phrases, terms, and sentences repeated throughout your site, or if you plan to update content frequently, make sure you take advantage of translation memory.

The "Change Order" Blues

A *change order* is what a vendor issues when additional translation, localization, or other modifications are required. Before your localization vendor begins any project, you both must agree on the scope of the project. If anything comes up later that falls outside that scope, you'll need to sign off on a change order.

These changes might be as simple as a few web pages that you forgot to get quoted initially or a few new graphics that you've decided to add. Change orders get more complex, however, if a company, in the middle of a localization project, decides to redesign its source-language site. Because many companies want their localized sites to match their source site, such a redesign can result in a lot of change orders.

More commonly, companies fail to fully estimate the size of their source-language sites, only to discover "new" content along the way. Change orders have a painful way of multiplying when you don't have a firm grasp of the size of your project. The best way to prevent this from happening is to conduct a "content audit" of your site so that your initial quotes more accurately reflect the project's scope. A *content audit* is simply a thorough analysis of all content—text and graphics—on your web site with an eye to what should or should not be localized. Ideally, the audit will result in a comprehensive listing of all HTML files and graphics that need to be localized, something that can easily be sent to a localization vendor for quoting. Many companies prefer to let localization vendors worry about selecting which files need to be localized, but this strategy is dangerous because it puts too much faith in the vendor. A vendor can't be expected to understand your company and the inner working of your web site. The more time you spend auditing your web site, the less time you'll spend singing the change order blues.

BEYOND THE BUDGET

In a perfect world, every company would localize its web site into every possible language. In the real world, however, costs get in the way—and costs play a major role in your web localization efforts. Because many companies are only just realizing the value of global web sites, the budgets they allocate typically fall well short of what's needed. You'll have to make the most with what you get and create localized web sites that justify additional investment. Keeping an eye on the many costs, hidden or otherwise, could make the difference between a profitable globalization effort and a painful one.

Figure 1   The Social Security Administration home page.

SOCIAL SECURITY ADMINISTRATION

The Social Security Administration (SSA) launched its multilingual gateway in July 2001, providing access to information in 14 languages (French was the most recent addition). So far, the most popular languages are Chinese, Korean, and Russian, respectively.

The SSA takes a rather unique approach to web globalization by relying primarily on localized portable document format (PDF) files instead of localized web pages. The exception to this rule is the Spanish site (see Figure 2), which does provide a large number of localized web pages. The SSA offers a more comprehensive Spanish site not just because Spanish is by far the second most popular language in the U.S., but because the SSA has Spanish-language expertise in house. It's not unusual for organizations to begin their localization efforts based not only on their audience and their needs, but on what in-house language expertise they happen to have on hand.

---

www.ssa.gov

Localized web sites: The SSA currently offers a Spanish web site and help sections in:

- Arabic
- Armenian
- Chinese
- Farsi
- French
- Greek
- Haitian–Creole
- Italian
- Korean
- Polish
- Portuguese
- Russian
- Tagalog
- Vietnamese

Figure 2 The SSA offers a comprehensive Spanish-language site.

ANALYSIS

Web localization isn't always about expanding beyond borders. Increasingly, American organizations are localizing their web sites for Americans, and the U.S. government is no exception. Although many governmental departments have been painfully slow to supply information in multiple languages, the SSA has made an aggressive effort to reach as many Americans as possible. The SSA doesn't have an enormous translation budget, but it still manages to provide information in 14 languages. Necessity breeds creativity, which in turn breeds PDFs.

The advantage of PDFs is that they can serve multiple purposes. They can be posted on a web site for download or can be printed for distribution at regional offices (see Figure 3). This strategy can save the SSA a great deal of money because it can update the PDFs periodically without having to worry about maintaining hundreds of web pages. Budgetary constraints aside, PDFs may in fact be necessary when you need to give the audience higher-resolution documents, such as forms or illustrations.

Figure 3   The SSA provides PDF documents in Farsi.

The potential downsides to PDFs are users not having Adobe Acrobat Reader installed or having very slow connections. Fortunately, the SSA keeps the bulk of the PDF files under 200KB, which keeps the download time relatively manageable. And, given that more than 200 million copies of Acrobat Reader have been downloaded over the years, more and more users can readily view the documents. PDFs are probably not the best long-term solution, though. The documents do serve more than one purpose, but they can't serve as many purposes as text stored in a content management system, something you'll read more about in Chapter 13, "Global Content Management."

A Globally Friendly Global Gateway

Finding the SSA multilingual home page isn't easy, but once you get there, you find a global gateway that puts the gateways of most Fortune 500 companies to shame. As shown in Figure 4, the gateway can't be missed. It's positioned in the middle of the page with a large type size. What makes the gateway so effective, however, is that the links to each language are given twice—first in English, and second in the native script. Why twice? Because most of the native script links are graphics, which aren't always displayed properly in browsers. The English links are all in text, so they are guaranteed to appear correctly. Global gateways are covered in much more detail in Chapter 11, "World Wide Design."

ARABIC	عربي
ARMENIAN	Հայերեն
CHINESE	中文
FARSI	فارسی
FRENCH	Français
GREEK	ΕΛΛΗΝΙΚΑ
HAITIAN-CREOLE	Kreyòl Ayisien
ITALIAN	Italiano
KOREAN	한국어
POLISH	Polski
PORTUGUESE	PORTUGUÊS
RUSSIAN	Русский
SPANISH	ESPAÑOL

Figure 4   A thorough, easy-to-read global gateway.

Q&A WITH SSA

Armando A. Garcia, Team Leader
Social Security Administration,
Office of Communications
Multilanguage Services

What criteria did you use to decide which languages to begin with?

We used 1990 census data to identify non-English languages spoken at home and where English was not spoken well. We validated the relevance of the language groups by using immigration figures from annual Census Statistical Abstracts. We also considered (from the 1990 census) such factors as high level of bilingualism for a language group. We considered United Nations data (UNESCO Institute for Statistics) on a language group's country of origin literacy level. We extrapolated the data to identify the languages and compared the list to our second defined audience—SSA beneficiaries. SSA electronically collects customer "language preference" management information data in our business process.

How many people manage the multilingual portion of your site and what are their titles?

The SSA Multilanguage Gateway web site is managed by two individuals: one who manages the site content and one who manages the web site itself. For each of these individuals, management of the Multilanguage Gateway is a collateral duty—that is, it is not his or her full-time job. In addition to the management responsibilities, approximately six staff members contribute to content creation and maintenance and web site development and maintenance. Again, these are collateral duties for these staff members. Based upon these staffing patterns, the site is managed by less than one full-time employee and maintained by fewer than two full-time employees.

What challenges did you encounter when creating the localized sites?

Creating Content: The terminology used by the SSA is unique. A translation glossary is a necessary tool for contracting out translations. Contracting out translations requires establishing a quality assurance review system of skilled/qualified employees to approve the translations. A company's technology infrastructure must be adequate to accommodate editable electronic (non-English character) documents.

Displaying Content: Displaying content of English characters on the Internet in HTML format is an easy task compared to displaying non-English (double-byte) characters. Standardizing the encoding of HTML documents by using Microsoft's Unicode character set may alleviate the difficulty, but compelling users to reconfigure PCs to reliably display Unicode characters is not as user-friendly an option as providing service with all the necessary components to reliably display a document. A second method of displaying content is either in image format or PDF; of these two, PDF offers better display resolution and printout capability. The downsides to these formats may be increased wait times for an image to display or requiring the installation of Adobe Acrobat Reader to view PDFs. This dilemma requires an organization to assess its technology and plan a strategy for best delivering public information over the Internet.

Managing Content: This requires resources/staff because of annual updates to publications. We are considering outsourcing this task.

What software tools did you use for localization? Any specific content management applications?

Microsoft Word 2000: This is the standard when dealing with contract translators. It is used to create editable non-English character documents and save them in several file formats, such as MS Word, Adobe PDF, and HTML.

Did you outsource the translation or did you do it in house?

Except for Spanish, we outsourced most of our translations. Occasionally, we will focus on one language and have a qualified employee translate material for us.

What advice would you give to other organizations seeking to add multilingual sections to their site?

Know your audience. Create a strategy to target that audience. Corporate internal [intranet] communications are easier to deal with than external [Internet] communications. A corporation can standardize PC/workstation configuration for browser display and create standardized encoded HTML documents to conform to the configuration. For the Internet environment, private business goals differ from public service goals. Business is driven by the profit margin of a campaign. If "an effort" allows a company to reach sufficient customers to sell its products profitably, then the venture is successful. In public service, one's enterprise is to reach all its customers. This may prove more perplexing than profit margins.

HANDS-ON: FRENCH, ITALIAN, AND GERMAN

Overview

This is the second of six Hands-On chapters. By now, you have completed "Hands-On: Spanish." Collectively, these chapters demonstrate the process (and challenges) of localizing an English-language web page into multiple languages. After completing all Hands-On chapters, you will have localized one web page into eight languages—the languages spoken by more than 80% of the world's population. If you'd like to try your hand at these exercises, all files used in these chapters are available for download; go to **www.bytelevel.com/beyondborders**.

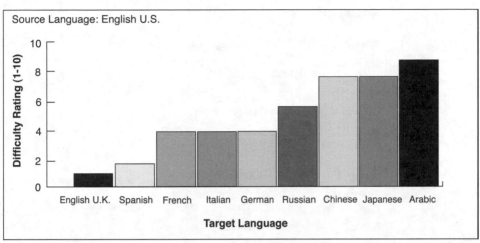

Figure 1 The difficulty ratings used in Chapter 1, "In the Beginning, There Was English."

For a full list of country and language codes, see Appendix D, "Language and Country Codes."

Speakers worldwide (source: *Ethnologue*, 14th Edition, 2000):

■ **French:** 77 million (51 million in France)

■ **Italian:** 62 million (55 million in Italy)

■ **German:** 128 million (75 million in Germany)

ISO language codes: FR, IT, DE

Difficulty rating: 4 (see Figure 1)

Major French locales:

Country	Language Code
France	fr-FR
Canada	fr-CA
Belgium	fr-BE
Switzerland	fr-CH
Haiti	fr-HT

French is spoken in more than 45 countries.

Major Italian locales:

Country	Language Code
Italy	it-IT
Switzerland	it-CH

Italian is spoken in more than 25 countries.

Major German locales:

Country	Language Code
Germany	de-DE
Switzerland	de-CH
Austria	de-AT

German is spoken in more than 35 countries.

FIRST THOUGHTS

In the "Hands-On: Spanish" chapter, you localized an English-language web page into Spanish. In this chapter, you're going to take that same English source page (see Figure 2) and localize it into three additional languages: French, German, and Italian. By focusing on languages (French, German, and Italian) rather than countries (France, Germany, Italy), you increase the size of your potential audience—from 188 million to 267 million (although regional language differences could lower this total somewhat).

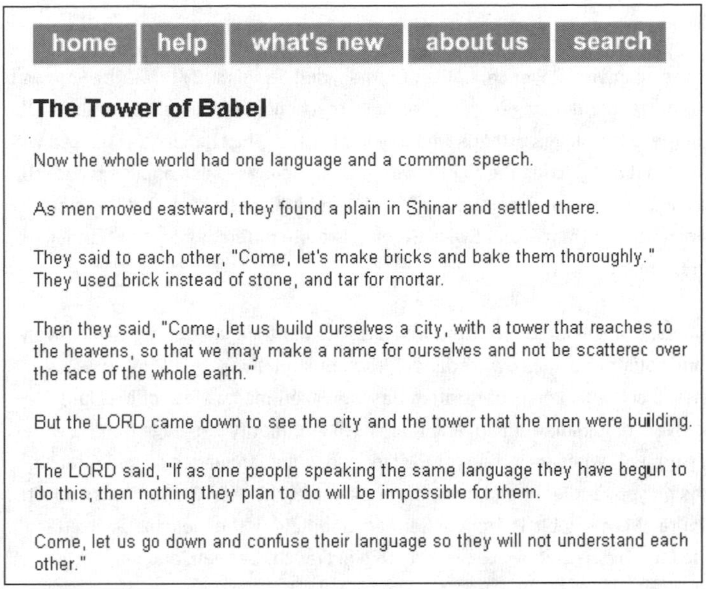

| home | help | what's new | about us | search |

The Tower of Babel

Now the whole world had one language and a common speech.

As men moved eastward, they found a plain in Shinar and settled there.

They said to each other, "Come, let's make bricks and bake them thoroughly."
They used brick instead of stone, and tar for mortar.

Then they said, "Come, let us build ourselves a city, with a tower that reaches to
the heavens, so that we may make a name for ourselves and not be scattered over
the face of the whole earth."

But the LORD came down to see the city and the tower that the men were building.

The LORD said, "If as one people speaking the same language they have begun to
do this, then nothing they plan to do will be impossible for them.

Come, let us go down and confuse their language so they will not understand each
other."

Figure 2 The English source page.

Because these three languages share the same character set as Spanish—
ISO 8859-1—there's no need to go through the technical details of the localization
process. You can follow the same workflow and use the same tools you used to create the Spanish web page. Instead, this chapter focuses on the general challenges
of localizing multiple languages simultaneously and the specific challenges of localizing European languages:

- **Inputting diacritics.** When working with European languages, you should be
  familiar with diacritics and how to input them.

- **Graphics with embedded text.** The text embedded in the navigation bar
  graphic is going to be more time-consuming to localize now that you're working with three languages. Should you create a text-only navigation bar?

- **Global gateways.** By the end of this chapter, you'll have four separate language
  web pages, in addition to the source page. What is your strategy for directing
  people to their localized web pages? It's time to build a global gateway.

FIGS

FIGS is the acronym for French, Italian, German, and Spanish. By localizing your web site into these four languages, you effectively reach most of Western Europe. Yet the reach of these languages extends well beyond Europe. The challenge you faced with Spanish—that of selecting the right flavor of the language—also applies to French, German, and Italian. For example, the French used in Canada is quite different from the French used in France, and Swiss German is quite different from the German used in Germany.

Sometimes, you'll need to localize a web site into multiple languages to effectively cover one country, such as Switzerland. Although a relatively small country, Switzerland certainly keeps translators busy; Switzerland has four official languages: French, Italian, German, and Romansch (a minority language that's a variation of German). When localizing for Switzerland, what languages do you offer? It depends on your audience and budget. For example, the IKEA Switzerland web site (see Figure 3) is available in French, German, and Italian; the Siemens Switzerland web site (see Figure 4), however, is available in French, German, and English.

Figure 3　The IKEA Switzerland web site is available in French, German, and Italian.

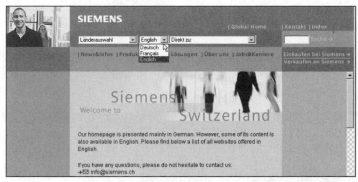

Figure 4   The Siemens Switzerland site, on the other hand, is available in French, German, and English.

DIACRITICS AND SPECIAL CHARACTERS

Although you don't need to be a linguistic expert to localize a web site, understanding the major diacritics and how they are used is helpful when you're working with European languages. Diacritics are those marks placed above and below characters, such as *A* or *n* or *e*, to create new characters, such as *á* or *ñ* or *è*. Diacritics are used to stress a syllable or alter its pronunciation in some way. Different European languages rely on different diacritics. All the diacritics required for the major Western European languages are included in the ISO 8859-1 and Windows 1252 character sets. Central and Eastern European languages require additional diacritics, which in turn require additional character sets. Fortunately, all diacritics are included in the Unicode character set.

Source for information on diacritics and accent marks: British & Foreign Bible Society, Machine Assisted Translation Team (**www.bfbs.org.uk**), *2002.*

There are four main types of diacritic marks:

- **Accent.** A mark above a character. In English, these marks usually appear only on foreign-loan words, and are often omitted (for example, fête, résumé).

- **Stress mark.** A mark above a character indicating where stress falls on a word (such as learnèd or blessèd).

- **Diaeresis.** A mark that indicates a change of vowel quality or marks the separate pronunciation of adjacent vowels (such as Zoë or naïve).

- **Ligature.** A character formed by combining other characters (for example, encyclopædia or phœnix). The ampersand symbol (&) was originally a ligature for the Latin *et* meaning "and." In printing, sometimes characters are combined into ligatures to take up less space (*ff* and *fi*, for example). Arabic relies extensively on ligatures.

The Accent Mark

The most commonly used diacritic is the accent mark. It is usually placed above vowels to mark changes in sound, vowel length, tone, stress, or pitch. These are common accents that appear above a letter:

- **Acute accent.** An ascending line above a letter (é, á).

- **Grave accent.** A descending line above a letter (è, à).

- **Circumflex.** An inverted *v* above the letter (ê, ĉ).

- **Dieresis.** A double dot above a letter (ë, ï); it's common in German, where it's called an *umlaut*.

- **Caron.** A small *v* over a letter (š, ě). This accent is common in Slavic languages, where it's used above consonants to soften them (it is called a *hacek* in Slovak, Slovene, and Czech languages).

- **Breve.** Like a smooth caron (ă, Ě); used in Romanian and Latvian.

- **Ring.** A small circle (å, Å), used in Czech and Scandinavian languages.

Common accents that appear below a letter:

- **Cedilla.** A mark underneath a letter (ç, ţ), usually used with a *c* in French and Romanian.

Common accents that appear above or below letters:

- **Tilde.** A squiggle above or below a letter (such as the ñ in the Spanish word "mañana").

- **Macron.** A bar, usually over a vowel (ē, Ā), used in Latvian and Maori.

Inputting Diacritics and Special Characters

Although not all diacritics have dedicated keys on the English keyboard, you can still input them in a variety of ways. Because every character has a numeric code point, you can enter that character by number. Using the numeric keypad on Windows, hold down the Alt key and type the appropriate number. The full code point chart is located in Appendix C, "Character Entities." Here are a few examples:

á	Alt+0225
ó	Alt+0243
ú	Alt+0250
é	Alt+0233
ñ	Alt+0241
í	Alt+0237
¿	Alt+0191

If you don't want to bother with numbers, there are keyboard shortcuts you can use. Here are some of the most frequently used shortcuts:

165

- To input an acute accent, press Ctrl+apostrophe ('), and then the letter (á).

- To input a grave accent, press Ctrl+grave accent (`), and then the letter (à).

- To input a tilde, press Ctrl+Shift+tilde (~), and then the letter (ñ).

- To input a cedilla, press Ctrl+comma (,), and then press the letter c or C (ç or Ç).

For more information on multi-lingual text input, see Chapter 12, "Creating Multilingual Content."

FYI

For an overview of European diacritics by language, go to **www.tiro.com/di_intro.html**.

MULTILINGUAL MULTITASKING

Localizing a web page into one language is relatively straightforward. Localizing a web page into multiple languages *simultaneously* is not always so straightforward. Instead of working with one translator and one editor, you'll work with no less than three translators and three editors. Managing all these people takes coordination and attention to detail; a project-tracking sheet won't hurt either. Take a moment to create a tracking sheet like the one in Figure 5. It doesn't have to be fancy—just an Excel sheet with the participants, stages, and dates. Notice how the sheet includes a number of "validation" stages. *Validation* is the process of reviewing a file before it goes to a translator and after it is returned. This step helps ensure that HTML code isn't accidentally altered and that all relevant text is translated.

	A	B	C	D	E	F
1						
2	**Project workflow**					
3						
4	**French**	**validated**	**translated**	**validated**	**edited**	**validated**
5	index.html	1-Feb	4-Feb	4-Feb	6-Feb	7-Feb
6						
7	**Italian**	**validated**	**translated**	**validated**	**edited**	**validated**
8	index.html	1-Feb	4-Feb	4-Feb	6-Feb	
9						
10	**German**	**validated**	**translated**	**validated**	**edited**	**validated**
11	index.html	5-Feb	7-Feb	9-Feb		
12						

For more information on managing translation, see Chapter 8, "Translation Management."

Figure 5   A very basic project tracking sheet, created in Excel.

Before sending off the HTML source page to the translators, prepare the glossary. In this case, you can simply expand the glossary you began in "Hands-On: Spanish" (see Figure 6) and let the translators fill in the blanks. Typically, the glossary should be translated and edited before any work begins on the HTML files.

	A	B	C	D	E
1	Glossary				
2					
3	**EN**	**ES**	**FR**	**DE**	**IT**
4					
5	Home	Principal	Accueil	Home	Home
6	Help	Ayuda	Aide	Hilfe	Aiuto
7	What's new	Novedades	What's New	Was ist neu	Novità
8	About us	Sobre nosotros	Au sujet de nous	Wir über uns	Circa noi
9	Search	Buscar	Recherche	Suche	Ricerca
10	Privacy Policy	Centro de privacidad	Données personnelles	Datenschutz	Privacy
11	Contact	Contactar	Contact	Kontakt	Contatto
12	Tower of Babel	Torre de Babel	Tour de Babel	Aufsatz von Babel	Torretta di Babele
13					
14					

Figure 6   The glossary now includes all FIGS.

Finally, even though you've yet to send a file to a translator, decide how the files will be organized and named once they're returned. Ideally, you should organize the files in separately named language directories, as shown in Figure 7. The ISO language codes provide an efficient, standardized naming system. Don't forget to update the hyperlinks within the HTML files to match the new naming system. As you did with the Spanish page, create "fr," "de," and "it" subdirectories for your target files. Rename the target files with the proper extensions and locate the navigation graphics in the main images directory.

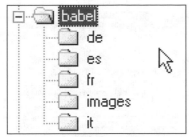

Figure 7 Each language resides
in a subdirectory.

Translator Feedback and Last-Minute Changes

Translator and editor feedback is critical to the success of your localization project.
For this project, the three editors who reviewed the web pages had significant comments. For example, feedback from the French editor included the following note:

> *In the navigation bar, "Accueil," "Aide," and "Recherche" are fine. "What's
> new" should be "Quoi de neuf." As for "About us," I believe that "Qui
> sommes-nous?" would be much better than "Au sujet de nous." Both "Quoi
> de neuf" and "Qui sommes-nous?" are very commonly used in French
> websites.*

167

Translation isn't always a matter of right or wrong. In this case, the French editor
distinguishes between a change that "should" be made and a change that "I
believe" would be better. Sometimes you, as the project manager, have to make
the final call on which changes should be made. A good translator always provides
recommendations and rationales—but sometimes the ultimate decision falls on
your shoulders.

Sometimes a translator or an editor for one language raises an issue that affects all
other languages. In this case, the German editor questioned why the words in the
navigation bar were not capitalized. Although lowercasing words may be considered
stylistic in the U.S., in Germany, it could be considered sloppy; German capitalization rules are not bent as frequently as they are in American English. To play it safe,
you decide to capitalize the words across all languages (see Figure 8). But you have
a small problem: the French and Italian graphics have already been localized.
Updating them will require opening the source graphic files in Photoshop, making
the edits, and exporting the graphics again. Instead, you decide to get rid of the
graphics altogether and simply use a text-based navigation bar, as shown in Figure
9. Then, if any more translation issues arise, which is to be expected, you can make
a quick change without generating all new graphics.

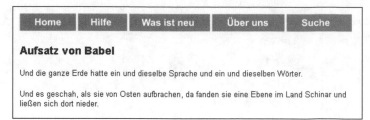

Figure 8   The German navbar, after capitalization.

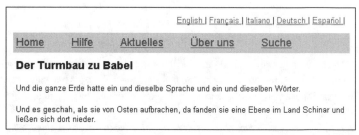

Figure 9   The German navbar, text only.

German Capitalization

The German language has more complex capitalization rules than the English language. In English, only proper nouns are capitalized, but in German, *all* nouns are capitalized, even common nouns.

GLOBAL GATEWAY

After localizing the source page into three target pages, you'll need to devise a strategy for directing users to their localized web pages. If you assume that most web site visitors speak English, the English-language web page should be the landing page. You also want visitors to find their localized web pages quickly, however, so the gateway should be easy to find and available on *all* web pages, as shown in Figure 10. This global gateway embedded at the top of every web page is very basic, but works better than most major corporate gateways because the language selection is far easier to find. Too many companies unintentionally hide their gateways.

For a more in-depth look at developing global gateways, see Chapter 11, "World Wide Design."

English | Français | Italiano | Deutsch | Español |

Home   Help   What's new   About us   Search

The Tower of Babel

Now the whole world had one language and a common speech.

As men moved eastward, they found a plain in Shinar and settled there.

English | Français | Italiano | Deutsch | Español |

Accueil Aide Quoi de neuf Qui sommes-nous ? Recherche

La Tour de Babel

Toute la terre avait une seule langue et les mêmes mots.

Comme ils étaient partis de l'orient, ils trouvèrent une plaine au pays de Schinear, et ils y habitèrent.

English | Français | Italiano | Deutsch | Español |

Home   Hilfe   Aktuelles   Über uns   Suche

Der Turmbau zu Babel

Und die ganze Erde hatte ein und dieselbe Sprache und ein und dieselben Wörter.

Und es geschah, als sie von Osten aufbrachen, da fanden sie eine Ebene im Land Schinar und ließen sich dort nieder.

English | Français | Italiano | Deutsch | Español

Home   Aiuto   Novità   Circa noi   Ricerca

La torretta di Babele

Tutta la terra aveva una sola lingua e le stesse parole.

Emigrando dall'oriente gli uomini capitarono in una pianura nel paese di Sennaar e vi si stabilirono.

Figure 10   The global gateway is now embedded at the top of all pages.

169

THINKING AHEAD

You've now created four localized web pages that combined have the potential of reaching nearly 600 million people. In the subsequent Hands-On chapters, you'll add more languages and begin using new character sets.

Credits: Céline Détraz provided translation and editing support for French and can be reached at **www.simply-said.com.** Gaby Chitwood provided translation and editing support for Italian; she is an ATA-accredited translator and can be contacted through **www.atanet.org.** Richard Nangle provided translation and editing support for German.

7

INTERNATIONALIZATION AND LOCALIZATION

The two terms most critical to the success of web globalization—internationalization and localization—are also the two most frequently misunderstood. Their odd-looking abbreviations (i18n and L10n) certainly don't help matters. Internationalization is the process of building a web site so that it can support multiple locales, while localization is the process of modifying that site for a specific locale.

At first glance, the two terms don't appear related at all. Internationalization implies taking a global approach to web development, but localization implies just the opposite. Yet these two terms are intimately linked, so much so that it can be difficult to tell where internationalization ends and localization begins. This chapter will help you not only differentiate between the two, but also understand how to successfully use them together.

THE I18N AND L10N OF AN AUTOMOBILE

The principles behind internationalization and localization extend beyond web development, even to something much more concrete, like a car. A car, like a web site, is expensive to design and build. To minimize costs and maximize returns, a car manufacturer often develops a car model that can be easily adapted to numerous countries, instead of developing new models for each country. Doing so requires internationalization. The internationalization stage is the "behind the scenes" stage. People don't buy internationalized cars; they buy localized cars. Internationalization mostly entails the extensive planning and testing that go into creating this global template of a car. For example, if the car will be sold in both the U.S. and the U.K., allowances must be made for placing a steering wheel on either side of the car. Some car manufacturers might decide during this process that some markets are just not worth the cost of localization efforts. It's a cost/benefit decision that you'll also have to make as you internationalize your web site.

After internationalization is finished, the car can be localized for each market. The more thorough the job you do of internationalization, the less time you'll spend on localization. Localization can be as simple as moving the steering wheel to the other side or could be as complex as deciding what color palette to offer. The line between localization and personalization is not always so clearly defined. Inevitably, you want your web site to be as customized as possible to your audience, but you can't do everything. Even car manufacturers don't offer every option imaginable, which is why car buyers do a fair amount of customization themselves. Just as in the internationalization stage, the decisions you make during localization are heavily dictated by costs and benefits.

The key to success is striking a balance between flexibility and profitability. Similar challenges face a web team: How global do you *need* to go? How local can you *afford* to go?

Microsoft Localizes the Xbox

Before launching its new Xbox gaming console in Japan, Microsoft localized the game controllers—moving the buttons closer together—to better fit the average Japanese user's hands.

Source: New York Times, *February 18, 2002*

THINKING GLOBALLY

Thinking globally requires big thinking. Put aside budgetary constraints for a moment and think of every possible country or region your company might want to target:

India?

Malaysia?

The Middle East?

Although these three markets might not be at the top of a company's globalization strategy, it's just a matter of time before they get there. There are more than 1.5 billion people in these three markets alone, and their buying power is exploding. Even if you plan to enter only a few European markets this year, you might someday end up like IBM, with 62 localized web sites. If you want to build a global company, you need to think global from the beginning.

Thinking Big

Coke has 26 localized web sites.
Lycos has 34 localized web sites.
IBM has 62 localized web sites.

173

What's Your Localization Timeline?

Creating a localization timeline for the next 5 to 10 years can be as simple as this example:

Sample Localization Timeline

> Year 1: Spanish-Mexico, Portuguese-Brazil
>
> Year 3: French-France, German-Germany
>
> Year 5: Japanese-Japan, Korean-Korea
>
> Year 8: Arabic-Middle East, Tamil-India

A localization timeline, including both language and region, helps you avoid a lot of the common technical, legal, and cultural potholes that await. For example, assume that you test your brand for the first four markets you're planning to enter. The initial launches work so well that you accelerate your rollout schedule and add a few new markets. Unfortunately, because you didn't test all potential markets initially, competitors have beaten you to them by launching similar brands and localized web sites of their own. With the Internet, anyone anywhere can spy on you. If you have global aspirations with your products or services, you need to make the investment upfront to ensure that you can launch in those markets without hitting regulatory and copyright obstacles. If you want to avoid the sort of conflict that Anheuser-Busch is involved in with Budvar (see sidebar), think big from the beginning.

When You Say Budweiser...

There is more than one company in the world brewing Budweiser (see Figure 7.1): the American giant Anheuser-Busch and the tiny Czechoslovakian brewer Budvar.

Figure 7.1 Budweiser Czechoslovakia and Budweiser U.S.: Similar names, different brands.

Needless to say, the big guy has won trademark battles in much of the world, but not all of it. Budvar has the right to Budweiser in Germany and Russia, so Anheuser-Busch promotes "Bud" instead. It's a nasty fight and very much ongoing. Since 1939, Budvar has been prohibited from selling its beer under the Bud, Budweis, or Budweiser name in North America. But that hasn't stopped it from going after A-B where it lives; it recently released a new product for the U.S. market: Czechvar.

Separating the Constants from the Variables

The main purpose of internationalization is to isolate the graphical and textual elements of a web site that change from locale to locale as well as within the locale itself. The way these elements are managed for each market—in terms of design and text—will be covered in later chapters. For now, you just want to make sure you've got a good understanding of what elements will change and what elements will not.

The Constants

A constant is anything that remains the same, no matter what market you localize for. It can be the design template that your site shares across all web pages, or it could be a collection of scripts and style sheets. It can also be a collection of what's called "corporate constants," such as brand names, slogans, logos, colors, and navigation menus. For example, in the Spanish banner ad for Volvo, shown in Figure 7.2, notice that the slogan "for life" remains in English. Very often, companies decide to maintain a global slogan regardless of the target market.

Figure 7.2   In the Volvo banner ad, the logo and slogan are constants.

175

Some companies also maintain unique colors across all locales, such as the Coca-Cola red or IBM blue or UPS brown. Despite how various cultures perceive colors, many corporations elect to err on the side of consistency.

The Variables

Variables include anything that changes from market to market or within a market. During the internationalization stage, you focus on isolating the variables and modifying your site so that they can be more easily adapted to each market. Variables include:

- Measurements and sizes

- Prices and currencies

- Dates, calendars, and time zones

- Product selection

- Contact information

- Images and icons

- Forms and input fields

The more variables your site consists of, the more challenging internationalization becomes. However, there is no rule that says you have to offer the same variables across all locales. To simplify internationalization and localization, you might decide to limit the number of variables available in each localized site. In fact, it's rare to find a company that provides the same level of functionality and support on its localized sites that it does on its source-language site.

Text Expansion and Contraction

When a block of text is translated into another language, it tends to expand or contract, depending on the target language. This phenomenon, known as *text expansion* or *text contraction*, occurs because translation is not a one-to-one process. The word *cat* in English translates to "gato" in Spanish, thus adding a character. In Chinese, a cat can be represented by just one character: 猫

Although much depends on the verbosity of the translator, general patterns are noticeable. English text often expands when translated into European languages— from approximately 15% in Spanish to as much as 35% in German (see Figure 7.3). Asian languages typically require fewer characters than their English equivalents, yet you might not see much contraction; even though you're working with fewer characters, they generally need to be displayed at a larger point size to ensure legibility. Text expansion and contraction become particularly acute when working with small amounts of text, such as with headlines or text in navigation bars. For example, *search* translated into French becomes "recherché," a 30% expansion.

Think about how text expansion will affect your site's design and functionality. Also alert your translators to places where space is tight on your site; they can often provide more austere translations, but they can't work miracles. If you don't give your web design enough room for text expansion, you'll face a painful redesign when localizing for European markets. The best way to avoid this problem is to follow Yahoo!'s lead and simply avoid embedding text into graphics; if you must embed text, allot plenty of room for the inevitable expansion.

English:	News
Italian:	Notizie
French:	Actualités
German:	Schlagzeilen
Japanese:	ニュース
Chinese:	新闻
Korean:	뉴스

Figure 7.3 The "news," when translated, either expands outside its allotted space or leaves room to spare, depending on the language and the style of translation.

Don't Forget the Back End

Some of the more complex text expansion problems are not so visible. It's not uncommon to discover, after your web site has launched, that users in Germany are having difficulty entering their complete addresses (because the fields won't allow for additional characters) or users in Japan are having problems inputting their names (because the database won't accept Japanese characters). Always make sure that you adapt the text fields to allow for longer names and other locale-specific issues.

Address fields are particularly challenging. There are more than 100 different address formats in use around the world (see sidebar "Return to Sender"). If you've developed a web order form for users in the U.S., you'll have to make some immediate changes to accommodate users outside the U.S. Countries such as the U.S., Canada, and Brazil have states, but most countries do not, so you shouldn't require that the state field be filled out. Better yet, offer a localized order form that does not include the state field. The ZIP code field is also challenging. For starters, the term *ZIP code* is unique to the U.S.; other countries call it a "postal code" or "postcode." In the U.S., a ZIP code is either 5 or 9 digits, but in other countries, a postal code can be anywhere from 3 to 7 digits and might include letters. And just to keep you on your toes, some countries, such as Ireland, don't even use a postal code. The technical issues of managing text in databases and web applications are complex, and beyond the scope of this book. Just be aware that you'll probably need to modify your databases to support new and longer input fields and additional character sets.

┌─ Return to Sender ─

With 112 different address formats in the world, odds are that you'll need to update your web site to accommodate entering and displaying addresses for different countries. And details count. For example, compare the following two addresses: the first for the U.S., the second for Germany.

JOHN DOE
55 COOLIDGE ST
BOSTON, MA 02151-4645

For the U.S., the standard is all uppercase letters, with the street number coming before the street name and the ZIP code on the same line as the city and state.

Herm
Gunther Meyer
Goethestrae 25

20002 HAMBURG

For the German address, the personal form of address, *Herm*, is written on a separate line, the house number follows the street number, and an empty line is inserted above the postal code.

*Source: "A Guide to International Address Management," GRC Database Information (**www.grcdi.nl**)*

Global Architecture

If you localize your English site for six locales, you might find yourself with six times as many web pages to manage. If you don't implement and maintain a sound structure, you may also find yourself struggling to manage all those new files. Many developers, because they begin localization with just one language, find that they've labeled the pages haphazardly, as shown in Figure 7.4.

Notice how the Spanish pages and directories are labeled inconsistently and in different languages, and are mixed together with the source-language pages. Consider how confusing this arrangement will be after the site grows to a few thousand pages. Now for an alternative approach, shown in Figure 7.5.

	A	B	C	D	E
1	Sample Web site architecture				
2					
3	/				
4		index			
5		index_espanol			
6		welcome.html			
7		bienvenidos.html			
8					
9		/about			
10			index.html		
11					
12		/about_spanish			
13			index.html		
14					
15		/products			
16			item1.html		
17			item2.html		
18					
19		/spanish_products			
20			item1.html		
21			item2.html		
22					

Figure 7.4   An architecture for trouble.

	A	B	C	D
1	Sample Web site architecture			
2				
3	/en/			
4		index.html		
5		welcome.html		
6				
7		/about/		
8			index.html	
9				
10		/products/		
11			item1.html	
12			item2.html	
13				
14	/es/			
15		index.html		
16		welcome.html		
17				
18		/about/		
19			index.html	
20				
21		/products/		
22			item1.html	
23			item2.html	
24				
25				

Figure 7.5   A better architecture.

By creating "es" and "en" parent directories, all locale-specific pages can be isolated from one another. Notice how filenames are mirrored in each directory. This strategy will come in handy when it's time to update content. If, for example, your welcome.html page needs updating, you know exactly where all the welcome.html localized pages are, no matter what the language. An added benefit is that pages don't need to be renamed, and developers can switch between languages by simply changing the "es" to "fr" or "de."

Business Rules

After you've effectively organized the site, think about how to organize the content itself. You may have certain product or service categories that make sense to Americans, but not to users abroad. Or, even if the categories do make sense, they might not be needed in your target markets. Just as Wal-Mart doesn't sell snow shovels in Florida, you shouldn't build a site that sells products that people in other countries don't need.

Business rules help you automate some of the complexities of interacting with multiple locales. Rules include anything from product selection and pricing to sales tax, shipping fees, and privacy restrictions. For example, you could have a Chinese New Year promotion planned for your Chinese market while you're simultaneously planning an Easter promotion for European and Latin American markets. Later in the book, you'll examine content management systems that have business-rule capabilities built in.

For more information on managing locale-specific content, see Chapter 13, "Global Content Management."

The better you understand the various constraints of each local market, the better you can prepare for them on a global scale.

Yahoo! and France

French law prohibits the sale of racist items, such as Nazi or Ku Klux Klan paraphernalia, yet until recently, Yahoo! regularly featured such items on its auction site. Using business logic, Yahoo! kept these items out of any auction that would be seen on the Yahoo! France site. However, in late 2000 a French judge said that this solution wasn't good enough, so in early 2001, Yahoo! banned the auction of such items altogether, joining the ranks of eBay and Amazon. Other countries don't share the same laws (or lack thereof) as the U.S., so expect your site to abide by many differing laws.

Loose Strings

Thinking globally has technical requirements as well as business requirements. For example, text strings might not seem important, but they can create major problems if overlooked. Often, web developers hard-code text strings into the scripts stored throughout a web site. For example, when you conduct a search on a site, you'll see a response similar to this:

Your search returned 15 results.

This string is actually composed of four elements, assembled dynamically:

"Your search returned"

"15" (generated automatically)

"result"

"s" (the *s* is added to "result" when the number of results is greater or less than 1)

This system works for English, but in some languages, such as French or Spanish, plurals aren't always formed by simply tacking an *s* to the end. In other languages, such as Chinese, there is no difference between plural and singular. To avoid this problem, the string should be rewritten as follows:

Number of results returned: 15

The process of chaining text strings together is called *concatenation*, and concatenation simply does not travel well. Every language has it own unique patterns and idiosyncrasies. Notice how the string **Results 1 - 10 of about 475,000** changes depending on whether you're using Google U.S. versus Japan (see Figure 7.6).

181

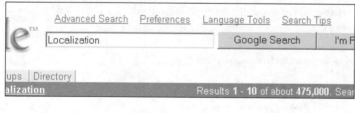

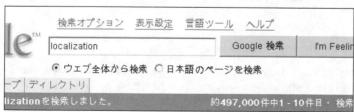

Figure 7.6 Google U.S. and Japan: Similar messages, differently constructed sentences.

Solving (and preferably avoiding) concatenation problems is a job for software developers. Increasingly, software developers take all these text strings and place them in a separate resource file or database. By keeping the translatable text separate from the software, the text strings can be easily translated and the developers don't have to spend their time searching for lost strings. This book won't attempt to delve any more deeply into this area, but just be aware that all those little text strings used throughout your web site—even though they might not cost a lot to translate—could cost quite a lot to internationalize.

ACTING LOCALLY

Internationalization generally focuses on those web site elements that remain invisible to the end user—architecture, databases, modular design—but localization focuses on those elements that are visible: text, images, and the manner in which they're presented.

If you consider how companies struggle to target their web sites toward various groups of users *within* the U.S., you can understand the challenge of localizing a site for new, global markets. Every locale is going to require its own degree of customization. Even within a market, there are always smaller markets that require an even finer level of customization. Some of the changes you make will be cosmetic; others will be highly technical. Given the complexity, it's not hard to imagine a time when entire books will be devoted to localizing web sites for each market.

For this book, the focus is on the macro issues. Although there is no limit to how localized a site can be, at a minimum, you should answer three questions:

> Do users understand your site?
>
> Can they find what they're looking for?
>
> Can they purchase what they find?

Do Users Understand Your Site?

For users to understand your site, you need to understand them. Localizing your message begins with understanding how your users think. Begin by asking the following questions:

- **What are their traditions, tastes, holidays, religions?** You won't want to promote your Halloween decorations to countries that don't celebrate Halloween.

- **How many have access to the Internet, and how do they access the Internet?** In Japan, more people access the Internet through their mobile phones than their PCs.

The better you understand your audience, the more focused your message will be. Along the way, however, be sensitive to anything that might confuse or offend your audience:

- **Colors:** Pay close attention to colors and their meanings. Just because black signifies death in the U.S. does not guarantee a similar meaning abroad. In China, white symbolizes death.

- **Flags:** Flags are best avoided because they are more political than cultural. The Canadian flag doesn't indicate whether a given web site is written in French or English and a Brazilian flag doesn't indicate Spanish or Portuguese. Unless you have a clear reason for using flags, you probably shouldn't.

- **Icons:** Web sites rely on icons to assist the user, such as the ubiquitous shopping cart icon. Yet imagine what a shopping cart means in a culture where people rarely use shopping carts. The famous garbage can icon on the Macintosh was not universally recognized because garbage cans around the world don't all look alike. The same goes for mailboxes. And in France, the house icon doesn't signify "home page" because they usually call their home pages the "welcome page."

- **People and their body language:** Some cultures are much less diverse than the U.S. and are keenly sensitive to photographs of people who do not reflect the general population. Also be sensitive to how the models are dressed and how they pose. An open palm may mean "stop" in the U.S., but is offensive to other cultures. *Body language is just as important as the written language.*

- **Writing style:** In the U.S., writers are expected to communicate messages in the first two sentences, yet this style might be considered rude in Asia, where the writing style is more subtle and the point of a message is typically located near the end of a paragraph, not the beginning.

- **Spelling and grammar:** The rules of language are rarely simple or straightforward. Hyphenation and spelling vary within the language itself (such as in English and Spanish), depending on where they're used. The use of accent marks can also be confusing. In Canadian French, the uppercase letters generally retain accent marks, but not so in France.

183

For more information about body language and culture-specific design, see Chapter 11, "World Wide Design."

To learn more about writing for a global audience, see Chapter 10, "Writing for the World."

Mind the (Language) Gap

A shared language does not save you from translation:

U.S.	U.K.
Sneakers	Trainers
Restroom	Loo
911	999
Cookie	Biscuit
Wrench	Spanner
Truck	Lorry
Elevator	Lift
Parking Lot	Car Park

Can They Find What They're Looking For?

Your web site needs to be usable to people around the world, yet not all people have the same Internet connections, browsers, web savvy, and preconceptions. To ensure that your site remains as usable in Norway as it is in Nebraska, pay close attention to the factors in the following sections.

Bandwidth

The broadband revolution is taking a little longer than expected. According to most analysts, the U.S. won't reach a critical mass in broadband usage until 2005 or later. The rest of the world, with the exception of parts of Asia and Europe, is much further behind in high-speed Internet connections. So if most of the world is still accessing the Internet at 56Kbps or slower, why do companies build sites that can be easily viewed only with broadband connections? Even if you're targeting businesses, which are more likely to use broadband connections, the percentage of broadband users outside the U.S. rarely justifies designing a bandwidth-hogging web site.

Note

Only 10% of households in France, Germany, and the UK will have broadband Internet access by 2005.

*Source: Gartner (**www.gartner.com**), February 2002.*

As shown in Figure 7.7, the weight of your web site in kilobytes directly affects the amount of time your audience must wait to view your site. If you want your site to be popular outside the U.S., keep its total weight at 70KB or lower. Given that the average web page weight for Fortune 500 sites is more than 90KB, odds are you have some graphics to remove. But the result will be worth it, not just for your foreign visitors, but even for a good portion of your domestic audience.

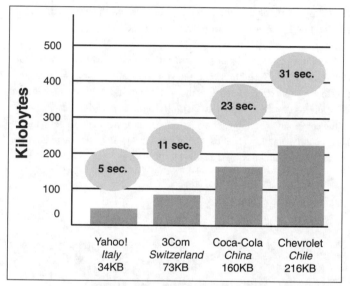

Figure 7.7 The weight and the waiting: Home page weight and download time when using a 56Kbps modem.

For more information on building web pages that don't keep international users waiting, see Chapter 11.

185

Measurements

While the world largely embraced the metric system, the U.S. largely ignored it. Today, Americans still measure their driving in miles per hour, their gas tanks in gallons, and the temperature in Fahrenheit degrees. Although these forms of measurement work fine in the U.S., they range from troublesome to meaningless in most other countries.

Paper sizes are also a source of frustration. The standard letter size in the U.S. is 8½×11 inches, but the rest of the world has a different idea of "standard." The A4 standard is actually much more common. Remember the International Standards Organization (ISO)? It has a standard for paper, too: A4 (specified by ISO 216). A4 is metric-based and, at 21cm×29.7cm (approximately 8¼×11¾ inches), is narrower and longer than the American letter.

FYI

For more information about international page sizes, go to **www.cl.cam.ac.uk/~mgk25/iso-paper.html**.

Why do paper sizes matter to web developers? If you want users to be able to print your web pages, you have to make sure the margins are narrower than usual. Also, many companies provide marketing brochures and white papers in PDF files for download. All too often, they are formatted in letter size, which only frustrates users who find that the pages print with the edges chopped off.

Clothing sizes could also use a bit of standardization, not just within the U.S., but globally. When Victoria's Secret first ventured into localization, it focused on developing a customer service page in each of the target languages. A good percentage of these pages was devoted to converting sizing information across locales, as shown in the conversion chart in Figure 7.8. In the future, Victoria's Secret plans to make this function dynamic so that users in a given locale are instantly presented with the local size, without having to convert it themselves.

Bra Size Conversions

US	UK	France	Australia	International
32AA	32A	85A	10AA	70A
32A	32B	85B	10A	70B
32B	32C	85C	10B	70C
32C	32D	85D	10C	70D
32D	32DD	85DD	10D	70DD
34AA	34A	90A	12AA	75A
34A	34B	90B	12A	75B
34B	34C	90C	12B	75C
34C	34D	90D	12C	75D
34D	34DD	90DD	12D	75DD
34DD	34E	90E	12DD	75E

Figure 7.8   Victoria's Secret conversion chart.

Numerical Notation

The number 2.455 means different amounts in different countries. In the U.S., 2.455 is less than 3; in Germany, it is more than 2,000. Blame numerical notation for the confusion. Not all countries use periods and commas in the same fashion.

In the U.S., the period indicates the decimal point; in Germany and other countries, the period is the thousands separator.

All too often, American companies expect users around the world to understand their numerical formats, yet numerical notation is not universal, as shown in the following chart.

Country	Notation
U.S.	123,456,789.00
France	123 456 789,00
Spain	123.456.789,00
Germany	123.456.789,00
Sweden	123 456 789,00
Russia	123 456 789,00

For a more comprehensive list of notation standards, see Appendix F, "International Notation Standards."

Phone numbers also have country-specific notation standards. Unfortunately, there's no international standard that all countries should follow. In fact, you'll often see notation differences *within* countries. In the U.S., for example, the number (555) 555-5555 can also be written as 555.555.5555 for purely stylistic reasons. When you feature phone numbers on your web site, try not to be stylistic. Your localized web sites should present phone and fax numbers in the formats that are most commonly used in each locale. Even more challenging than displaying phone numbers is making sure you can properly accept phone numbers. Make sure that input forms on your site don't force users to adhere to the American 10-digit phone number format, as the form in Figure 7.9 does.

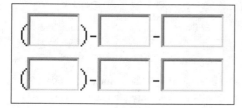

Figure 7.9   Phone number entry fields need to be localized. This one is not globally friendly.

As you can see, some countries don't even have 10-digit phone numbers:

Country	Notation
Hong Kong	1234 5678
Singapore	123 4567
Sweden	12 345 67 89
France	12-34-45-67-89
Poland	(12) 345.67.89
U.K.	1234 567899
U.S.	(123) 456 7890
Brazil	5102 1800
Germany	1234 567-8

Dates and Times

The Gregorian calendar that the Western world relies on is hardly the only calendar in use around the world. There are also the Islamic, Hebrew, Buddhist, Ethiopian, Hindu, and Japanese "Genko" calendars. Each calendar has its own unique holidays, which often vary from year to year. The way dates are represented is rarely consistent, even between countries that share a common calendar. For example, when is the Fourth of July not the Fourth of July? It all depends on the locale, as shown in the following chart:

Country	Notation
U.S.	7/4/2002
France	4/7/02
Germany	4.7.02
Japan	2002 年 7 月 4 日
ISO 8601	2002-07-04

For a more comprehensive list of notation standards, see Appendix F.

There has been a global push toward adopting the ISO 8601 standard for date formats, which follows the formula **YYYY-MM-DD** (February 1, 2002, is represented as 2002-02-01). But until everyone follows this standard, there is bound to be confusion. For the time being, a more practical solution is to simply spell out the name of the month and use the full four digits for the year, such as February 1, 2002. This notation prevents any ambiguity, even between differing calendar systems.

There's also global ambiguity about how times are represented. The U.S. is the only major country to use the 12-hour a.m./p.m. notation. The 12-hour notation is prone to error; for example, is 12:00 midnight or midday? With 24-hour notation, known in the U.S. as "military time," 12:00 is always midday and 00:00 is midnight. This system is widely used around the world, although the exact notation varies regionally. ISO 8601 also recommends a standard time format: **HH:MM:SS**. As with the date format, the larger units start on the left.

Finally, there's the pesky challenge of working with time zones. There are 24 global time zones, but many countries set their own time zones. For example, Canada has one time zone that spans three American time zones. Other countries have half-hour time zones. Do not assume that people in other countries will understand that "EST" means Eastern Standard Time. You could refer to GMT (Greenwich Mean Time), yet this is hardly universally understood and has since been replaced by the Coordinated Universal Time (UTC). In other words, if you must display times on your site, make sure they are fully localized for the end user.

Rules and Regulations

Every country has its own unique regulations. Although there are efforts underway to "harmonize" regulations globally, for the time being, you need to rely on legal experts in each local market to help you play by the rules. Here are some regulatory issues to consider:

- **Privacy laws:** Europe has much stricter rules than the U.S on collecting and sharing customer list information.

- **International advertising laws:** In the U.S., head-to-head comparisons are commonplace, but Germany and Japan don't allow comparative advertising. Also, many countries prohibit price competitions and lotteries, and place tight restrictions on direct mail marketing.

- **Liability:** What if a translator makes a mistake that leads to an injury in another country? What are your responsibilities and liabilities, and how should you be prepared?

- **Labeling:** Should your packaging include any regional or country-specific markings or terminology? For example, the European Union closely regulates packaging labels for the health care industry. If you don't abide by these rules for even one country, you are prohibited from entering *any* of the EU countries.

Can They Purchase What They Find?

Now that a web user has found a product, you need to ensure that he or she can easily purchase it (and receive it). Currency conversion is the first challenge.

The user naturally wants to know what the product or service costs in his or her currency. At the least, you can supply a link on your site to one of the many free currency conversion sites on the Web, such as xe.com (**www.xe.com/ucc**), shown in Figure 7.10. Ideally, you save your customers the added work and provide the conversion dynamically so that all they see are prices in their currency.

Figure 7.10   Do-it-yourself currency conversion.

A lot of companies mistakenly assume that because credit cards are universally used, they can just take credit card orders. However, credit cards are not universally used or trusted. In Germany, money orders are a popular method of payment. Wire transfers are also common, particularly in B2B transactions.

If you want to collect payment in Japan, you had better consider doing a deal with the convenience store chain 7-Eleven. Only about 10% of Japanese use credit cards; they prefer bank transfers, COD, and, increasingly, payment at their local 7-Eleven stores. Since 1999, web users in Japan have been able to order goods online and pay for them at 7-Eleven stores. With nearly 9,000 locations throughout Japan (compared with 400 in the U.S.), 7-Eleven is a major force in Japanese payment collection (see Figure 7.11).

Figure 7.11   7-Eleven Japan: More than just Big Gulps.

After you've offered the necessary payment options, you'll need to collect applicable taxes, clear customs for products that need to be delivered, and make allowances for the occasional return. With so many issues to be resolved, there's also a growing list of application service providers that provide full-service global payment collection, tax collection, customs clearance, and fulfillment.

Searching and Sorting

Enhancements need to be made to your search engine so that users entering a local term will get the relevant response. For example, "jumper" is another name for "sweater" in the U.K., but if you enter **jumper** in Lands' End's U.K. search engine, it returns no results, even though Lands' End offers a wide array of sweaters. Your translators and editors should play an active role in highlighting such terminology issues, which you can add to your terminology glossary as the project progresses. There are a number of technical solutions to making search engines locally friendly, but first you need to do the groundwork of building the terminology glossary.

Accented characters can also pose problems for search engines. The characters *e* and *é* are not considered equal to a search engine, but a web user might not make that distinction. For example, an American web user may want to search for the company Vésper, but type **vesper** into the search engine. How will the search engine know what the user is looking for? It all depends on the search engine and how well it has been prepared for handling different language and characters. For example, when entering **vesper** into Google, the top result just happens to be the company Vésper (see Figure 7.12).

191

Figure 7.12　If you want to find the company Vésper using Google, just enter **vesper**. Google doesn't get confused by the missing accent mark. Would your search engine?

Sorting might seem trivial, yet you'd be surprised how it affects the way people find things: Online dictionaries and site maps rely on sorting, for example. Suppose you have a dictionary of terms on your site. After you translate that dictionary, many of your terms might need to be re-sorted. When sorting, characters with accents typically follow their base characters, as shown here:

cable

câble

câblé

Not all characters sort in ways that make sense in English, however. For example, in Danish, the character æ follows *z*, and in Icelandic, the character ð falls between *d* and *e*. Sorting Asian languages is particularly challenging, as rules are based on a complex combination of phonetics, radical order, and number of pen strokes.

Different Languages, Different Characters

As you work with other Latin-based languages, prepare to use a variety of characters not often used in English.

Spanish: á, ch, ll, ñ, ó, ú, ü

French: à, â, ä, ç, é, è, ê, ë, î, ï, ô, œ

Danish: ñ, æ, ø, å

Swedish: å, ä, ö

Czech: á, c, e, š, r, ž, é, u, ú, í, ý

And don't forget punctuation marks, such as:

- Guillemets (French quotation marks, also used in Spanish): « and ».
- French uses the colon (:), but requires a space to be inserted on both sides.
- Spanish uses upside-down question marks and exclamation points to preface sentences, as in ¿ ... ? and ¡ ... !

Uppercase, Lowercase, and Neither

Different languages have different rules for lowercase and uppercase characters. Some languages, such as Arabic, Chinese, and Hindi, do not even have separate cases. Many American web designers make frequent use of all upper-case or all lowercase headlines for stylistic effect. However, a lowercase headline appears sloppy in a country such as Germany, where capitalization rules are more rigidly observed (see sidebar "Capitalization Case Study: German").

Capitalization Case Study: German ─────────────────────────────

German follows slightly different capitalization rules than English. The beginnings of sentences, proper names, and *all* nouns (including adjectives and verbs used as nouns) are capitalized. The second person formal pronoun *Sie*, the polite form of address, is capitalized in all contexts. However, the second person familiar pronouns *du*, *dich*, *dir*, *ihr*, and *euch* are not capitalized. The first person pronoun *ich* as well as adjectives that refer to nationality, such as *russisch* (Russian) or *amerikanisch* (American), are also not capitalized.

English has its many quirks, and so do other languages. The way to be prepared for these many quirks is to work with people who understand the target languages thoroughly and understand how the target languages will influence the functionality of your source-language web site.

THE GLOBAL/LOCAL INTERNET

With this chapter, you now have a wide-angle view of the key issues in adapting a web site for the world and for a locale. There will always be a natural tension between internationalization and localization, a tug-of-war between global efficiency and local customization. As long as you don't sacrifice one for the other, however, you'll be well on your way to creating a successful, globalized web site. The following chapter delves into the most important, and most noticeable, component of localization: translation.

193

8

TRANSLATION MANAGEMENT

Translation is an art and, like any art, is much more challenging than it appears. In fact, translating a web page sometimes requires more effort than writing a web page. Writing requires proficiency in only one language, but translating requires a proficiency in two languages. And translating a web page requires proficiency in at least three languages: the source language, the target language, and HTML.

Although there is an art to translation, managing translation is a science. To master this science, you don't need to be multilingual, but you do need to be good at multitasking. This chapter will show you how to manage translation projects and how to ensure quality every step of the way. But before diving into the science of translation, let's take a moment to appreciate the art.

IN THE BEGINNING, THERE WAS TRANSLATION

The Bible is by far the most translated (and retranslated) written work. Originally written largely in Hebrew and Greek, the Bible has since been translated into just about every language, including more than 50 English-language editions. What's interesting about the many English-language editions is how much they differ from one another. Granted, not all translators worked from the same source text, but of those who did, the resulting translations still vary widely. Did someone make a mistake along the way? Isn't there supposed to be *one* correct translation?

Not necessarily. The following passage from Genesis, taken from two translations, exhibits the subtle and not-too-subtle differences between translations:

King James Version: Genesis

In the beginning God created the heaven and the earth.

And the earth was without form, and void; and darkness was upon the face of the deep. And the Spirit of God moved upon the face of the waters.

And God said, Let there be light: and there was light.

New International Version: Genesis

In the beginning God created the heavens and the earth.

Now the earth was formless and empty, darkness was over the surface of the deep, and the Spirit of God was hovering over the waters.

And God said, "Let there be light," and there was light.

Both translations are technically correct, yet stylistically different. Translation is as much about style as it is about accuracy; it reflects the personalities, perspectives, abilities, and goals of the translators involved. In the case of the Bible, some translators aimed for a user-friendly translation, relying on accessible language, while others strove for a more literal, word-for-word translation. Still others translated the Bible with a particular philosophical or evangelical point of view.

As you manage translation projects, focus on what's right for your audience and your company. If you're translating dosage instructions for a new pharmaceutical product, you'll make accuracy the priority. If you're translating promotional text for a new brand of candy, you'll want a translation that's more clever than clinical.

Managing Translation When You Don't Speak the Language

Some people feel uncomfortable in places where they don't speak the language. Managing translation will make you feel, at times, as though you *are* lost in a strange country, or many strange countries. Don't worry. In the translation industry, nobody can know everything. There are just too many languages and too many technologies. We're all learning as we go, which is what makes the field exciting—but it's not a field for people afraid to ask questions.

When managing translation projects, act as you would in a strange country: Ask lots of questions. So what if you get strange looks from your translators and editors. Take advantage of their expertise while you have them around. If you try to bluff your way through the process, you risk letting serious mistakes slip by. You also miss out on learning more about the languages you're managing.

The translation industry is populated by specialized experts who often grow weary of people asking them "silly" questions. But you're the boss, and your questions are not silly because you need to understand as much as possible about the languages you're managing. After all, once you launch your web site in a dozen languages, the rest of your staff will probably have the same "silly" questions—and then you'll be the expert.

HOW TRANSLATION WORKS

197

Whether you manage freelance translators or outsource everything to a translation or localization vendor, you need a solid understanding of the translation process. Fundamentally, the process is simple; it is the logistics that can grow complex, depending on the number of web pages and languages in your project. What follows are four steps that must take place, regardless of how many languages you're translating and who manages the process:

1. Set goals, budget, and schedule.
2. Create a translation/localization kit.
3. Select translators or a translation agency; the following steps will be managed by an in-house project manager (web globalization manager) or a vendor project manager.
4. Execute the project
    - Create "frozen" copy of web files for localization.
    - Prepare files for translation.
    - Validate files.
    - Send files to translator.
    - Validate translated files.
    - Send translated files to editor.
    - Validate edited files.
    - Post edited files on beta site for review and testing.

■ Integrate final comments and changes.

■ Conduct final review of finished web pages.

See Chapter 9, "Computer-Aided Translation (CAT)," for more on translation memory.

■ Align translated files in translation memory.

■ Prepare for ongoing maintenance.

Now you just have to decide who is going to manage the process. As shown in Figures 8.1 and 8.2, a translation or localization vendor can save you time and trouble. What's the difference between a translation vendor and a localization vendor? A *translation vendor* generally focuses on the text translation only, while a *localization vendor* manages the text translation as well as graphics and web page localization. Often, the difference is purely semantic, as the majority of translation vendors now manage web localization. This chapter, however, focuses just on the text translation component of localization.

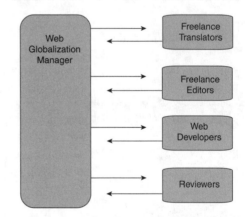

Figure 8.1 Translation workflow (in house).

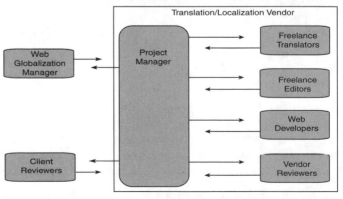

Figure 8.2 Translation workflow (outsourced).

The in-house workflow in Figure 8.1 assumes that you'll rely on freelance translators, but this isn't always the case. Some companies hire full-time translators
depending on the amount of translation needed annually. The workflow requires a
large commitment of time from the web globalization manager. He or she is responsible for making sure the text keeps moving from translator to editor to reviewer. It's
a critical job and one that companies often decide to outsource to a translation or
localization vendor, illustrated in Figure 8.2. Using a vendor does not eliminate the
need for an in-house web globalization manager, who works closely with the vendor
project manager to make sure files are sent and returned correctly and according to
schedule. The globalization manager can also facilitate client reviews, if needed.

The translation workflow is a component of
the web globalization workflow, covered in
Chapter 5, "Web Globalization Workflow."

Setting Goals, Budgets, and Schedules

Before you begin hiring translators (or a translation vendor), you have some big
decisions to make. First, as covered in Chapter 6, "Let's Talk Budget," you need to
align your goals for the localized web site with your budget. If you believe that web
localization is going to be an important component of your web strategy from now
on, you need to invest in developing in-house expertise; in other words, you need to
invest in a full-time web globalization manager (or assign the role to an existing
employee). You might still decide to outsource work to a vendor, but at the least, you
need to make an internal commitment. If you aren't quite ready to make the commitment—or you view a localized site as ancillary to other, more important, web initia-
tives—you're probably better off outsourcing the work to a vendor who can manage
the process for you. Be aware that hiring a vendor does not ensure trouble-free
localization. Not all vendors are equally competent, and not all clients are equally
organized. The key to success is understanding your organization's strengths and
weaknesses as well as the strengths and weaknesses of vendors. The schedule also
plays a major role in your strategy. If you have never localized a web site before, it's
probably going to take you longer to do so than hiring a vendor with translators and
vendors already lined up (see sidebar "Setting Deadlines").

199

Setting Deadlines

A healthy dose of reality is critical when setting deadlines. A translator can manage, at best, about 2,000 words per
day. An editor can manage up to twice that amount per day. If you've got 10,000 words, you're looking at five days
minimum, plus extra time for editing and client review. The complexity and number of web pages involved also
affect turnaround time. Finally, you need to make allowances for working with translators and editors based in other
countries. Just because your U.S. office has a file ready for translation at noon doesn't mean your translator in Japan
will be ready to get started (in fact, he or she will be asleep).

If you want to speed up the process, you can work with multiple translators and editors simultaneously. Remember,
though, that with more players, you increase the chance of inconsistency and make the logistical process that much
more challenging.

The "Hands-On: Spanish" chapter will take you, step by step, through managing a translation project.

Putting Together the Localization Kit

The *localization kit* (also known as a translation kit) includes all files to be translated and comprehensive instructions on what to do with them. The term was coined by the software industry and now is commonly used by the web globalization industry. The reason you need to create this kit is simple: Translators can't read your mind, and translation vendors can't instantly know how your web site works and how it should work when localized. Even if you decide to do everything yourself, you should still spend the time to put this kit together. Among the items you'll need to include are the following:

- All HTML/ASP files to be translated

- All text strings to be translated (from databases or programming scripts)

- All graphics that require localization

- All source files for these graphics (that is, Illustrator or Photoshop files)

- Terminology glossary (see the following section "Creating the Terminology Glossary)

- Style guide

In addition to the files, you need to include detailed instructions on how to manage the files. Vendors should assist you in developing these instructions; many provide checklists that the client must complete before work can begin. Keep in mind that some of these tasks go beyond mere translation. Your instructions should include answers to the following questions:

- **What is the file-naming system and organization structure for the site?** Are you going to set up subdirectories for each language? And how will all the links be managed so that they remain valid in the localized site?

- **How does your site design accommodate text expansion?** You might need to redesign aspects of your web site to allow for text expansion. The alternative to a redesign is working closely with your translators to make sure the target text does not exceed any character-length limitations. If the translators are aware of space limitations, they can work to translate as succinctly as possible; they can also alert you when they run into instances where the source text must be edited down to ensure that the target text remains within the character-length limit.

- **Do you have a global gateway?** You will likely need to provide translated links on an English-language site that direct users to their localized web sites.

- **Do you have a style guide?** Every company has its corporate rules and occasional quirks. Ever wonder why Lands' End has the apostrophe on the wrong side? Make sure your translators understand your company's stylistic quirks so that they don't inadvertently change them.

- **How will you test the site?** Many vendors post localized web pages as they're completed on a server for clients to review, yet not all web sites can be so easily staged. Some rely heavily on databases that cannot be easily replicated on a vendor's server. In these cases, it becomes critical that the client and vendor set clear guidelines on previewing and testing web pages so that mistakes don't slip through.

Creating the Terminology Glossary

The *terminology glossary* (also known as the translation glossary) is critical to maintaining a consistent and usable web site. You develop the glossary by exhaustively scouring your site and transcribing any terms, slogans, and navigational wording that need to be consistently translated (or not translated) throughout the site, such as:

- Corporate brand names and slogans

- Technical and clinical terminology

- Acronyms

- Text used for navigation menus and buttons

- Text embedded in graphics

If a word is *not* to be translated, it should be noted in the glossary so that translators know to leave it as is. The glossary is the first document you translate. You should put a lot of effort into translating and editing the glossary because it will become the essential reference for every translator on the project. The glossary can be as simple as a spreadsheet, as shown in Figure 8.3.

	A	B	C	D	E	F	G
1							
2	**Terminology glossary**						
3							
4	**Context**	**EN_US**	**DE**	**ES**	**FR**	**IT**	**PT_BR**
5							
6	Company name	Theo's Computer Shack	Theo's Computer Shack	Theo's Computer Shack	Theo's Computer Shack	Theo's Computer Shack	Theo's Computer Shack
7	Company slogan	Simply the best	Simply the best	Simply the best	Simply the best	Simply the best	Simply the best
8	Computer hardware	hardware	Hardware	hardware	matériel	hardware	hardware
9	Computer software	software	Software	software	logiciel	software	software
10	Graphic button for users who need help filling out registration form	hint	Tipp	pista	truc	suggerimento	dica
11	Computer keyboard	keyboard	Tastatur	teclado	clavier	tastiera	teclado
12							
13							
14							

Figure 8.3 Sample terminology glossary. Notice how some terms remain the same across languages.

When working with text embedded in graphics, you might need to prepare for text expansion. One approach is to figure out how many characters a graphic can contain without having to be modified and then giving translators this number as a margin to work within. If the translators find that they cannot stay within the margin, they can contact you so that you can edit or change the source text; you can also decide to expand the graphic or remove it altogether. With specific goals and limitations, your translators and editors will be more effective, and you will spend less time sending files back and forth.

Managing File Flow

The flow of files between project managers, translators, editors, and reviewers is an all-consuming job once the project begins. A number of content management tools can assist with this process and save a great deal of time; these tools are covered later in the book (see Chapter 13, "Global Content Management"). Assuming you manage the workflow yourself, develop a system to document the flow of each file between all parties. The Excel spreadsheet in Figure 8.4 includes a column for each stage of the localization process, for each file. When each stage is completed for a file, the date is entered.

	A	B	C	D	E	F	G	H
1								
2	**Project workflow**							
3								
4	**file name**	**validated**	**translated**	**validated**	**edited**	**validated**	**reviewed**	**tested**
5								
6	**root directory**							
7	index.html	1-Feb	4-Feb	4-Feb	6-Feb	7-Feb	8-Feb	9-Feb
8	company.html	1-Feb	4-Feb	4-Feb	6-Feb	7-Feb	8-Feb	9-Feb
9	products.html	1-Feb	4-Feb	4-Feb	6-Feb	7-Feb	8-Feb	9-Feb
10	services.html	5-Feb	7-Feb	9-Feb	9-Feb			
11	about.html	5-Feb	7-Feb	9-Feb	9-Feb			
12	new.html	5-Feb	7-Feb	9-Feb	9-Feb			
13								
14	**products directory**							
15	1.html	9-Feb						
16	2.html	9-Feb						
17	3.html	9-Feb						
18								
19								

Figure 8.4 This basic project workflow tracks the progress of each file.

The workflow can be expanded to include target dates and completion dates, as well as notes on files that require special attention. The primary focus of this document is to avoid overlooking any file or letting any deadline slip. It's not unusual for large projects to entail more than 400 files in various languages, all bouncing around between translators, editors, and you. The better you prepare for the deluge, the less deluged you'll feel.

203

Translating Versus Editing

Just as every writer needs a good editor, so does every translator. Translators cannot be expected to get everything right the first time. In fact, you should expect translators to miss a few things here and there. That's why you'll also need an editor to review the translator's work with a copy of the source text as reference.

At a minimum, every page of your web site should be reviewed by two target-language experts: a translator and an editor. Some vendors rely on an additional editor if the material is particularly complex or mission critical. As a general rule, the more proofreaders you rely on, the less room for error.

Editors rely on translators to do a good enough job with the translation so that they can focus on the larger issues, such as terminology, consistency, and style. It's important that they are free to communicate with one another, if necessary, and that the project manager communicates any concerns to all translators and editors.

Conducting the Client Review

The *client review* is your opportunity to make sure everything is perfect before the web page goes live. Of course, you can't conduct a client review unless you have someone on staff who is fluent in the target language.

Multinationals often rely on their in-country offices for reviews. If you don't have that luxury, you can arrange for an independent freelance editor to conduct the review on your behalf. It would also be an ideal opportunity for you to develop a relationship with a secondary translation firm to proof the work of your primary translation firm.

The review, if not well managed, can create more problems than it solves. People in foreign offices generally conduct reviews in addition to their normal jobs, so reviews take a back seat and turnaround times suffer. Some client reviewers get overly critical of the translations, making changes to the style instead of looking for actual mistakes. Here are a few suggestions for working with reviewers:

- Instruct the reviewers to focus on accuracy of the translation, with a close eye on terminology.

- The reviewers shouldn't rewrite text to suit a personal style. Although they should alert you if the style doesn't suit the corporate style, they should primarily focus on accuracy.

- They need to meet their deadlines.

- Be wary of reviewers who say translation is "awful" or "perfect." Always ask for specific examples.

Validating Files

When translators go into HTML files and start rewriting text, the odds of an HTML tag accidentally being overwritten increases. And the less a translator understands about web development, the more likely it is that he or she will try to translate something that should not be translated, such as an HTML tag or a line of programming code. *Validation* provides an orderly process of making sure translators don't introduce errors into your web pages.

If you validate a file before it goes out to translators and after it comes back, you can catch these problems when they occur and make sure they are not repeated. The first validation stage occurs when you "freeze" files for translation. Freezing simply means making a copy of the web site. Given that sites are so dynamic and that translation can take several weeks, you need to record exactly when you copied the files for translation so that when you launch them later, you'll know what elements have changed since the freeze.

Validation doesn't have to take more than a few seconds per file. If all you do is preview the file in a web browser, that could well be sufficient. So much depends on the complexity of your web pages. If files are more complex, you might need to load the web pages for previewing on a staging server, instead of just previewing them on a hard drive.

When working with translators and editors, insist that they use software that won't introduce errors into your web pages. Microsoft FrontPage, for example, is notorious for surreptitiously adding unwanted HTML tags and other assorted garbage to web pages. Macromedia Dreamweaver is also known to add tags without the user knowing it. Although these features can be disabled, many translators are better off *not* using HTML editors and working instead from web editors designed specifically for translation, such as TRADOS TagEditor (**www.trados.com**). Another solution, although time-consuming, is to work with Microsoft Word files and actually highlight the text that needs to be translated.

205

SELECTING A TRANSLATOR

If you decide to manage the localization process yourself, you'll need to select translators. With thousands of translators around the world, the challenge isn't so much finding a translator as it is finding the *right* translator. Before looking out of house, take a moment to look in house; check with your marketing, documentation, or regulatory departments. You may already have designated translators (or a designated vendor) and not even know it. Most multinational companies have translated their print materials for decades. Perhaps you can batch translation projects together and save money based on the added volume; you'll also ensure consistency across all communications—print and electronic.

If you have no in-house connections, the Internet is a wonderful place to start looking. Andres Heuberger, president of ForeignExchange Translations (**www.fxtrans.com**), regularly hires translators and editors for more than 30 languages. He recommends that you begin with the regional and national translator associations: "A good listing can be found at **www.notisnet.org/links/orgs.htm**. Next, check out online translator directories, such as Aquarius (**www.aquarius.net;** see Figure 8.5) and ProZ (**www.proz.com**). These sites allow searching by numerous criteria, including subject matter expertise."

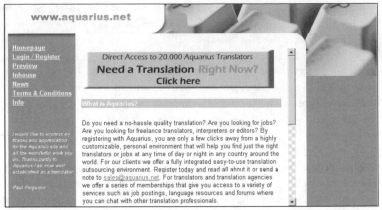

Figure 8.5   Aquarius.net.

Finding a Translator Online

Aquarius.net is a portal for translators looking for work and clients looking for translators. According to Santi van der Kruk, chief operating officer of Aquarius, the portal has 19,000 registered freelance translators, 2,700 translation agencies, and 1,500 translation clients.

"The agencies and clients use the system mostly to recruit long- or short-term resources or to outsource their projects online," notes van der Kruk. "Translators use the system to bid on projects and market themselves to the agencies and clients. The system functions as a meeting place and information database for all parties." Although the site has 125 registered languages, the most popular are "PFIGS"—Portuguese, French, Italian, German, and Spanish.

Heuberger stresses that your translators should be native speakers of the target language: "German translation should be done by a native German speaker and not by an American who has lived in Germany for five years." When looking for a translator, he recommends that you specify the following:

- Language pair (such as English to German, French to Spanish)

- Volume of work (how many words distributed across how many pages)

- Your deadline

- Your target budget (typically expressed as a per-word rate)

- Required expertise and background

- References (always check references)

- Any special instructions, such as need for onsite work, use of particular soft-ware application, and so forth

The Translator Test

There are hundreds of "mom and pop" translation shops around the world and thou-sands of freelance translators, all claiming to offer high-quality translation. How do you tell them apart? For starters, you give them a test.

The American Translators Association (**www.atanet.org**) offers an accreditation pro-gram that sets a baseline you can begin with. But translation vendors usually admin-ister their own tests, too, and so should you. If it's a web site you want to be trans-lated, supply a web page or two to translate. Vendors and translators alike should offer to take free tests, and you should expect this because it's your only way to evaluate their performance.

In addition to a test, you can set some basic standards that every translator must meet. Heuberger sets the following criteria for the translators he hires:

- 3+ years experience as a professional linguist

- 2+ years of subject or industry-specific experience

- Experience translating more than 100,000 words in the specified field or industry

- Outstanding references

- Strong track record of maintaining strict schedules and rapid turnaround

Although these qualifications limit the number of translators at your disposal, Heuberger says the process actually saves time. "By using pre-qualified translators, we run into fewer mistakes and rarely run into scheduling conflicts. Experienced translators know how to manage their workload and their schedules. They also have the wisdom to raise the right project-specific questions early enough in the process to allow time for corrections and editing."

SELECTING A TRANSLATION VENDOR

When you hire a translation or localization vendor, you are, in effect, also hiring a number of translators, editors, and web programmers. To be safe, select two translation vendors, not just one. Always have a backup firm ready and waiting. This strategy will come in handy if your first vendor gets overbooked with work or if you find the quality lacking. Also, having a second vendor in the wings keeps your primary vendor more focused on pricing and service.

Questions to Ask Your Translation Vendor

Do you outsource? And to whom? Ask for their credentials.

How many employees do you have? Try to match the size of your account with the size of the agency.

What is your rate of turnover? Some agencies have a high rate of employee burnout caused by high workloads; this affects quality and service.

How long have you been in business? The translation industry is highly fluid, with vendors here one day and gone the next. Try to select a vendor with a stable, profitable track record.

What languages do you manage? Some agencies specialize in only one or two language pairs. Although you may get higher quality with these shops, they won't be able to expand with you as your site expands into new markets.

What clients do you have? Ask for references and check them carefully. Review sample translations.

How do you control quality? Ask for detailed statistics on how they monitor themselves and ensure that errors, once spotted, don't occur again.

Who is my dedicated contact? You need someone you can call any time you have a question or need an update on your account. During a project, it's wise to have regularly scheduled calls with your contact to check on progress.

Can you conduct a sample translation for us? Any vendor who is worth hiring will gladly take a test. Also, get your client reviewers, if you have them, involved now. You can also get their "buy in" on the vendor you select.

What translation tools do you use? You might need a vendor that uses the same software you're using. Make sure they have the software, skills, and support in place before you send them electronic files.

Do I retain ownership of the translation memory? Translation memory is covered in Chapter 9; for now, just know that you want to own it.

What's Your Specialty?

Despite what they might say, no translation vendor can be an expert at everything. Translation firms tend to concentrate on certain industries. Firms such as ForeignExchange and Luz (**www.luz.com**) focus heavily on the medical industry, the Detroit Translation Bureau (**www.dtbonline.com**) focuses on the automotive industry, and Crimson Financial Translation (**www.financial-translation.com**) focuses, naturally, on the financial industry.

The more specialized your industry, the more likely it is you'll need to work with a specialized vendor. For example, not many translators have the skills to understand the instructions on medical devices, let alone translate them. Says Heuberger, "Medical device manufacturers must navigate a virtual maze of global regulations. Entire departments are set up to keep tabs on FDA rules in the U.S. as well as CE Marking requirements in the European Union and similar regulatory hurdles in Japan, Australia, and elsewhere."

The World's Largest Translation Company

Based in Luxembourg, the European Union Translation Centre (**www.cdt.eu.int**) claims to be the largest single translation agency in the world. It employs more than 60 full-time translators and thousands of freelancers in translating official documents into the 11 languages of the member countries: Danish, Dutch, English, Finnish, French, German, Greek, Italian, Portuguese, Spanish, and Swedish (with more expected). The number of pages translated has grown from 20,000 in 1995 to 260,000 in 2000.

Translation Costs

Pricing in the translation industry is anything but consistent. Some vendors price a job low just to get your business, but others price it higher, assuming you'll want to negotiate it down. Other vendors may place a premium on their rates because of their degree of specialization and reputation. The best way to understand the Byzantine quoting process is to simply get lots of quotes. Some vendors offer quotes automatically, as shown in Figure 8.6. Although web-based quotes are a helpful feature, don't rely on them exclusively. Web sites are too complex for automatic quotes to be accurate.

Figure 8.6 Instant quotes courtesy of Berlitz.

Your "per word" costs vary depending on whether you manage the translators and editors or you outsource those tasks. If you manage the process yourself, you can expect to save anywhere from 25% to 40% off what translation vendors charge. For example, for English to Spanish translation, you might hire a translator who charges 11–14 cents per word and an editor who charges 3–5 cents per word. If you outsource the job to a vendor, however, you'll pay anywhere from 22 to 40 cents per word (see Table 8.1). Some vendors also tack on a small project-management fee.

Table 8.1 Sample Translation Rates

Language Pair	Rate ($U.S.)
English → Bulgarian	0.24
English → Chinese (Simplified)	0.29
English → Chinese (Traditional)	0.29
English → Croatian	0.24
English → Czech	0.24
English → Danish	0.28
English → Dutch	0.24
English → Finnish	0.28
English → French	0.24
English → French (Canada)	0.24
English → German	0.24
English → Greek	0.28
English → Hungarian	0.24
English → Italian	0.24
English → Japanese	0.38
English → Korean	0.28
English → Norwegian (Bokmål)	0.28

Language Pair	Rate ($U.S.)
English → Polish	0.24
English → Portuguese	0.24
English → Portuguese (Brazil)	0.22
English → Russian	0.24
English → Slovak	0.24
English → Slovenian	0.24
English → Spanish	0.24
English → Spanish (Latin-American Spanish)	0.22
English → Swedish	0.28
English → Turkish	0.28
Bulgarian → English	0.24
Chinese (Simplified) → English	0.27
Chinese (Traditional) → English	0.27
Danish → English	0.26
Finnish → English	0.28
French → English	0.28
French (Canada) → English	0.24
Spanish → English	0.22

Note: Price is per word and includes translating and editing, based on word count of less than 5,000.
Source: Berlitz (**www.berlitzit.com**), February 2002.

Specialization, Quantity, and Costs

In addition to the complexity of the project and the language, two other variables affect localization costs: industry specialization and project size. Some industries are more challenging to translate for than others. For example, there are few translators in the world who understand the inner workings of an automobile engine; if General Motors needs someone to translate its engine maintenance guide into Russian, there's a very limited pool of talent from which to choose, which naturally increases costs. The more specialized—legal, medical, scientific, technical—the text, the more translators charge. The following chart shows how specialization can affect costs:

Categories	Increase
Business	25%
General	No increase
Legal (certified)	50%
Legal (not certified)	25%
Scientific	50%
Technical	15%

Source: Berlitz (**www.berlitzit.com**), February 2002.

However, you can often offset these increases with an increase in the volume of work. Translators generally discount their rates by a few cents per word for larger projects. What is a large project? It depends on the vendor. A 100-person vendor might view a 200,000-word project as large, but a large project to a five-person vendor could be 20,000 words. The size of a project depends not just on word count, but also on number of target languages. A 5,000-word project might not sound substantial, but if it's being localized into 15 languages, it turns into a 75,000-word project.

Quality Matters

Maintaining quality translation can, at times, feel like shooting at a moving target. So many people have different opinions on what constitutes "quality" translation. To keep yourself sane, work on establishing a series of quality audits to make sure mistakes aren't slipping by. A quality audit could consist of hiring another transla-tion agency to proof your primary translation agency. However, you might want to keep costs even lower by simply hiring a freelance translator to tell you what your site is saying to him or her; this process, often called *back-translation*, also func-tions as a basic type of focus group.

The Art of Translation

In the following chart, a sentence of German text is translated into English three different times, with varying degrees of success. Not only is the "bad" translation grammatically incorrect, but it also makes the mistake of assuming that the German word *analog* should be translated into German as "similar" instead of being left as is. Context is critical in translation; in this case, the word *analog* is a technical term that should not be translated. The "so-so" example is more technically accurate, but difficult to read. The "excellent" translation is accurately trans-lated *and* grammatically correct—the sign of a translator who not only understands both languages well, but can write elegantly in both languages.

Source Text in German	Bad Translation	So-So Translation	Excellent Translation
Die arithmetische Herleitung des Meßsignals gemäß der Gleichung (1) wird vorzug-sweise mit Hilfe von entsprech-enden analogen Bauelementen für die auszuführenden arithmetischen Operationen durchgeführt.	The arithmetic derivation of the measuring signal according to Equation (1) is preferably performed with the help of the similar corresponding components for the arithmetic operations to be performed.	The arithmetic derivation of the measuring signal according to Equation (1) is preferably performed with the help of the corresponding analog components for the arithmetic operations to be performed.	The measuring signal is computed according to Equation (1) preferably using analog units for the corresponding arithmetic operations.

Source: Accurapid Translation Services (**www.accurapid.com**).

After you've built in safeguards, you need to track the mistakes that do slip past. Many translation vendors and their clients don't keep track of the number of mistakes made on a given project, let alone what types of mistakes were made. Counting and classifying mistakes is a reliable way to measure quality. Just as an automaker strives to produce "zero defect" cars, you should strive to produce zero-defect translations. How do you define defects? It's up to you and your translation vendor. They can be factual errors, grammatical errors, and HTML errors, for example. By collecting and classifying them, you can conduct quarterly reviews with your client to look for patterns and ways to prevent them from recurring.

Quality management systems can be implemented companywide, such as ISO 9000—a family of international management standards. (The ISO 9000 standards are explained in detail at **www.iso.ch**.) Several thousand companies around the world have adopted some type of ISO 9000 system. The process can be difficult to institute, as it often requires a reorganization of a company's workflow as well as frequent internal audits. To be certified as "ISO 9000 compliant," companies must hire outside registrars to ensure that they are playing by the rules. Many ISO 9000–compliant companies demand ISO 9000–compliant translation vendors, and there are several agencies out there who do have the credentials (see Figure 8.7).

8.7 Excel Translations bears the ISO mark.

Six Sigma is a more recent, less rigid quality management system, made popular by General Electric. Regardless of whether you actually invest in any quality management system, take time to study how they work and how your project management can benefit from quality control systems. The very nature of managing quality might not appear too exciting, but these systems can help prevent those heart-stopping moments when incorrect translations slip by.

FYI

For more information on how General Electric uses Six Sigma, go to **www.ge.com/sixsigma**.

How to Read a Quote

Translation quotes, when they are priced on a per-word basis, are easy to understand. Web localization quotes, however, are not always as clear. These quotes may include not only translation, but also project management, graphics localization, and software localization. There's no universal standard for quoting web localization projects. For example, some vendors separate the translation costs and editing costs, and others group them together. And because many localization vendors also quote software localization projects, it's not unusual to see a web localization project quoted using software-specific terms. Vendors are not necessarily trying to mislead their clients; each vendor typically has its own method of quoting that it feels is best, but none of these methods seems to agree with the others. What follows are tips for reading a quote and for reading between the lines. Remember that shorter is not always better. Some vendors like to keep their quotes short in an effort to make them easy to read and easy to produce, but short quotes can be dangerous because of what they don't include. Always make sure your quote covers the following elements:

- **What files are included?** Ask for a detailed list of all HTML and graphics files included in the project. Some vendors supply this type of list automatically. Ideally, the list will even break down word counts on a per-HTML page basis; this type of quote allows you to better understand which HTML pages are going to be more expensive to localize than others. The list also helps you identify any HTML pages that might be missing.

- **How was the word count calculated?** If there's one thing you can be sure of when you get multiple quotes, it's that none of them will estimate the same word count. It's not uncommon to see significant word count variances between vendors; they're not necessarily trying to trick you—each vendor uses its own word count tools and methodology. But do ask your vendors what tools they used to arrive at their counts. Ask if any text was left out of the quotes, such as **<META>** tags or page titles. To see a word count tool in action, refer to the "Hands-On: Spanish" chapter.

- **Detailed schedule.** The quote should include a project completion date along with project milestones that allow you to track its relative progress.

■ **Translation memory discount?** If you have a translation memory that you've been building from previous translation jobs, give it to the vendor for an additional discount. You shouldn't have to pay for the same translation twice. The vendor scans the new source text against your translation memory to see the percentage of repetition between the two. This percentage is used to calculate the discount.

■ **Language breakdown.** If you're quoting a localization project that includes more than one language, the quote should be broken down by language.

■ **Assumptions.** Assumptions provide a measure of protection for you and your vendor. They could include assumptions about the date you'll deliver files to the vendor and return files sent for review. Read these assumptions in detail to make sure nothing is being left out of the quote that you want included.

■ **"Technology fee" and other confusing costs.** If you see a quote listing a cost such as "technology fee" or "software QA," ask your vendor for details. It might be a legitimate project management cost, but you should be clear on everything.

215

Read the Fine Print

In the end, all vendors have the same basic costs they must charge through to you. The question then becomes "How are the costs listed on the quote?" Some vendors include a project management fee; others include the project management fee as part of the translation costs. The key to understanding these quotes is to get lots of them and to ask lots of questions.

What Your Translation Vendor May Not Be Telling You

With all this back and forth between translators, editors, and reviewers, it's little surprise that so many companies outsource everything to translation or localization firms. Before you start sending out RFPs (request for proposals), however, you should be aware of some not-so-pretty practices in the industry.

The translation industry is not regulated. There's no standards group that rates vendors or the translators they hire, so much of the responsibility for ensuring quality falls on the clients. Most translation vendors are reputable and reliable, but you need to be prepared for those who aren't.

The Translator Next Door

Translation vendors often rely on freelance translators, but not all freelancers are equally qualified. Vendors obviously want to hire the best translators, but they also want to keep costs down; however, the best translators generally command higher rates. The degree to which vendors control costs (by hiring less experienced translators) could make the difference between a skillful translation and a sloppy one.

If you're spending a lot of money on translation, you have a right to demand full disclosure as a way to safeguard your investment; ask to be involved in selecting the translators working on your project or at least in reviewing their credentials. You might think your translator is Sven, the smart fellow you met at the initial kick-off meeting, but how do you know that Sven is actually working on your project? It's common practice in this industry for work to be farmed out to lower-price translators. A savings of a few pennies per word can add up to major profits. Be sure the translator your vendor uses is Sven, not the intern.

Translators also engage in outsourcing. For example, you hire Diego to translate your web pages into Spanish, but he hires his colleague Fernando to help without your knowledge. Your editor begins noticing inconsistencies in the translations, and your web developer discovers that errors have been introduced into the code (because Fernando doesn't understand HTML). Inconsistency is often a sign that multiple translators are at work on your project.

Translation Inflation

Once you've come to depend on a translation vendor, you'll find that leaving your vendor becomes increasingly difficult. You develop relationships; your vendor gets to know your terminology and corporate style. All this is well and good, until your vendor begins to raise prices. Often, the client doesn't notice the increase right away, as ongoing translation work is usually less expensive than the initial translation. Although inflation is a fact of life in all businesses, keep an eye on the rate of inflation. Take time periodically to get an additional quote or two on a project, just for comparison, and let your vendor know what quotes you received. A reputable vendor welcomes the opportunity to remain competitive—not just on quality, but on price.

The Less You Know, the More You Pay

Education is the antidote to overpricing in the translation/localization industry. The more you know about how vendors work and what they charge, the more effective you'll be at controlling costs. Often, cost overruns have less to do with vendors overcharging than with clients not fully understanding the process. Rush charges, for example, are a constant source of client frustration, but easily avoided with proper planning and education. The translation industry has historically been slow to educate clients about exactly what they do. There has been a general fear that once clients know what goes on behind closed doors, vendors will no longer be wanted or needed. However, not all vendors subscribe to this line of thinking. Many play an active role in educating their clients about what they do and the value they bring to the process; these are the vendors you should seek out. As you begin evaluating both translation and localization vendors, don't be afraid to ask lots of questions. Increasingly, a vendor's role is about providing not only translation, but education.

THE ART AND SCIENCE OF TRANSLATION MANAGEMENT

Translators are as important to the communications process as the writers themselves. If a product description or a mission statement or a marketing brochure is a work of art, should its translation be any less? As you begin managing translators and translation agencies, you'll come to appreciate the artistic elements of web localization. Just be sure not to lose sight of the science behind the art. So much of translation relies on rules and deadlines and clear instructions, and so few companies have perfected the process. Although the lack of quality in the translation industry presents opportunities for companies that do get it right, it also presents dangers for companies that don't know where to start. In the next chapter, you'll learn the many ways that computers aid in the translation process and how you can make the most of them.

9

COMPUTER-AIDED TRANSLATION (CAT)

Given the complexities and costs of managing translators and editors, you might wonder why the software industry hasn't figured out a way to replace these folks altogether. You're not alone. Computer scientists have been trying to put translators out of business since the early 1950s. But the better they get at developing translation software, the clearer it becomes that computers are better at *assisting* translators than *replacing* them. This chapter explains how computers can be used to augment the efforts of your translators, and, in some cases, replace them altogether.

TRANSLATORS AND COMPUTERS

Computer-aided translation (CAT), like many terms in the translation industry, means different things to different people. For the purposes of this book, CAT refers to any of the following applications:

- Computer-based bilingual and multilingual dictionaries

- Terminology management software

- Translation memory (TM) software

- Machine translation (MT) software

The first three types of tools are designed to assist translators. The fourth tool, machine translation, may be used to replace translators altogether. Tools are not without their tradeoffs. When used incorrectly or inconsistently, CAT tools can cause more problems than they solve. In translation, there's an inherent tension between speed and quality. CAT tools clearly help accelerate the translation process, but as shown in Figure 9.1, you must balance speed with quality. Before you use any tool, the question you need to ask is *Do the rewards justify the risks*?

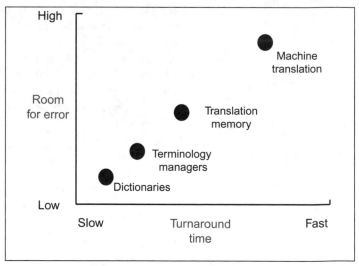

Figure 9.1 The risks and rewards of computer-aided translation.

Dictionaries and terminology managers assist in translating specific words or terms. A computer-based dictionary automates the process of looking up terms, and terminology managers store previously translated terms so that they don't have to be looked up again. Both tools save translators a fair amount of manual work and can result in reduced turnaround times. However, this chapter focuses on the two tools most commonly associated with CAT: translation memory and machine translation. Both applications promise dramatic savings in turnaround time and costs, but in markedly different fashions. This chapter will help you understand how best to make use of these applications and decide whether you should use them at all.

TRANSLATION MEMORY DEMYSTIFIED

Web sites often contain a good deal of repeated text: product descriptions, company slogans, legalese. Once you translate a sentence, you shouldn't have to pay for it to be translated again. *Translation memory* is software that stores previously translated sentences for reuse. Think of TM as a recycle bin for your translated text.

What makes TM so valuable is not just that it recycles text, but that it helps you track changes to already translated text. After a web site has been translated and stored into memory, all you have to do from that point is let the software scan the web pages and isolate new or modified sentences. You then send the changed files to the translators and editors, and they need translate only those few sentences, not entire web pages. TM can play a critical role in the maintenance of localized web sites, a topic covered in more depth in Chapter 13, "Global Content Management."

TM also aids in consistency. No matter how many different translators and editors are involved on your web site, if they're all using TM, the software guides them to use the pretranslated terminology and sentences. Not only do you save time, but you increase overall quality. In fact, consistency is the first benefit you'll notice when implementing translation memory. After all, when you begin implementing TM, you have to first build up a memory of translations that you can reuse.

How Translation Memory Works

The TM workflow is circular in nature. After you translate each web page, the source and target sentences, or segments, must be aligned and then stored in the memory. A *segment* is the fundamental unit of text that can be stored into memory—typically a sentence. *Alignment* is the process of connecting the source and target segments into pairs; many TM applications automate much of the alignment process by breaking down the source and target files into segments and then connecting them (see Figure 9.2). A translator must review the alignment and make any modifications before the new language pairs are added to the memory. Before translating additional web pages, they must be scanned by the TM software to look for any matches in the memory that can be reused, or "leveraged." Sentences that do not have any matches must be translated, and the cycle begins again (see Figure 9.3).

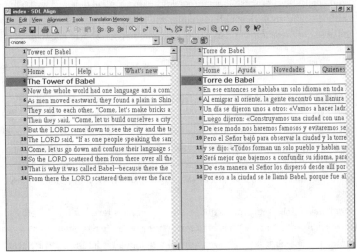

Figure 9.2 Using SDLX, a TM package, the English source and Spanish target pages from the "Hands-On: Spanish" chapter are aligned. Notice how the sentences are broken into segments.

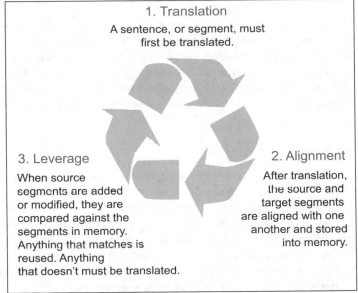

Figure 9.3 Translation memory: please recycle.

There are a number of TM applications on the market, with three groups of users: translators, translation vendors, and translation clients. Each group has a slightly different view of what makes a TM product useful. A client, for example, is more concerned with the memory aspect of an application, and a translator might be more concerned with price and usability. The following list includes some of the more well-known TM applications:

Déjà Vu (**www.atril.com**)

Trans Suite 2000 (**www.cypresoft.com**)

TRANSIT (**www.star-transit.com**)

TRADOS 5 (**www.trados.com**)

SDLX (**www.sdlintl.com**)

ForeignDesk, a free, open source product (**www.foreigndesk.net**)

MultiTrans (**www.multicorpora.ca/emultitrans.html**)

In this section, you'll see how one of the more popular packages on the market, TRADOS 5, works. According to Jochen Hummel, co-founder and chief technical officer of TRADOS, more than 3,000 companies and thousands of freelance translators currently rely on TRADOS software. TRADOS, like most TM packages, does not focus solely on HTML files; it can also process Word, QuarkXPress, and FrameMaker files, to name a few.

The TRADOS workflow (see Figure 9.4) stresses the separateness of the translation memory from the documents to be translated. By keeping memory separate, you are free to use it to leverage the memory against any document: XML, PDF, or RTF. Suppose your marketing department needed to translate a brochure; they can use the same memory you created for your web site and not only save money, but maintain consistency companywide. Larger companies sometimes develop multiple memories, each devoted to a separate business unit or specialty.

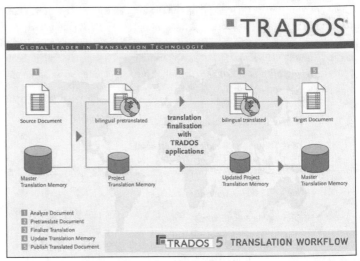

Figure 9.4 In the TRADOS workflow, notice how the memory exists separately from the documents.

Suppose you need to translate a web page from Japanese into English. In Figure 9.5, TRADOS "preprocesses" the web page by comparing each sentence to its memory. If a segment matches a stored segment perfectly, it is termed an exact, or 100%, match. At this point, TRADOS replaces the source segment with the translated segment. Anything less than an exact match is called a *fuzzy match*. Even a comma out of place results in a fuzzy match. Fuzzy matches are given a rating based on just how "fuzzy" they are, and then the closest matches are presented to the translator for review. The translator can then elect to use one of the suggestions or modify it as needed. Generally, when new text is processed, fuzzy match parameters are set, usually at 80% or higher, so that only the most likely matches are displayed. Anything below that margin is left for manual translation.

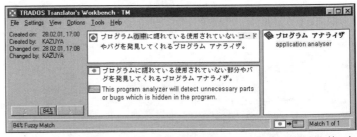

Figure 9.5 Analyzing English and Japanese segments using TRADOS Workbench, the project management component of the TRADOS suite.

The web page is edited in TagEditor, the TRADOS editing environment. TRADOS enables the translator to view source and target segments side by side, as shown in Figure 9.6. To translate a web page, you simply move along, one sentence at a time. Exact matches are already replaced with target text; fuzzy matches feature suggested segments. You can accept the suggestion or translate the segment manually. When the page is fully translated, the source segments are automatically removed from the file.

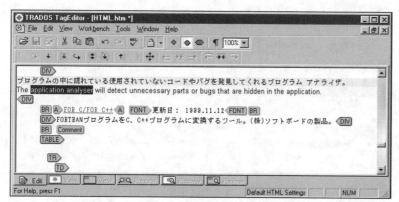

Figure 9.6 TRADOS TagEditor allows you to view the HTML document line by line. Notice how the HTML tags are "locked down" so that they cannot be altered.

Note in this figure how TRADOS hides the HTML tags, such as **<FONT>** and **<TABLE>**. This "lockdown" feature preserves the integrity of the HTML coding; it's such a useful feature that vendors sometimes use TRADOS software even if they aren't using memory.

When to Use Translation Memory

Translation memory is not for everyone. For starters, it's expensive: Packages run from $1,000 to $2,500 per license. Furthermore, if you don't incorporate TM throughout your entire translation workflow, you risk creating more problems than you solve. For example, if your translator uses TRADOS but your editor doesn't, any translation changes made by the editor won't be stored in the memory. Or suppose your site has been launched and your foreign office makes changes to the site without alerting you; those changes also won't make it into the memory. The greater the variance between the translations on your site and the translations in your memory, the less valuable your memory.

To prevent inconsistencies from creeping in, every round of translation must include a stage of "realignment," in which final changes are incorporated back into the memory. This time-consuming but vital process is often overlooked. If you don't think you can convince all parties to maintain the memory, then don't bother trying to use one. Assuming that you do have full support from your company and your translators, ask yourself four questions before purchasing the software:

- **How much text is there?** Run a word count of your web site. If your site contains less than 40,000 words, you might not get a return to justify the investment.

- **How frequently is text repeated?** Some web sites have more repetition than others. The degree of repetition in your site will give you an idea of what to expect in translation savings.

- **How stable is the site?** There's little sense in using translation memory if the text of your web pages changes or expires frequently. A news portal, for example, where content expires daily, might not benefit at all from TM.

- **Will other departments benefit from TM?** If your marketing and product support departments also manage translation, consider sharing costs and memory. The more parties in your company that rely on translation memory, the higher the odds that you'll be able to justify the investment.

The Future of Translation Memory

Translation memory, as it increases in size, increases in value to your company. But suppose you decided to switch translation vendors, and your vendor refused to return your memory. Some vendors claim ownership of the translation memory because it's a product they helped develop. As a rule, make sure your contract guarantees that you retain full ownership of the translation memory. Many vendors had relied on the memory as a sort of leash to retain their clients, but clients are a lot more sophisticated now, so this practice is rapidly fading.

Restrictive memories are being replaced by *open source memories*. Recently, the Localisation Industry Standards Association (LISA) published an open standard for how translation memory should be managed: the *Translation Memory eXchange (TMX) format*. It is defined as a Document Type Definition (DTD) in Standard Generalized Markup Language (SGML). TMX mandates vendor-neutral conventions for storing translation memories so that they can be easily exchanged between any tool that adheres to this standard. Most tool makers, such as TRADOS and SDL, support this standard.

TMX offers some exciting possibilities. For example, companies within an industry could share some of their memories so that they all save on translation costs and are all using more consistent industry terminology. A company might also want to share its memory so that other companies promote its proprietary terminology.

"Microsoft actively shares its terminology databases with its partners because these terms also carry Microsoft's marketing message," says Hummel. To support its .NET initiative, Microsoft would rather supply its partners with its preferred terminology in all languages than risk the terms being mistranslated.

Although TMX is designed for sharing translation memories, a new file format is being developed that will enable sharing any localizable content. The XML-based Localization Interchange File Format (XLIFF) promises to allow vendors and clients to share files freely without worrying about application compatibility. The format is still very much under development and currently applies primarily to software developers, but it's another important sign that the localization industry is moving toward common format standards that promise to make your life easier.

FYI

For more information about TMX, go to **www.lisa.org/tmx**. For more information about XLIFF, go to **www.opentag.com/xliff.htm**.

227

MACHINE TRANSLATION DEMYSTIFIED

Machine translation is what most people think of when they imagine computers replacing human translators. MT requires no human intervention; you simply input text and the software outputs the translation. MT software relies on a sophisticated parsing engine that analyzes the source text and translates it in real time. A number of MT applications are available; the following are a few of the more popular packages:

> IBM WebSphere Translation Server (**www-3.ibm.com/software/speech/ enterprise/ep_8.html**)
>
> SYSTRAN (**www.systran.com**; you can try this software free at **http://world.altavista.com**)
>
> SDL Enterprise Translation Server (**www.sdlintl.com**; you can try this software free at **www.freetranslation.com**)

Although MT is by far the fastest and cheapest alternative to relying on human translators, it's also the most prone to error. In fact, it is so prone to error that translation agencies rarely use it, if at all. Some experts doubt that MT will ever replace human translators. Translation is in many ways as challenging as writing itself. To effectively translate a sentence, you have to understand it first. Computers do not understand text; they merely do a passable job of *pretending* to understand text. For now, machine translation is ideal for conveying the "gist" of a message, which is good enough for many people.

Let's Go "Gisting"

The best way to understand the strengths and weaknesses of machine translation is to watch it in action. Let's try the most popular source for free translation, AltaVista Babel Fish (see Figure 9.7), at **http://babelfish.altavista.com**.

Figure 9.7   The Babel Fish window allows you to input text for translation or a URL.

Babel Fish offers web and text translation of 19 language pairs—from Chinese into English to French into German. According to AltaVista, Babel Fish is used more than one million times each day; the most popular language pair is Spanish into English.

Translating Web Pages

If you search using AltaVista and come upon a web page that's not in English, as shown in Figure 9.8, you can have it translated instantly.

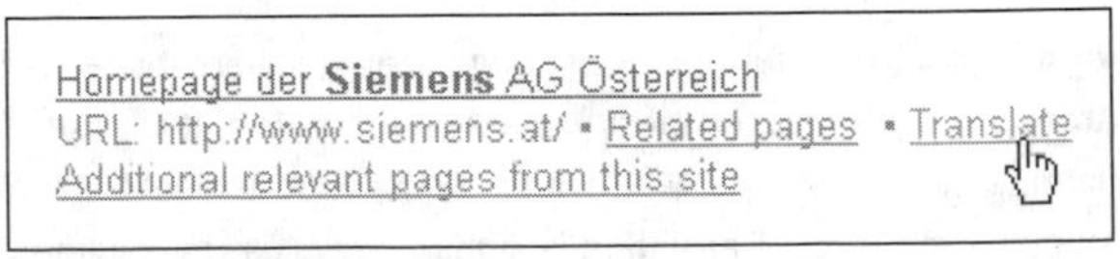

Homepage der **Siemens** AG Österreich
URL: http://www.siemens.at/ • Related pages • Translate
Additional relevant pages from this site

Figure 9.8   AltaVista search result for the Siemens home page with a **Translate** link.

Click the **Translate** link, and you'll be taken to the Babel Fish page with the translation options preselected (see Figure 9.9).

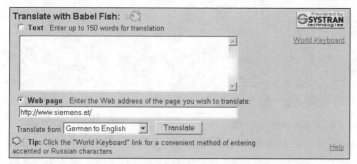

Figure 9.9 Babel Fish page with the Siemens URL entered and German to English translation option selected.

Babel Fish doesn't always work as planned. Don't be surprised if you click the **Translate** link and find a blank page, as shown in Figure 9.10. MT doesn't work as well with more complex or graphics-intensive web pages—yet another argument for why simpler is better in global web designs.

Figure 9.10 Babel Fish page "translated."

Now compare two web pages that Babel Fish was able to successfully translate: the Boston.com home page and the Target home page. Notice that the Boston.com page seems nearly fully translated, but the Target page appears to have changed hardly at all (see Figure 9.11). Why the variance? Blame the images. The Target page uses multiple images with embedded text.

Figure 9.11 The Target page at the top reflects few changes because most of the text is embedded within images and, therefore, "untranslatable."

Take a moment to view your company's web site through Babel Fish. Does it look more like Boston.com or Target? Even if you decided against translating your web site, if you did nothing but reduce the number of images with embedded text, you would make it much easier for people using Babel Fish to read your site.

Translating Text

Babel Fish also translates raw text, up to 150 words at a time. A popular way to illustrate the limitations of MT is to conduct a "round trip" translation, in which you translate text into a target language and then back again.

1. Go to **http://babelfish.altavista.com**.

    Type **I'm hoping we can hang out a bit this Friday.** into the text translation window. Set Babel Fish to translate English to Spanish (see Figure 9.12).

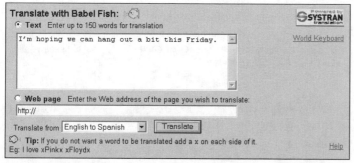

Figure 9.12 Enter text for translation.

2. Click the *Translate* link.

    Babel Fish will return this sentence: "I.m que espera podemos colgar hacia fuera un dígito binario este viernes." Notice how *bit* translated into "digito binario," a literal translation, instead of "poco," a more accurate translation (see Figure 9.13). Because MT isn't aware of the context of the sentence, it doesn't know to properly translate a word such as *bit*. Context is everything in translation, and is typically where MT falls short of success.

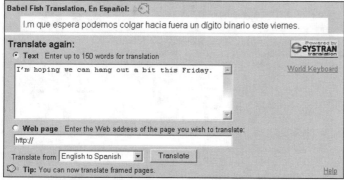

Figure 9.13 View the translated text.

3. Now take the translated text and copy and paste it back into the text translation window.

4. Change the settings to "Spanish to English" and translate again.

Here's what you end up with (see Figure 9.14): "I.m that hopes we can outside hang toward a bit east Friday." Round-trip translation is not a fair test because it only compounds errors made after the first translation pass, but it does give you a taste for MT and just how problematic it can be. To see how MT falls short when translating one-way, from Italian to English, see the sidebar "Machine Versus Translator."

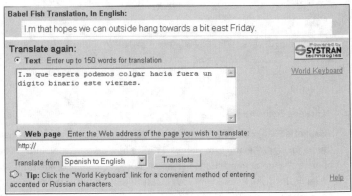

Figure 9.14 From here to there and not quite back again.

Machine Versus Translator

When compared side by side, machine translation fails to measure up to a qualified human translator. The following example illustrates what the same Italian text looks like after translation by Babel Fish as well as a professional translator.

Source Text in Italian	Machine Translation	Human Translation
Bisogna procedere coi piedi di piombo quando si scrive (e si legge) di biblioteche "elettroniche", "digitali" o "virtuali", termini che si sprecano, di questi tempi, anche nelle riviste e nei programmi televisivi più divulgativi, senza che sia sempre chiaro a chi legge (e talvolta nemmeno a chi scrive) a cosa ci si stia effettivamente riferendo.	It must proceed with the lead feet when law) of "electronic " libraries, " " virtual " digitalises " is written (and or, terms that are wasted, of these times, also in the reviews and the television programs more divulgativi, without that is always clearly to who law (and sometimes to who does not write) to what is effectively reporting to us.	Extreme caution must be used when writing (and reading) about "electronic," "digital," or "virtual" libraries, these terms being liberally used today even in the most popular magazines and TV programs, while it is not always clear to the reader (and sometimes not even to the author) what is actually being discussed.

*Source: Accurapid Translation Services (**www.accurapid.com**).*

Machine Translation Goes Corporate

Although Babel Fish is wildly popular with web users, corporations are less enthusiastic. Most companies want web users to understand considerably more than the gist of their web pages. SYSTRAN, the developer of the MT software used in Babel Fish, has since discovered a growing niche where MT can play an important role in global business: customer support.

The global software developer Autodesk recently began using SYSTRAN to help provide multilingual online customer support. According to the research firm IDC, Autodesk chose MT as a cost-effective solution to offering extensive customer support across a number of languages. Autodesk supplies users with an extensive customer support library of 10,000 articles of approximately 1,000 words each. To translate these many articles manually was not a realistic option; instead, SYSTRAN machine-translates the articles and caches them for instant download. Although MT can't provide the level of quality that human translation provides, Autodesk felt that the tradeoff was worth it.*

When a Little Translation Is Better Than No Translation

If you want to offer a translated web site but don't have the budget for translators, you can embed the button shown in Figure 9.15 in your home page and let users translate the web page themselves. SYSTRAN offers this service free for up to five web pages. If you want to include additional web pages, SYSTRAN offers several pricing and service options (**www.systranlinks.com**).

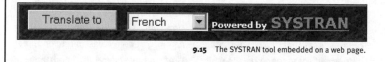

9.15   The SYSTRAN tool embedded on a web page.

Although many companies don't use MT applications externally, they do use them internally. MT allows employees of multinationals to share information across languages, such as reports and email messages. According to SYSTRAN, employees from Ford, DowCorning, and PriceWaterhouseCoopers all rely on MT to communicate globally.

---

*"Systran Enables Multilingual Customer Support for Autodesk," Mary Flanagan and Steve McClure, IDC Bulletin #25019, June 2001.

When Machines *and* Humans Fail

Some concepts and words are so unique to a culture that word-for-word translation is impossible. For example, how would you translate the following words into equivalent, compact English words?

Word	Language	Meaning
saudade	Brazilian, Portuguese	Wistful longing
fusto	Italian	Man who dresses provocatively
bol	Mayan	Stupid in-laws
bardo	Tibetan	Plane between birth and death
suilk	Scottish	Swallow noisily
ta	Chinese	To understand deeply and take lightly

Source: They Have a Word For It, *by Howard Rheingold, Sarabande Books, 2000.*

OF TRANSLATORS AND MACHINE TRANSLATORS

All this talk about machine translation and the march of technology can make translators a little nervous. It's not easy working in a profession where so many companies want to replace you with computers, but translators need not worry. Just as desktop publishing tools didn't put designers out of business 15 years ago, computer-aided translation tools won't put translators out of business. If anything, these tools will make the translators who know how to use them more valuable, not less. Even machine translation, though it has clearly found a growing niche, isn't likely to endanger human translators. Ironically, it too could make the services of translators that much more valuable. As more people come to rely on Babel Fish, they will come to realize the limitations of computers and the importance of the human touch.

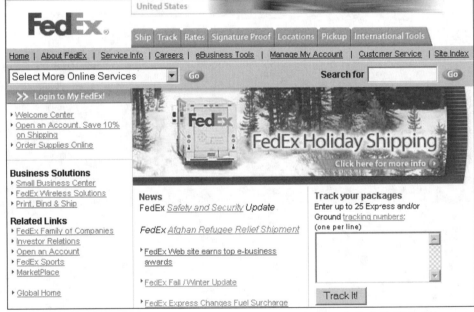

Figure 1 The FedEx U.S. English home page.

FEDEX

FedEx delivers more than three million packages daily to more than 200 countries. To effectively serve all its customers in all these countries, FedEx developed 204 country-specific web sites. The sites range in depth from just a few localized pages on the Grenada site to dozens of localized pages on the Brazil site. FedEx also recently introduced the FedEx Global Trade Manager (www.fedex.com/us/international), an impressive collection of international shipping tools and resources (see Figure 2).

---

www.fedex.com

Localized web sites: FedEx offers 204 country-specific web sites, with functionality incorporated into 188 sites. All sites are available in English. In addition, the top 37 markets are translated into local languages, which include:

- Arabic
- Canadian French
- Chinese (Simplified)
- Chinese (Traditional)
- Dutch

- English
- French
- German
- Italian
- Japanese

- Korean
- Portuguese
- Spanish (Latin America)
- Spanish (Castilian)
- Thai and Hebrew are planned

Figure 2 The FedEx Global Trade Manager provides international resources and shipping documents for 20 countries.

ANALYSIS

The FedEx site is enormous and enormously complex. What makes the localization of this site impressive is not so much the front-end translation (which is clearly lacking on many sites) but the back-end functionality. Consider the challenge of providing users around the world with web sites that display shipping rates in local currencies and delivery dates and times in the correct formats. As discussed in Chapter 7, "Internationalization and Localization," some of the biggest obstacles a company may face during globalization have little to do with translation. For example, translating the German FedEx home page is relatively easy (see Figure 3), but localizing the functionality behind that home page is not always so easy. In Figure 4, a customer can access shipping rates in euros (€) and deutsche marks (DM) as well as a localized delivery schedule.

Figure 3 The FedEx Germany front end: looks like a local web site.

Figure 4   The FedEx Germany back end: Acts like a local web site.

A Grand Gateway

When you first visit FedEx, you're presented with a global gateway splash page (see Figure 5). The list of all 204 countries is hidden behind a pull-down menu. The countries are listed alphabetically, except for the U.S.A. link, which is at the top of the list to save the majority of users from scrolling down. A pull-down menu is not the ideal solution for a global gateway because it hides the names of the countries and presents residents of Venezuela, Zambia, and Zimbabwe with a rather lengthy scroll. In addition, the purpose of the pull-down menu might not be clear to non-English speakers because the text on this page is all in English; positioning an icon of a globe next to the menu would alleviate this problem. The good news with this gateway is that you should need to see it only once. After selecting your country, the preference is stored on your computer, so when you return to the FedEx site, you are taken directly to your preferred country. As gateways go, the FedEx site is better than most because it places a priority on getting web users to their localized web sites.

Figure 5 The FedEx global gateway forces users to choose a country before entering the web site.

If you should want to get back to the gateway, you can click the "Global Home" link, which is a bit challenging to find at times (see Figure 6). An easy fix would be to position the same globe icon that would ideally be used on the global gateway at the top of every web page. The icon would provide an easy link for web users who need to get back to the gateway.

Figure 6 Getting back to the global gateway
isn't always so obvious.

Getting Organized

Although this might not be the most glamorous feature of the web site, FedEx does
an excellent job of organizing its country sites (see Figure 7). Imagine the challenge
of creating a labeling system for 204 web sites that an entire web development staff
can easily remember and manage. FedEx wisely follows the ISO country code abbreviations for labeling. If you want to brush up on your country code abbreviations
(see Appendix D, "Language and Country Codes"), go to **www.fedex.com/us** and try
substituting other codes for the **us**, such as **ar** for Argentina or **la** for Laos. This
degree of standardization makes it easier for the people managing the site; instead
of wondering whether the Saudi Arabia directory is named "saudi" or "saudiarabia"
or "saudi_Arabia," you have to know only the "sa" country code.

Figure 7 A standardized naming structure makes site management much easier. Notice how the French URL
specifies **fr**. Should you want to skip over to the
equivalent German page, simply substitute **de** in
place of **fr**.

A Work in Progress

In terms of translation, the FedEx site is very much a work in progress. Many of the localized sites are still offered in English only, and even some of the translated web sites are light on translated content. For example, compare the two FedEx pages in Figure 8.

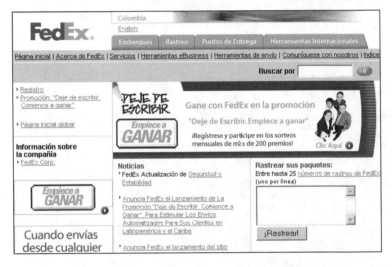

Figure 8   The FedEx Colombia page (on top) is fully translated; on the bottom, the FedEx Sweden page in still in English.

Nevertheless, the FedEx site represents an enormous investment in resources and exhibits many best practices that other companies can learn from.

Q&A WITH FEDEX

Virginie Lasnier, Marketing Advisor
FedEx Corporate Services

Some localized sites do not contain translated text. What was the rationale behind, say, not using Arabic for the Egypt site?

FedEx will localize all 204 sites in phases. The rollout plan and phases are based on the following criteria:

- *FedEx operation in the local countries, such as local strategy and volume*
- *Economic forecast*
- *Web penetration*
- *Cost/ROI analysis*
- *Competitive forces*
- *Available resources in the local country to provide localized content and news*
- *Ranking of all global and local web development projects worldwide and resource allocations*

Do you find based on your tests and feedback that users are comfortable with the global gateway?

The global gateway page is an excellent way to showcase global service capabilities to customers. In our experience, users do prefer to have direct access to their local page or site. However, if accessing a local site requires placing a cookie on their machine, the users complain that they have to delete the cookie, in some cases, to visit the U.S. site. We are working on an alternate solution that will meet all customers' needs.

What are the most popular countries selected?

The top five are the United States, Canada, Great Britain, Japan, and Germany.

Did you spend a great deal of time when you began planning the global design to accommodate the many languages involved?

Yes, it was a conscious decision. All design decisions take into consideration translations and right-to-left languages. We had to reject several designs because in certain languages, like German, the word length would not fit on tabs or looked odd. (As shown in Figure 9, the orange tabs can be resized to fit expanded text.)

243

Figure 9 In the German and Finnish navigation bars, notice how the orange tabs are designed so they can be enlarged to accommodate text expansion.

The choices of naming convention, tab and category labels, product names, length of word, customs, and local meaning were all taken into consideration. We spent several months in planning and testing options with our customers.

Are the localized web sites hosted in each country or centrally?

All localized sites are hosted centrally, not locally, in order to maintain consistency, brand management, and global application development. However, we use a mixture of local, regional, and U.S. development for management of content and translations.

Is email customer support also handled within each country and in the native language?

Webmaster email support is handled at the regional or local level, mostly in local languages. There are some exceptions. Successful localized email functionality that is highly integrated with customer service, while maintaining the global brand, is critical to a successful global site. FedEx is continuously improving in this area.

Do you manage translation in house or do you work with a vendor?

We use local, regional, and U.S translation vendors, depending upon the size of the project.

Do you use content management software? What were your challenges with setting it up to manage multilingual content?

Yes. We are in the process of upgrading our system. It is highly challenging to manage the complexity of our U.S. site as well as each local site's needs and challenges. There are no tools in the market right now that offer an easy-to-implement solution for translation and multi-language site management, particularly for sites like FedEx's with high numbers of pages, high traffic, and component bases with owners in several countries.

The key challenge was migrating a site of FedEx's size to a new content management software tool. We had to rethink all our processes, such as how to manage several translation agencies at the local level, having multiple local and regional content owners, and training all participants.

How do you measure success for each of your localized sites?

Success is measured by

245

- *Increase in hits, visits, return visitors*
- *Reduction of calls to customer services*
- *Site load time*
- *Online tracking and shipping or applications usage (cost savings, ROI, shipping volume, yield)*

HANDS-ON: RUSSIAN

Overview

This is the third of six Hands-On chapters. By now, you have completed Hands-On chapters for Spanish as well as French, Italian, and German. After completing all the Hands-On chapters, you will have localized one web page into eight languages—the languages spoken by more than 80% of the world's population. If you'd like to try your hand at these exercises, all files used in these chapters are available for download; go to **www.bytelevel.com/beyondborders**.

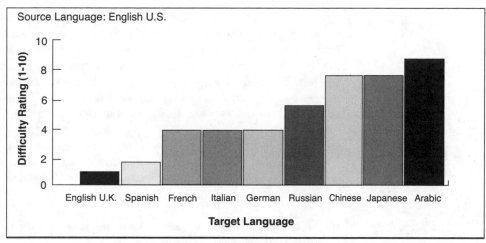

Source Language: English U.S.

Figure 1 The difficulty ratings from Chapter 1, "In the Beginning, There Was English."

For a full list of country and language codes, see Appendix D.

Speakers worldwide : 167 million (approx. 150 million within Russia); Russian is widely spoken in more than 30 countries.
(source: *Ethnologue*, 14th edition, 2000; **www.ethnologue.com**)

ISO language code: RU

Difficulty rating: 6 (see Figure 1)

Major Russian locales:

Country	Language Code
Russia	ru-RU
Bulgaria	ru-BG
Ukraine	ru-UA

FIRST THOUGHTS

Logistically, creating a web page in Russian isn't much different from creating a web page in Spanish or French, which is why the workflow isn't repeated in this chapter. Linguistically and technically, however, the localization process can be very challenging. If you don't speak Russian, the language can be a little intimidating. French and Italian, for example, largely rely on characters that English speakers are already familiar with, but Russian uses an entirely new script: Cyrillic. The Russian alphabet contains 33 Cyrillic characters, most of which are based on Greek characters. The Cyrillic script is used by more than 50 languages, including Georgian, Ukrainian, Belorussian, and Bulgarian. There are, however, minor differences in the exact character sets used by each language. For example, Ukrainian and Russian share most of the same Cyrillic characters, but not all; therefore, they have historically relied on different character sets: KOI8-R for Russian and KOI8-U for Ukrainian.

Because there are no Cyrillic characters in ISO 8859-1 (the Latin 1 character set), a new character set is required. However, selecting that character set and manipulating the characters present many technical challenges for English-speaking web developers:

- **Which character set?** You can build a Russian web page using one of several character sets, but the question becomes: Which one?

- **How do you create a Russian graphic?** You might wonder why you need to bother with graphics, because you removed the navigation bar graphic for the FIGS pages (see Figure 2). As you'll see, character set conflicts in the global gateway will force you to create a few new graphics.

- **What about Unicode?** Unicode was designed to prevent character set conflicts. As an exercise, you'll see firsthand how Unicode saves you time and frustration.

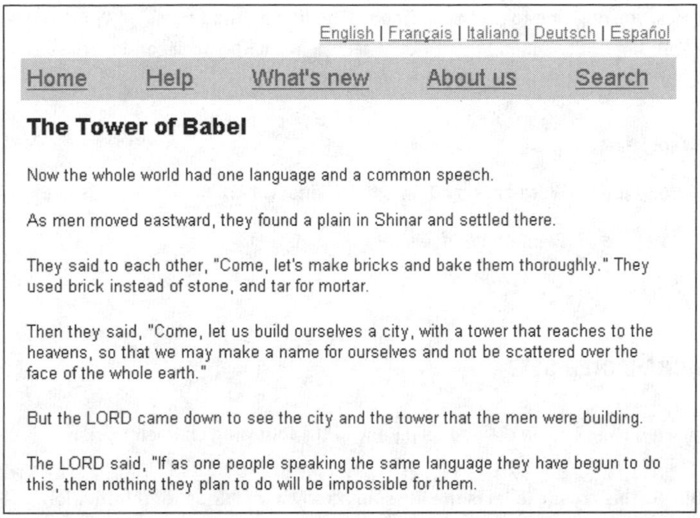

English | Français | Italiano | Deutsch | Español

Home   Help   What's new   About us   Search

The Tower of Babel

Now the whole world had one language and a common speech.

As men moved eastward, they found a plain in Shinar and settled there.

They said to each other, "Come, let's make bricks and bake them thoroughly." They used brick instead of stone, and tar for mortar.

Then they said, "Come, let us build ourselves a city, with a tower that reaches to the heavens, so that we may make a name for ourselves and not be scattered over the face of the whole earth."

But the LORD came down to see the city and the tower that the men were building.

The LORD said, "If as one people speaking the same language they have begun to do this, then nothing they plan to do will be impossible for them.

Figure 2   The English-language source page, after being modified for the FIGS languages.

TOOLS

The easiest way to create a Russian web page is with a Russian operating system and Russian software. But assuming you don't have the budget or the patience to install an entirely new system, this chapter focuses on the easiest and cheapest workarounds for Windows users. Mac users can follow along; although the software and steps vary, the strategies are still valuable.

Your choice of tools is limited to those that support Cyrillic characters. Fortunately, Word 97 and 2000 do support Cyrillic characters, regardless of whether you're using the Windows 98, ME, or XP operating system.

Text Tools

Operating system: Windows ME

HTML: Word 2000

For graphics, you're going to try two methods. The first method relies on Word and a screen-capturing utility called SnagIt (**www.techsmith.com**). The second method relies on the Microsoft Paint application that ships with Windows XP.

> **Graphics Tools**
>
> Method 1: Word 2000 and SnagIt on Windows ME
>
> Method 2: Paint on Windows XP

WHICH CHARACTER SET?

A Russian web page can be created using any of the following character sets:

- **KOI8-R:** This cryptic label is the Russian acronym for "Code for Information Exchange, 8 bit." This character set, developed in Russia, was the dominant character set for a long time.

- **Windows 1251:** Commonly called Cyrillic Windows, 1251 is a Windows Codepage similar in nature to Codepage 1252 for Latin characters. As Windows has taken over in Russia, so has 1251.

- **ISO 8859-5:** The international standard, this 8-bit character set is much like ISO 8859-1. Unlike 8859-1, however, it hasn't been widely embraced in the technical community.

- **Unicode:** This super-character set is still not widely used on the Internet because older browsers do not recognize it.

Confused? You're not alone. Although any of these character sets will work, when developing a web page, you should select the character set that the majority of local users can view properly. At one point, this choice might have been KOI8-R, but this character set is rapidly fading from view; it is, in many ways, Russia's version of ASCII. Normally, I would recommend selecting an ISO standard, but among major Russian sites, Windows 1251 appears to be the overwhelming favorite. Unicode is the ideal solution in theory, but in reality, many Russian users are still using older browsers that do not support it.

FYI

For more information about Cyrillic script and character sets, visit the following sites:

The Cyrillic Charset Soup (**http://czyborra.com/charsets/cyrillic.html**)

Windows 1251 description (**www.microsoft.com/typography/unicode/1251.htm**)

Extensive resources on the Russian language and Windows (**http://ourworld.compuserve.com/homepages/PaulGor**)

CHARACTER SET CONFLICTS

HTML allows you to specify only one character set (encoding) per web page. For web pages that feature only Cyrillic and ASCII characters, this is no problem: You specify Windows 1251. But there *is* a problem with the Tower of Babel page: At the top of the web page, the global gateway includes two characters that are not included in 1251—*accented* Latin characters. Compare the 1251 and 1252 character sets in Figure 3 to see the problem.

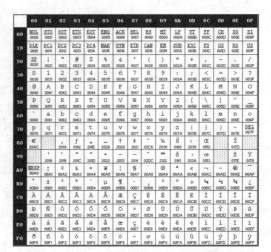

Figure 3   Notice how the characters of Windows 1251 (left) and 1252 (right) vary. In particular, notice that 1251 does not include accented Latin characters.

Most major character sets share the same batch of ASCII characters in the first 128 code points. The upper 128 code points are typically where character set conflicts arise. As shown in Table 1, the accented characters in 8859-1 and Windows 1252 conflict with the Cyrillic characters in Windows 1251, but the basic Latin characters present no conflicts. Also note that KOI8-R uses different code points for Cyrillic characters than 1251.

Table 1   Cyrillic Character Set Conflicts

Code Point Decimal (hexidecimal)	Windows 1252 (Western European Windows) and 8859-1 (Latin 1)	Windows 1251 (Cyrillic Windows)	KOI8-R
65 (41)	A	A	A
97 (61)	a	a	a
241 (F1)	ñ	C	Я
231 (E7)	ç	3	Г

Character Set Conflicts in Action

To truly understand character set conflicts, you need to witness them for yourself. In the following two exercises, you'll create the global gateway using 8859-1 (Latin 1) and again using Windows 1251 (Cyrillic). In both exercises, you'll see the limitations of each character set.

First, you'll need Russian text. Given the character set issues, managing the flow of text between you and the translator and editor is critical. It's important that you know what tools your translator is using and, more important, which character set. For this exercise, you will use Russian text translated from the Tower of Babel page, using the Windows 1251 character set. The quality of the translation is irrelevant at this point, but it's important to use the 1251 character set. You can quickly generate sample Russian text on your own in that character set by using machine translation software from Rustran at **www.rustran.com**. After you have Russian text to work with, you'll need to do a bit of copying and pasting.

FYI

Russian machine translation sites:

www.rustran.com

http://translation2.paralink.com (allows a choice of encodings)

http://world.altavista.com (Russian-to-English translation only)

The Hidden Dangers of "Copy and Paste"

When working with more than one character set, the simple act of copying and pasting text into HTML documents or graphics is not so simple. Software applications generally default to using the same character set that your operating system uses.

Defaulting to one character creates problems when you're working with different character sets, and the problems become most acute when you're working with different character sets at the same time.

Fortunately, many software applications do a fair job of guessing which character set you're using at any given time. Windows 2000, for example, supports a wide range of character sets; the key is in how well you manage this feature. Not all software is so sophisticated. For example, what you see in Figures 4 and 5 is what happens when you copy and paste Cyrillic text into Dreamweaver. Copying Cyrillic text isn't a problem, but pasting it into Dreamweaver is. As shown in Figure 5, the pasted text appears as a bunch of question marks.

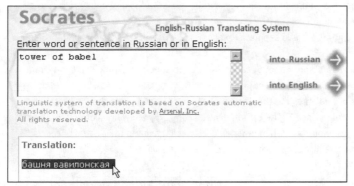

Figure 4 Copying the Cyrillic text from the Rustran machine translation web page is easy.

253

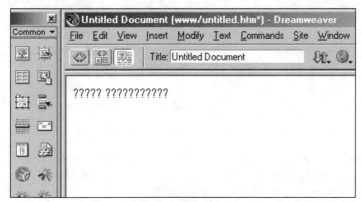

Figure 5 Pasting the Cyrillic text into Dreamweaver 4 is not so easy. The text appears as question marks because the application does not support pasting Cyrillic text. You'll need to go back to a text editor again.

Using Latin Character Set 8859-1

In this first exercise, you'll copy and paste Cyrillic and Latin text into a new HTML document. First, create the target HTML page in Microsoft Notepad, WordPad, or another basic text editor that supports the Latin 1 character set. Do not use Microsoft Word, as it often tries to function as a WYSIWYG editor and ends up creating additional problems. Make sure you have the correct **<META>** charset tag at the top of the HTML page, as shown here:

<meta http-equiv="content-type" content="text/html; charset=8859-1">

Next, open a document that contains Cyrillic text encoded in Windows 1251; this could be as simple as copying text from a web page, as shown in Figure 4. At this point you now have two separate text sources: a Latin 1 source and a Cyrillic source.

Open Microsoft Word 2000. Because Word 2000 supports Cyrillic *and* Latin characters simultaneously, you'll copy all text into this application. First, copy and paste the Latin 1 HTML text into the document. Next, copy and paste the Cyrillic text into its correct place (see Figure 6). You need to copy only a few lines of text for this exercise, but make sure the European gateway links retain their correct accents. If the characters disappear, you'll know something is amiss.

```
<table bgcolor="dddddd" align="right">
<font face="arial, helvetica" size="2">
<a href="babel.html">English</a> |
<a href="fr/babel_fr.html">Français</a> |
<a href="it/babel_it.html">Italiano</a> |
<a href="de/babel_de.html">Deutsch</a> |
<a href="es/babel_es.html">Español</a> |
<a href="ru/babel_ru.html">Русский</a>
</font>
```

Figure 6   The Russian text (circled) has been pasted into the global gateway.

Next, save the document as "encoded" text. When you save as encoded text, a dialog box opens offering you a choice of encodings (see Figure 7). Select Western European (ISO), which is Microsoft's way of saying ISO 8859-1. You can preview the text in the dialog box before you commit to an encoding. In this case, notice that the Cyrillic text is highlighted in red with this warning: "Text marked in red will not save correctly in the chosen encoding." Proceed anyway.

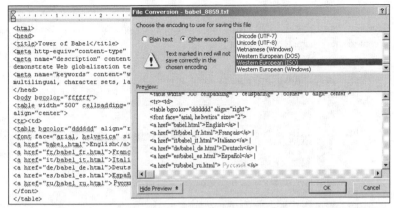

Figure 7 Saving as encoded text: Western Windows. Word warns that the Cyrillic characters won't retain their encoding.

Complete the save procedure, and then change the extension of the saved file from **.txt** to **.html** and view it in a web browser. Your gateway should look like the one in Figure 8.

255

English | Français | Italiano | Deutsch | Español | ???????

What's new   About us   Search

Figure 8 Using **charset=8859-1**, the Russian text is not displayed correctly.

An HTML page allows for only one character set. So if you save the file as 8859-1, the page can't display Cyrillic characters. Because most of the text on this web page will consist of Cyrillic characters, you'll need to use the Cyrillic Windows character set 1251.

FYI

Test how your browser views different Cyrillic encodings at **www.dimka.com/ru/cyrillic/**.

Using the Cyrillic Character Set Windows 1251

This second exercise follows the same basic steps as before: Open a new Word document, and then copy and paste the Cyrillic and Latin 1 text into this document. This time, however, include a **<META>** tag that specifies the Windows 1251 Codepage:

```
<meta http-equiv="content-type" content="text/html; charset=windows-1251">
```

When you save the Word document as encoded text, select Cyrillic (Windows), as shown in Figure 9. Notice that the Cyrillic characters now appear correctly, but the accented Latin characters do not.

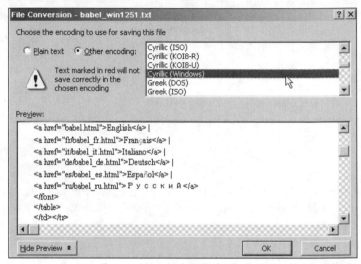

Figure 9   Saving with the Cyrillic (Windows) encoding. Word warns that the accented Latin characters won't retain their encodings.

After you've saved the file and changed the file extension to **.html**, preview the page in a web browser. Instead of the Cyrillic characters not being displayed, you should be missing the accented marks on the European text, as shown in Figure 10.

Figure 10   Notice that the accented Latin characters don't appear correctly when using **charset=windows-1251**.

You've now witnessed character set conflicts firsthand. The question, then, is how to avold them on the Babel web page. You have two choices for displaying both Cyrillic *and* accented Latin characters on one web page: Use Unicode as the encoding, or use Windows 1251 and embed the text that won't display properly into graphics. Because Unicode isn't supported on older browsers, you'll need to create a few small graphics for your navigation bar. The next section illustrates how to do this.

HOW TO CREATE A RUSSIAN GRAPHIC

To display accented characters on the Russian page, they must be embedded in graphics; this includes the **Français** and **Español** links. However, you also need to consider how you're going to display the **Русский** link to the Russian page on the Latin 1 web pages. Therefore, it makes sense to create three graphics. For the French and the Spanish text, this is a simple matter of copying and pasting the text into a graphic. For the Russian graphic, however, the Cyrillic characters are a lot more challenging. Word 2000 handles Cyrillic characters just fine, but many software applications, such as Photoshop 6, Dreamweaver 4, and Illustrator 10, do not. So for this exercise, you'll try two different methods that assume you don't have the latest software and aren't going to buy Russian software.

Method 1: Word and SnagIt

Copy and paste the French, Spanish, and Russian text into Word 2000, and then use SnagIt (or another screen-capturing utility) to take a picture of that image. Save the screen grab as a GIF file to create a graphic for the French, Spanish, and Russian links, as shown in Figure 11. A quick alternative to using screen-capturing software is to press Alt+Print Screen on a Windows system. This key combination captures a picture of the screen in bitmap format. You can then paste it into a graphics application and edit it as needed; it's a more cumbersome process than using SnagIt, but the end result is the same.

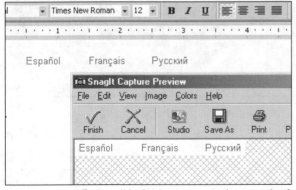

Figure 11   Using SnagIt, you can capture the exact portion of the screen that you need.

Method 2: XP and Paint

All versions of Windows include Microsoft Paint, a very basic graphics tool. Windows XP, however, includes a surprisingly multilingual version of Paint because of Microsoft's push to support Unicode across all applications. Even though Paint is quite limited in graphics capability, it's sophisticated in character set support. For the purposes of this chapter, it too will work just fine to create a graphic of the French, Spanish, and Russian links. Simply copy the text and paste it into a new Paint file (see Figure 12). Save the image as a GIF file.

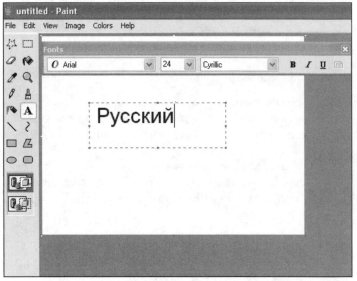

Figure 12   Microsoft Paint, which ships with Windows XP, supports all major languages.

FYI

Cyrillic Font Resources

www.ccss.de/slovo/eurocp.htm

http://koi8.pp.ru/

LOCALIZATION NOTES

When you deviate from the Latin 1 character set, a host of new challenges, small and not so small, typically emerge. When working with new character sets, making sure your translators, editors, designers, and writers are aware of the complexities and how to minimize them is important. Make sure your translation teams support the same encoding throughout the process. If you don't understand the language, you might not notice that the encoding has changed because the differences are sometimes subtle.

Needless to say, character set conflicts make it apparent how valuable globalization management systems (GMSs) can be. A typical GMS application would allow your translators and editors to input and edit text directly through a web-based interface, ensuring that the text encoding remained consistent and saving you from any worry about encodings. Assuming, however, that you don't have this luxury, there are a few tips to keep in mind when managing different character sets.

Globalization management systems are discussed in Chapter 13, "Global Content Management."

One Character Set per Glossary

In the previous Hands-On chapters, you have added a new column in your Excel glossary for each new language, but with the addition of yet another character set to your Babel page, it makes sense to create a new glossary for each additional character set. If not, Excel will encode the document's text in Unicode to ensure that the different character sets are all displayed properly. It won't tell you that it's doing this; it just does it. So if you want to copy and paste this text into your document, the text will be encoded in Unicode, not Cyrillic Windows. If this happens, you can "transcode" the text back to Cyrillic Windows by using the "save as encoded" process covered earlier. As a rule, try to keep character sets as is throughout the localization process to reduce the room for error.

Avoid *<font face>*

When working with different character sets, you'll likely be working with different fonts, and the people viewing your web site will likely be using fonts you might not be familiar with. As a result, you should avoid specifying a **<font face>** in the HTML code. Always keep in mind that web users outside the U.S. often rely on very old operating systems, browsers, and freeware fonts. Many developers avoid specifying a font by name entirely, opting instead for general font attributes, such as **<font face="sans-serif">**.

Your Server and Your *charset*

Web servers, when sending web pages to the world, also send out headers that tell browsers which charsets to expect. Some servers default to the localized operating system they are running. For example, most U.S. servers assume a Latin 1 character set, but you don't want your Russian web pages to have a Latin 1 charset heading. You might have to configure your server so that it knows exactly which pages have which encoding. Some servers deduce this information automatically, but be sure to test your server before taking your localized pages live.

The Importance of *charset*

The Lucent web page in Figure 13 does not have a **charset** attribute, and it shows. The English browser does not recognize the encoding, so it displays gibberish instead. Note that the Cyrillic text that does display correctly has been embedded into a graphic. You can manually adjust the web page's encoding so that it's displayed correctly, but if the web developer had simply added the **charset** attribute, this adjustment would not be necessary.

Figure 13 The browser doesn't display the text of the Lucent web page because the **charset** is not specified.

Titles and *ALT* Tags

Many web browsers still struggle to display Cyrillic characters properly in **ALT** tags and in the titles of web pages; instead of Cyrillic characters, you end up with more question marks. As you can see on the left in Figure 14, the title of the Tower of Babel page appears as a string of question marks when using Internet Explorer in Windows ME. But there's hope: Using Internet Explorer in Windows XP, the title of the Tower of Babel web page, when encoded in Unicode, is displayed correctly, as shown on the right in Figure 14. Keep in mind that these examples illustrate what users of English-language web browsers will see, not necessarily what's seen by users of Russian-language web browsers, which generally do much better in this regard.

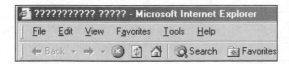

Figure 14   Notice how the title of the Tower of Babel web pages appears as question marks in Windows ME but as Cyrillic characters, as intended, in Windows XP.

Test and Test Again

Preview your web page in both Netscape Navigator and Internet Explorer, particularly older versions. A good method of looking for character set conflicts is to preview your page in Netscape Navigator 4.08 (or earlier). It's much less forgiving than Internet Explorer. IE does a best guess if there's a character set conflict, defaulting to Unicode and tweaking the text so that it is displayed correctly, as shown in Figure 15. Netscape is much less tolerant. In some cases, it simply gives up and shows a blank screen (see Figure 16).

261

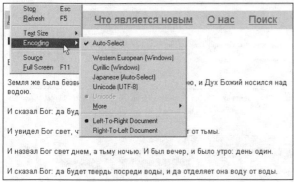

Figure 15   IE, if it notices a character set conflict, defaults to Unicode (grayed out in this figure because IE has detected no conflict) and tweaks the text in an attempt to fix the problem.

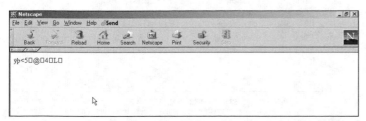

Figure 16   Older versions of Navigator, if they encounter a conflict, often give up and display something like this.

> **Don't Forget** *lang*
>
> Always tag your HTML pages for the language they include. In this case, you'll begin at the top of the web page with **<HTML lang="ru_RU">**. This tag helps search engines, particularly language-specific search engines, find your site.

Live Editing

Finally, after you've copied the translated text into your target document and moved it to the server, have the editor conduct one more round of editing. No matter how careful you are, this final pass will catch minute problems more often than not. For people who are completely unfamiliar with Cyrillic characters, it can be difficult to spot transcoding errors. As shown in Figure 17, the editor for this web page, Natalia Kisseleva, caught a few mistakes in the translation. She emailed the revised text, but it arrived scrambled. As you can see, character sets and encodings are something you need to be aware of throughout the entire process. Fortunately, Microsoft Outlook supports viewing the text in more than one encoding. After you change the encoding from Western European (Windows) to Cyrillic (Windows), the new text appears correctly, as shown in Figure 18.

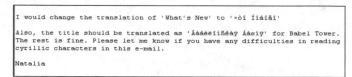

Figure 17 The email message from the editor doesn't display correctly in Microsoft Outlook.

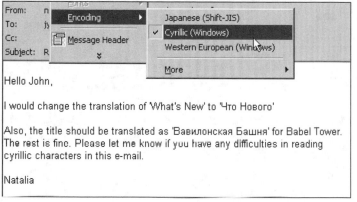

Figure 18 After changing the encoding for the email, the Cyrillic words are displayed correctly, ready to be copied into the HTML document.

WHAT ABOUT UNICODE?

With all this talk about character set conflicts, spending a moment to see how Unicode promises to solve these problems is useful. The final Hands-On chapter goes into more depth on Unicode, and you'll combine text from every localized web page into one web page.

For now, simply copy the text from your HTML page and paste it into a new Word 2000 document. Make sure that both the Cyrillic characters and accented Latin characters are displayed correctly. Update the **<META>** tag to read:

```
<meta http-equiv="content-type" content="text/html; charset=utf-8">
```

Finally, save as encoded text with the Unicode UTF-8 option selected, and preview the page in a web browser. All characters should be displayed correctly, as shown in Figure 19. It's easy to see why Unicode has gained such a strong following.

Figure 19   When you save the text with the Unicode
encoding, there are no character set conflicts.

HEADING EAST

Congratulations! With Russian complete (see Figure 20), you now have five web pages with the potential reach of nearly 800 million people. In the next Hands-On, you're going to move farther east to the Asian languages.

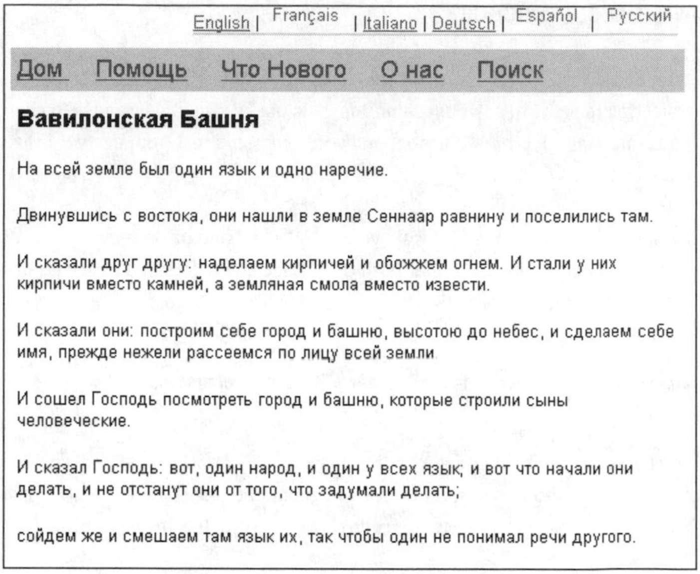

English | Français | Italiano | Deutsch | Español | Русский

Дом　　Помощь　　Что Нового　　О нас　　Поиск

Вавилонская Башня

На всей земле был один язык и одно наречие.

Двинувшись с востока, они нашли в земле Сеннаар равнину и поселились там.

И сказали друг другу: наделаем кирпичей и обожжем огнем. И стали у них кирпичи вместо камней, а земляная смола вместо извести.

И сказали они: построим себе город и башню, высотою до небес, и сделаем себе имя, прежде нежели рассеемся по лицу всей земли

И сошел Господь посмотреть город и башню, которые строили сыны человеческие.

И сказал Господь: вот, один народ, и один у всех язык; и вот что начали они делать, и не отстанут они от того, что задумали делать;

сойдем же и смешаем там язык их, так чтобы один не понимал речи другого.

Figure 20　The target Russian-language page: The global gateway isn't very elegant-looking, but it will be fixed in the next Hands-On chapter.

Credit: Natalia Kisseleva provided translation and editing support. She is an ATA-accredited translator and can be contacted at **www.atanet.org.**

10

WRITING FOR A GLOBAL AUDIENCE

Writing for a global audience demands a global writing style—a style that is clear, concise, culture-neutral, and easy to translate. Too often, companies translate their source-language web sites without giving much thought to the text. Just because text is effective in the source-language site is no guarantee it will be effective in the target-language site, no matter how well it's translated. Given the cost and complexities of translation, you can save a lot of time and money by investing resources into your source text before it becomes target text. This chapter will help you fine-tune your writing for the world and show you some of the systems companies rely on to create "globally friendly" text.

WRITING FOR TRANSLATION

Writing for the world requires writing for translators. They are an important audience, and often overlooked. If they don't clearly understand what you're trying to say, neither will the rest of the world. Spend the time preparing the text so that they understand it and can easily translate it. The following guidelines will help you create translation-ready, globally friendly text:

- **Keep it short.** The ideal sentence length is between 5 and 25 words. A word limit forces writers to communicate in shorter sentences, generally resulting in clearer sentences.

- **Avoid Americanisms, clichés, puns, word play, and slang.** Words and phrases such as "home run," "phat," and "on the wagon" don't travel well, sometimes not even within the U.S., let alone outside it.

A Few Bad Phrases...

Clichés should be avoided in any language, particularly when they are destined to be translated into another language. Some of the more common ones to avoid include:

- Time is on our side.
- Down to the wire.
- Throw caution to the wind.
- Time is money.
- A walk in the park.
- Waking up on the wrong side of the bed.
- Don't let the cat out of the bag.
- If the shoe fits.

- **Avoid marketing lingo and acronyms.** The world has not yet embraced such industry buzzwords as "action item," "viral marketing," and "killer app," and acronyms such as CRM (customer relationship management) and ASAP are not globally understood. Furthermore, translating these terms can be difficult (and prone to error); for example, "viral marketing," in another language, could easily end up sounding like something one would rather avoid than catch.

- **Don't be cute.** Humor is highly culture-specific and rarely translates well.

- **Punctuate properly.** Sloppy punctuation, in addition to confusing both readers and translators, can wreak havoc on machine-translation software.

- **Write in complete sentences.** Sentence fragments might make sense in English, but they are difficult to translate.

- **Be specific.** Ambiguity almost always leads to translator questions.

- **Avoid analogies and metaphors that aren't relevant to other cultures.** For example, "feeling like you hit a home run" won't mean much to people who don't even know what a home run is.

- **Spell check manually as well as automatically.** Spell check software catches only misspelled words; it won't always catch misplaced words. When writing for translation, misplaced words could do more damage than misspelled words, as they can change the meaning of the sentence.

- **Be consistent.** Don't describe the same object twice using different terms. If you're talking about a yacht in one sentence, don't call it a pleasure craft in the next sentence and a boat in the third. Although you might feel the urge to describe the same object differently to avoid sounding repetitive, you'll find that translators often prefer repetition to creativity.

269

LANGUAGE, SIMPLIFIED

Language is inherently challenging to translate because it is so inherently flexible. In the English language, for example, a noun is rarely just a noun. Consider the word *test*, which is both a noun (taking a test) and a verb (when you test someone). Language would be a lot easier to translate if it were simplified or controlled. If *test* were used only as a noun, for example, translators (machine and human) would have less room for error because any sentence using that word would be less ambiguous.

Many companies cannot afford to leave room for ambiguity, so they develop what's known as a *controlled language* (*CL*). A controlled language, also known as simplified language, is basically a thorough and rigid style guide. A CL can improve the clarity and consistency of source-language text and improve the quality of the translated text (as well as the speed at which it's translated). To ensure that writers follow the CL rules, many companies rely on CL software. As shown in Figure 10.1, you can purchase software that can be customized to enforce your company's specific CL.

Figure 10.1 Software to help you keep it simple. Maxit is a software tool that can be customized to scan your text files according to your company's simplified/controlled English rules.

Many companies rely on CL as a means of prepping text for machine translation (MT) software. By creating source text that follows more predictable patterns, MT software can be remarkably effective; as demonstrated in Chapter 9, "Computer-Aided Translation (CAT)," it's the unpredictability of text that generally confuses MT software. The CL workflow, as shown in Figure 10.2, varies depending on your needs. Companies that use CL tend to produce a high volume of text with a low tolerance for error. And the text is not the sort of text you'll find in a marketing brochure; it's usually technical and practical in nature. Two companies that have had success with CL are General Motors and Boeing.

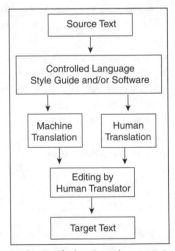

Figure 10.2 Controlled language workflow: By enforcing rules on the source text, the target text can be more consistently and rapidly produced.

Controlled Language and General Motors

General Motors developed a CL program primarily to reduce the translation costs of its service manuals. Known as the Controlled Automotive Service Language (CASL), it set parameters for English text so that it would be more effectively and less expensively machine-translated into Canadian French. Kurt Godden, who managed CASL at GM, says, "The model year 2000 Chevrolet Metro service manual was written in CASL English, machine-translated to French, edited by trained translators, and delivered to the market in both CASL English and French on time and under budget."

According to Godden, the Chevy Metro project involved five organizations, three companies, and three countries, so the challenges in this project were more organizational than technical. The participants must buy into the new process and change their behavior to support it. Despite your best management skills, a CL project cannot succeed if you don't have the full support of your writers. Fortunately, General Motors did have writer buy-in. "We anticipated a certain amount of resistance from the writers, but were surprised by their enthusiastic reception," says Godden. "They loved the project, found the software quite easy to use, and told us that it dramatically improved the quality of their writing. They were so enthusiastic that we actually made a 20-minute video that included many author interviews to use during the training of the other 300 to 400 authors."

Although many companies develop CLs with the goal of incorporating machine translation, some companies rely on CLs purely to improve the quality and consistency of their human translation. "If you talk to professional translators, they will always tell you that it is extremely important to have high-quality source text in order to obtain high quality translations," says Godden. "They will even give you lists of source language features to avoid in order to make their job easier." If you do decide to incorporate machine translation, you'll still need human translators to provide a round of editing after the machine translation is complete. Even the best-controlled language needs a little work after machine translation, but Godden says the work is minimal enough to justify the investment: "In my opinion—and there is evidence to back this up—using controlled language will provide a positive ROI for both human and machine translation. But only if the controlled language is defined properly, and implemented correctly."

Simplified English and Boeing

Because the official language of the aerospace industry is English, Boeing doesn't need to translate its documentation. However, Boeing does need a controlled language, in this case known as Simplified English (SE). The aerospace industry produces voluminous, mission-critical airline maintenance manuals in English, yet

271

airline mechanics around the world are not all native English speakers. In the late 1970s, the European Association of Aerospace Industries (AECMA) worked with its member companies to develop a CL that would be used for all documentation. Simplified English ensures that the text is easy for non-native speakers to understand. Richard Wojcik, associate technical fellow at Boeing, was involved in creating the rules that documentation writers now follow.

Initially, there was a fair amount of resistance to these rules. This is understandable, particularly because the Simplified English manual is more than 300 pages long. "There are a lot of different groups in Boeing who must use Simplified English," says Wojcik. "I have encountered attitudes that range from extreme opposition to enthusiastic acceptance. Most engineers seem to fall into a middle category. If they are told that Simplified English is necessary, then they make a good-faith effort to do the best they can to comply." The Simplified English rules can easily take a month to learn (see the sidebar "Simplified English, in Depth"). Key features of the rules include the following:

- Sentence length (20 or 25 words maximum)

- Paragraph length (6 sentences maximum)

- Noun cluster length (3 words or less)

- Missing articles not allowed

- Multiple commands not allowed in a single sentence

In 1990, these rules were incorporated into the Boeing Simplified English Checker software. This tool helps writers and editors quickly evaluate their text.

Simplified English, in Depth

Richard Wojcik highlights two of the SE rules and explains their importance:

- **RULE: 2.3 When appropriate, use an article (the, a, an) or a demonstrative adjective (this, these) before a noun.**

This is especially useful to non-native speakers because English often does not place suffixes or prefixes on words to indicate what part of speech or grammatical role they have. For example, the word "clean" in "clean surfaces" could be either a verb or an adjective. If you say "Clean the surfaces" or "the clean surfaces," then the reader knows immediately whether "clean" is a verb or an adjective.

continues

┌─Simplified English, in Depth   (continued)─────────────────────

■   **RULE: 2.1 Do not make noun clusters of more than three nouns.**

English speakers, especially engineers, love to create long noun clusters in an effort to describe the function, shape, or location of objects. The problem is that English does not always attach suffixes or prefixes that indicate the grammatical roles of words in noun clusters. So non-native English speakers find it difficult to figure out how to interpret sequences like "main gear onboard door retraction winch handle." Simplified English forces writers to reword such monstrosities into more digestible chunks— for example, "the retraction winch handle to the inboard door of the main gear."

Source: Richard Wojcik, Boeing, 2002.

In the past year, Boeing offered its SE Checker as a commercial product and has received a great deal of interest (see Figure 10.3). "This increasing demand for controlled language has been driven by the need to compete in global markets," says Wojcik.

Figure 10.3   The Boeing Simplified English Checker web site: This tool is now being sold to other companies who want to automate their CL programs (**www.boeing.com/assocproducts/sechecker**).

Know When to Use It, When to Lose It

The controlled language movement has gained momentum—even within the U.S. government (see Figure 10.4). And the movement is not unique to the U.S.; Sweden has pursued a similar program to make its government documents easier to read, and Germany has pursued simplified spelling for years, though not without resistance. In industries and companies where poorly translated languages can put lives at risk, CL is rapidly becoming a necessity.

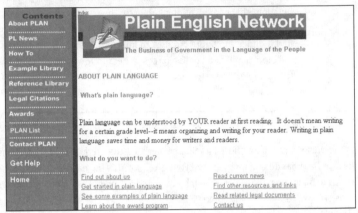

Figure 10.4   Plain English: A group of U.S. government volunteers are campaigning to make their government a little more reader-friendly.

CL is not appropriate for all organizations, however. If you're still struggling to develop an efficient writing and translation workflow, you probably don't want to add controlled languages into the mix. But if your company is ready and prepared to make the investment, be sure to pick the right projects. For example, controlled languages work best with text that is less marketing oriented and more product focused. Projects such as maintenance manuals and product-support web pages are among the best choices for developing controlled languages. Finally, the success of CL requires a high-level champion within your organization. CL issues are so complex and so challenging that you'll need to educate a lot of people before the dream becomes a reality.

ONE WORLD, MANY STYLES

A global writing style may be easy to translate, but can also be a little too boring or ineffective for specific locales. That's okay, because after you've developed a global style, you can then add any number of local styles.

- **The global and the local:** In addition to modifying the message you send to each market, you can modify the style of writing. American writing, when translated literally into Asian languages, often comes across as too strong, too informal, and a bit rude. Asian writing rarely announces the thesis in the first few sentences or takes a combative stance. A marketing brochure that criticizes the competition might come across as more abrasive than persuasive to an Asian audience. To avoid this problem, work with translators who are qualified to rewrite the text to better suit the audience (without changing the meaning of the text).

- **The literal and the loose:** Sometimes you need text to be translated with no deviation; other times you can let your translators have a little fun. The following paragraphs were taken from different sections of the Adobe web site. Notice how they differ in tone and overall complexity.

Adobe Illustrator Marketing Text

Adobe Illustrator defines the future of vector graphics with groundbreaking creative options and powerful tools to publish artwork on the Web, in print, everywhere. Produce superb web graphics using symbols and innovative slicing options. Explore creative ideas with live distortion tools. Publish in record time with dynamic data-driven graphics and other productivity features.

Adobe Illustrator Product Support Text

Problem: When you try to draw a new path or continue a selected path with the pencil or paintbrush tool in Adobe Illustrator, a nearby object is reshaped or deleted instead.
Solution: Move the pencil or paintbrush tool until a small "x" appears next to the cursor, and then begin drawing the new path.

275

The first paragraph relies on engaging language, such as "Explore creative ideas" and "Defines the future," and the second paragraph relies on more utilitarian language, such as "Move the pencil" and "When you try to draw." Each paragraph might require a different translator; some translators are better at literal translation, and others are more creative. Literal translation is necessary for documentation, legalese, or anything you might want to have machine-translated. For marketing materials, however, you want the resulting text to sound a lot more engaging than an instruction sheet.

Keep It Short

On the Internet, words are cheap. If you want to add a few extra pages of promotional text, just tack on a few extra web pages. Adding pages to a product catalog could cost thousands of dollars, but there are few, if any, added costs to additional web pages. Just because you can easily add a few extra web pages, however, doesn't mean you should. Steve Krug, author of *Don't Make Me Think* (New Riders Publishing, 2001), advocates ruthless editing to web pages. By simply cutting the fat from your text, you will...

- Reduce the noise level of the web page.

- Emphasize the useful content that remains.

- Make web pages shorter and therefore more easily scanned.

I'd like to add yet another benefit to the mix: *You'll save a lot of time and money*.

On the *multilingual* Internet, words are not so cheap. A few extra web pages, when translated into several languages, can quickly cost a few hundred extra dollars. Suddenly, wordiness has a price, and a little ruthless editing isn't such a bad idea. Consider the following paragraph from the web site of the telecommunications company, Global Crossing (**www.globalcrossing.com**). With a little creative editing, it can by reduced by nearly half:

Before: 97 words

Welcome to the world of Global Crossing. The premier provider of state-of-the-art digital communications and networking services to global enterprises. Enabling corporations and governments to link with partners, clients, suppliers, employees and the global community. Empowering them with an IP infrastructure that can support any voice, data or multimedia application. Increasing their efficiency by expanding their reach. Our seamless, fiber-optic network spans nearly 100,000 route miles and connects its users to more than 200 major cities. So no matter where you are or where you want your information to go, Global Crossing makes that connection a reality.

After: 59 words

Global Crossing provides digital communications and networking services to global enterprises. Our seamless, fiber-optic network spans nearly 100,000 route miles and 200 major cities, enabling corporations and governments to link with partners, clients, suppliers, employees and the global community. No matter where you are or where you want your information to go, Global Crossing makes that connection a reality.

The second paragraph contains the same amount of information as the first paragraph, just a bit less hyperbole. First, the sentence "Welcome to the world of Global Crossing" sentence was dropped, and then empty words and phrases, such as "empowering," state-of-the-art," and "premier provider," were edited out. The result is a paragraph that conveys the same message in less time and, best of all, costs 40% less to translate.

- **Editing saves money.** Editing goes to your bottom line. If you could shave just 20% of the text from your 100,000-word web site, you would save anywhere from $3,500 to $5,000 per language. If you're planning on launching five localized sites, that's a savings of up to $25,000. If the site is constantly adding text, consider adding a full-time editor; the person's salary could well be covered by reduced translation costs.

- **Editing saves time.** Editing takes time initially, but it saves time overall. Suppose you spend an extra day editing a new product description before translation. If the resulting text is a bit shorter and clearer, your translators will have fewer questions and less text to translate, resulting in a faster turnaround time. That one day of editing could save you several days of translation.

Edit Before You Translate

The translation firm ArchiText (**www.architext-usa.com**) offers an editing service called Abreve that edits down the source text before translation, sometimes by as much as 40% (see Figure 10.5). Although this service adds upfront costs to the project, ArchiText claims clients still end up saving money.

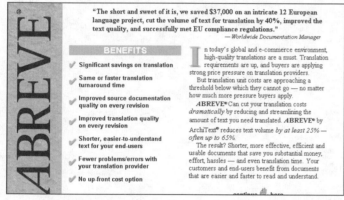

Figure 10.5 A translation company that also edits.

ELEMENTS OF STYLE

A poorly written web page will be reflected in poorly written translations around the world for all to see, but a well-written web page has the potential to increase sales and set you apart from your competitors (who probably have their share of poorly written web pages).

Too many organizations invest more resources in the visual elements of a web site than the textual elements. Although global web design is important and will be covered in the following chapter, it's not more important than text—and often it's less important. As you manage localization projects, don't underestimate the power of the written word, in any language.

11

WORLD WIDE DESIGN

As if it wasn't hard enough designing for users within one country, now you've got to worry about users in other countries. Although you can't please everyone, you can develop an understanding of how different cultures interact with your web site and perceive its visual elements, such as colors and icons. Design is a language all its own and, like all languages, is not shared by everyone. The first half of this chapter focuses on making your site globally usable, the second half on making your site locally acceptable.

■ **Usability:** Before people around the world can use your web site, they first have to find your web site. And when they get there, the site has to be usable, no matter what language they speak or how sophisticated their web skills.

Questions:

Can your international audience find their localized web sites?

Do the web pages load quickly on their browsers?

Do the visual elements communicate the intended meaning?

■ **Acceptability:** People have a hard time accepting web sites that they don't trust. The site itself may be usable, but if it isn't culturally sensitive, it still might not get the sale.

Questions:

Is the design culturally sensitive?

Do the visual elements create a positive impression?

Does the site appear credible and trustworthy?

BUILDING THE GLOBAL TEMPLATE

Increasingly, companies rely on global design templates to both streamline resources and promote a consistent message globally. The localized IBM web sites, shown in Figure 11.1, share a template that includes a navigation system, color scheme, and typeface, and still allows room for localized content and promotions. A *global template* supports the inherent need of multinational companies to convey a global image, but with a local touch. A template also supports a distributed web management structure; while the global design team manages the global template, the local design teams are free to manage the local portions of their web sites. However, a global template may not work for your organization; you might decide to create a completely localized web site for each locale.

281

Figure 11.1 IBM's global template allows local variations while retaining a global consistency.

Honda does not rely on a global template, as shown in Figure 11.2. The only element tying these sites together is the Honda logo. It's likely that Honda relies on local web teams who operate their sites independently of one another. This strategy is not necessarily a bad one. Local web teams can be more effective if they are free to design and redesign their sites to serve their audiences. Nevertheless, the prevailing trend is to not reinvent the wheel for each market. A global template enables companies to make the most of one design, to centralize control, and to convey a consistent image to the world.

Figure 11.2 Honda relies an entirely new web design for each locale.

BUILDING THE GLOBAL GATEWAY

Much overlooked in web design is the navigation system that directs users to their localized sites. Too often these "global gateways" are buried at the bottom of home pages, as shown with Compaq in Figure 11.3. Picture a user who doesn't speak English visiting this page. Will that person have the patience to search for the pull-down menu, and will that person even understand what the pull-down menu is for?

Figure 11.3   Can you find the Compaq gateway?

Now picture that same person visiting the Giant Bicycles home page: The first page the person sees is a "splash gateway" with the phrase **Select your country of residence** written in seven languages above the pull-down menu (see Figure 11.4). There is no chance of this person missing out on his or her locale. If the locale does not exist, this too is easily deduced. Don't underestimate the importance of a global gateway; it plays a critical role in the success of your localized web sites. A successful global gateway requires much more than just a pull-down menu or splash page; it requires a combination of design elements and technologies that, when used together, ensure that users find their localized web pages as quickly and effortlessly as possible.

Figure 11.4   You can't miss the Giant Bicycles gateway.

Degrading Gracefully, Globally

Graceful degradation is the practice of building web pages so that they adapt themselves to the user's browser. If a user has the latest browser, the web page makes use of the latest HTML features, but if not, the web site degrades gracefully so that older browsers can still access the site's basic features. A classic example of this strategy is a web site that presents Flash pages to users with Flash viewers and HTML pages to those who do not. The benefit of graceful degradation is that nobody gets left out. Your global gateway should also degrade gracefully. The four strategies shown in Figure 11.5 can be used in tandem to ensure that users are directed to their appropriate web pages. If the first strategy doesn't work, you move on to the next strategy, and so on.

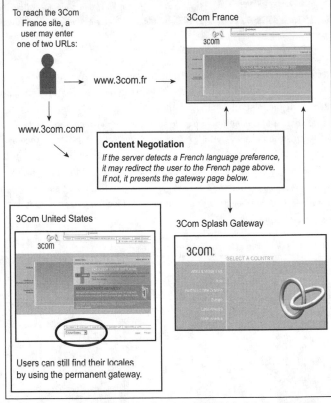

Figure 11.5   Graceful degradation in global gateways.

These best practices for graceful degradation of global gateways are explained in the following sections:

1. **First, use the front door.** In a perfect world, people would go to their localized sites by typing in locale-specific URLs, like **www.yahoo.co.jp** for Japan and **www.amazon.de** for Germany.

International domain names are covered in detail in Chapter 14, "Mastering Your (Country) Domain."

2. **Then use content negotiation.** If people don't try the front door, you can kindly escort them to their localized sites with the help of content negotiation. Content negotiation is a still-developing technique for detecting the browser's language preference and serving the web page with the matching language. Once you serve the matching web page, you should store a cookie on the user's computer so you can remember his or her language preference.

3. **Have a splash gateway ready.** If content negotiation fails, which happens occasionally, send users to a splash gateway where they can select a country or language. After making a selection, this preference should be stored as a cookie on their computers so that they don't have to keep clicking through the gateway every time they return to the site.

4. **Design a permanent gateway.** Finally, embed a gateway prominently on every web page of your site—and display it in such a way that non-English speakers understand how to use it.

Content Negotiation Explained

Servers and browsers send a lot of information back and forth that web users never see. For example, the browser tells the server the types of documents it can accept, and the server tells the browser what types of documents are available. During these exchanges of information, the browser can also tell the server what language web page to send, and, if properly configured, the server will do just that.

This process is known as *content negotiation*. Although there are various flavors of content negotiation currently in use and in development, I'll focus on the most commonly used method: server-driven negotiation. With server-driven negotiation, the server responds to the **accept_language** HTTP header. In the header example shown in the following line, it tells the server that Brazilian Portuguese is the preferred language, and, if it isn't available, to send U.S. English.

HTTP_ACCEPT_LANGUAGE = pt-br, en-us

If neither language is available, the server sends whatever default page it's configured to serve. The **accept_language** of your browser typically matches your operating system's default language, but Internet Explorer and Netscape allow you to manually change the setting (see Figures 11.6 and 11.7). You can list one or many preferred languages. The language at the top of the list is the language you want to see first when you visit a web site.

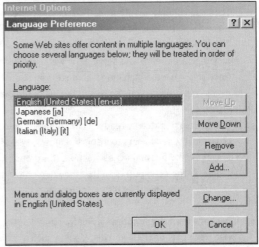

Figure 11.6   To change language preferences in Internet Explorer, go to Tools, Internet Options.

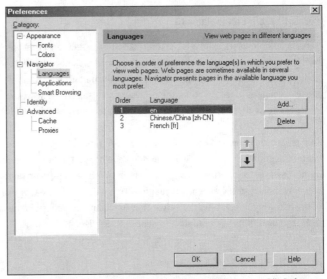

Figure 11.7   To change language preferences in Netscape Navigator, go to Edit, Preferences.

For content negotiation to work, the server must be configured to respond to the **accept_language** header. Although Apache and Windows 2000 servers support content negotiation, not all companies make use of this feature. Deciding which browser is supposed to get which language adds overhead to the server and can slow down response time. The Internet Engineering Task Force (IETF) is developing a more robust solution, known as transparent content negotiation, which is supposed to lighten the load on the server. Many companies aren't waiting for a better solution. Google, one of the world's busiest web sites, make extensive use of content negotiation for the languages it supports.

FYI

To Learn More About Content Negotiation...

- Visit the IETF Working Group at **www.imc.org/ietf-medfree/index.html**.

- The HTTP description of content negotiation is located at **www.w3.org/Protocols/rfc2616/rfc2616-sec12.html**.

- To configure the Apache server for content negotiation, visit **http://httpd.apache.org/docs/content-negotiation.html**.

- For tips on using Active Server Pages (ASP) to support content negotiation, check out **http://msdn.microsoft.com/msdnmag/issues/0700/localize/localize.asp**.

Older browsers do not support content negotiation, so don't rely on it exclusively. Even if you do offer content negotiation, you'll find browsers that request languages your site doesn't offer. You'll need to specify a default page to serve if the requested language isn't available—and make sure a global gateway is clearly located on this page. An excellent site to play with content negotiation is **www.trigeminal.com**. The site is localized into 48 languages, so you can test a wide range of language preferences. First, set your browser's language preference to Japanese, and then refresh the web page and watch the language adjust to your preference (see Figure 11.8).

Figure 11.8   Content negotiation in action at **www.trigeminal.com**.

Cookies

Think of *cookies* as name tags for computers. These name tags are sent by web servers to the computers of web site visitors. Many web sites rely on cookies to maintain a more personal relationship with their visitors. A cookie can be used to remember your name when you return to the site as well as to track your buying preferences. Language preference is often added to the list of data stored in cookies. After you know a person's language preference, your site no longer has to present a splash gateway when he or she returns. Look for the language preferences in the following two cookies:

Burton cookie
languageID JP
www.burton.com/
0 3892912128 29505807 951062016 29455304 *

eTrade cookie
ghome
customer:en_US:US
etrade.com/
0 953329280 31869445 48765728 29455457 *

The Burton cookie specifies a Japanese language preference, and the eTrade cookie specifies U.S. English. Cookies are a wonderful development for web sites, but users don't always trust them. Some browsers are set to block cookies, so always have a backup plan ready. For browsers that do accept cookies, make allowances for users who might want to change their language preference later. That's why a permanent global gateway is crucial; it's the only simple way a user can escape out of a given language.

Gateways

You can't go far on the Internet today without running into a global gateway. It might be hidden at the bottom of a web page or could be an entire web page, forcing you to make a selection before moving forward. Figure 11.9 shows a few examples of global gateways.

Figure 11.9   Global gateways are a common site on the Internet.

There's a healthy debate raging over whether to use a splash gateway for first-time visitors, as E*TRADE does, or skip the splash page and get right to the home page, with a gateway readily available, as in the Palm site (see Figures 11.10 and 11.11). Neither approach is necessarily right or wrong. You have to decide which approach works best for you and your users. If the majority of your users speak one language, it may make sense to skip the splash page and go straight to their language, like the Palm home page. Those who don't speak the default language then navigate to their localized pages by using the gateway. However, if you want to treat all your users equally and leave no room for error, you must use a splash page.

Figure 11.10   Palm treats all first-time visitors to its .com address as English speakers. The gateway is located in the upper-right corner.

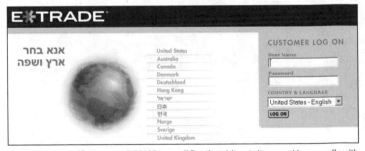

Figure 11.11   E*TRADE treats all first-time visitors to its .com address equally, with a splash gateway.

THE ART OF THE GLOBAL GATEWAY

The difference between an average gateway and an excellent gateway is measured, ultimately, in traffic. Most companies do a poor job of directing users to their local-ized web sites, so it's best not to blindly imitate other sites. There are a number of subtle but important issues, discussed in the following section, to be aware of as you design your gateway strategy.

Country or Language or Both?

If you've localized your web site according to language, you'll need a language gate-way and, if you've localized by country, a country gateway. But what if you've done both? Ikea, shown in Figure 11.12, uses a country gateway initially; after users select a country, it then presents a language selection. This hierarchy is important for countries with more than one official language, such as Canada or Switzerland.

Figure 11.12   Ikea presents a country selection first, and then a language selection when users get to the country site.

To Pull Down or Not to Pull Down?

Pull-down menus are not an ideal solution for gateways because they hide the most important information: the languages or countries. The common argument for using a pull-down is that the site doesn't have enough room to list all the choices, but Macromedia effectively displays 13 choices relatively unobtrusively (see Figure 11.13).

Figure 11.13 A better solution than a pull-down menu.

The other problem with a pull-down menu is that it, like your HTML page, is limited to one character set. That means unless you use the Unicode character set, you'll have difficulty representing all languages in their native scripts. Because Unicode is not yet a realistic option for most companies, they use only Latin characters in the pull-down menu. It's for this reason that you often see "Japanese" on a pull-down menu instead of actual Japanese characters. The only workaround is to follow Symantec's lead, shown in Figure 11.14, and embed non-Latin text in graphics separate from the pull-down menu.

Figure 11.14 Symantec uses graphics with embedded Asian text because the pull-down menu supports only the display of Latin text.

When Words Fail

The phrase "select your language" or "select your country" doesn't mean much to people who don't speak English. Yet many companies rely on these phrases for their gateways. As an alternative, use a visual element that says "global" without relying on words, such as a globe icon or a map. For example, the Palm gateway relies on a visual of a world map, and UPS relies on a globe icon (see Figure 11.15).

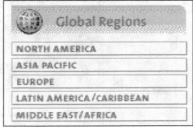

Figure 11.15   Palm (on the left) uses a world map to make its gateway clear to non-English speakers. UPS (on the right) uses a globe icon, a visual that takes up even less real estate than a world map.

Translate Your Gateway

Translating the text of a global gateway might seem obvious, but many web sites fail to do it. For example, the link to a Spanish-language site should read **Español** rather than **Spanish**. The same philosophy applies to country links (use **Deutschland** rather than **Germany**) and any other text or instructions on the gateway. As illustrated in Figures 11.16 through 11.18, not all web sites do an equally good job of translating gateways.

Figure 11.16   Best: Notice the use of regional maps and how country names are translated into the local languages.

Figure 11.17   Good: Some of the country names are translated, but not all.

Figure 11.18   Bad: None of the country names are translated into
the local language.

And Just to Be Safe...

Yahoo! offers an introductory splash page for people who click on the Japan link
from the **.com** page; the splash page instructs web users on how to download the
necessary Japanese font and properly view Japanese text (see Figure 11.19). If
someone comes in through the **.co.jp** address, this Informational page is not presented, as it is assumed that person already knows the basics.

Yahoo! Japan

Yahoo! Japan is a site much like Yahoo! but tailor-made for Japanese users. You'll find lots of Japanese sites you haven't seen before, and the list keeps growing!

Note: You need to be able to view Japanese characters through your Web browser in order to properly view Yahoo! Japan.

- Windows Users
  - **Windows 95** and NT users will need Japanese language support (e.g., UnionWay or AsiaSurf) and a browser that supports Japanese (e.g., Netscape Communicator or Microsoft Internet Explorer).
  - **Windows 3.1** users will need Japanese language support (e.g., UnionWay) and a browser that supports Japanese (e.g., Netscape Communicator or Microsoft Internet Explorer).
- Macintosh users (running System 7.1 or later) need to load the Japanese Language Kit (available through most Apple resellers) as well as a browser that supports Japanese (e.g., Netscape Communicator)

Figure 11.19 Yahoo! helps users download the font they need to view Japanese characters.

DESIGN FOR SLOW CONNECTIONS

After people make it to their localized web sites, they don't want to wait endlessly for the web pages to load. Yet most of them do just that, day after day, because companies have built "overweight" web sites. An *overweight web site* is one that uses too many graphics or too much complex scripting (or both). Put simply, the greater the weight, the greater the wait. Although overweight web sites can be a mild frustration for users in the United States, they are major obstacles in countries where high-speed connections are less common. In fact, even in the U.S., only 10% of all homes have high-speed connections.

When Is a Web Site Overweight?

The heavier a web page, the longer visitors must wait for it to load. Whether end users grow irritated depends on how long they are accustomed to waiting for an "average" web page to load. The average weight—89KB—was calculated by weighing the home pages of 300 major web sites across several industries (see Table 11.1). The weighing process entailed adding up the total weight (in kilobytes) of all graphics, HTML text, and scripting. Many home pages were lightweight, such as Lycos at 30KB and Yahoo! at 37KB, but the majority of pages were badly overweight, ranging from 80KB to well over 400KB.

Table 11.1 Selected Web Site Weights (in Kilobytes)

Site	Weight
Charles Schwab	45KB
Gap	89KB
Barnes and Noble	109KB
Monster.com	156KB
Victoria's Secret	173KB
CNN	198KB

Although you want a site that loads more quickly than your competitor's, you should go one step further and study the Internet as a whole. Sites also need to be competitive with the most-visited sites on the Internet, such as Yahoo! or Lycos. These web sites, although they might not be direct competitors, have conditioned consumers not to wait too long for a web page to display. To give you an idea of how weight affects download time, the Yahoo! home page takes approximately five seconds to load using a 56Kbps modem. Contrast that to the Victoria's Secret site, which takes more than 12 seconds to load. Now imagine what a user in Germany with a 28Kbps modem must go through to view that same site. To keep the weight off your web site, use the following strategies:

- **Remove unnecessary graphics.** The majority of sites use graphics recklessly. The average home page uses 28 graphics, a remarkably high number, given that Yahoo! uses only 4 graphics.

- **Remove unnecessary functionality.** The many bells and whistles that web pages feature often require a great deal of scripting, sometimes hundreds of lines worth. Even scripting can lead to unnecessarily overweight web pages.

- **Set a weight limit (and maintain it).** If something is added to your home page, something else must be removed. This "zero sum game" discipline might be challenging to enforce at first, but over time it will prevent the inevitable flood of added products and announcements from dragging down your site.

Weight Loss Begins at Home

Most companies prefer to develop localized sites that maintain the same look and feel of their source-language site. If the home page is overweight, however, the localized sites will only exacerbate the problem (see sidebar "Oracle Versus ESPN").

Oracle Versus ESPN

The ESPN English home page is three times heavier than the Oracle English home page, primarily because of its reliance on graphics (see Figure 11.20).

Figure 11.20 ESPN English (weight: 185KB) and Oracle English (weight: 35KB).

continues

Oracle Versus ESPN   (continued)

When localized into Spanish, both sites retain the same look and feel (see Figure 11.21). Unfortunately, ESPN also retains its weight, resulting in frustrating waits for users with slow connections. ESPN, in striving to maintain the same look and feel in the Spanish-language site, developed a site that means longer waits for users around the world. Ironically, ESPN caters to consumers, who generally have slower connections than Oracle's audience, which is businesses.

Figure 11.21   ESPN Spanish (weight: 186KB) and Oracle Spanish (weight: 37KB).

Graphics are not the enemy, but when taking a site global, they can quickly become a liability. If your company can agree to setting and maintaining strict weight limits, you can ensure that your audience will not be left waiting.

Text and Graphics Don't Mix

Embedding text within graphics is common in web design, yet it often leads to time-consuming and expensive localization projects. Suppose you localize a web site into five languages and the navigation bar has 10 buttons, each with embedded text. Localizing this navigation bar will require creating 50 new buttons (10 per language). Localization firms may charge anywhere from $25 to $100 per graphic—resulting in anywhere from $1,250 to $5,000 in costs.

Considering that some sites use upward of 40 graphics with embedded text, the costs can quickly add up. Had these buttons been mostly converted to text-only links, the cost and time savings would be substantial. Now consider the ongoing maintenance costs of all those graphics. Should the text in one button change, it must be replicated across every language. Companies with frequently updated web sites would be wise to ensure that their most dynamic text is not embedded within graphics.

The Use (and Abuse) of Flash

Flash is an animation software tool that allows developers to create effects ranging from animated banner ads to full-scale web sites. To view a Flash file, users must have the necessary plug-in installed (available free). Macromedia claims that more than 95% of all U.S. web users have this plug-in installed, yet having the plug-in installed doesn't make up for a slow connection. It's common practice to develop introductory pages that warn the user of the impending Flash graphics and provide links for downloading the plug-in from the Macromedia site.

Loading, Please Wait...

Although Flash can be used to create compact graphics, it can also be used to create enormous graphics, which more often than not seems to be the case. Typically, a company develops a Flash site in addition to an HTML site and serves the Flash site only to browsers with the Flash plug-in installed. The flaw with this system is that usually no distinction is made as to the user's connection speed, so if you have Flash installed, you get the heavier, slower-loading site, regardless of your connection speed. Many web sites do not bother to offer HTML alternatives (see Figure 11.22), and this approach discriminates against users with slower connections.

This site requires the Flash 5 plugin. Click the Hanro-logo above to enter. If you don't see the Hanro-logo, click here to download the Flash plugin.

Figure 11.22   Hanro provides its site in German and English, but users without Flash will never know because there's no HTML alternative.

Macromedia (**www.macromedia.com**) offers the following guidelines when using Flash:

■ **Avoid unnecessary intros.** Flash introductions only get in the way of the user and what the user wants: the home page. If you find you must use an introduction, make the "skip intro" option easy to find.

■ **Provide logical navigation and interactivity.** You must build navigation, such as the much-used Back button, into your Flash web site. If you don't, users will get confused, irritated, or both.

■ **Don't overuse animation.** Unless your web site is selling a product or service that requires animation, you probably don't need to use much animation on your site. Animation can quickly lead to an overweight web site, so use it judiciously.

■ **Use sound sparingly.** Sound files also add considerably to the site's total weight and rarely add much to the end user's experience. If you must use sound, give the web user the option of turning it on (instead of forcing the user to turn it off).

■ **Target low-bandwidth users.** Macromedia recommends that the home page (including Flash files, HTML, and images) should be less than 40KB total. Many web sites use Flash files that weigh in excess of 100KB.

The Danger of DHTML

Dynamic HTML (*DHTML*) is a combination of scripts and standards that have evolved to make web pages more animated and interactive. Put simply, DHTML enables a web page to Interact wIth the user long after It has been fully downloaded. The most popular technologies used in DHTML are JavaScript and cascading style sheets (CSS).

Developers use DHTML to create effects as simple as rollovers, requiring only a few lines of code, to complex pull-down menus, requiring several thousand lines of code. The Victoria's Secret site uses DHTML to create pull-down navigation menus (a sample is shown in Figure 11.23). The danger with DHTML is using too much of it.

Figure 11.23 Victoria's Secret relies on extensive DHTML for its navigation menu.

To create this level of functionality, Victoria's Secret used more than 20 text pages of scripting, adding up to 43KB. The entire Yahoo! home page, at 37KB—text and graphics combined—weighs less than the scripting on the Victoria's Secret site. In addition to sheer weight, DHTML taxes the speed of the browser. Think of DHTML as a small software application. When it's first loaded into your browser, it must initially boot up. The more complex the script, the longer this process will take, further delaying the display of a web page. Although DHTML can produce impressive functionality, if overused it can also cause sluggish web pages and frustrated users around the world.

301

Designing for Languages That Move in a Different Direction

Hebrew and Arabic are bi-directional (bidi) languages. The text reads from right to left, with numerals and English-language words reading from left to right. Until recently, web browsers didn't properly support the display of bidi text, so developers had to create "visual" pages that were in fact written backward. Today, an Arabic or Hebrew web page can be written natively and displayed correctly in IE 5 and higher or Netscape 4.61 and higher. Chinese can be written from left to right or top to bottom. However, HTML does not support vertical text display, so you'll have to embed text in graphics to create this effect.

You'll learn more about bidi and Asian text and web pages in "Hands-On: Chinese and Japanese" and "Hands-On: Arabic."

CULTURALLY SENSITIVE DESIGN

Although it's dangerous to make sweeping statements about any culture—after all, not all Americans enjoy baseball and apple pie—often you can identify personalities and predispositions common to the majority of people. Twenty years ago, cultural anthropologist Geert Hofstede set out to identify and classify these personalities and predispositions. He surveyed more than 100,000 IBM employees in more than 60 countries. In his groundbreaking book, *Culture's Consequences, International Differences in Work-Related Values*, he theorized that because the employees all shared a common corporate culture, any major differences and similarities between nationalities could be largely attributed to national culture. Based on the research, Hofstede identified five dimensions of culture:

- Power-distance

- Collectivism vs. individualism

- Femininity vs. masculinity

- Uncertainty avoidance

- Long- vs. short-term orientation

Aaran Marcus, president of the global design firm Aaron Marcus & Associates, and Emilie Gould, professor at Rensselaer Polytechnic Institute, applied Hofstede's dimensions of culture to the practice of web user interface design. You can read the full paper at **www.amanda.com,** but I'll touch on two of these dimensions in the following sections.

Power-Distance

Power-distance (PD) reflects the extent to which people within a culture accept (or expect) unequal power distribution. Hofstede claimed that high PD countries exhibited centralized power structures and clearly defined class distinctions, and low PD countries viewed people as equals. Based on this model, Marcus identified the following design implications:

- Access to information—PD cultures value highly structured designs.

- Focus on expertise, authority, experts—Designs that incorporate official seals and certifications appeal more to high PD cultures.

- Prominence is given to leaders over citizens in high PD cultures.

To see how these issues are reflected in web designs, Marcus highlights two university web sites, shown in Figure 11.24: one for a high PD country, Malaysia, and the other for a low PD country, the Netherlands.

Figure 11.24 University sites in Malaysia, a high PD country, and the Netherlands, a low PD country.

Notice how the Malaysia site features the university's official seal and photographs of faculty, administration, and monumental buildings all within a formal, structured design, and the Netherlands site emphasizes the students amid a loose, almost chaotic design.

Femininity Versus Masculinity

Hofstede examined the traditional roles assigned to gender across cultures. Some cultures have a higher masculinity (MAS) index value than others, as shown in the following list. A high MAS index emphasizes division of labor and roles between genders, and cultures with low MAS ratings blur the differences between the genders.

Country	MAS Value
Japan	93
Austria	79
South Africa	63
U.S.	62
Israel	47
France	43
South Korea	39
Sweden	5

Marcus points to the Woman Excite web site for Japan, shown in Figure 11.25. Japan, with the highest MAS value, is the only country that Excite developed a "woman-only" web site for. Other countries, such as the U.S. and U.K., have sites designed for both genders.

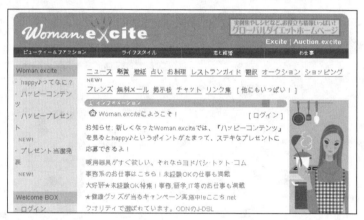

Figure 11.25   The only Excite site developed solely for women is in Japan.

Marcus notes that a culture with a high MAS value might respond better to a navigation interface that stresses exploration and control, and sites with low MAS values would put an emphasis on visual aesthetics.

┌─Just Undo It ───────────────────────────────────────

Nike experienced firsthand the importance of imagery and symbolism in international marketing. The company emblazoned a new line of shoes with the word *Air* written to resemble flames or heat rising off blacktop. The shoes had names such as Air Bakin', Air Melt, Air Grill, and Air B-Que. What Nike did not realize was that the logo's squiggly lines resembled Arabic script for *Allah*, the Arabic name for God. Under threat of a worldwide boycott by Muslims who considered it a sacrilege, Nike recalled the shoes and agreed to build several playgrounds in Muslim communities as part of its apology.

*Source: Web of Culture (**www.webofculture.com**).*

Colors

Don't underestimate the power of color—both positive and negative. From your web site to your logo, take the time to view the colors you use through the eyes of your target audience. For example, the color purple has different meanings in different countries:

U.S.	nobility, bravery
Israel	divinity, the sea
Turkey	nature
Brazil	mourning
England	royalty
Japan	royalty

For a comprehensive chart of colors and what they signify around the world, see Appendix B, "Global Color Chart."

Blue appears to be the most universally positive or neutral color. However, if every web site relied on blue, no web site would ever stand out. When selecting colors, you need to balance cultural acceptability with your unique marketing goals. For instance, just because Asians associate white with death doesn't mean you can't use plenty of white space on your web site. Americans associate black with death, yet there are plenty of black web sites (although most Fortune 500 companies avoid black). By paying close attention to the significance of color, you'll be better prepared to emphasize (or de-emphasize) your corporate colors as you enter new markets.

Icons

It wasn't too long ago that the shopping cart icon first appeared. In the U.S., where shopping carts are a fixture of suburban life, Americans need little education on what this icon represents. But consider this icon in a culture where it's not such a common sight. Is the shopping cart truly the best icon for residents of Paris or Madrid or Moscow, or would a shopping basket be more appropriate (see Figure 11.26)? And what should a mailbox icon look like on a web site? Because different countries use different mailboxes, even this seemingly innocuous icon can present challenges (see Figure 11.27).

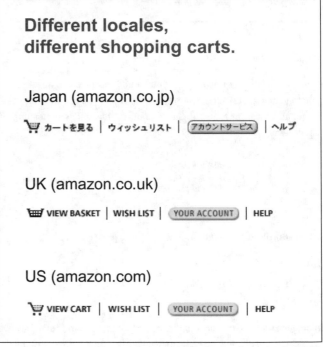

Figure 11.26　Amazon localized its shopping cart icon for the U.K.

Not everyone has a mailbox like this...

or this...

or this.

This icon is the most universally recognized:

Figure 11.27   You've got mail.

307

Not all icons should be avoided. In fact, in some cultures certain icons can have a positive effect. A study by the market research firm Cheskin (**www.cheskin.com**) found that specific icons play an important role in establishing trust for web users, but that the icons vary by culture. For example, Americans recognize the VeriSign logo as a sign of security on web sites. Although VeriSign isn't as well known in Latin America, the word *VeriSign* looks similar to the word *verdad* for "truth," and thus generates a certain level of trust. On the other hand, the TRUSTe logo, while also recognized by Americans, carries little significance to Latin American web users.

Latin American and Brazilians respond much more positively than Americans to credit card icons on web sites. The word *Visa* is enough for most Americans to trust a web site, but Latin American users want to see the actual Visa credit card icons (see Figure 11.28). Cheskin claims that credit card companies play the largest role in establishing a sense of security for users on e-commerce web sites. It recommends that sites clearly display credit card icons. Of the symbols tested, the Visa symbol was the most recognized overall.

Figure 11.28   Terra Honduras prominently displays the Visa credit
card icon.

—Wave the Flag Cautiously —

As icons, flags convey a great deal of meaning, and not always the meaning you intend. After all, what language does the U.S. flag represent? English? There are many people in the U.S. who might disagree. And you'll find this true for other countries as well. Conversely, what flag do you use to represent Spanish? As shown in Figure 11.29, all eight flags represent Spanish-speaking countries.

Relying on flags can also pose a problem with global gateways. Boston Scientific offers localized sites for a number of countries and one region: Latin America. Although the countries can be represented by flags, as shown in Figure 11.30, Latin America poses a bit of a problem.

continues

Wave the Flag Cautiously   (continued)

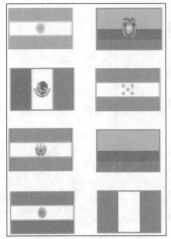

Figure 11.29   Which of these flags do you use to denote Spanish? All of them.

Figure 11.30   The gateway for the Boston Scientific web site relies on flags, but runs into a bit of a snag. Notice the artificial flag for Latin America.

309

If your audience can be defined purely by geographic boundaries, flags can work well, as discussed in the Monster.com Spotlight. Generally, however, it's wise to avoid them.

Photographs

A photograph is worth a thousand words, but in what language? Photos can add value to a localized site. For example, a photo of the Eiffel tower offers a comfortable, albeit clichéd, image for French users. However, be careful if you consider using photographs of people. Unless your company's spokesperson is Michael Jordan—arguably the most recognized human being on the planet—you're probably better off avoiding using photos of people. There are just too many risks involved when using people because many cultures are sensitive to the ethnicity and dress of the models. Then there are the ways models pose. They might be posed in an offensive way to some cultures. The open palm, fingers extended in a certain way, the bottom of the shoe—any of these poses will offend some group of people around the world. In Brazil and Spain, for example, the "OK" hand sign (see Figure 11.31) is considered offensive.

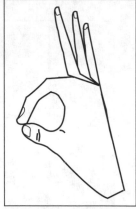

Figure 11.31 The use of this gesture
is not okay in many cultures.

Offensive poses around the world:

Bottom of the foot/sole of the shoe

Left hand

Open palm

Practically any combination of outstretched fingers

GLOBALLY USABLE; LOCALLY ACCEPTABLE

When designing for the world, be sensitive to the practical demands of each
locale. An animation-free site might not win you any design awards, but it will load
faster in India. Also, be sensitive to the cultural demands of each locale. Germans
may find your web design clever, while Japanese find it confusing. If you want your
design to be effective, you need to understand the visual languages of the world—
not just how people speak, but how they see.

12

CREATING MULTILINGUAL CONTENT

To create web pages in multiple languages, you need software that supports multiple languages. Until recently, however, most English-language software supported only the Latin 1 character set. Latin 1 works fine for creating English and Western European web pages, but it's useless with languages such as Arabic, Russian, or Japanese. And although software has come a long way in the past two years, there are a still a number of obstacles to be aware of. This chapter explains many of the limitations you'll face when using software to create multilingual content and offers a few helpful workarounds.

THE GOLDEN AGE OF MULTILINGUAL SOFTWARE

We stand at the threshold of the age of Unicode-friendly software. Because Unicode supports all major languages, any software application that supports Unicode will support your web localization efforts. Unfortunately, not all software fully supports Unicode. Not yet, at least. Although Windows 98 provided partial Unicode support, it wasn't until 2000 and XP that Microsoft offered native Unicode support for consumers. Today, Microsoft offers full support for Unicode in not only its operating system, but also its Office suite and FrontPage web development software. Apple also offers full Unicode support, but because of its low penetration worldwide, the focus in this chapter will be primarily on Windows applications.

For more information on Unicode, see "Hands On: Unicode."

The Achilles' heel of Unicode support is not the operating system, but the software applications that run on the system. For example, even if you have Windows XP, you won't be able to input Japanese text into Dreamweaver because the English-language version of Dreamweaver doesn't support double-byte text.

The tricky part about working with different languages is that you need to understand their underlying character sets before you can figure out whether you have the software to support them. Everything depends on your target languages. For example, if you're localizing for just French and Spanish, odds are the software you have right now will work perfectly fine. If you're planning on working with the double-byte Asian languages, however, you might have to consider upgrading. Even a single-byte script, such as Arabic, may not be well supported in your application. It's not just a double-byte issue, but a character set support issue.

For a list of languages and their corresponding character sets, see Appendix E, "Encodings."

MANAGING MULTILINGUAL TEXT

There is more than one way to turn a source HTML page into a target HTML page. The method you use depends largely on the software you have on hand as well as the skill level of your translators and editors. In general, there are four methods for managing text in web pages and graphics, each with its own advantages and disadvantages.

Method 1: Working Within the File

The most straightforward way of turning a source HTML page into a target HTML page is to work within the file itself. You send the HTML file to a translator, who returns it as a translated HTML file, as shown in Figure 12.1. This method requires little intervention on your part because the file should be returned to you ready for posting to a server for testing. You still might have to alter HTML code, such as hyperlinks, but the translated text itself should require no further modification. If your software doesn't support double-byte character sets, or languages such as Arabic or Russian, working within the file might be your only feasible solution. However, the danger of relying on this method is that you place a great deal of faith in your translators and editors. If they aren't skilled at working in HTML files, they could accidentally delete a critical piece of HTML code or translate an HTML tag, such as **<BODY>** or **<TABLE>**, causing significant problems.

Figure 12.1 An HTML page, before and after translation. This page is taken from the "Hands On: French, Italian, and German" chapter.

315

Method 2: Copying and Pasting

Assuming the translator cannot (or should not) work within the HTML file, you can also extract the text and have it translated separately, as shown in Figure 12.2. The best way to send the file to the translators and editors is as an RTF file (see the Note box "Get to Know RTF"). When the text is returned, you manually copy and paste it into the HTML file. This method is clearly a lot of work, but you'll need to do a little copying and pasting if you localize your own graphics. For HTML pages, this is not the best method, but it does ensure that your translators don't damage the HTML markup text. Of course, this method doesn't ensure that you or your web developer won't also damage any of the translated text. The problem with *both* Methods 1 and 2 is that you leave your HTML text vulnerable to manual errors.

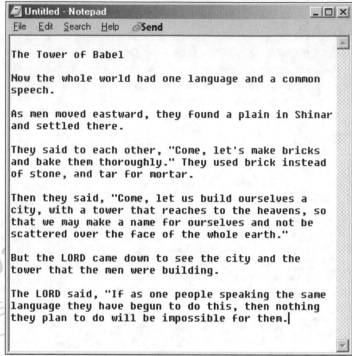

Figure 12.2 Text extracted from the HTML file, ready for translation. This text is the source text from the Hands-On chapters.

Method 3: Isolating and Automating

If you take the best parts of Methods 1 and 2 and build them into a software-based content management system, you will end up with a globalization management system (GMS). A GMS is a software application that separates the translatable text from the HTML code so that nobody can do damage to the code. Although a GMS application sounds awfully nice, it can also be expensive and sometimes rather inflexible. For smaller sites and budgets, you'll most likely be using Method 1 or 2, or a customized combination of both.

See Chapter 13, "Global Content Management," for a more in-depth look at this method.

Method 4: Directly Inputting

If you understand the language, you can input the translated text yourself. In fact, as you localize graphics, you might choose to skip the copy-and-paste method and manually enter the text yourself; of course, you'll first need to know how to input text that isn't supported on an English keyboard.

Get to Know RTF

Rich text format (RTF) is a platform-neutral file format commonly used in the translation industry. All major text editors support it (see Figure 12.3). RTF preserves the integrity of the text, no matter what language is used, and helps you avoid any of those nasty file conversion errors that occur when a translator is using one version of a text editor and you're using another.

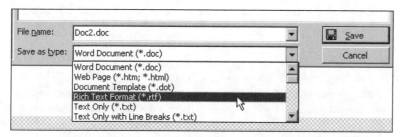

Figure 12.3   Saving a file in RTF format.

CREATING MULTILINGUAL WEB PAGES

317

The degree of success you have developing multilingual web pages depends on the software (and version) you're using. Macromedia Dreamweaver and Microsoft FrontPage are the two most popular visual development tools on the market, but they are not equally strong in managing various languages. Although FrontPage 2000 fully supports the input and display of Unicode text, Dreamweaver does not (see Figures 12.4 and 12.5).

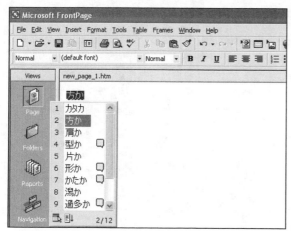

Figure 12.4   FrontPage 2000 supports the input of Japanese text...

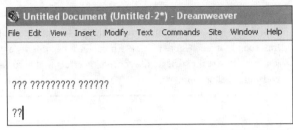

Figure 12.5 ...but Dreamweaver does not. Instead of displaying Japanese characters, Dreamweaver displays question marks.

To avoid any unpleasant surprises in your localization project, first identify the character sets you'll need to support, and then select the software applications that support them. Most software developers have embraced Unicode, so it's just a matter of time before these issues are a thing of the past. Unfortunately, many applications are not there yet. In Table 12.1, for example, many English-language software applications currently do not support the display and input of double-byte character sets.

Table 12.1 Support for Double-Byte Character Sets in Windows (English-Language Applications)

Product	Windows 98/2000/XP
Macromedia Dreamweaver 3 and 4	No
Microsoft FrontPage 2000/2002	Yes
Adobe GoLive	No
Macromedia HomeSite 5	No
Macromedia FreeHand	No
Macromedia Flash	No
Adobe Illustrator 9 and 10	No
Adobe Photoshop 5	No
Adobe Photoshop 6	Yes
Microsoft Word 97	Yes
Microsoft Word 2000	Yes

┌─ **FYI** ──┐

  ■ Dreamweaver localization tips: **www.macromedia.com/support/dreamweaver/manage/localization_design**

  ■ FrontPage support information: **www.microsoft.com/frontpage**

  ■ An excellent all-around Unicode resource: **www.hclrss.demon.co.uk/unicode/htmlunicode.html**

└──┘

When Text Editors Will Do

Many web developers prefer making web pages the old-fashioned way—using text editors. Text editors are ideal for creating multilingual web pages because so many of them support Unicode. For example, Word 2000 offers full support for entering and editing Japanese text, which means that even if you don't have the latest operating system or web development tools, you can still create a Japanese web page. In addition, Word 2000 offers a wide range of export encodings, so you can input and edit most major languages (see Figures 12.6 and 12.7).

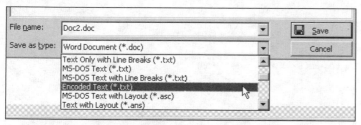

Figure 12.6 Using Word 2000, you can save a document as "Encoded Text."

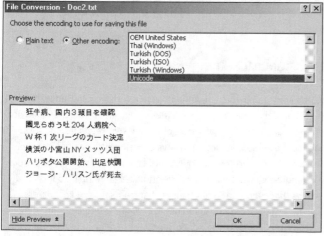

Figure 12.7 After selecting the Encoded Text option, you can select from a wide range of encodings.

When Using FrontPage...

FrontPage is notorious for wreaking havoc on non-English web pages. By default, on English systems, FrontPage assumes that the web page uses the Latin 1 character set. Unless you instruct it otherwise, when you save the document, it converts any non-Latin characters into numeric entities—and you'll lose the native encoding of your document. Just be sure that when you work with different encodings, you adjust the page properties, as shown in Figure 12.8.

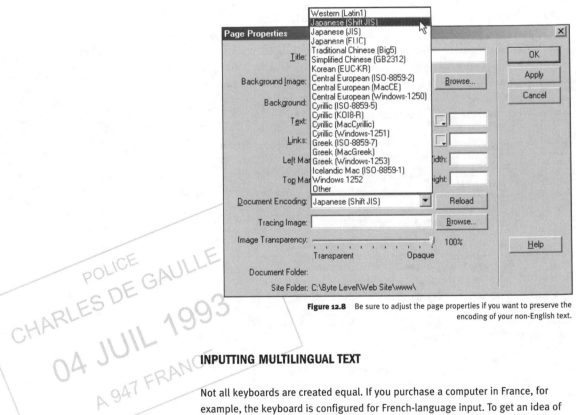

Figure 12.8   Be sure to adjust the page properties if you want to preserve the encoding of your non-English text.

INPUTTING MULTILINGUAL TEXT

Not all keyboards are created equal. If you purchase a computer in France, for example, the keyboard is configured for French-language input. To get an idea of what a French keyboard looks like, Microsoft offers a *visual keyboard*, as shown in Figure 12.9. Notice the addition of accented keys as well as the positions of the characters; as you can see, the "qwerty" keyboard layout that English users are familiar with is hardly a global standard. Microsoft offers more than 40 localized operating systems that support a wide range of character sets and keyboards. Given such a wide range of keyboards, you might wonder how to input non-English characters using a U.S. English keyboard. Fortunately, there are a number of input methods you can use.

Figure 12.9 The French visual keyboard provided by Microsoft.

Using Character Entities

When ASCII ruled the Internet, web developers who wanted to display Western European characters or symbols, such as the trademark symbol (™), relied on character entities. *Character entities* allowed a web page written in the ASCII character set to display characters outside that character set. There are two types of character entities: *named* and *numeric*. To display a character such as the division sign (÷), the named entity **÷** is a lot more convenient than the numeric entity **÷**. When using numeric entities, you have to know the precise code point; with named entities, you simply have to know what character you're referring to.

Named entities have the advantage of being independent of the page's encoding; in other words, the browser does not have to know which character set is being specified to know what **&** is supposed to represent. The disadvantage of named entities is that there are only a limited number from which to choose. Table 12.2 lists the more commonly used named and numeric entities.

Table 12.2 Selected Named and Numeric Character Entities

Named Entity	Numeric Entity	Character
&cent;	&#162;	cent symbol
&pound;	&#163;	pound sterling symbol
&yen;	&#165;	yen symbol
&copy;	&#169;	copyright symbol
&reg;	&#174;	registered symbol
&acute;	&#180;	acute accent
&cedil;	&#184;	lowercase c with cedilla
&iquest;	&#191;	inverted question mark
&Aelig;	&#198;	capital AE diphthong (ligature)
&Ccedil;	&#199;	capital C with cedilla

continues

Table 12.2   Continued

Named Entity	Numeric Entity	Character
&ETH;	&#208;	capital Eth, Icelandic
&szlig;	&#223;	small sharp s, German (sz ligature)
&icirc;	&#238;	small i, circumflex accent
&iuml;	&#239;	small i, dieresis or umlaut mark

The full list of character entities is located in Appendix C, "Character Entities."

*Source: World Wide Web Consortium (**www.w3c.org/TR/html401/sgml/entities.html**).*

Numeric entities, on the other hand, can be used to display the entire Unicode character set. For notation, you can use decimal (**メ**, for example) or hexadecimal (such as **メ**) numbers, although the standard for Unicode is hexadecimal. With numeric entities, you can create a web page with a dozen different languages by using nothing but numbers.

More Than One Way to Make an Ampersand

There are three ways to display an ampersand in HTML:

- **&**   named entity

- **&**   numeric entity (decimal)

- **&**   numeric entity (hexadecimal)

Entities in Action

If you have Internet Explorer 5.0 or greater, you can save web pages to your computer in your choice of encodings. This feature can be useful for learning how text is displayed in web pages. To try it out yourself, visit the Yahoo! Japan home page at **www.yahoo.co.jp** and save this web page to your computer in two different encodings. First, save it as Japanese (EUC) encoding (see Figure 12.10). Explorer defaults to this encoding because it's the native encoding of the web page. Next, save the page as Western European (Windows) encoding (see Figure 12.11).

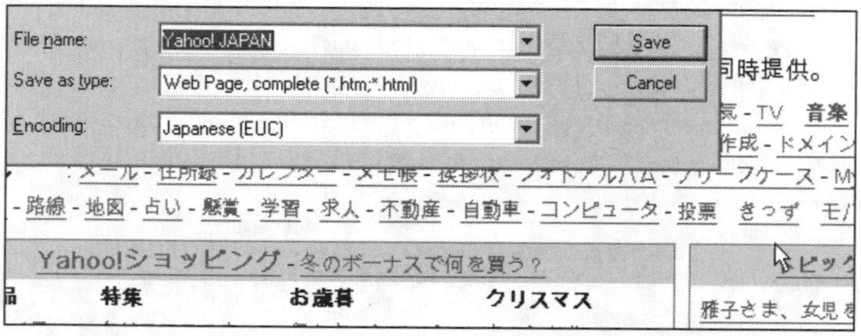

Figure 12.10 Save as Japanese (EUC).

Figure 12.11 Save as Western European (Windows).

Now view both pages in your web browser. In a browser, both pages look the same; however, if you view the source text of both pages in Notepad, you'll see a major difference. The EUC page retains its native encoding (and therefore looks scrambled in Notepad), but the Western European version relies on all numeric entities (see Figure 12.12).

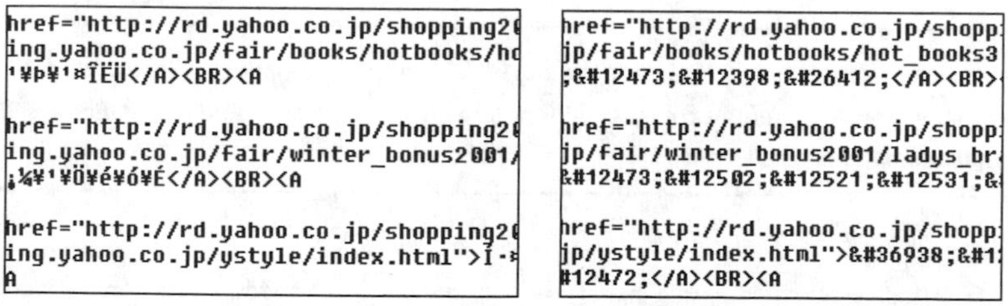

Figure 12.12 The EUC page on the left retains its native Japanese encoding, which looks scrambled in Notepad. On the right, the Western Windows page uses numeric entities to represent Japanese characters.

Inputting Accented Characters

As ASCII fades from the Internet, so does the need for character entities. After all, the Internet's default character set is now Unicode, so why not input all characters directly using the Unicode encoding? Unfortunately, older browsers do not recognize Unicode, but most browsers in use today do recognize the Latin 1 or Windows 1252 character sets. So at the very least, you can directly input characters from Western European languages—even the accented characters. Users of the Windows operating system can enter accented characters by holding down the Alt key and simultaneously entering a four-digit number. The number corresponds to the Windows 1252 Codepage. After entering the four-digit number, release the Alt key and the character will appear on the page. This chart includes some of the more commonly used accented characters:

Character	Hold down the Alt key and enter:
á	0225
ó	0243
ú	0250
é	0233
ñ	0241
í	0237

You can also input punctuation and special characters, such as:

¶	0182
®	0174
¿	0191

The full list of accented characters and code points is located in Appendix C, "Character Entities."

Pay Attention to Accents

Accented characters can be easily confused if you don't understand the language. Too often, the marks end up facing in the wrong direction, so proof your work carefully. For more information on inputting accented characters, visit **http://home.netscape.com/eng/intl/accentinput.html#method1**.

This system of inputting characters, four-digit number by four-digit number, works for the occasional character, but what if you want to input pages and pages of text? This is when visual keyboards come in handy.

Using Visual Keyboards

Even though an English-language operating system comes with an English-language keyboard, Microsoft provides visual keyboards that allow you to modify how your keyboard functions. The implementation varies depending on the operating system, but I'll focus on the combination of Windows ME and Office 2000. There are actually two components to the visual keyboard feature: the keyboard driver and the visual keyboard you view onscreen as you type. People who already know the layout of a French keyboard, for example, simply need to modify the keyboard driver. To do so, click Start, Settings, Control Panel, double-click the Keyboard icon, and select the Language tab (see Figure 12.13).

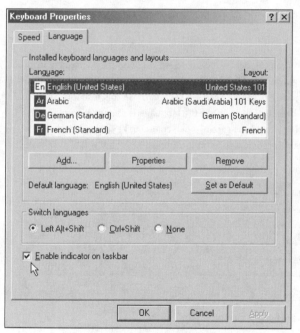

325

Figure 12.13 Configuring language input in Windows ME.

If you're not familiar with keyboard layouts for different languages, you can activate a visual keyboard on your screen. Microsoft supplies the visual keyboard software as part of Office Tools. You can download Microsoft Visual Keyboard for Office 2000 at **http://office.microsoft.com/Downloads/2000/viskeyboard.aspx** (see Figure 12.14).

Figure 12.14 Downloading visual keyboard support.

Once you activate more than one keyboard driver, you'll notice a language icon (displaying the language code) in the taskbar (see Figure 12.15). By double-clicking this language icon, you can toggle between keyboards. In this example, the visual keyboard has also been activated. When the language is changed, so too is the layout of the visual keyboard. Be careful when changing keyboards, as any keyboard shortcuts you're accustomed to on the English keyboard will also change.

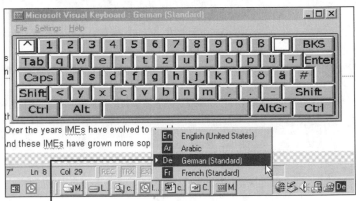

Language icon

Figure 12.15 When toggling between keyboard languages, the visual keyboard, if activated, will also change.

Microsoft Multilingual Support

- An overview of Office 2000 multilingual features: **http://office.microsoft.com/assistance/2000/oflangs.aspx**

- To set up your keyboard to work in another language in Office 2000: **http://office.microsoft.com/assistance/2000/OKeyboard.aspx**

- To set up multilingual support in Office XP:
  http://office.microsoft.com/assistance/2002/articles/oWebOffice2002Worldwide.aspx

---

Using Input Method Editors

Keyboards work well with a small range of characters, but how do you input Chinese, a language that includes more than 5,000 characters? No keyboard can effectively represent all Chinese characters, so computer users must rely on software known as an *input method editor* (*IME*). The IME works with the keyboard to input an unlimited range of characters. If you want to input double-byte characters on an English-language system, Microsoft offers free IMEs for download at **www.microsoft.com/windows/ie/downloads/recommended/ime/default.asp** (see Figure 12.16).

Downloads for Office 2002/XP		Downloads from Other Provide
Title	**Date ▾**	**Type**
Office XP Add-in: Microsoft Clip Gallery Download Now! 2601kb / 16 mins For users who have upgraded to Office XP, this add-in installs Clip Gallery to provide access to previously downloaded clip art.	04-May-2001	▦ Add-in
Office XP Tool: Global IME (Simplified Chinese) Download Now! 23491kb / 140 mins Use the Microsoft Global Input Method Editor for Office XP (Simplified Chinese) to input Simplified Chinese text in your documents, worksheets, presentations, mail messages, publications, and Web pages.	27-Apr-2001	▦ Add-in
Office XP Tool: Global IME (Traditional Chinese) Download Now! 8987kb / 54 mins Use the Microsoft Global Input Method Editor for Office XP (Traditional Chinese) to input Traditional Chinese text in your documents, worksheets, presentations, mail messages, publications, and Web pages.	27-Apr-2001	▦ Add-in
Office XP Tool: Global IME (Japanese) Download Now! 57874kb / 345 mins Use the Microsoft Global Input Method Editor for Office XP (Japanese) to	27-Apr-2001	▦ Add-in

Figure 12.16   Downloading the Chinese IME for Windows XP.

IMEs can't overcome the limitations of the software in which they're used, however. For example, even though you may be using a Japanese IME on Windows 98, you won't have any luck inputting Japanese text into a graphics program, such as Adobe Illustrator, Photoshop, or Macromedia Flash. These software applications simply don't support double-byte input.

For more information about Asian text input, see "Hands-On: Chinese and Japanese."

327

The Microsoft Japanese IME

A Japanese IME converts keystrokes into phonetic (kana) and ideographic (kanji) characters and words. As keystrokes are entered, the IME attempts to guess which character or characters the keystrokes should be converted into. Because many Japanese words have identical pronunciation, the Japanese IME's first suggestion might not be what the sentence requires. For this reason, the IME might offer a list of homophones (similar-sounding words) from which the user can choose (see Figure 12.17). In some cases, the homophone that the user selects becomes the IME's first suggestion the next time around.

*Source: Microsoft Japanese Input Method Editor (**www.microsoft.com**).*

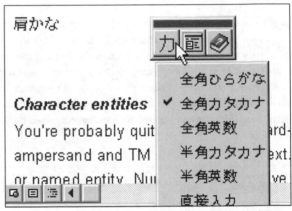

Figure 12.17 The Japanese IME (on Windows ME) provides a list of choices.

Note that the Microsoft IME for Windows 9x/ME is designed to support Microsoft applications, such as Internet Explorer, Outlook, or Word 2000. It won't necessarily work with applications from other companies.

Windows XP: One Giant Step Forward

Windows XP Professional offers an impressive array of language support, both in terms of multilingual input and management (see Figures 12.18 and 12.19). For more information, visit **www.microsoft.com/windowsxp/pro**.

Figure 12.18 Windows XP developed new language support features and new IMEs for Asian languages.

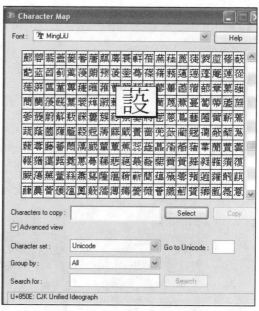

Figure 12.19 The XP character map feature allows you to view—and input—the full range of characters by font or by character set.

329

WHEN CHARACTER SETS COLLIDE

In a few years, hopefully, this chapter will be made obsolete by Unicode. When all major software applications support Unicode, you'll no longer need to worry about which application supports which character set. Unicode will make multilingual software more accessible, more affordable, and less intimidating. But until this chapter is made obsolete, study up on your character sets. Better yet, take a shot at working with double-byte character sets in the chapter "Hands-On: Chinese and Japanese."

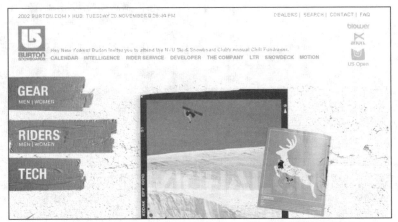

Figure 1   The Burton global home page.

BURTON SNOWBOARDS

Based in Burlington, Vermont, with offices in Urawa, Japan and Innsbruck, Austria, Burton is one of the world's leading manufacturers of snowboards, clothing, and accessories. Burton snowboards are distributed in 35 countries.

www.burton.com

Localized web sites:

- English
- French
- German
- Italian
- Japanese
- Polish
- Spanish

ANALYSIS

Being a niche company doesn't preclude you from taking your company global. Burton has invested heavily in its global web site, both in response to its growing global markets and as a means of expanding them. The Burton site still has a ways to go; much of the text is not translated, including some key menu items. Nevertheless, Burton has a competitive advantage over its competitors, many of whom have made no attempt at web localization.

Many companies do not put enough thought into how they will direct users to their language-specific web sites. Burton, however, does an excellent and stylistic job of building a "global gateway." When users first visit the Burton site, they arrive at the gateway page shown in Figure 2. After users select a language, a cookie is stored on their computers so that this page is not seen again. The next time they visit, they go directly to the localized site. For example, the German home page is shown in Figure 3.

Figure 2   The Burton global gateway.

Figure 3   Burton's German home page.

The use of cookies on global gateways is an excellent method of not only directing users to their localized content, but also for tracking your users' usage habits. As David Buckland of Burton notes in the Q&A, Burton has found that the Japanese section is much more popular than the other localized sites.

The only flaw with relying solely on cookies is that after a user has selected a language preference, Burton does not make it readily apparent how to switch to a different language preference. The "language" link is located on the bottom of the web page, as shown in Figure 4. For instance, if a user mistakenly selects Japanese, he or she might not be able to easily figure out how to get out of that language and back to the English page. Many localized web sites, such as Amazon.com (see Figure 5), place the language links at the bottom of every web page so the user can easily switch languages.

Figure 4   The "language" link at the lower-right side of the home page, is not translated for each localized site, making it difficult for people to switch to a different language.

Figure 5   The global gateway at the bottom of the Amazon Japan web page.

Q&A WITH BURTON SNOWBOARDS

David Buckland,
Internet Project and Development Manager Burton USA

Explain your role in managing the web site.

I manage the overall project and the developers working on the site. After a site goes live, I work with global marketing departments on enhancements and providing tools to enable them to manage global content and updates.

Describe your localization strategy.

Our site is geared more toward languages than specific regions. Regional content managers have access to admin tools that allow them to manage language-specific content.

When did you launch the localized sites?

We launched five localized web sites on August 1, 2001. The Polish site was launched in late 2001.

Have the sites been a success?

The sites generate between 20,000 and 25,000 unique visitors per month. The popularity of each web site breaks down as follows:

- *66.8% English*
- *16% Japanese*
- *8.6% German*
- *4.2% French*
- *2% Italian*
- *1.7% Spanish*
- *1% Polish*

I notice that the main navigation bar isn't translated (though the rollovers are). Did you have a reason for not translating these graphics?

Marketing requested that the product hierarchy and general navigation not be translated, which is consistent with our catalog. Many consumers prefer to have the site in English since the Burton voice is native to the English language.

Do you have plans for eventually translating all the content on your site?

Not at this time.

What challenges did you encounter when creating the localized site?

Coordinating translations in six different languages is always a challenge. It is a ton of content, considering the size of the Burton line.

Are you going to expand into other languages?

We plan to add Russian in 2002 and Korean in 2003.

What software tools did you use for localization?

Everything was built in-house using Microsoft tools. All language content is fed via a SQL 2000 database.

What advice would you give to other growing companies with tight budgets that want to add localized portions of their site?

For our sites, it doesn' t make sense to make each "localized section" a separate site. It saves a ton of time and maintenance costs to build each page once and pull the language content from the database.

Regarding the "Dealers" menu, I see that it provides local contacts, but the user must navigate English buttons first. Does this present problems for your users or are you gradually planning to localize it?

For now, I have heard of no plans to localize it. Our global offices have not mentioned this as a significant roadblock for our consumers finding shops.

And finally, since you've localized, do you find an increase in multilingual emails or support questions?

As a global company, we have been consistently interacting with our consumers around the globe for many years. The web site did not substantially change this. If anything, global requests have decreased due to the multilingual information that our site provides.

335

HANDS-ON: CHINESE AND JAPANESE

Overview

This is the fourth of six Hands-On chapters; by now, you have completed Hands-On chapters for Spanish; French, Italian, and German; and Russian. Collectively, these chapters demonstrate the process and challenges of localizing an English-language web page into multiple languages. After completing all the Hands-On chapters, you will have localized one web page into eight languages—the languages spoken by more than 80% of the world's population. If you'd like to try your hand at these exercises, all files used in these chapters are available for download; go to **www.bytelevel.com/beyondborders**.

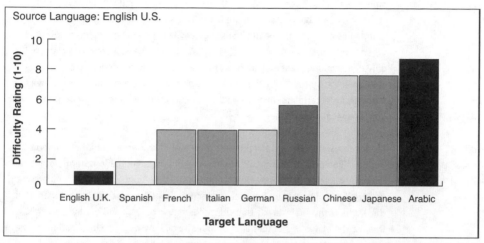

Figure 1 The difficulty ratings from Chapter 1, "In the Beginning, There Was English."

For a full list of country and language codes, see Appendix D.

Speakers worldwide (source: *Ethnologue*, 14th edition, 2000; www.ethnologue.com):

- **Chinese:** 1 billion+ (874 million Mandarin speakers in China)

- **Japanese:** 126 million (121 million in Japan)

ISO language codes: ZH, JA

Difficulty rating: 8 (see Figure 1)

Major locales:

Country	Language Code
China	zh-CN
Taiwan	zh-TW
Japan	ja-JP

FIRST THOUGHTS

The research firm Gartner Dataquest predicts that in 2003, Asia-Pacific will have more Internet users, at 183 million, than the U.S., at 162 million. What makes this statistic remarkable is that at 183 million, Asia is only just getting started. Companies have already begun investing heavily in Japanese-language web sites. When Yahoo! first looked overseas, Japan was one of the first countries chosen. Not only does Japan represent a major world market, but its residents have readily embraced the Internet. Whether by mobile phone or PC, the Japanese truly love the Internet, for entertainment as well as shopping. There are already more than 40 million Japanese Internet users.

China represents perhaps the greatest potential of any world market. With more than a billion people sharing a common written language, the long-term potential is enormous. Currently, Internet penetration is still quite low, at about 33 million, but if only 25% of China gets an Internet connection, it will become the largest market in the world. Many analysts say that this milestone is only a handful of years away. Despite the marvelous potential of both markets, however, web localization can be very challenging for native-English speakers. The languages are complex, and English-language software tools don't make things any easier.

- **More languages; more character sets.** Japanese and Chinese have relied on a bewildering array of characters and character sets over the years. You'll need a basic understanding of how computers manage all these characters and which character sets you should use.

- **How to display and input text.** Even if you won't be inputting Asian text, it's useful to understand how a standard keyboard can be used to input thousands of characters.

- **What about that global gateway?** With two new languages to add, the gateway is going to get a little more complex. In this chapter, you will create a more consistent-looking, graphics-only gateway to improve the gateway's appearance (see Figure 2). By upgrading to the latest version of Photoshop, the process will become a lot more manageable.

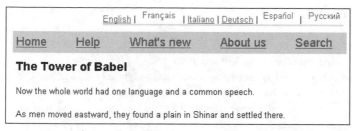

Figure 2   The English-language source page has an inconsistent-looking global
gateway, a problem that will be fixed in this chapter.

TOOLS

Although Chinese and Japanese rely on many more characters than the Russian language, you can still use the same tools you used to create the Russian web page. To
create the graphics, you should use Photoshop 6 or higher, as this version offers
support for a much wider range of characters, including Japanese and Chinese. For
this exercise, the following applications will be used:

339

Operating system: Windows ME

HTML: Word 2000

Graphics: Photoshop 6.01

CJK

CJK stands for Chinese, Japanese, and Korean. Localization experts commonly use the acronyms CJK (and CJKV,
which also includes Vietnamese).

JAPANESE PRIMER

Japanese is a complex written language, using a combination of syllabaries, Chinese characters, and, occasionally, Latin characters. A syllabary is a group of phonetic characters that represent syllables. English relies on an alphabet of 26 letters, but Japanese relies on an alphabet of roughly 100 syllables, collectively known as *kana*. Many Japanese brand names, when transliterated into English, can be easily broken down into these syllables, such as "Su-zu-ki" or "To-yo-ta." In all, the Japanese language relies on four unique sets of characters:

■ **Hiragana**: A syllabary used to represent words of Japanese origin. Notice in Figure 3 how the characters flow like handwriting.

あ	い	う	え	お
a	i	u	e	o
か	き	く	け	こ
ka	ki	ku	ke	ko
さ	し	す	せ	そ
sa	shi	su	se	so
た	ち	つ	て	と
ta	chi	tsu	te	to
な	に	ぬ	ね	の
na	ni	nu	ne	no

Figure 3 Twenty-five of the 46 basic hiragana characters and their Latin equivalents.

■ **Katakana**: A syllabary used to represent words imported from other languages. These characters are more angular and boxlike, as shown in Figure 4.

ア	イ	ウ	エ	オ
a	i	u	e	o
カ	キ	ク	ケ	コ
ka	ki	ku	ke	ko
サ	シ	ス	セ	ソ
sa	shi	su	se	so
タ	チ	ツ	テ	ト
ta	chi	tsu	te	to
ナ	ニ	ヌ	ネ	ノ
na	ni	nu	ne	no

Figure 4 Twenty-five of the 46 basic katakana characters and their Latin equivalents.

- **Kanji:** Nearly 2,000 Chinese characters. If you were to break down a typical Japanese sentence, kanji would account for roughly 40% of the characters, with kana making up the rest.

- **Latin:** Occasionally, Latin characters are used to represent brand names and personal names.

If you look at the Japanese web page in Figure 5, you'll see all four writing systems mixed together. Japanese text is traditionally written vertically, from right to left, but on the Internet, it's written like English—horizontally, from left to right.

Figure 5 Notice the mix of writing systems on the Lycos Japan home page.

CHINESE PRIMER

Chinese uses just one writing system: a collection of characters known as hanzi. Chinese is the world's most popular language, spoken by more than a billion people, but there is a significant difference between written Chinese and spoken Chinese. Mandarin, the official spoken language of the Republic of China and Taiwan, is by far the most popular globally. Yet Cantonese, a language that sounds nothing like Mandarin, is widely used throughout Hong Kong. Fortunately, the various dialects (some of which are shown in the following list) share the same basic written language. Even the written language poses its challenges, however.

Chinese Dialects	Number of Speakers in China (in millions)
Hakka	33
Jinyu	45
Mandarin	867
Min Nan	25
Wu	77
Yue	52
Total	1,099

Source: Ethnologue, *14th edition, 2000.*

Chinese: Traditional and Simplified

Chinese began as a pictographic and ideographic language, in which each character represented an object, idea, or concept, as shown in Figures 6 and 7.

Figure 6 The pictograph for "wood," on the left, looks like a tree; on the right is the pictograph for "fire."

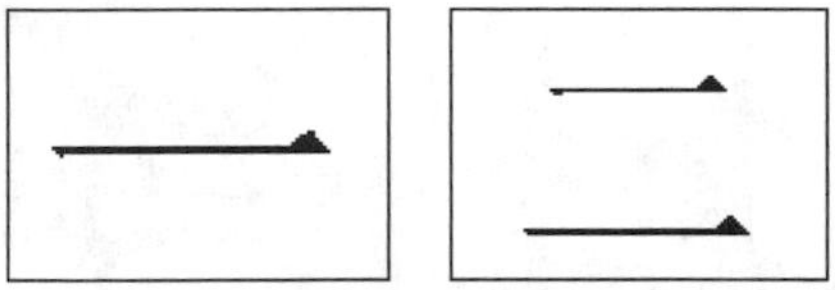

Figure 7 Ideographs for "one" (left) and "two" (right).

Today, ideographs and pictographs make up a minority of Chinese characters. Most characters represent syllables, much like Japanese kanji. The building blocks of Chinese characters are called radicals; some are characters in their own right, as shown in Figure 8.

一	丨	丶	丿	乙	亅	二	亠	人	儿
1	2	3	4	5	6	7	8	9	10
入	八	冂	冖	冫	几	凵	刀	力	勹
11	12	13	14	15	16	17	18	19	20
匕	匚	匸	十	卜	卩	厂	厶	又	口
21	22	23	24	25	26	27	28	29	30

Figure 8 Thirty of the more than 200 Chinese radicals.

*Source: James Kass (**http://home.att.net/~jameskass/chiradtest.htm**). This site includes a user-friendly directory of all Unicode characters.*

343

Today, roughly 56,000 Chinese characters are in use, although it is estimated that you need to know only between 2,000 and 3,000 characters to read a Chinese newspaper. Still, that's a lot of characters to remember, so in the 1950s, the Chinese government set out to "simplify" the language. The government reduced the number of strokes in many of the characters (see an example in Figure 9) and eliminated other characters outright. Many traditional characters were left as is, so you can have a traditional and simplified character that look exactly alike.

Figure 9 The character for horse in Traditional Chinese (left) and Simplified Chinese (right).

This "simplification" resulted in two different, but overlapping, written languages. If you want to reach all Chinese people, you need to use both written languages. Simplified Chinese is used in Mainland China and Singapore, and Traditional Chinese is used in Taiwan, Hong Kong, and Macao, as well as most overseas communities.

Transliteration Explained

Transliteration is a method of representing the sounds of words in one language by using the characters of another language. Transliteration is important for personal and brand names. Coca-Cola, for example, was initially transliterated into Chinese characters that, when pronounced, sounded like "ko-ko ko-le." Transliteration systems, like languages, have evolved over the years. During the 19th century, the major method of transliteration into English (or *romanization*) from Chinese was the Wade-Giles system. It has since been replaced by Pinyin, the official transliteration system of Mandarin. This evolution explains why Peking is now called Beijing and Taoism has recently evolved into Daoism. The transliteration of Japanese characters is called Romanji.

FYI

Resources on Asian Languages and Computing

www.chinesecomputing.com

http://zhongwen.com

www.mandarintools.com

DISPLAY AND INPUT OF ASIAN TEXT

Because Japanese and Chinese rely on so many characters, the standard single-byte character set won't suffice. The character sets used for Asian languages are traditionally called *double-byte character sets* (*DBCSs*) and, more recently, *multibyte character sets* (*MBCSs*). The extra byte makes it possible to represent thousands of characters instead of the few hundred allowed by a single-byte character set. When working with double-byte character sets, everything you do gets a little more complicated. For starters, you need fonts that include these additional characters. You

can download them for free from Microsoft (**http://windowsupdate.microsoft.com**) or
Netscape (**http://home.netscape.com/eng/intl**).

Text Display

Fonts are not much of a worry for web developers because you can assume your
Asian end users have them installed by default on their systems. The problem you'll
run into is with people in your own U.S. office who might not have the fonts installed.
Some companies develop introduction pages or buttons with instructions for how to
download the necessary fonts. (See the Yahoo! page in Figure 10 for an example.)

Downloading the necessary fonts could take a bit longer than expected. Asian fonts
are usually much larger, in kilobytes, than Latin fonts because of the significant
increase in glyphs. The free Windows font MS Mincho is more than 8MB, compared
with 278KB for the basic Arial font. When you work with Unicode, the fonts usually
grow even larger.

Yahoo! Japan

Yahoo! Japan is a site much like Yahoo! but tailor-made for Japanese users. You'll find lots of Japanese sites you haven't seen
before, and the list keeps growing!

**Note: You need to be able to view Japanese characters through your Web browser in order to properly view
Yahoo! Japan.**

- Windows Users
  - ○ **Windows 95** and NT users will need Japanese language support (e.g., UnionWay or AsiaSurf) and a browser
    that supports Japanese (e.g., Netscape Communicator or Microsoft Internet Explorer).
  - ○ **Windows 3.1** users will need Japanese language support (e.g., UnionWay) and a browser that supports
    Japanese (e.g., Netscape Communicator or Microsoft Internet Explorer).
- Macintosh users (running System 7.1 or later) need to load the Japanese Language Kit (available through most Apple
  resellers) as well as a browser that supports Japanese (e.g., Netscape Communicator)

Figure 10   People clicking through to the Yahoo! Japan page from the global
English home page will see this page, with instructions on downloading the necessary font.

To ensure that the text displays properly on the end user's browser and is correctly
indexed by search engines, don't forget to include the language code at the top of
the page, such as **<HTML lang="jp-JP">** for Japanese. Chinese is not so simple
because ISO does not provide codes that distinguish between Traditional and
Simplified. As a workaround, the tag zh-TW (Chinese-Taiwan) is generally used to
denote Chinese (Traditional) because Taiwan relies on Chinese Traditional, and
zh-CN (Chinese-China) is used for Chinese (Simplified).

Text Input

There are two ways to get Asian text into your web pages: You can copy and paste it in, or you can input it directly. Most web developers take the copy-and-paste approach, particularly when creating graphics that require embedded text. Generally, copying and pasting Asian text works well in current Windows and Mac operating systems, but inputting Asian text is not so simple. Naturally, your keyboard won't suffice for inputting thousands of characters on its own. Enter the input method editor (IME), a software tool that sits in between your keyboard and your application. You can purchase off-the-shelf IMEs or use the IMEs that Apple and Microsoft offer with their operating systems. IMEs generally do not come pre-installed on English-language operating systems, so you'll need to do a little legwork first, but the effort is well worth it. For example, the Windows XP IME is very sophisticated and a good learning experience for non-Asian language speakers (see Figures 11 and 12).

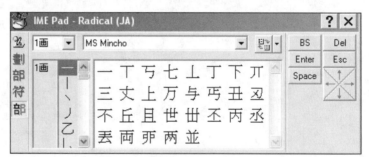

Figure 11 The Chinese IME for Windows XP provides both keyboard and handwriting input methods.

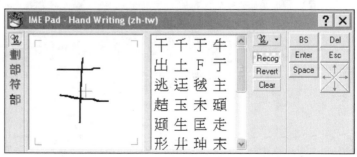

For more information on text Input and display, see Chapter 12, "Creating Multilingual Content."

Figure 12 You draw a character, and the software provides a list of suggested matches.

WHICH CHARACTER SET?

More than 20 Chinese and Japanese character sets and encodings have evolved over the years, making localization very confusing. Particularly confusing is the difference between a Chinese encoding and a Chinese character set. As mentioned in Chapter 2, "Navigating the Multilingual Internet," the character set is a group of characters, and an encoding is the mapping of characters to numbers so that computers can display them. Sometimes a character set and an encoding are one and the same, as with Big5 and GB-18030; you can call these coded character sets. Figure 13 charts the more popular character sets and encodings and shows what languages they represent. For a thorough explanation of Asian character sets and encodings, get a copy of Ken Lunde's book, *CJKV Information Processing* (O'Reilly and Assoc., 1999).

Language	Popular Character Sets and Encodings		
Chinese Simplified	**GB-2312-80** GB-18030-2000 (new standard) HZ-GB-2312 EUC (Unix)	**GBK** (Microsoft Codepage 936)	**Unicode**
Chinese Traditional	**Big5** (Microsoft Codepage 950)		
Japanese	**Shift-JIS** (Microsoft Codepage 932) EUC-JP (Unix) ISO-2022-JP		

Figure 13   Character sets and encodings for Asian languages.

So which character sets should you use? I suggest following the lead of the more popular Asian web sites, such as Lycos and Yahoo! (see Figure 14). For Chinese Traditional, both web sites use Big5; for Chinese Simplified, both use HZ-GB-2312. For Japanese, the overwhelming favorite across most sites is Shift-JIS.

347

Figure 14 Yahoo! Traditional Chinese in Big5 (top) and Yahoo! Simplified Chinese in HZ-GB-2312.

FYI

For more information on Asian character sets, go to: **http://kanji.zinbun.kyoto-u.ac.jp/~yasuoka/CJK.html**

GRAPHICS

At this point, the Babel global gateway is an inconsistent hodgepodge of text and graphics. Japanese and Chinese web pages will necessitate adding two more graphics. To ensure that the gateway looks consistent across all language pages, it makes sense to simply convert all text links to graphics. Photoshop 6 works reasonably well with Asian characters (see Figure 15). Text input is a little unstable at times, but copying and pasting shouldn't be a problem.

Figure 15 Copying Chinese text into Photoshop (left). Photoshop 6 also supports Cyrillic characters (right).

The many language graphics take up quite a bit of screen real estate. As global gateways grow, many web designers and developers tend to migrate to a pull-down menu to save space, but pull-down menus are not globally user friendly because they hide the language names. And unless you use Unicode as the encoding (as explained in "Hands-On: Unicode"), you cannot display all languages in their native scripts in a pull-down menu. Although language links do take up precious real estate, they are vital links to additional precious real estate, so make them as visible as possible.

After you've created all your graphics, you'll also need to input **ALT** tags, as shown in the following code, so that browsers without graphics support can display the alternate text instead.

```
<a href="ru/babel_ru.html"><img src="images/ru.gif" border="0"
➥ alt="Russian"></a> |
<a href="jp/babel_jp.html"><img src="images/jp.gif" border="0"
➥ alt="Japanese"></a>
```

ALT tags are also critical for web users with disabilities, who rely on machine-readable text. However, as mentioned in the "Hands-On: Russian" chapter, English browsers still don't fully support the display of **ALT** tags in different character sets. If you want to avoid people seeing question marks instead of Asian text, for the non-Latin graphics, use Latin names. It's not the best solution, but it's the best we have for now.

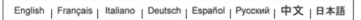

Figure 16 The finished gateway—only Arabic remains.

LOCALIZATION NOTES

The process of localizing for Japanese and Chinese is similar to the Russian web page. The steps are as follows:

1. Copy the HTML text into a new Word document.

2. Copy the Japanese or Chinese text into the new document.

3. Make sure the correct **<META>** charset label is added.

4. Save the document as "encoded text," and select the correct encoding.

5. Change the extension of the new document from "txt" to "html," and pre-view the page in a various web browsers.

Why not use a WYSIWYG (What You See Is What You Get) web editor, such as Dreamweaver or FrontPage? For starters, many web editors still do not fully support Asian text, such as Dreamweaver 3 or 4 or FrontPage 97. FrontPage 2000 does support Asian text, and you'll try it out in the "Hands-On: Arabic" chapter.

Numeric Entities as an Alternative

Although numeric entities are not an ideal alternative to inputting Asian text, they do offer an option for those who don't have Asian text support. Here's a section of text from the Cannondale Japan web page (**www.cannondale.co.jp**; see Figure 17). Notice how the numbers are in decimal format; numerical entities can be in either decimal or hexadecimal notation.

```
<span lang=JA; class="normal">&#12418;&#12398;&#12496;&#12522;&#12456;
&#12540;&#12471;&#12519;&#12531;&#12398;&#20013;&#12363;&#12425;&#12362
;&#36984;&#12403;&#12356;&#12383;&#12384;&#12367;&#12371;&#12392;&#1236
4;&#12391;&#12365;&#12414;&#12377;&#12290;</span>
```

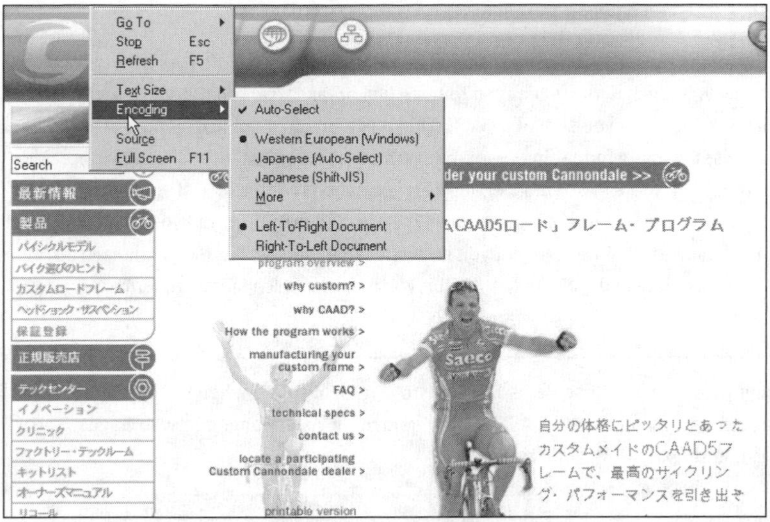

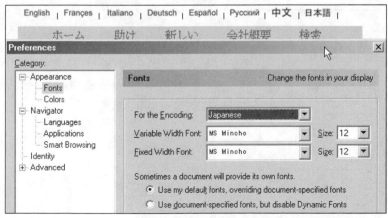

Figure 17   Notice how the encoding of the page is Western Windows, yet the Japanese text is displayed properly. Although some of the text is embedded in graphics, other text is displayed through the use of numerical entities.

Problems with Netscape?

If you're using a pre-6.0 version of Navigator, don't forget that you'll need to adjust the preferences, one language at a time. If you don't, you'll end up with empty boxes, as shown in Figure 18. Make sure the language corresponds to a font (such as MS Mincho) that includes the necessary glyphs. You might also want to increase the type size because Asian characters look muddy at smaller sizes.

Figure 18   Netscape 4.8 won't display Japanese or Chinese web pages correctly unless you modify the preferences.

Line Breaks and Word Wrapping

Because Chinese and Japanese scripts usually do not include spaces between words, many web designers are tempted to force line breaks to accommodate a particular layout. However, you should avoid forcing a line break in the text; let the end user's browser manage formatting. Even though Japanese, for instance, allows line breaking almost anywhere in a sentence, there are exceptions to this rule. If you let the text flow as is, the end user's browser manages the line breaking, and you won't insert any mistakes. Just be sure that you correctly label the web page with the **lang** attribute (such as **lang=ja_JP**) so that the browser knows which language formats to apply.

FTP Carefully

The common method for uploading files to the web server is File Transfer Protocol (FTP). When using it, however, make sure you've selected binary upload as opposed to ASCII when uploading Asian-language web pages (see Figure 19). ASCII will result in scrambled text.

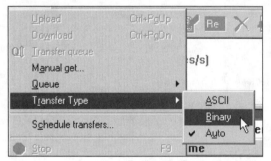

Figure 19   Make sure Binary is selected for the transfer type when you FTP files to your server.

ALMOST THERE...

Now that you've added Chinese and Japanese web pages (see Figure 20), you have expanded your potential audience to more than two billion people! But you still have one more language to add: Arabic.

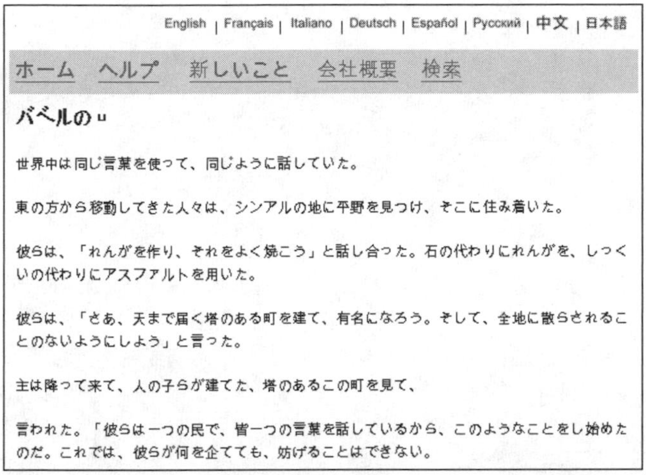

English | Français | Italiano | Deutsch | Español | Русский | 中文 | 日本語

ホーム　ヘルプ　新しいこと　会社概要　検索

バベルの ᵾ

世界中は同じ言葉を使って、同じように話していた。

東の方から移動してきた人々は、シンアルの地に平野を見つけ、そこに住み着いた。

彼らは、「れんがを作り、それをよく焼こう」と話し合った。石の代わりにれんがを、しっくいの代わりにアスファルトを用いた。

彼らは、「さあ、天まで届く塔のある町を建て、有名になろう。そして、全地に散らされることのないようにしよう」と言った。

主は降って来て、人の子らが建てた、塔のあるこの町を見て、

言われた。「彼らは一つの民で、皆一つの言葉を話しているから、このようなことをし始めたのだ。これでは、彼らが何を企てても、妨げることはできない。

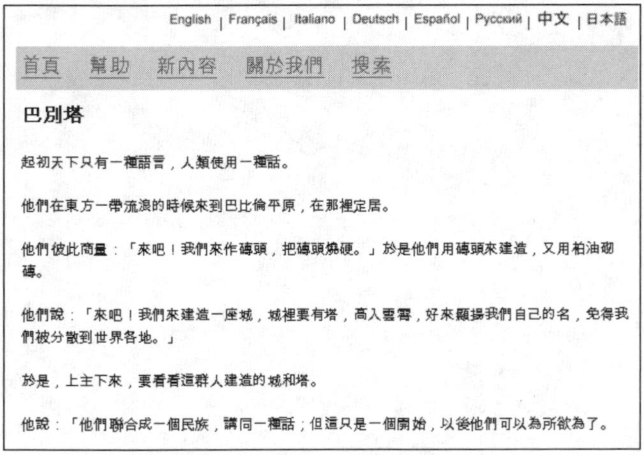

English | Français | Italiano | Deutsch | Español | Русский | 中文 | 日本語

首頁　幫助　新內容　關於我們　搜索

巴別塔

起初天下只有一種語言，人類使用一種話。

他們在東方一帶流浪的時候來到巴比倫平原，在那裡定居。

他們彼此商量：「來吧！我們來作磚頭，把磚頭燒硬。」於是他們用磚頭來建造，又用柏油砌磚。

他們說：「來吧！我們來建造一座城，城裡要有塔，高入雲霄，好來顯揚我們自己的名，免得我們被分散到世界各地。」

於是，上主下來，要看看這群人建造的城和塔。

他說：「他們聯合成一個民族，講同一種話；但這只是一個開始，以後他們可以為所欲為了。」

Figure 20 The completed Japanese (top) and Chinese (bottom) web pages.

353

Credits: Gang Li, Ph.D., provided translation and editing support for Chinese, and Nisiki Hayasi, Ph. D., provided translation and editing support for Japanese. They are both ATA-accredited translators and can be contacted through **www.atanet.org**.

13

GLOBAL CONTENT MANAGEMENT

If you localize a 300-page web site into five languages, you'll end up with a 1,500-page web site. That's a lot of new content to manage. If your company doesn't have a content management system in place already, by the time you've finished localizing your web site, you might very well need one. This chapter explores some of the challenges of managing localized web sites and some of the software available to help.

MANAGING LOCALIZED WEB SITES

When a localized web site goes live, the real work begins. Much of the work that goes into maintaining a localized web site is represented in Figure 13.1. This localization maintenance loop begins when changes are detected on the source-language site. Companies typically want any changes made to the source-language site reflected across all localized sites — and quickly.

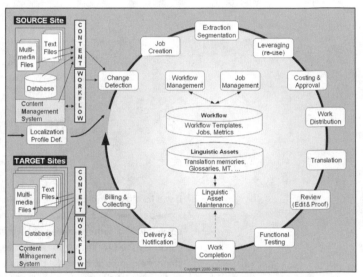

Figure 13.1 The localization maintenance loop: Maintaining localized web sites is often more challenging and expensive than the initial localization.

*Source: i18N Inc. (**www.i18n.ca**), ©2000–2002.*

After a change is detected, the following steps may be required:

1. Job creation

2. Extraction of text for translation

3. Leveraging text against any translation memory

4. Costing and approval

5. Distribution of files to translators

6. Translation

7. Review (editing and proofing)

8. Functional testing

9. Work completion

10. Delivery and notification

That's a lot of steps just to keep the localized web sites current, and as more changes are made to the source-language site, more iterations of the localization loop are required. Historically, the steps were managed manually, but as companies strive to reduce turnaround time, many of these steps are automated. Regardless of whether you manage localization maintenance by hand or by computer, however, the principle challenges remain the same:

■ **Update control.** You need to know who has updated what pages of your web site at all times, and it would be even more helpful to know exactly which item was changed. Was it a graphic? A paragraph? A few strings from the database? After you locate what content has changed, you have to decide whether the change should be replicated across all localized sites or just selected sites. Given the rate at which web sites are edited and expanded, content management is a full-time job, perhaps several full-time jobs.

■ **Error control.** With so many pages in so many languages to manage, the odds of mistakes slipping by increase dramatically. Rarely is there one person who can keep an eye on all pages, particularly if multiple languages are involved. If a web developer accidentally inserts a typo into a Japanese web page, who on your staff is going to catch it?

■ **Turnaround time.** Translating a source-language web page into a target-language web page takes time, but time is often a luxury you don't have. The more automated your translation workflow is, the more quickly you can get translated content onto the site. Instead of weeks, companies that automate content management can drop turnaround time to days or even hours.

■ **Business rules.** Business rules are policies and procedures that control a company's behavior. For example, a business rule might dictate that you offer repeat purchasers a 20% discount or that you sell some products in certain markets only. To implement these rules on a web site, across more than one locale, you'll need either a very, very organized Webmaster or a content management system.

Content Management Systems

A *content management system* (*CMS*) means different things to different organizations. Some companies purchase off-the-shelf software packages while others build

357

their own. Some systems are designed to support e-commerce, customer relation-ship management, and fulfillment; other systems simply automate basic web development tasks. The key features and potential benefits of CMS include:

- **Separation of form and content.** Not everyone understands HTML, nor should they. The promise of many content management systems is to make it possible for people to contribute and edit content without knowing any HTML. To achieve this goal, the CMS separates the web site's content from the HTML markup code. Companies often store the content in databases to be dynamically inserted into web pages as needed. The benefit of this sys-tem is that the content can be updated by anyone and be repositioned for multiple platforms. With dynamic updating, suddenly a job listing can be posted on your site, shared with other web sites, or accessed by mobile phone or PDA (see Figure 13.2).

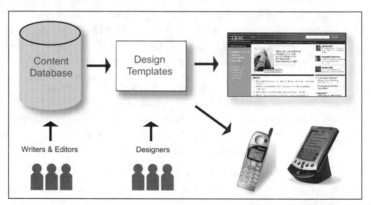

Figure 13.2   A content management system (CMS): By separating content and presentation, the content can be easily adapted to different channels, such as web pages, cellphones, and PDAs.

- **Access privileges.** CMS enables the site to be opened up to a wider range of content providers without opening it up to additional risk. For example, certain sections of the web site can be opened for interdepartmental collabo-ration, and others can be restricted to just the web team.

- **Decentralized management.** A CMS can be configured to support multiple web developers and content providers in multiple offices. This arrangement is ideal for multinationals, in which foreign offices may want ownership over their localized web sites.

- **Quality control.** An approval process can be established so that web pages don't go live without being viewed by copyeditors and managers.

- **Versioning.** CMS systems can store different instances or versions of the site—future and historical. This feature allows you to quickly "fall back" to an earlier site if something breaks on the current site. Versioning also enables you to develop, preview, and test sites that are planned for the following weeks or months.

- **Personalization.** A CMS system can present a more customized selection of content for web visitors, based on their past browsing and buying habits. Personalization, although complex to implement and manage, can directly increase sales or indirectly increase customer retention.

FYI

Popular CMS Vendors

Broadvision (**www.broadvision.com**)
Documentum (**www.documentum.com**)
FileNET (**www.filenet.com**)
Gauss (**www.gaussvip.com**)
Interwoven (**www.interwoven.com**)
Mediasurface (**www.mediasurface.com**)
Microsoft Content Management Server (**www.microsoft.com/ cmserver**)
Vignette (**www.vignette.com**)

359

Globalization Management Systems

As companies began localizing web sites for new markets, the need arose for content management systems that could also manage ongoing web localization—hence the introduction of *globalization management systems* (*GMSs*). A GMS adds a layer of content management to the process, thus ensuring that source content is translated, graphics are localized, and any changes to the source text are isolated and translated (see Figure 13.3). Some of the key benefits promised by a GMS include:

- **Less manual work.** The logistics of sending files back and forth between translators, project managers, and editors can be overwhelming and very time consuming. A GMS reduces file sharing, sometimes dramatically, and also helps project managers easily track the progress of files through the localization workflow. Some GMS packages enable translators to do their work through web-based interfaces, although these systems are not so successful when translators do not have dependable Internet connections.

- **Faster turnaround.** A GMS can be configured to alert translators when a new page needs to be translated, then alert the editor after it has been translated, and then alert the project manager when it's ready to go live. This level of automation helps accelerate the localization process.

- **Quality control.** As with a CMS, checks and balances can be installed to ensure quality. For example, before a localized web page goes live, a formal sign-off from the project manager might be required.

- **Vendor management.** Large web sites often require managing hundreds of independent translators or multiple translation firms. A GMS application can help you track the quality of a given translator as well as price fluctuations over time. You can analyze historical costs broken down by vendor, language, or file type. This information helps keep costs in line and helps you estimate future costs.

- **Translation memory management.** A GMS supports translation memories across the entire company and can implement rules and procedures that make sure the memory remains current.

- **Change detection and synchronization.** If you have a large decentralized web site and are using a CMS, it's possible to know whether someone changed text on a web page somewhere, but sometimes difficult to know which line of text was changed. A GMS can scan the modified page through translation memory to isolate the exact text string that was changed. This feature alone can save project managers significant resources.

- **Versioning.** Versioning is helpful for project managers because they can see what new content is coming and allocate resources accordingly.

FYI

Popular GMS Vendors

Convey Software (**www.conveysoftware.com**)
Glides (**www.glides.com**)
GlobalSight (**www.globalsight.com**)
Idiom (**www.idiominc.com**)
SDL (**www.sdlintl.com**)
Uniscape (**www.uniscape.com**)

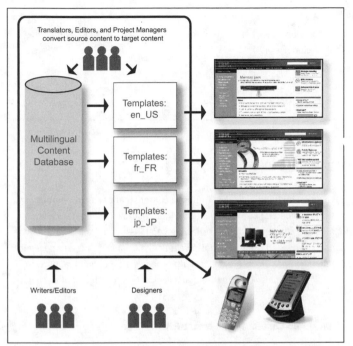

Figure 13.3 A globalization management system: Translators, editors, and project managers are incorporated into the workflow.

The Blurring of CMS and GMS

Implementing a CMS is difficult. Implementing a CMS *and* a GMS is, for many companies, not worth the effort or the cost. As a result, many GMS and CMS vendors have begun working more closely together to create more tightly integrated solutions. As localization management features are integrated into popular CMS applications, it's likely that the term "GMS" will fade away entirely (along with a few GMS vendors). Therefore, I'll stick with the term CMS for the rest of the chapter.

Although the blurring of terms can be confusing, the software you'll have to choose from is even more so. In truth, no one CMS vendor or one software package will work for every company, and some companies will be better off developing their own solutions. Perhaps the best way to arrive at your company's solution is to patiently and thoroughly examine what's out there.

┌─ CMS Meets GMS ─────────────────────────────────

Recent partnerships between content management firms and global management firms include:

Documentum + Lionbridge
Interwoven + Uniscape
Vignette + SDL

└──

CMS VENDORS UP CLOSE

Even if you plan on building your own in-house content management solution, it's useful to study commercial applications to understand how vendors tackle the many globalization challenges. In the following sections, you'll look briefly at two vendors who have tackled the globalization challenge from two different perspectives: Documentum and Idiom. Please note that these are just two of many vendors you should get familiar with before making a content management decision.

Documentum 4i Web Content Management Edition

Documentum is one of the giants in the content management industry. Although it originally focused on English content management software, it has since invested heavily in providing support for globalization. Documentum partnered with the localization firm Lionbridge to ensure that its software supported localization workflow, instead of creating an entirely new workflow (see Figure 13.4).

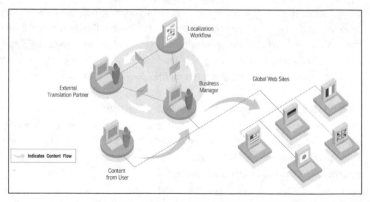

Figure 13.4 Documentum integrates globalization workflow into a company's existing content management workflow.

The Documentum 4i Web Content Management Edition creates, manages, and delivers web content in multiple languages and ensures that the appropriate relationships between source and target content are maintained. Documentum provides the WebPublisher interface, shown in Figures 13.5 and 13.6, for project managers. The interface helps focus the teams on the most pressing issues and also limits room for error.

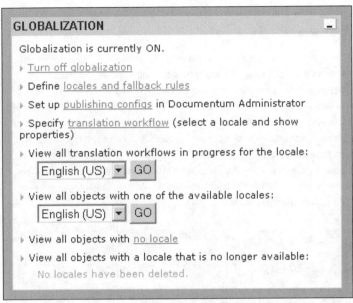

Figure 13.5 WebPublisher allows you to view the status of content translation.

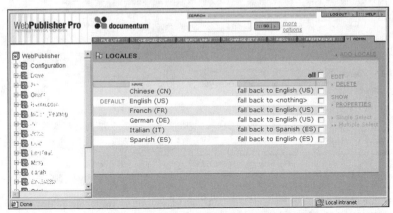

Figure 13.6 WebPublisher allows you to specify the default language and "fallback" rules. If, for example, a web page is not available in a target language, the server can be told to "fall back" to a backup language.

Documentum costs around $100,000, which puts it out of reach for many small companies. However, according to Documentum, more and more mid-sized companies are embracing its products because the long-term returns and cost savings easily justify the investment. In addition, Documentum offers its software in modules, so companies can start relatively small and build from there as their needs, and web sites, grow.

Idiom WorldServer 5

Documentum began as a CMS vendor, but Idiom began as a GMS vendor. Idiom claims that its understanding of globalization's unique challenges gives it an advantage over companies that have just recently expanded their English-only products into this globalization field. Its latest product, WorldServer 5, is designed to support enterprise globalization in any language. One of the strengths of WorldServer is its complex business rules support. You can establish intricate relationships between your source and target content and how it is used and reused, as shown in Figure 13.7. After you establish a relationship, WorldServer enforces it across any locale. WorldServer also offers web-based project-management features and supports translation memory.

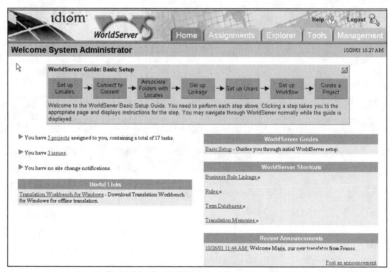

Figure 13.7   The WorldServer interface allows project managers to establish workflows and business rules.

One of the ongoing challenges for translators is knowing how translated text will appear in the context of the web page. WorldServer offers the ability to preview target web pages as they're being localized. WorldServer also supports versioning so that a translator can view an older version of a translated page, if needed. In addition, Idiom supports the wide-scale use of translation memory, as shown in Figure 13.8. Idiom, like Documentum, is not inexpensive to purchase and install. Yet companies are increasingly coming to realize that automation, properly implemented, can save time and money over the long run.

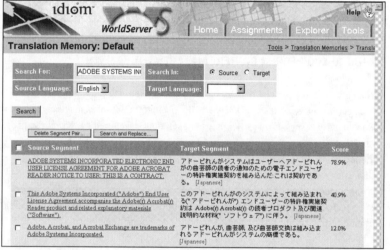

Figure 13.8 WorldServer supports translation memory—in this case, between English source text and Japanese target text.

GMS on the Cheap

Just because your company doesn't have the budget to afford a high-end globalization management package, you can still develop a homegrown solution. In fact, many companies get by just fine without purchasing specialized software. For example, if you have Dreamweaver or FrontPage, you can do quite a bit already. These two tools can be used to replicate many of the features of high-end content management systems, such as:

- **File checking.** Ensures that localized content is not modified without the project manager's knowledge.

- **Site synchronization.** Aids in maintaining consistency across all locales.

- **Template management.** Templates can be built and managed for each locale.

To manage workflow, you may already have a project-management tool on hand, such as Microsoft Project. Simply build a workflow tailored to your company and make sure that everyone adheres to it. Whether you purchase a high-end GMS, rent a GMS, or build your own, the challenges are the same: managing all those files and languages as efficiently as possible while making as few mistakes as possible.

365

> **Caveat CMS**
>
> Before you invest in a CMS application, invest the time in understanding the major content management vendors and solutions. The AIIM (Association for Information and Image Management) is a great place to start. AIIM, which now calls itself the Enterprise Content Management Association, holds an annual conference that draws all the major CMS vendors. For more information, go to **www.aiim.org**. In addition, the publication *Multilingual Computing & Technology* frequently covers the challenges of globalization management (**www.multilingual.com**).

WHAT TO LOOK FOR IN CONTENT MANAGEMENT SOFTWARE

The content management industry is going through a tough period of consolidation. For instance, what's now known as the Microsoft Content Management Server was, in early 2001, known as NCompass Resolution, developed by NCompass Labs. Also that year, the content management firm Divine acquired two other content management firms: Eprise and Open Market. Many experts believe that consolidation will result in stronger companies offering better products, but for the time being, it can be frustrating for clients who find their products frequently changing owners. Before selecting a vendor, invest the time to talk with companies that are already using various packages; ask them the following questions:

- **How flexible is it?** Can your IT department integrate the software into existing systems and customize it to your needs, or are you going to have to hire a consultant every month to make these changes?

- **Does the software support partial or subset localization?** For example, you might not want to fully translate some web pages; the system should support this option and exempt designated text from the translation cycle. Or you might want to create subset sites, such as "Spanish_Mexico, Spanish_Argentina, Spanish_Spain" that share some Spanish text but also contain unique translations. A management system should be able to accommodate these complex but realistic scenarios.

- **Does the system detect changes to source or target content?** You have to know when something has changed in any language, in any part of the site. You also need to know who changed it, at what time, and to what extent. If not, you'll fail to build an effective translation memory, and errors will inevitably slip by.

- **How are files sent out for translation?** Is this an automatic process? How prone to error is this process?

■ **Can your translators use it?** Too often, companies purchase systems that not all vendors are able to use because the system is not user friendly or requires a high-speed Internet connection, for example.

■ **Can your translation agencies use it?** If you're outsourcing all translation, you'll want to integrate the agency into the process, and this includes giving project managers some degree of access to the application. The ideal package allows multiple levels of access so that you can keep an eye on the outside project managers who are keeping an eye on the translators and editors.

■ **Does the software allow for metadata?** The software should provide a system for inserting comments and instructions to the translators and editors within the files. These notes are vital to ensuring quality throughout the process.

■ **Does the software support standards?** There is a standards group for nearly everything web related, including content management. The IETF World Wide Web Distributed Authoring and Versioning (WebDAV) Working Group has published a number of standards at **www1.ics.uci.edu/pub/ietf/webdav**. Standards by themselves don't guarantee better software, but they sometimes open the door to increased competition and compatibility among vendors and products.

367

SO MANY LANGUAGES; SO LITTLE TIME

Content management becomes an issue only when you have content to manage. For companies just embarking on web localization, content management is easily overlooked. But don't overlook the importance and complexity of maintaining localized web sites, particularly when it comes time to allocate budgets. Eventually, you'll need to update the localized web sites, and you'll need the staff and, possibly, the software to make it happen.

Now that you understand how to develop and manage a localized web site, it's time to begin promoting and supporting your localized web site. The next chapter, "Mastering Your (Country) Domain," will teach you how to register your company's domain name in just about any language and any country.

14

MASTERING YOUR (COUNTRY) DOMAIN

The Domain Name System (DNS) functions as the virtual phone book of the Internet. Just as everyone with a phone has a name and matching phone number, every computer connected to the Internet has both a domain name and matching Internet Protocol (IP) number. Without the DNS, people who want to visit Amazon.com would have to type in its IP address: 207.171.181.16. The DNS offers a user-friendly alternative to remembering those cumbersome IP addresses.

Unfortunately, when working with a global audience, the DNS is not nearly as user friendly. For instance, which address should French speakers enter when they want to find your French-language web site: .com or .fr? And how are Chinese speakers supposed to find your Chinese-language web site when your URL is in English, not Chinese?

On the World Wide Web, .com isn't always good enough. This chapter will help you make your web address more accessible to a global audience through the use of country domain names and internationalized domain names. First, let's review the DNS.

DNS 101

The DNS is a global network of servers structured a lot like an inverted tree (see Figure 14.1). At the top of this tree is the appropriately named root server, which contains a master list of all domain names and their matching IP addresses. The process of translating, or resolving, domain names into numbers is shared by thousands of DNS servers scattered throughout this tree and around the world, each responsible for a specific domain. You don't need to worry about how domain names are resolved, just how domain names fit together.

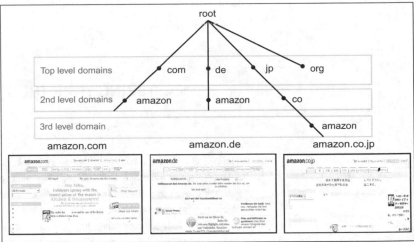

Figure 14.1 The Domain Name System: Not all countries administer their domains in exactly the same way. Notice how Japan adds a domain for specifying the nature of the organization—in this case, .co for commercial enterprise.

The hierarchical structure of the DNS is reflected in the domain names we use. Domain names consist of domains and subdomains, separated by periods. At the far right of the address is the top-level domain (TLD), such as .com, .org, .jp, or .de. There are two types of TLDs: generic top-level domains (gTLDs) and country code top-level domains (ccTLDs). Some examples of top-level domain names are shown in the following list:

Generic TLDs	Country Code TLDs
.com	.jp
.org	.uk
.net	.de
.biz	.fr
.info	.es

Following the top-level domain are typically the domain names we know and love (and occasionally fight over), names like Amazon and eBay. There are exceptions to this rule, as shown in Figure 14.1 with Amazon Japan. Notice how Japan inserts a new second-level domain: a .co for commercial enterprise. The U.K. also uses this model. Just be aware that not all countries administer their domains in exactly the same manner. When you register a domain name, you are not registering just the domain; you are registering the domain *and* a top-level domain. Given the growing number of top-level domains available, selecting which TLDs to register and which to skip can be daunting.

Every top-level domain opens a new front door to your web site:

amazon.com

amazon.co.uk

amazon.fr

amazon.net

amazon.de

Each of these domains is a new front door to your web site. The implications are significant, legally and strategically. Many companies register their domains along with numerous ccTLDs to protect their brand name abroad. If you're expanding abroad, the ccTLD does a lot more than just protect your brand name; it helps promote your brand name. For example, country-specific search engines often give preference to URLs with country-specific domains.

Emerging Domains

In November 2000, the Internet Corporation for Assigned Names and Numbers (ICANN) selected the following seven new gTLDs. The first two are now available, with the rest to follow.

- .biz (for business purposes)

- .info (unrestricted)

- .aero (for the entire aviation community)

- .coop (for cooperatives)

- .museum (for museums)

- .name (for personal names)

- .pro (for professionals)

For More Information About the DNS...

The DNS Resource Directory (**www.dns.net/dnsrd**) is an excellent reference.

The Internet Corporation for Assigned Names and Numbers (ICANN; **www.icann.org**) manages the gTLDs and accredits the registrars who are allowed to register them.

InterNIC (**www.internic.org**) manages the master "phone book" of IP addresses.

The Internet Assigned Numbers Authority (IANA; **www.iana.org**) manages the ccTLD names, although each country has the authority over how those names are used.

COUNTRY CODE DOMAIN NAMES

Companies that are serious about expanding into new countries should consider expanding into new domains. Currently, there are more than 240 ccTLDs; these codes are assigned by the Internet Assigned Numbers Authority (IANA) according to the ISO 3166 country abbreviations (see Appendix D, "Language and Country Codes").

Although anyone anywhere can register a generic TLD, a country has sole authority over how its ccTLD is used. For instance, Japan only recently allowed non-residents the right to register .jp domain names. Some country domains are popular for reasons that have nothing to do with the country. The nation of Tuvalu sold the rights to its .tv domain outright. Remember those "Get your .tv domain today!" advertisements? The Polynesian island of Niue has the .nu domain name, which is popular in Scandinavian countries, where *nu* translates to "now." Table 14.1 gives you an idea of which country domains are the most popular, based on the number of Internet hosts.

Table 14.1   Most Popular Country Domains

Domain	# of Hosts	Country
jp	5,887,096	Japan
ca	2,685,100	Canada
de	2,399,004	Germany
uk	2,349,710	United Kingdom
us	2,147,936	United States
it	2,015,621	Italy
au	1,865,350	Australia
nl	1,763,133	Netherlands
fr	1,404,617	France
tw	1,280,032	Taiwan
se	1,038,108	Sweden
br	1,025,067	Brazil
es	921,505	Spain
fi	872,618	Finland
mx	701,374	Mexico

*Source: Internet Domain Survey (**www.isc.org/ds/**).*

373

HOW TO REGISTER GLOBALLY

Registrars in search of new revenue sources, now that the .com domain has been staked out, see a bright future in registering ccTLDs. The more mainstream registrars, such as Register.com and VeriSign, offer a wide range of country domains (see Figure 14.2); you can also register through a country-specific registrar (see "Where to Get Registered").

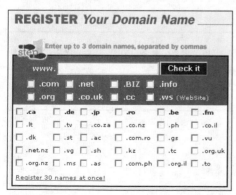

Figure 14.2   Registration alphabet soup: Register.com offers registration of 43 top-level domains.

Where to Get Registered

For a complete list of approved ccTLDs, go to:

www.iana.org/cctld/cctld-whois.htm

For the list of accredited registrars around the world, go to:

www.internic.net/language215.html

Why Register Yet Another Domain Name?

In case your boss needs a little convincing, here are the key reasons you need to consider registering domains for each country you're planning to enter:

- **Trademark protection.** It's less expensive to register a ccTLD now and sit on it a while than to wait, miss out on the domain, and then have to plead your case before the World Intellectual Property Organization (**http://arbiter.wipo.int/domains**). Giorgio Armani recently lost out to the armani.ca domain and Pepsi lost out on the pepsi.co.kr domain.

- **Usability.** Just as Americans are predisposed to think .com when they first guess at a web address, outside the U.S. it's not unusual to see people who guess at an address by using their country code domains first.

- **Marketability.** In the end, you want your audience to think of your company as a local company. A ccTLD is a step in that direction.

- **Searchability.** Local search engines give preference to web sites that use country-specific domain names. So if you want to do well on Russia's leading search engine, you really cannot afford not to invest in a .ru domain.

Consistency Counts

Domains are sometimes inconsistently used, as shown in these two Yahoo! domain names:

Yahoo! Japan: **http://www.yahoo.co.jp/**

Yahoo! China (Simplified): **http://cn.yahoo.com/**

FYI

A useful tool for getting familiar with the world's
many ccTLDs is the Global Web Explorer:
www.guernsey.net/~sgibbs/www.html.

INTERNATIONALIZED DOMAIN NAMES

The DNS, like the rest of the Internet, was never designed to support all the languages of the world. The current DNS allows only for a subset of the ASCII character set, specifically:

> A through Z (and a through z)
>
> 0 through 9
>
> hyphen

Consider the dilemma of the French car manufacturer, Citroën. If someone tries to visit Citroën's web site by typing **www.citroën.com,** he or she will be disappointed; the DNS doesn't recognize characters such as ë or ã, for example. As a result, web users must type **www.citroen.com**. Although this might seem like a trivial detail to many English speakers, it is anything but trivial to French speakers.

Citroën is relatively fortunate, for most of the characters in its name *are* included in ASCII. Consider how frustrating it must be for companies with names in languages that use no ASCII characters at all.

Entrepreneurs Rush In

In 1999, a startup company named i-DNS.net began registering the first internationalized domain names (IDNs). Suddenly, a company could register a web site in Chinese or Japanese characters. Within six months, i-DNS.net claimed that it had registered more than 50,000 names and was expanding its services from Asian countries to include more than 30 languages worldwide. Although the DNS supports only ASCII domain names, i-DNS.net developed software that converts IDNs into *ASCII-compatible encodings* (*ACEs*), which are resolved by domain name servers. Compare the differences between the DNS and IDNs in Figures 14.3 and 14.4.

375

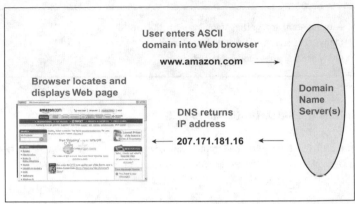

Figure 14.3 How the current DNS works: ASCII characters are turned into a numeric IP address and that address is used to locate the web server.

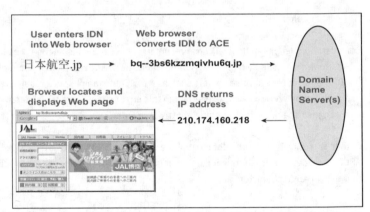

Figure 14.4 How IDNs work: Notice how the IDN is not retained in the browser address window.

Companies that register IDNs are actually registering only the ACE conversions of the IDNs, such as **bq--3bs6kzzmqivhu6q.jp** for Japan Air Lines. It's not an elegant solution, but it's catching on. In November 2000, VeriSign also began registering IDNs using an ACE conversion scheme, and claims that it has registered more than a million IDNs so far.

┌─ To Make Matters More Complicated... ───────────────────

Now that vendors offer IDNs, domain registration gets that much more complicated. For example, i-DNS.net offers two types of IDNs, as shown in Figure 14.5.

Location: http://简体中文. 雅虎. 公司

Location: http://삼성 .회사

Location: http://พีเอชนิค.พาณิชย์.ไทย

Location: http://简体.雅虎.com

Location: http://삼성.com

Location: http://ヤフー.com

Figure 14.5   i-DNS.net supports partial or fully internationalized
domain names.

In one type, the ".com" is translated, and in the other type, it's left in English. Although it makes perfect sense to translate the entire domain name, TLD and all, keep in mind that ICANN hasn't authorized it yet. According to Paul Hoffman at the IETF, "The IDN Working Group's work allows you to localize all parts. When we are done, ICANN will start work on internationalized root names for ccTLDs."

377

The Problem with Plug-ins

The drawback to the i-DNS.net solution is that you can't take advantage of IDNs until you download a plug-in (called iClient) that manages this IDN-to-ACE text conversion. "Plug-ins are not a broad-based solution," said Chris Dobbrow, senior vice president of global application sales for RealNames, a company that claimed to have found a broad-based solution.

RealNames offered a proprietary web addressing system known as Keywords (see Figure 14.6). Keywords were marketed as a more user-friendly form of domain names because they didn't require such details as **http://** or **.com**. You could simply enter the company's name, such as **Yahoo**, and be taken directly to that company's web site. Keywords worked as a sort of intermediary to the DNS system. RealNames had built its own network of servers that resolved the Keywords to their IP addresses. Because RealNames built its software to support Unicode, it could also register multilingual keywords.

Sample Keywords

Sony (Japanese): 中国万网

Hyundai-Motor.com (Korean): 현대자동차

Figure 14.6 Sample RealNames keywords.

Keywords were not without their drawbacks. A company had to register a Keyword before people could take advantage of it, and web users needed to have Internet Explorer installed (RealNames didn't work with Netscape).

A NEW RESOLUTION

In June 2001, RealNames partnered with VeriSign to offer resolution of IDNs. Illustrated in Figure 14.7, this strategy appeared to be the most promising so far because it side-stepped the drawbacks of both Keywords *and* plug-ins. Yet despite such promise, RealNames folded in June 2002 when Microsoft decided not to renew its contract with them. Rumor has it that Microsoft is going to build IDN resolution capability into its next generation of Explorer. Until then, companies that had registered multilingual domain names are left in limbo. VeriSign is now promoting a free plug-in that you can use in Explorer or Outlook to resolve IDNs, but this is a short-term solution. The long-term solution is a web browser that has IDN resolution built in and a DNS that fully supports IDNs, which brings us to the ongoing struggle over standards.

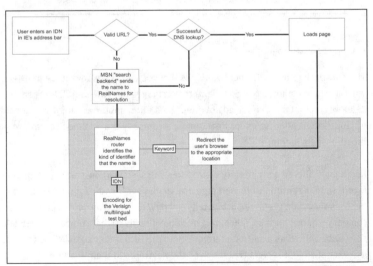

Figure 14.7 How RealNames handled IDNs: Using Internet Explorer, a web user entered an IDN. If the browser didn't recognize the name as valid, which happened with IDNs, it sent the name along to RealNames for resolution.

*Source: RealNames (**www.realnames.com**).*

The Search for Standards

Nobody can say for sure just how the DNS will react when asked to resolve IDNs on a massive scale, which is why the Internet Engineering Task Force (IETF) is involved. The IETF has been studying IDNs for more than two years; it is trying to recommend a protocol that not only enables IDNs to work, but also does not threaten the health of the existing DNS.

Given that the DNS currently resolves about a billion domain names a day, changing the DNS is a little like changing a tire on your car while driving. The DNS is a critical component of not just the Internet, but also email, Telnet, and FTP. As Paul Hoffman, director of the Internet Mail Consortium and technical advisor to the IETF IDN Working Group, puts it, "The IETF needs an IDN solution that works for all protocols, not just web browsers."

Overall, there are two schools of thought as to how to proceed: One school suggests we take this opportunity to build a brand-new DNS altogether; the other school wants to find a solution that leaves the DNS as is. John Klensin, who is currently technical advisor to the IETF IDN Working Group and chair of the Internet Architecture Board, was one of the people involved in deciding which characters would be in the *original* DNS. Ever wonder why the underscore character is not allowed in a domain name? "We didn't want it to be confused with the hyphen," says Klensin.

The problem with the DNS, says Klensin, isn't so much the DNS itself, but our expectations of what it should accomplish. The DNS was never intended to be anything more than a machine identifier. Instead of trying to upgrade the DNS so that it successfully navigates all these cultural, linguistic, political and legal issues, which he views as "hopeless," he proposes creating a new layer to the DNS.

Possible Solutions

This added layer would function as a sort of user-friendly directory and insulate the end user from having to deal with the messy details of the DNS. "We've made a horrible mistake of exposing URLs and domain names to the man on the street," says Klensin. The DNS doesn't allow for ambiguity, only yes or no. With a directory layer, users would find a more user-friendly DNS. For example, if you entered an incorrect domain name, this layer could display a pick list of options for you, instead of that error 404 page we've all seen enough of.

Although Klensin's solution certainly makes the most sense, it's not certain how much work or time would be required to make it a reality, and it's doubtful that vendors and the public will patiently await its development. As a result, the IETF is leaning toward a faster workaround that leaves the DNS as is. That solution appears to be Internationalized Domain Names for Applications (IDNA).

Because the DNS requires that a domain name be in an ACE format, IDNA proposes that client applications, such as a web browser, manage the character conversion internally. Says Hoffman, "IDNA makes the most sense of any of the proposed approaches. It requires no changes to DNS servers. More important, it puts no additional load on the DNS, particularly on the root servers."

If IDNA were implemented, software vendors would then have to build this functionality into their applications—not just web browsers, but email, Telnet, and FTP clients. The process would take some time, but because the DNS remains untouched, there should be no rude interruptions as these applications are deployed. IDNA is fully backward-compatible. If you entered a domain name, such as **newriders.com,** into the browser window, the application would simply skip the conversion and send the name out to the domain name server.

The IDNA proposal isn't perfect. When you input, for example, the Sega IDN (セガ. jp), the Sega web page appears; however, the browser address window displays the ACE, not the IDN. This is known as "name leak," shown in Figure 14.8.

Figure 14.8 Instead of displaying **www.sega.com**, the address window displays the ACE equivalent.

Hoffman concedes that name leak is an unfortunate side effect of IDNA. "When ACE names leak to users, the names are ugly. However, lots of ugly things in Internet protocols that should be hidden from users leak out—HTTP content types, for example." Nevertheless, it appears that IDNA will become a reality, as both Netscape and Microsoft have indicated that they will build support for the final standard into their browsers.

So what should you do now? You can wait for the IETF and ICANN to set standards for IDNs, or you can take your chances and register an IDN right now. Many companies are taking their chances. After all, the global markets are a vital source of revenue. Anything that will make your web site more easily accessible could pay for itself very soon. VeriSign is quick to note that even if the standards do change dramatically, it will do its best to make sure current registrants do not lose names they've registered. Before rushing off to the registrar, however, take time to study your domain name and the market you're entering.

Although internationalized domain names are complicated, messy, and uncertain, they also appear inevitable. For the Internet to be truly local—on a global scale— IDNs provide the missing link.

BEYOND THE .COM

Although ".com" might always be your company's primary address on the Internet, why limit yourself to just one address? If you invest the resources into localizing your web site for new markets, consider localizing your URL as well. The DNS is not the most user-friendly system. By registering a country domain or multilingual domain, or both, you can make the DNS a little more user friendly for your customers, no matter where they live or what language they speak—and you may gain a few new customers as well.

Befrienders International

Working to prevent suicide worldwide with 31,000 volunteers in over 40 countries

NEED TO TALK? | FIND A HELPLINE | HELPING A FRIEND | SUICIDE MYTHS | WARNING SIGNS

HOME | ABOUT US | CONTACT US | GET INVOLVED | FEEDBACK | DONATE ONLINE

HELP AND SUPPORT

Feeling Suicidal Or Depressed?

Worried About A Suicidal Friend?

The Warning Signs Of Suicide

Suicide Helplines - Online Directory

FURTHER INFORMATION

Suicide Statistics

Arabic
Chinese
Dansk
Deutsch
Español
Français
Magyar
Nederlands
Português
Russian
Suomi

Figure 1   Befrienders International home page.

BEFRIENDERS INTERNATIONAL

Founded in 1974, Befrienders International offers free confidential counseling for the depressed and suicidal by phone and email. Based in London with a network of 375 support centers in 41 countries, this non-profit organization relies on private and public donations as well as a global network of trained volunteers.

www.befrienders.org

Localized web sites:

- Arabic
- Chinese
- Danish
- Dutch
- Finnish
- French
- German
- Hungarian
- Portuguese
- Russian
- Spanish

ANALYSIS

Befrienders proves that you don't need to be a Fortune 500 company (with a Fortune 500 budget) to build a global web site. Befrienders offers web support in 11 languages, including the challenging languages of Arabic and Chinese. Combined, the localized sites account for more than half of the world's population and more than two-thirds of all Internet users.

Simple Is Good

The Befrienders web site keeps things simple. As a rule, if you want to hold down localization costs, simpler is better. In this case, the web site is almost entirely text-based, resulting in web pages that load more quickly and can be localized more quickly. By avoiding graphics with embedded text, Befrienders saves a lot of time and potentially a lot of money. As you've seen in the Hands-On chapters, editing text within graphics can be challenging because of text expansion issues as well as the inability of many English-language software applications to support Asian, Russian, or Arabic text. Befrienders also saves money (and ensures quality) by relying on a network of international volunteers to proof and edit translations.

The Global Gateway: Almost There

The global gateway occupies a major portion of the home page, making it hard to miss and easy to read (see Figure 2). The available languages listed in the gateway, with the exception of Chinese and Arabic, are translated into the target languages—an often-overlooked step toward ensuring usability. Chinese and Arabic are more challenging to display because they require different character sets (and different fonts on the user's end). In fact, the only way to effectively display all these languages on one web page is for a web developer to use the Unicode character set and a web user to install a font that contains all the necessary scripts. Although Windows 2000 and XP ship with the necessary fonts, it's best to assume for now that most users don't have this luxury. The ideal workaround is to create graphics of these two links in the native scripts, thus ensuring that users in any country with any font can view the language properly.

Arabic
Chinese
Dansk
Deutsch
Español
Français
Magyar
Nederlands
Português
Russian
Suomi

Figure 2 The global gateway is impossible to miss and, with the exception of Arabic and Chinese, easy for native speakers to read.

The only noticeable drawback to the Befrienders site is the splash page, shown in Figure 3, that all users encounter before arriving at the home page. This page is available only in English, which could lead many users to assume that the subsequent pages are only in English, too. The global gateway should always be clearly located on the first page that users encounter. According to Befrienders, a solution is in the works.

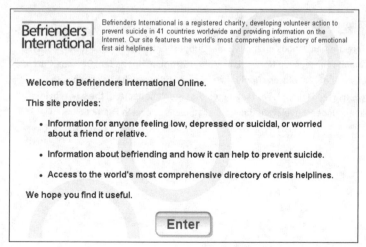

Befrienders International is a registered charity, developing volunteer action to prevent suicide in 41 countries worldwide and providing information on the Internet. Our site features the world's most comprehensive directory of emotional first aid helplines.

Welcome to Befrienders International Online.

This site provides:

- Information for anyone feeling low, depressed or suicidal, or worried about a friend or relative.

- Information about befriending and how it can help to prevent suicide.

- Access to the world's most comprehensive directory of crisis helplines.

We hope you find it useful.

Enter

Figure 3 The Befrienders splash page.

Managing Expectations

Although Befrienders has not yet localized all its content into all languages, it does an excellent job of letting you know what is and isn't offered in your language. For example, if you select the Español link on the global gateway, you are taken to a splash page (shown in Figure 4) that tells users what to expect.

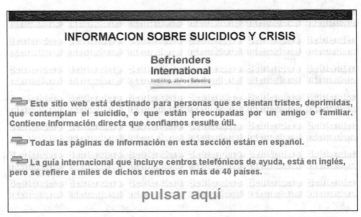

INFORMACION SOBRE SUICIDIOS Y CRISIS

Befrienders
International
listening, always listening

Este sitio web está destinado para personas que se sientan tristes, deprimidas, que contemplan el suicidio, o que están preocupadas por un amigo o familiar. Contiene información directa que confiamos resulte útil.

Todas las páginas de información en esta sección están en español.

La guía internacional que incluye centros telefónicos de ayuda, está en inglés, pero se refiere a miles de dichos centros en más de 40 países.

pulsar aquí

Figure 4   The locale splash page notifies Spanish speakers of which sections are available in Spanish and which are not.

Email Support

Many larger organizations offer customer support only in English, but Befrienders offers email counseling in Norwegian, Malay, Estonian, Hungarian, German, Dutch, and Polish. The local offices supply the support and the web site provides the instructions (see Figure 5). For languages that aren't supported, the site provides disclaimers under the relevant links; an example is shown in Figure 6.

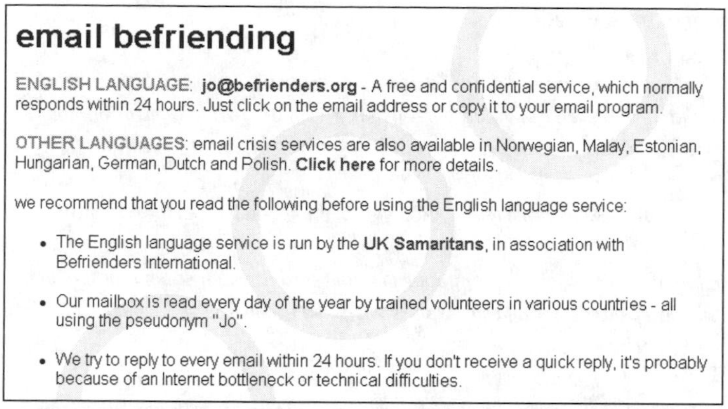

email befriending

ENGLISH LANGUAGE: **jo@befrienders.org** - A free and confidential service, which normally responds within 24 hours. Just click on the email address or copy it to your email program.

OTHER LANGUAGES: email crisis services are also available in Norwegian, Malay, Estonian, Hungarian, German, Dutch and Polish. **Click here** for more details.

we recommend that you read the following before using the English language service:

- The English language service is run by the **UK Samaritans**, in association with Befrienders International.

- Our mailbox is read every day of the year by trained volunteers in various countries - all using the pseudonym "Jo".

- We try to reply to every email within 24 hours. If you don't receive a quick reply, it's probably because of an Internet bottleneck or technical difficulties.

Figure 5 Befrienders email support page.

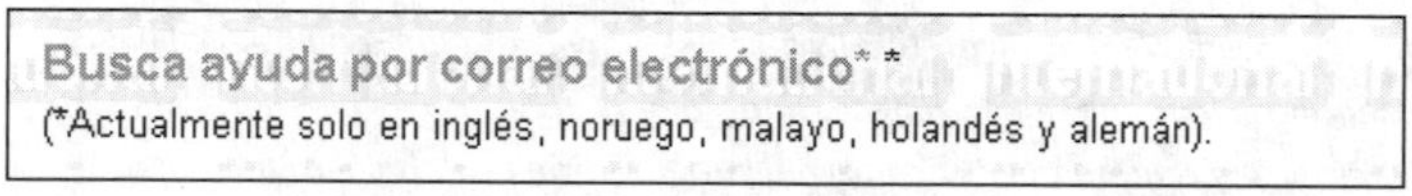

Busca ayuda por correo electrónico* *
(*Actualmente solo en inglés, noruego, malayo, holandés y alemán).

Figure 6 Befrienders doesn't offer email support for Spanish and lets you know this when you click through.

Q&A WITH BEFRIENDERS INTERNATIONAL

Eric Jarvis, Assistant Manager
Befrienders International Online

Explain why you chose the languages that you offer.

The site was originally developed in English; the first additional languages chosen were Spanish and German. Both languages were chosen because they account for a large number of web users and because there are few resources available in these languages. It also helped that the webmaster was fluent in German. Portuguese was chosen because we have numerous befriending centers in Brazil, and Danish because we were running a large program in Denmark. Finnish and Dutch were chosen because they are languages from countries with a high level of Internet use.

Any additional languages planned?

Japanese, Swahili, Bengali, and Hindi are imminent. No decisions have been made on what languages to add after that. Likely contenders are Greek, Hausa, Italian, Javanese, Korean, Serbian, Tamil, and Vietnamese.

Who manages the translation?

We use a translation agency to produce a fairly direct translation of what we send them in English, and then use volunteers, usually from our own organization, to judge whether the text matches the aims and objectives of our organization.

Since translation is so expensive, how did you manage such an extensive site?

Sponsorship. Budgeting for new languages is built into the sponsorship proposal each year. Translation is not all that expensive, given the extra traffic that is brought to the site by each new language.

What unexpected challenges did you face when localizing for so many languages?

The biggest problem is character representation for non-Western languages. This is not something we have dealt with totally successfully. There are a number of ways of representing a language like Chinese, and none is accepted as a general standard. We currently tend to use Unicode, but other options will have to be added to the site in the near future. In general, site management has been dealt with by thinking ahead rather than by using software to manage the site by brute force.

Of all the languages, which is the most popular in terms of usage?

English is first by a clear margin, and Spanish is second by a long way. German and French are neck and neck for third and fourth. Arabic is next, having recently overtaken Dutch and Portuguese.

It takes a long while to establish a new language with the search engines, so popularity of usage is partly a matter of how long we've had the pages published and how much time we spend on promoting them.

How do you measure success for each of your localized sites?

At present, we judge simply on site usage. We can't make any useful comparisons by measuring extra calls to member centers. We have no befriending centers in Finland, for instance, and only two in Arabic-speaking countries. We aim to make the usage of the various translations correspond closely to the online population in each language.

Any advice for a company that is planning a web globalization project?

Think ahead. What you do when you add Spanish next month will affect what you will need to do when you add Korean next year. So try to take it into account from the beginning. Look into issues such as character sets before you choose which languages you will add. It is much easier and cheaper to work in languages that are at least vaguely recognizable.

Make sure you get everything you will need into the translation—that also means the descriptions and keywords you will use to submit to search engines, and the name of the language to go in your languages menu (we forgot that with Arabic).

389

HANDS-ON: ARABIC

Overview

This is the fifth of six Hands-On chapters. By now, you have completed Hands-On chapters for Spanish; French, Italian, and German; Russian; and Chinese and Japanese. Collectively, these chapters demonstrate the process (and challenges) of localizing an English-language web page into multiple languages. After completing all Hands-On chapters, you will have localized one web page into eight languages—the languages spoken by more than 80% of the world's population. If you'd like to try your hand at these exercises, all files used in these chapters are available for download; go to **www.bytelevel.com/beyondborders**.

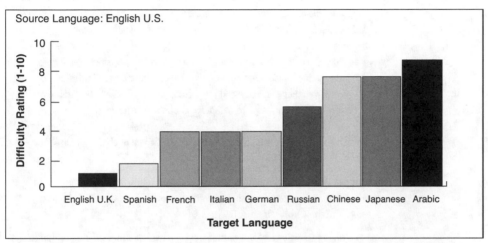

Source Language: English U.S.

Figure 1 The difficulty ratings from Chapter 1, "In the Beginning, There Was English."

For a full list of country and language codes, see Appendix D, "ISO Country and Language Code Charts."

Speakers worldwide: 181 million; Arabic is spoken in more than 20 countries.

(Source: Ethnologue, *14th Edition, 2000;* ***www.ethnologue.com****)*

ISO language code: AR

Difficulty rating: 9 (see Figure 1)

Major Arabic locales:

Country	Language Code
Saudi Arabia	ar-SA
Egypt	ar-EG
Jordan	ar-JO
Kuwait	ar-KW

FIRST THOUGHTS

Arabic belongs to the Semitic family of languages, which also includes Hebrew and Amharic (primarily spoken in Egypt). Arabic, the language of the Qur'an, is widely used throughout the Muslim world. Like Chinese, Arabic has many dialects. An Arabic speaker in Morocco might not be able to understand an Arabic speaker in Iran, although they share a common written language. Arabic uses considerably fewer characters than Chinese or Japanese, yet that does not make it any less challenging for web localization. In fact, Arabic poses some of the greatest web localization challenges because of poor software support and an acute shortage of Arabic translators. The American Translators Association lists only 65 English-to-Arabic translators in its online directory (**www.atanet.org**), compared with more than 1,200 English-to-Spanish translators. Not coincidentally, Arabic is also one of the more expensive languages to translate. Despite the costs and the challenges, more and more companies are developing Arabic web pages, but not without running into a number of obstacles, including:

- **Which character set?** Once again, you have a choice of character sets. And once again, they conflict with one another.

- **How to manage bi-directional text.** Arabic text reads from right to left and occasionally left to right. You'll learn how to manage bi-directional text in HTML and learn how browsers display it.

- **The final gateway.** Last, but not least, you have one more graphic to add to the global gateway (see Figure 2). Unfortunately, Photoshop doesn't handle Arabic script, so you'll need to learn a workaround solution.

Figure 2   The gateway for the Tower of Babel page, with just one more language to go ....

TOOLS

English-language software still provides little support for Arabic. Photoshop and Illustrator come up short, as do Dreamweaver and Adobe GoLive—which leads you back to the following tools:

Operating system:	Windows XP
HTML:	FrontPage 2000
Text:	Word 2000
Graphics:	Microsoft Paint

ABOUT ARABIC

Although Arabic uses only 28 characters, it's a lot more complex than a language like English because the characters themselves exhibit properties you might not have encountered before. Arabic is a cursive script, in which most characters join together, end to end. This "joining" property means that characters change shape based on their positions within a word. Most Arabic characters have three forms: initial, medial, and final. To see how joining works, the three characters shown in Figure 3, when combined, form the Arabic word for "river": *nahr*.

Figure 3 The three characters seen individually.

When the characters are joined together (which happens automatically in a text editor), they change shapes, as shown in Figure 4.

Figure 4 When combined, the characters change shape and form the Arabic word for river.

Arabic Character Sets

Over the years, more than a dozen Arabic character sets have evolved. The first widely adopted Arabic set was AMO 708, which was gradually replaced by the ISO standard, ISO-8859-6. Not surprisingly, Microsoft developed its own Codepage 1256 (Arabic Windows), used in Figure 5. Also not surprisingly, these two sets conflict with one another. Most web developers now use 1256. However, in this chapter, you're going to deviate from Microsoft's Codepage and use Unicode. Some Arab web sites are now developed using Unicode because it sidesteps the entire ISO/Microsoft Codepage conflict. Given that the Internet revolution is still in its infancy throughout the Arab Middle East, Unicode might actually be the best character set to begin with, as new web users generally have the more recent, Unicode-compliant web browsers. Current versions of Netscape Navigator and Internet Explorer (for Windows and Macintosh) correctly display both Arabic Windows and Unicode character sets.

Figure 5   The MSN Saudi Arabia site naturally uses Windows Codepage 1256, also known as Windows (Arabic).

FYI

Arabic Internet Resources

Arabic language resource (**http://i-cias.com/babel/arabic**)

Arabic and Unicode (**www.hclrss.demon.co.uk/unicode/arabic.html**)

Windows Codepage 1256 (**www.microsoft.com/globaldev/reference/sbcs/1256.htm**)

Online Arabic dictionary and translation (**http://english.ajeeb.com**)

MANAGING BI-DIRECTIONAL TEXT

Arabic is a bi-directional (bidi) script. Arabic text flows from right to left, but Arabic numerals and Latin text appearing in Arabic text retain their left-to-right orientation, as shown in Figure 6.

Figure 6 What a "bidi" language looks like.

Before browsers supported bidi display, web developers created "visually ordered" pages, in which they entered text in the reverse order. This method was painstaking—imagine typing a paragraph backward, one letter at a time. Fortunately, current browsers display bidi text quite well, assuming that you encode and tag the web page properly. The web browser ensures that the text flows in its correct direction, yet it won't flip the layout of the web page unless you specify it.

HTML 4 provides the bi-directional attributes: **"ltr"** for left to right and **"rtl"** for right to left. You can use them for an entire page, by inserting **<HTML dir="rtl">**, for example, or you can denote text direction as needed, such as **<SPAN dir="ltr">**. The advantage of these attributes is that you can also use them as needed to flip the layout of your web page, as shown in the global gateway in Figure 7.

Figure 7 What's wrong with this picture? The text is aligned left instead of right.

To flip a left-to-right text layout to a right-to-left layout, add **"dir=rtl"** to the **<HTML>** tag. Also, don't forget the **<LANG>** tag:

<HTML dir="rtl" lang="ar">

Because you're targeting only the Arabic language, you don't need to add the country code in the preceding tag. After you insert the direction tag, the page should look like Figure 8.

Figure 8 With the text direction tag inserted, the page flows correctly. Notice how the scrollbar also moves to the other side.

The default text direction for all web pages is left to right, so you need to add the **"rtl"** attribute whenever necessary. Flipping the scrollbar to the other side of the page is a relatively new feature of web browsers, known as *mirroring*. You can actually force page mirroring by choosing View, Encoding on IE's menu (see Figure 9).

Figure 9 If you want to force page mirroring, you can override the page settings with your browser. This feature is active only for pages that display bidi text.

The problem with the **dir** tag is that it flips everything on a web page, including graphics. Notice how the graphics in the global gateway of Figure 8 are also flipped. You might not want this degree of flipping, or mirroring, to occur because it throws the notion of global usability out the window. Fortunately, you can nest **dir** tags within one another, as shown in Figures 10 and 11. You can insert the tag **<SPAN dir="ltr">** around the global gateway so that the graphics retain the same positions they have on the other language web pages.

```
</head>
<body bgcolor="ffffff">
<table width="500" cellpadding="5" cellspacing="5" b
<tr><td><span dir="ltr">
<table bgcolor="dddddd" align="right">
<a href="../index.html"><img src="../images/en.gif"
<a href="../fr/babel_fr.html"><img src="../images/fr
<a href="../it/babel_it.html"><img src="../images/it
<a href="../de/babel_de.html"><img src="../images/de
<a href="../es/babel_es.html"><img src="../images/es
<a href="../ru/babel_ru.html"><img src="../images/ru
<a href="../cn/babel_cn.html"><img src="../images/cn
<a href="../jp/babel_jp.html"><img src="../images/jp
<a href="../ar/babel_ar.html"><img src="../images/ar
</table></span>
```

Figure 10 If you insert **<SPAN dir="ltr">** around the global gateway, the graphics will retain the same layout as on the other language web pages.

Figure 11 Now the Arabic text flows properly, and the gateway remains consistent across all languages.

LOCALIZATION NOTES

In previous Hands-On chapters, much of what you've done is copy and paste text from the translator into the target web pages, but when using Arabic, this strategy can lead to trouble. If your software does not support the joining and bidi properties of the Arabic characters, the words will look flipped and separated from one another, as shown in Figure 12 using Photoshop. In this case, the Arabic word for *river* was pasted into Photoshop and all properties were lost.

For this exercise, you need to be careful about the software you use. Word 2000 and FrontPage 2000 in Windows XP do maintain the proper display of Arabic characters, even after copying and pasting.

397

Figure 12 The Arabic word for *river* does not appear correctly in Photoshop 6.

The Final Gateway

All you need now is just one more graphic to complete the global gateway. Inserting Arabic text into that graphic could be a lot harder than it seems, however, because none of the major English-language graphics applications—Photoshop, Illustrator, or Freehand—support Arabic text. Just as you did in the "Hands-On: Russian" chapter, you'll have to revert to using Microsoft Paint in Windows XP (see Figure 13). Although Paint works fine for a simple graphic or two, it's not going to be useful for the more complex graphics on most web sites. As a result, you might want to consider outsourcing the graphics localization entirely or installing localized Arabic software, such as the Arabic version of Photoshop. For a full list of which language versions of Photoshop are currently available, go to **www.adobe.com/products/photoshop/languages.html**. Be aware that software developers don't always release all localized versions of a software application at the same time. For more information on which localized software applications are currently available, you can also visit World Language at **www.worldlanguage.com**.

Figure 13 Microsoft Paint (in Windows XP) comes to the rescue with full Arabic support.

Help Your Web Users

Because Arabic has only recently been supported in web browsers, instructing web users in how to display the web pages is often helpful. The Befrienders web page (see "Spotlight: Befrienders," prior to this chapter) includes a handy instruction page, shown in Figure 14. To create a helpful instruction page, take the time to pre-view your Arabic web pages using a wide range of browsers and versions. Also, make sure you remove any Arabic font from your system beforehand so that you can better understand what a new user might experience when first visiting your site.

399

Figure 14 The page at the top gives users a "help" option. Clicking on the "Can't see Arabic?" link displays a detailed explanation (at the bottom) on how to find fonts and adjust browsers.

Form Input Issues

Supporting user input on web pages can be tricky. You have to be prepared for a host of encodings. When someone fills out a form and submits it, the text input generally matches the encoding of the user's system. So a user in Japan enters text in one encoding, and a user in Jordan enters a different encoding. Web developers need to either instruct users to follow a rigid input method, which really isn't practical, or develop scripts that convert all input into one encoding, such as UTF-8. Encoding conversion relies on mapping tables. To see how the Arabic character set 8859-6 maps to Unicode, go to **www.unicode.org/public/mappings/ISO8859**.

What About Hebrew?

Hebrew, because it is a bidi language, presents many of the same challenges as Arabic (see an example in Figure 15). Hebrew does rely on different character sets: 8859-8 and Windows Codepage 1255.

Figure 15   The Office Depot home page in the U.S. and Israel.

A GOOD BEGINNING

With Arabic complete, your web page now comfortably speaks to a potential audience of 2.2 billion people and more than 80% of all web users (see Figure 16). Even with eight languages, however, you're only just getting started. The Hands-On exercises neglected to tackle a host of localization challenges, such as date and currency formatting, form inputs, interactivity, and so forth. But now that you have a solid grounding in the basics, particularly character set/encoding issues, you're fully prepared to take on the more complex challenges that await.

Figure 16   The finished Arabic web page.

Credit: Andrew Freeman provided editing and technical support. He is a Ph.D. candidate in Arabic Linguistics at the University of Michigan and can be reached at **www-personal.umich.edu/~andyf**.

15

SUPPORTING INTERNATIONAL CUSTOMERS

International customer support is often viewed as the final stage of web globalization. Although this stage doesn't take place until after the site is launched, it is one of the most important stages. Would you order from a web site that didn't offer an easy way to return the product? Would you order a product that wasn't priced in your local currency?

You should plan for customer support well before you begin translation. This chapter shows you the challenges you'll face when supporting a global audience and some options and vendors available to help.

LIMITED SUPPORT AND LOCALIZED FAÇADES

Given how challenging and expensive it can be to effectively support customers within the U.S., don't expect to offer all types of support when you leave the U.S, and don't lead your web site visitors to assume you offer more support than you do. Some companies develop *localized façades*, in which only the first few pages are translated, accompanied by limited, or no, customer support (see Figure 15.1). Localized façades, it is argued, are better than no localized web pages at all. However, web pages that create false expectations and frustrated users could actually be worse than no web pages at all. If you can afford only a few localized pages, go a step further and let your visitors know what support options you offer and don't offer.

Figure 15.1   The Siebel Brazil home page is a localized façade; the **Clique aqui para saber mais** link on the home page to the left (which means "click here to learn more") takes you to the English-only page on the right—not a nice way to manage expectations.

CUSTOMER SUPPORT CHANNELS

Customer support means different things to different people. One person might want to pick up the phone to get more information, while another goes straight to your web site. Ideally, customer support includes all major communications channels: web, email, phone, retail. Realistically, you might not have the budget to cover all channels. Customer support typically begins with your web site, as it is usually your international customer's first point of contact.

Web-Based Support

The knowledge base has become a familiar feature on many web sites, sometimes one of the most popular features for visitors. Knowledge bases, which are basically collections of support materials, FAQs, and tutorials, are popular with site managers as well because they often pay for themselves by reducing the strain on other, more costly, support channels.

IBM Leverages Web to Reduce Call Volume

Since 1996, IBM Personal Systems Group has offered a localized technical "self-support" web site. The primary goal of the site was to decrease the number of calls to the international call centers. The localization required translating more than 85,000 files. According to IBM, the cost of maintaining the site in each language is paid for by the first 45 calls deflected each day.

*Source: Lionbridge (**www.lionbridge.com**).*

The knowledge base you offer depends on your customers and what kinds of support they need. Symantec has a Q&A support section, shown in Figure 15.2, that presents a series of questions designed to lead you to your answer. This interface is ideal for people who don't want to spend a lot of time searching through the web site, but more sophisticated web users might find the limited support options frustrating.

405

introduzione

Per facilitare l'individuazione delle risposte ai quesiti di supporto tecnico e servizio clienti, l'impostazione di questo sito prevede lo svolgimento di una serie di fasi guidate. La maggior p clienti trova la risposta nelle fasi iniziali. Se non si riesce a trovare una risposta, nell'ultima fa possibile contattare un tecnico o un rappresentante del servizio clienti di Symantec.

Per passare alla fase successiva fare clic sul pulsante giallo "continua" nella parte inferiore d ciascuna pagina.

selezionare prodotto e versione

Per iniziare, selezionare il prodotto e la versione, o fare clic qui se il problema non è correlato a un pro

1 | Norton Internet Security |

2 | 2001 Family Edition 3.0 | come trovare la versione

3 (continua)

Figure 15.2 Symantec uses a simple Q&A interface with few options.

Autodesk takes a different approach—offering you far more choices as well as a search engine, so you can be the one asking the questions (see Figure 15.3). Included among the support features are a knowledge base, newsletter, and collection of support topics from the past seven days.

Figure 15.3 Autodesk's German support site is more complex and feature-rich.

Email Support

If your company has no system in place for responding to emails in foreign languages, you're not alone. The research firm IDC and localization firm Wordlingo conducted a test of how companies respond to emails in various languages. In 2001, they studied 247 Fortune 500 and Forbes International 800 companies located around the world. Of the companies studied, more than 90% failed to respond to emails that were not in their native language. English email messages sent to countries with a native language other than English received a response rate of 44%, but U.S. companies responded at a rate of 8%. As expected, emails sent in Spanish were the most likely to receive a reply in Spanish, although none of the companies replied appropriately to Japanese emails.

If your company cannot offer multilingual email support, let your visitors know. A simple message above your contact addresses might not prevent visitors from sending you emails that you can't answer, but it's a start. If you do offer multilingual support, you should also let your visitors know, as they might assume otherwise. Lands' End does an excellent job of instructing customers how to email them. Even the sample email addresses are localized (see Figure 15.4).

Figure 15.4 Lands' End Italy and U.K. email support pages: Even the sample addresses are localized.

Managing Multilingual Email

Email messages are a lot like web pages in that they rely on character sets. If your support team doesn't have the correct fonts installed to support the full range of global character sets, you might have trouble displaying email messages from around the world. Fortunately, email clients such as Microsoft Outlook alert you when the email requires a new font (see Figure 15.5).

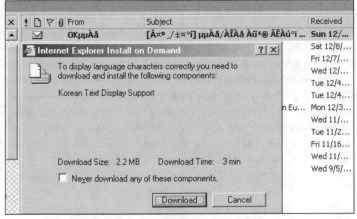

Figure 15.5 Microsoft Outlook alerts you if you don't have the necessary font to display the characters. In this case, a Korean email triggered the download dialog box.

407

Phone Support

Phone support, once seen as a financial drain by many organizations, is increasingly being viewed as a profit center. Companies have learned that effective phone support can drive additional sales and retain customers. In addition, no matter how usable your e-commerce web site is, there will always be people who would rather phone in orders. Of course, making it easy for people to call in often requires creating country-specific or international toll-free numbers. Lands' End creates country-specific toll-free numbers and clearly posts them on every web page of each localized site (see Figure 15.6). If you offer toll-free support for your American customers, consider offering it to everyone.

Figure 15.6   Lands' End Italy and U.K. phone support is made clear on every web page.

As companies evolve globally, so do call centers. It's not unusual for a customer in the U.S. to dial an 800 number and speak with a support person in India or New Zealand. Managing call centers that support multiple languages is particularly challenging. Companies such as Gateway and Dell have established European multilingual call centers, in which calls are allocated to language-specific personnel based on country of origin. Someone calling from Italy will speak to someone who speaks Italian, even though that support person might be based in Ireland. Pan-European centers allow a company to serve a market of 17 countries, without having to open 17 different call centers. In addition, countries throughout Europe are working to standardize toll-free numbers so that your web site can announce one toll-free number throughout Europe. Some of the more popular service providers are listed here:

Popular Contact Center Service Providers

Convergys (**www.convergys.com**)

eGain (**www.egain.com**)

Sitel (**www.sitel.com**)

Stream International (**www.stream.com**)

Sykes (**www.sykes.com**)

Many call centers have transformed themselves into "contact centers," as they expand their range of offerings to include email, billing, and promotional support. Convergys is one such company; through its 41 worldwide contact centers, it manages more than a million contacts each day by phone, email, web chat, mail, and fax. Global, integrated customer support is a rapidly growing market. According to the research firm Datamonitor, the number of contact centers in Europe, Middle East, and Africa (EMEA) will grow from 1,000 in 2000 to 7,000 in 2005.

FYI

For more information about customer support resources, visit the Service & Support Professionals Association (SSPA) at **www.supportgate.com**.

Phone Support by Interpretation

Another customer service option is to hire someone to act as interpreter on your phone support calls. Language Line (**www.languageline.com**) provides interpretation services in more than 140 languages, 24 hours a day. This service enables you to offer multilingual support without having to hire and train multilingual support staff.

409

PAYMENT

To sell goods online to international customers, your web site needs to offer localized currencies and payment collection.

Self-Service Currency Conversion

Ideally, your web site manages currency conversion dynamically, so that all your customers see are the localized prices. If you can't afford this level of functionality, however, you can make it relatively easy for customers to do the conversion themselves. Simply include a link to a free currency converter, such as Oanda (**www.oanda.com**) or XE (**www.xe.com**), shown in Figure 15.7.

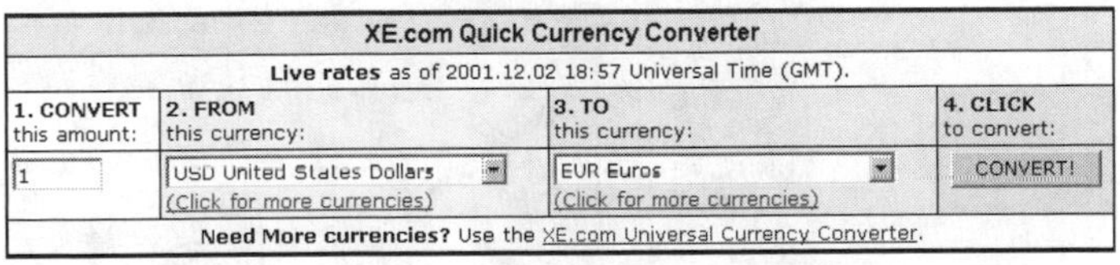

XE.com Quick Currency Converter			
Live rates as of 2001.12.02 18:57 Universal Time (GMT).			
1. CONVERT this amount:	**2. FROM** this currency:	**3. TO** this currency:	**4. CLICK** to convert:
1	USD United States Dollars ▼ (Click for more currencies)	EUR Euros ▼ (Click for more currencies)	CONVERT!
Need More currencies? Use the XE.com Universal Currency Converter.			

Figure 15.7   XE allows you to convert 164 currencies.

The problem with making customers do the conversion is not just the added hassle, but the perceived risk. People want to know exactly how much will be charged to their credit cards; should currency rates fluctuate between the time of ordering and the time the card is debited, the customer might be in for a pleasant (or painful) surprise.

Dynamic Currency Conversion

A much more user-friendly option is dynamic currency conversion, in which customers see prices only in the local currency. There are vendors that will supply you with the tools to embed the functionality into your site, and then you simply need to get a daily update of the currency exchange rates. Oanda provides a subscription service, FXCommerce, that enables you for $40 per month to offer items in localized currencies (see Figures 15.8 and 15.9).

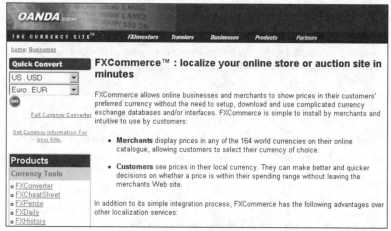

Figure 15.8 The Oanda currency conversion tool, FXCommerce, offers users a more dynamic currency conversion.

Figure 15.9 Using Oanda's conversion tool.

Get to Know the Euro

On January 1, 2002, 12 national currencies, including the franc, deutsche mark, and lira, were replaced by just one: the euro. The euro (abbreviated EMU for European Monetary Unit) is now the dominant currency of the European Union (EU), a market made up of more than 400 million people (see Figure 15.10). Even the U.K. is now considering adopting the euro. The euro promises to make it easier to do business in the EU.

Figure 15.10 For information about the euro, go to **www.euro.ecb.int**.

The euro will only continue to gain momentum as additional countries join over the next few years. Although many are lamenting the loss of their native currencies, they aren't lamenting the savings in hassles and bank fees when traveling across borders.

Even with the advent of the euro, there are still many currencies in the world, so the ISO developed the currency abbreviation standard, ISO 4217. A few of the abbreviations are shown in this list:

Japan, yen	JPY
EMU, euros	EUR
U.S., dollars	USD
Russia, rubles	RUR
India, rupees	INR

*For more information, visit **www.xe.com/iso4217.htm**.*

411

Credit Cards: Not Everywhere You Want To Be

Credit cards may be ubiquitous in the U.S., but in many countries, they are not the preferred means of payment. For instance, in Germany people generally prefer using debit cards to credit cards. However, many American companies won't accept debit cards issued by foreign banks, so a lot of Germans who might want to purchase from your site are out of luck.

FYI

More than 70% of all Germans are reluctant to provide credit card details online (source: Taylor Nelson Sofres Interactive).

The Japanese also have an aversion to using credit cards online, and many young people simply don't have credit cards. As a result, the 7-Eleven chain of convenience stores accepts payment for goods ordered from online merchants, and the service has been remarkably successful. With more than 8,000 stores throughout Japan, 7-Eleven is a major payment channel for e-commerce; it also offers the online shopping portal 7Dream.com, where people can shop online, and then pick up their goods and pay at their nearest 7-Eleven store (see Figure 15.11). But it's not the only channel: Amazon.co.jp now offers a cash-on-delivery (COD) payment option, which allows customers to pay with cash when their packages arrive.

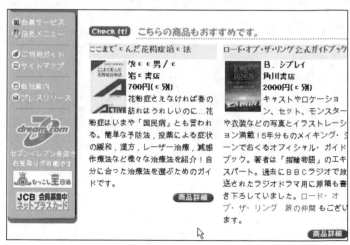

Figure 15.11   The esBooks web site allows shoppers to pay for and pick up their purchases at their local 7-Eleven.

Despite local variances, credit cards are still the dominant means of payment worldwide. You can select from a number of vendors for support of online processing.

FYI

Selected Credit Card Payment Vendors

> WorldPay (**www.worldpay.com**)
>
> Citibank Worldlink (**www.citibank.com/gct/worldlink**)
>
> VeriSign (**www.verisign.com**)
>
> PlanetPayment (**www.planetpayment**)

---

mCommerce

Increasingly, people are paying for products with their cellular phones, a method known as *mCommerce* (short for "mobile commerce"). In Japan, NTT DoCoMo has more than 30 million subscribers to its i-Mode phone service. Using i-Mode, users can automatically debit their bank accounts to make purchases online or at vending machines. Amazon and Yahoo! support i-Mode, as do countless local merchants. i-Mode launched in Europe in early 2002 and is expected in the U.S. by early 2003. Even if i-Mode doesn't take off outside Japan, operators are developing comparable services that promise the same level of functionality. The success of these applications will hinge largely on the markets in which they are launched. In countries where PC penetration remains low—such as Asia and most of Latin America—mobile phones are the primary conduit to the Internet. For these countries, mCommerce seems like a natural evolution, but for countries where mobile phones will compete against already entrenched PCs, mCommerce will likely play a more complementary role. For instance, although it's doubtful that most Americans will abandon their PCs for phones to shop at Amazon, it's not unlikely that they will rely on phones for services that PCs cannot offer, such as purchasing movie tickets while on the way to the movie theater.

FYI

For more information on mCommerce, go to **www.epaynews.com**.

PayPal Goes Global

PayPal (**www.paypal.com**) has grown into a popular method of exchanging money between individuals and, increasingly, businesses and their customers. For small businesses looking for an easy way to expand payment collection outside the U.S., PayPal currently supports 37 countries (see Figure 15.12). PayPal has become such a success that Citibank recently launched a similar service, c2it (**www.c2it.com**), which is available in 30 countries.

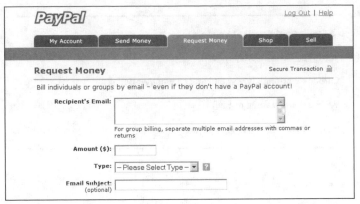

Figure 15.12   PayPal allows you to bill people in 37 countries.

Taxes

Managing taxation of cross-border e-commerce—a complicated and seemingly ever-changing process—should be handled by an expert. The Organization for Economic Cooperation and Development (**www.oecd.org**), composed of 30 countries including the U.S., is currently grappling with global taxation issues. According to David Hardesty, vice president of the accounting firm Markle Stuckey Hardesty & Bott, these issues include the following:

■ Characterization of digital transactions

■ Taxation of a foreign company when its only presence in a country is a web site

■ Information sharing

■ Methods of collecting tax

As more of the world embraces e-commerce, the governments of the world will have to embrace a *harmonization* (or standardization) of their many confusing tax laws. "Tax harmonization is currently in process, especially in Europe, where they have been engaged in harmonizing their tax systems for many years," says Hardesty. "As e-commerce causes more cross-border sales of goods and services, pressure will mount for all developed countries to harmonize their tax systems."

FYI

For more information, visit eCommerceTax at **www.ecommercetax.com,** or Global VAT Online at **www.globalvatonline.pwcglobal.com.**

DELIVERY (AND RETURNS)

Delivering goods internationally can be a daunting task, not just because of the distances involved, but because of the paperwork—declarations, invoices, waybills. Fortunately, there are global delivery companies that offer an impressive range of services. They can help you fill out the correct forms, provide your customers with precise delivery dates and times, and supply customer service contacts.

Pay close attention to the level of service that your providers offer. If you don't have an office in another country, your only point of personal contact is the person delivering the product; he or she becomes an extension of your company and can either help or hurt your success internationally.

Need to Deliver Down Under? Be Aware of Australian Regulations ...

- A shipment of videotapes is subject to censorship and requires the title of the video on the airbill and commercial invoice.

- A shipment of laboratory/biological specimens, samples, or minerals is unacceptable.

- Any shipment with a value greater than AUD 250.00, or duty and tax assessments greater than AUD 49.00, is assessed an additional Australian customs and administration fee of AUD 35.00.

- A shipment of plant and animal-derived products is subject to quarantine. Any shipment requiring quarantine is assessed an additional AUD 80.00 by Australian quarantine services, whether the shipment is destroyed, abandoned, or returned.

*Source: Airborne Express (**www.airborne.com**).*

FedEx recently launched the Global Trade Manager (**www.fedex.com/gtm/ international**). As shown in Figure 15.13, it includes information on required shipping documents for 20 countries. UPS also provides extensive international support (see Figure 15.14).

415

Figure 15.13 The FedEx Global Trade Manager provides a wide range of news and resources.

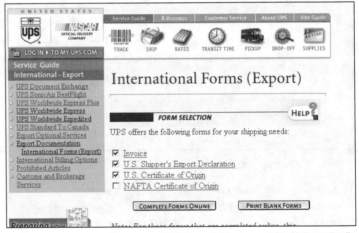

Figure 15.14 UPS tells you what forms you need to ship internationally.

FYI

Selected International Shipping Vendors

FedEx (**www.fedex.com**)

UPS International (**www.ups.com/using/services/intl/intl-guide.html**)

United States Postal Service (**www.usps.com/ibu/postalfin**)

Airborne Express (**www.airborne.com**)

On your web site, make it clear how goods will be shipped, how long they will take to arrive, and who your customers should contact if they don't arrive. More importantly, let your customers know how they can return goods; most of the major vendors also provide pick-up services. Finally, you should offer a money-back guarantee to help alleviate any worries of your international customers.

GLOBAL CRM

Effective *customer relationship management* (*CRM*) is the Holy Grail for many companies and often just as elusive. The challenge is simple: Treat each of your customers as though he or she is your only customer. To achieve this goal, companies purchase software from the likes of PeopleSoft, Siebel, and SAP—systems that integrate their sales, marketing, accounting, and customer service databases into one centralized, coordinated tool. If someone calls your customer support line, your support person should know if the caller is a prospect or a client, and, if a client, every detail about that person. CRM software can implement business rules that enable companies to treat their customers with customized levels of service and support, based on factors such as purchasing history, location, and internal goals. Integrating all these separate systems across languages and borders presents a number of challenges and rewards.

First, the rewards. According to Richard Cross, president of the marketing consulting firm Cross World Network (**www.crossworldnetwork.com**), 3Com saved money *and* time through its global CRM program. Cross credits 3Com's investment in a globalized, standardized database that helped it manage relationships across product lines and country borders. This added level of intelligence and integration helped 3Com accomplish the following:

- Reduce marketing costs by 85%.

- Double and even triple response rates from direct response campaigns.

- Identify and target opportunities within the customer bases of acquired companies.

- Minimize under- and overmarketing to individual customers.

Such returns are not easy to come by, however. Implementing global CRM is one of the biggest challenges a company can face, as it affects all parts of the organization and, if not done correctly, can do more damage than good. For global CRM to be successful, a company must have global support. Employees must be trained to use the software, and the software should be viewed as a business enabler, not

417

just another annoying database to maintain. Cross recommends that each office have a senior-level "data champion" who works to ensure that countrywide standards are implemented.

Privacy Matters

Integrating databases across borders makes sound business sense, but might violate local privacy laws. Several European countries have much stricter data-sharing laws than in the U.S. For example, if you have London and New York offices, the London office can't simply email its local database if its users haven't given full permission. Data privacy laws are constantly changing, too. Fortunately, however, many CRM applications can be built so that certain customer fields can be restricted to certain offices. The key is just keeping up on the many changing rules and consulting with an attorney before collecting or sharing data.

Global CRM is clearly the goal of any company that wants to be a global leader, but don't make any hasty CRM decisions. Done correctly, both the company and its customers benefit. Done poorly, companies waste precious resources, and customers end up feeling more cut off.

ALL SUPPORT IS LOCAL

Web globalization would be a lot easier if you didn't have to worry about all those non-Internet issues. Yet these very issues will make or break your web site and, ultimately, your company. This is the perfect time to invest heavily in global customer support. So few companies are doing a good job at it that you can quickly gain a competitive advantage and begin to build a loyal, global customer base. Now that you know how to support your customers, the next chapter focuses on driving even more customers to your site.

16

PROMOTING YOUR SITE GLOBALLY

Most companies measure the effectiveness of a localized web site not by the quality of the translation, but by the number of visitors and, ultimately, the number of sales. If you want to ensure that your site succeeds by these measures, you need to invest appropriate planning and resources into promotion. Although there are many ways to promote a web site, this chapter focuses on the more "web-centric" promotions: search engines, banner ads, and email.

SEARCH ENGINES

Registering your site with search engines and directories should be the first thing you do once your site goes live. But where to begin? Outside the U.S., there are a myriad of country and language-specific search engines. The localized versions of Yahoo!, MSN, and Lycos are familiar, but there are countless other sites you've probably never heard of, some of which are enormously popular in their countries.

Search Engine Versus Directory

Before you begin registering your web site, you should understand the difference between a search engine and a directory. A search engine relies on software programs called "spiders" or "bots" to scour the Internet and literally index every page they find. Each search engine uses a different methodology to determine which web pages are most relevant.

Search engines rely on computer-generated indexes, and directories rely on human-generated indexes. Human beings act as the gatekeepers to the directory, deciding which sites get in and which sites get ignored. Popular directories include Yahoo! and LookSmart; popular search engines include Google, AllTheWeb, and Ask. Some web sites offer both search engines and directories. For example, Google is known as a search engine, although it now offers a directory, too. Knowing the difference between a search engine and a directory affects how you go about submitting your site. Search engines, such as Google, generally allow automatic submissions, and directories, such as Yahoo!, generally require manual submissions. In fact, Yahoo! requires a submission fee for businesses, with no guarantee that your site will make it into the index. Fortunately, Yahoo! is not as popular in other countries as it is in the U.S. Figures 16.1 and 16.2 show a couple of examples of search engines popular in other countries.

FYI

For information on global search engines:

Search Engine Colossus (**www.searchenginecolossus.com**)

Search Engine Watch (**www.searchenginewatch.com**)

Search IQ (**www.zdnet.com/searchiq**)

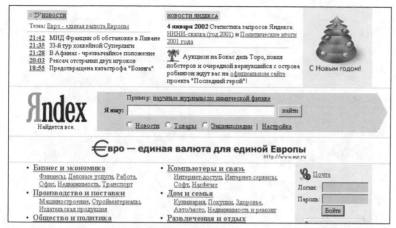

Figure 16.1 Want to drive traffic to your Russian site? Begin with the largest search engine in Russia, Yandex.

423

Figure 16.2 Want to drive traffic to your Brazilian site? Begin with Cadê.

So Many Search Engines, So Little Time

In the end, it really doesn't matter if the site is a search engine, directory, or some hybrid portal, as long as it's popular in your target country. But it's not easy figuring out which sites are most popular when you look to new markets. Many research firms have only recently begun measuring the popularity of search engines outside the U.S. The following list shows a few of the available search engines around the world:

Asia

Country	Search Engine	URL
Pan-Asia	Yahoo! Asia	**asia.yahoo.com**
Taiwan	Sina	**www.sina.com.tw**
Japan	Goo	**www.goo-ne.jp**
South Korea	Naver	**www.naver.com**

Europe

Russia	Yandex	**www.yandex.com**
U.K.	SearchUK	**www.searchuk.com**
France	Voilà	**www.voila.fr**
Germany	Fireball	**www.fireball.de**
Italy	Virgilio	**www.virgilio.it**
Poland	Arena	**www.arena.pl**
Spain	Olé	**www.ole.com**

Latin America

Regional sites	Terra	**www.terra.com**
Regional sites	Starmedia	**www.starmedia.com**
Argentina	Grippo	**www.grippo.com**
Brazil	Cadê	**www.cade.com.br**
Colombia	Ubicar	**www.ubicar.com**
Mexico	Iguana	**www.iguana.com.mx**

Africa/Middle East

Arabic language	Arab Bay	**www.arabbay.com**
South Africa	Zebra	**www.zebra.co.za**
Israel	Walla	**www.walla.co.il**
Jordan	Al Bawaba	**www.albawaba.com**

*Source: Search Engine Colossus (**www.searchenginecolossus.com**).*

The research firm Jupiter Media Metrix now ranks search engines in all Western European countries. As you can see in the following chart, there are quite a few other search engines and portals that you may need to get familiar with if you're planning on entering Europe:

Country	Search Engine/Portal	URL
Denmark	Jubii	**www.jubii.dk**
U.K.	MSN UK	**www.msn.co.uk**
Norway	Sol	**www.sol.no**
Switzerland	MSN US	**www.msn.com**
Sweden	MSN Sweden	**www.msn.sw**
Spain	MSN Spain	**www.msn.es**
Italy	IOL	**www.iol.it**
Germany	T-Online	**www.t-online.de**
France	Lycos France	**www.lycos.fr**

*Source: Jupiter Media Metrix (**www.jupitermmxi.com**), 2001–2002.*

Given the chaotic nature of the search portal industry, keeping up with all the players is a full-time job. T-Online is owned by Deutsche Telekom. Sol, which stands for Scandinavia Online, manages portals in Sweden, Norway, Finland, and Denmark. Terra Lycos is the result of a merger of Terra Networks and Lycos in late 2000. Terra Lycos and Yahoo! are currently the two largest global portals. Yahoo! may be stronger in the U.S., but Terra is much stronger in Latin America and parts of Europe. In early 2002, Yahoo! purchased the leading Brazilian search portal, Cadê, in an effort to bolster its Latin American presence.

Searching by Language; Searching by Country

Search engines are not mutually exclusive. Just because you're based in the U.S. and using Google doesn't mean you won't find a site from a company in Japan. That means you might have to register your web site at search engines from other countries. For example, even if you register your Swiss site at MSN Switzerland (MSN.ch), you're not going to reach everyone in Switzerland. As illustrated in the following chart, you'll need to register your site at other search engines/portals. For countries with more than one official language, you'll need to register with more than one language, too.

Search Engines/Portals	Site Reach
MSN.com	27.2%
MSN.ch	25.3%
Yahoo.com	21.5%
Search.ch	18.5%
Google.ch	17.8%

continues

Continued

Search Engines/Portals	Site Reach
Yahoo.de	12.8%
MSN.de	12.6%
Google.com	11.8%
Yahoo.fr	7.7%
Altavista.com	7.1%
Netscape.com	6.1%
Lycos.fr	6.0%
T-online.de	5.6%
Netscape.de	5.4%
Altavista.ch	3.2%
Google.de	2.9%
Altavista.de	1.9%

*Source: Jupiter Media Metrix (**www.jupitermmxi.com**), October 2001.*

Google: A Global Search Engine

No matter what language site you develop, don't forget Google. Google claims to have indexed more pages than any other web site and allows users to search by 27 languages. You can even modify your search interface to match your preferred language (see Figure 16.3). Translation is on the way. You can also have a little fun with the "Bork, bork, bork!" option (see Figure 16.4).

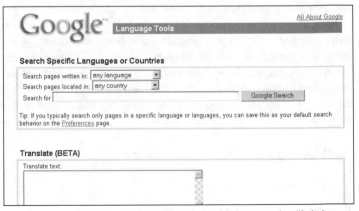

Figure 16.3   Google language tools: Search by language and modify the language of your search interface.

Use the Google Interface in Your Language

Set the Google homepage, messages, and buttons to display in your selected language via our <u>Preferences</u> page. Google currently offers the following interface languages:

• Afrikaans	• Elmer Fudd	• Icelandic	• Maltese	• Spanish
• Albanian	• English	• Indonesian	• Marathi	• Swahili
• Arabic	• Esperanto	• Interlingua	• Nepali	• Swedish
• Basque	• Estonian	• Irish	• Norwegian	• Tagalog
• Bengali	• Finnish	• Italian	• Pig Latin	• Tamil
• Bork, bork, bork!	• French	• Japanese	• Polish	• Telugu
• Bulgarian	• Frisian	• Kannada	• Portuguese	• Turkish
• Catalan	• Galician	• Korean	• Punjabi	• Ukrainian
• Chinese (Simplified)	• German	• Latin	• Romanian	• Vietnamese
• Chinese (Traditional)	• Greek	• Latvian	• Russian	• Welsh
• Croatian	• Hacker	• Lithuanian	• Scots Gaelic	
• Czech	• Hebrew	• Macedonian	• Serbian	
• Danish	• Hindi	• Malay	• Slovak	
• Dutch	• Hungarian	• Malayalam	• Slovenian	

If you don't see your native language here, you can help Google create it by becoming a volunteer translator. Check out our <u>Google in Your Language</u> program.

Figure 16.4 Set your own language interface preference, including Bork, the speaking style of the Swedish Muppet cook.

If You Don't Speak the Language

It's not easy selecting and submitting to search engines if you don't understand the languages. But it's also not inexpensive to hire experts to do the submitting for you. As an alternative, you can ask your translators or the staff in your foreign office to assist in the process. At the very least they can help you generate a list of target search engines. Who better to know what search engines are popular in a country than the translators based in that country?

You can go one step further and ask the translator or colleague to manage the site submission as well. This strategy is not ideal if you're truly serious about generating high rankings. For this you will need experts, people who fully understand how the search engines and directories work, and how to optimize your site accordingly. The experts can also help you and your translators draft effective keywords for each search engine and market. For example, if you're a shoe retailer and you want to do well in a U.S. search engine, the keyword "sneaker" is obvious. But you won't want to use that same keyword in the U.K., where sneakers are called "trainers."

┌─FYI

Popular search engine submission services and firms:

Arial Global Reach (**www.arialglobalreach.com**)

GlobalPromote (**www.gloprom.com**)

Global Reach (**www.global-reach.biz**)

International Crossing (**www.internationalcrossing.com**)

NetBooster (**www.netbooster.co.uk**)

Submit It (**www.submit-it.comv**

Zen Hits (**www.zenhits.com**)

If you have to keep costs down, you can rely on an automatic bulk web site submission service. There are hundreds of free and paid services from which to choose. One such service is Submit It (**www.submit-it.com**), which submits your site to search engines in more than 25 countries. However, this might not include the search engines you need and can't include the directories that require manual submissions. Here are some tips for search engine success:

- **Get your translators involved.** Ask your translators, editors, and agencies about the search engines they use in their countries. For a nominal fee, you can even have them do the submission for you instead of hiring a specialist. It's not the ideal solution, but it's a start.

- **Use plenty of static content.** Increasingly, web pages are assembled dynamically, with content drawn from databases. The problem with dynamic web pages is that web bots can't spider them. Although there is a technique you can use to cache preassembled web pages specifically for the web bots, a much simpler approach is to build a number of permanent, static web pages that include plenty of text.

- **Register local domain names.** Country-specific domain names typically carry more significance to a foreign search engine than a .com or an .org. (See Chapter 14, "Mastering Your (Country) Domain," to learn more.)

- **Don't forget the <META> tags.** Search engines scan the **<META>** tags at the top of a web page to help them index the site. The most important **<META>** tags are **Keywords** and **Description,** both of which should be translated. Don't forget to translate your page title as well.

- **Localized keywords.** A direct translation of the keywords on your source site won't necessarily work on foreign search engines. And although you should avoid slang and colloquialisms when localizing sites, these words might help a great deal in terms of searching. Ask your translators to localize as well as translate the text. If you're Nike, for example, ask them to brainstorm all the different ways of saying "running shoe" in that country.

- **Don't forget the lang tag.** The **lang** tag is becoming more important these days. Search engines rely on these tags to tell them the web page's language. Many search engines can guesstimate the language based on character set and the text itself, but you shouldn't count on it.

BANNER ADS (AND OTHER PROMOTIONS)

The banner ad can be as simple as a small graphic at the top of a web page or as complex as a fully customized web page. Before you start designing ads, exercise the same degree of care you took when localizing your web site. Advertisements that rely on humor, cultural stereotypes, and location-specific visuals do not travel well globally. However, you might not even want to develop ads that travel globally. The key question is whether you want people in each country to view the web site and brands as global or as local? The promotions you develop will fall into one of two overall strategies:

> Promoting a global brand with localized promotions

> Promoting a local brand with localized promotions

If you want your brand to be recognized globally, you should keep the same name and create localized promotions on a country-by-country basis. This approach is by far the most popular, but it's not always the best. You might find that some brand names don't travel well, in which case you'll need to localize the name or create (or purchase) new brands for each market. Some multinational companies use both strategies, such as Procter & Gamble (P&G), which markets both global and local brands. One of the more popular brands of diapers in Russia is the P&G product Pampers. Although Pampers is a true global brand, P&G also markets one of the most popular toothpastes in Russia, yet this one you might not be familiar with: Blend-a-Med (see Figure 16.5).

429

Figure 16.5 Blend-a-Med is a local product promoted by a global company, Procter & Gamble.

Localize Your Slogans

The UPS slogan "Moving at the speed of business" does not travel well globally. According to Don Laurvick, vice president of business development, the "speed of business" concept didn't connect with cultures outside the U.S. In Europe and Asia, the slogan is "Consider it done."

*Source: SAM Magazine (**www.sammag.com**).*

Global Brand, Localized Promotions

The ideal for many companies is to take their products global, rather than create new products for each market. After all, once you've gone to the expense of developing a product, it makes sense to try to sell as much of it as you possibly can. Sometimes you can keep manufacturing centralized and increase profit margins simply from economies of scale.

FYI

For more information on global advertising and samples of international banner ads, go to Ad Age Global (**www.adageglobal.com**).

Although the product remains the same, the marketing message typically changes. For instance, if you're selling computers globally, you might find that Americans are motivated by the mention of high-speed processors, and Germans are motivated by the mention of money-back guarantees. Even if you have a brand with global appeal, you'll still need some level of localization to ensure that the brand sells well in all markets. Britney Spears, who has become a powerful global brand all her own, relied on localized promotions (see the sidebar "Britney Spears: Global Name, Local Promotion").

Britney Spears: Global Name, Local Promotion

To promote Britney Spears's latest album, Yahoo! developed a web page localized into numerous languages and promoted on its localized portals. Notice how the template remains the same, yet the message and various promotions, shown in Figure 16.6, vary by locale.

continues

Britney Spears: Global Name, Local Promotion (continued)

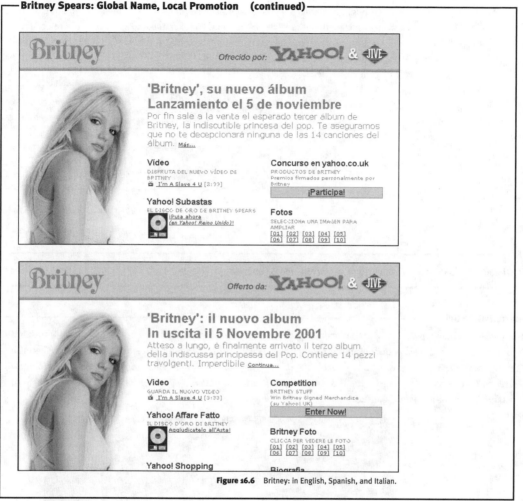

Figure 16.6 Britney: in English, Spanish, and Italian.

Advertising agencies have responded to the needs of their increasingly globally minded clients by partnering with or purchasing agencies in foreign markets. Local agencies are generally more in touch with the subtleties of their market and may be better at developing advertising that people connect with. You'll often see cultural variances between the types of advertising used in other countries. For example, British advertising relies more on humor, often using sophisticated visual and linguistic puns. French advertising is known for extravagant or odd imagery at times and, of course, sensuality. Japan has a strong visual aesthetic; some Japanese print ads would look at home in a museum of graphic arts. Assuming you don't have the budget to hire local agencies, you can begin with the promotions you already have, localizing them for each new market. For example, in Figure 16.7, the telecommunications company Alcatel simply modifies one banner ad for different markets by translating it.

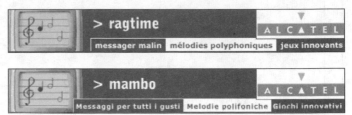

Figure 16.7 Alcatel promotes the same mobile phone locally by running a banner ad on Lycos France (top) and one on Tripod Italy (bottom).

FYI

View banner ads from around the world at **www.adageglobal.com**.

Harry Potter Goes Local

Harry Potter is much more than a global phenomenon—he's a local phenomenon. The books have been translated into numerous languages, with book titles, chapter titles, character names, and places localized for each country (see Figure 16.8). For example, the British book title *Harry Potter and the Philosopher's Stone* was localized to *Harry Potter and the Sorcerer's Stone* for the U.S. And in Japan, Harry Potter is Halley Potter, which is easier for Japanese speakers to pronounce (see Figure 16.9).

Figure 16.8 The Harry Potter web site is localized into nine languages.

continues

┌─ **Harry Potter Goes Local** (continued) ──────────────────────

Figure 16.9 On the Japanese Harry Potter site, the name "Harry," when transliterated into Japanese characters, becomes "Halley."

For more examples of how Harry travels globally, visit:

www.eulenfeder.de/int/gbint.html

www.cjvlang.com/Hpotter/index.html

433

When running banner ads, you'll need to evaluate the best portals to advertise on in each market. Although U.S.-based portals such as Yahoo! and MSN still dominate the world in terms of overall audience, Asian-based portals are gaining ground. As more and more Asians embrace the Internet, it's safe to assume that the leading portals five years from now may not be based in the U.S. at all. Table 16.1 lists the leading portals in late 2001, according to Nielsen/NetRatings (**www.netratings.com**).

Table 16.1   Leading Portals

Rank by Unique Audience in Country of Origin	Country of Origin	Local Property
1	U.S.	AOL Time Warner
2	U.S.	Yahoo!
3	U.S.	MSN
4	U.S.	Microsoft
5	U.S.	Lycos Network
6	U.S.	Excite@Home
7	U.S.	eBay
8	U.S.	About-Primedia
9	U.S.	Amazon

continues

Table 16.1   Continued

Rank by Unique Audience in Country of Origin	Country of Origin	Local Property
10	U.S.	Walt Disney Internet Group
11	Japan	Yahoo!
12	Korea	Daum Comm Corp
13	U.S.	Vivendi Universal
14	U.S.	InfoSpace
15	Korea	Yahoo!
16	U.S.	CNET Networks
17	U.S.	eUniverse Network
18	U.S.	Google
19	Korea	Korea Telecom
20	Korea	DreamWiz

AOL Gets Local

AOL is offered in 16 countries in eight languages. Its strongest overseas market is Europe, particularly the U.K., where it's the number-one ISP. Much of this success can be attributed to a highly localized spokesperson, Connie. Connie was created as a very British, very unintimidating character and has become something of an icon (see Figure 16.10). Although she is completely fictitious, people request signed photos.

WHAT IS AOL?

AOL is an exciting online service which provides access to a huge range of exclusive content and services. It includes fun and easy-to-use communication tools such as email and Instant Messenger and a full range of help and support options for all Internet users, whatever their experience. The AOL service is open only to members; to find out more about becoming a member, click on the 'Try AOL For Free!' button at the bottom of any page in the Showcase.

We also have a very different online site called AOL.co.uk, which is the homepage on the Web for AOL. This acts as a home-away-from-home for AOL members, but is open to anyone with Internet access.

Figure 16.10   Connie, the very British spokesperson for AOL in the U.K.

Source: Washington Post, May 2001.

Localized Brands, Localized Promotions

Although launching (or purchasing) brands country by country might not be the most efficient strategy, it could be effective in the long term. Millions of people are happy to drink the global beer Budweiser, but many people would rather stick with their local brands, such as in Boston, Tremont, or Harpoon. Local brands might not have global clout or the revenues that match, but they do have a glamour all their own and often command much higher price margins. Before you assume that you need global ads for global products, study the countries and the people in those countries; perhaps they don't want a global brand after all.

Focus on Local Needs and Demands

"Even for a company with global brands, there is no such thing as a global consumer. For instance, in Japan consumers demand choice—and change. There are more than 500 soft-drink manufacturers in Japan, 7,000 different products on the market at any given time, and more than 900 new products each year."

Source: Doug Daft, CEO of Coca-Cola.

435

Have a Georgia and a Smile

Coca-Cola may be a global giant, but it can be as savvy as any local company. For example, the best-selling noncarbonated beverage in Japan is Georgia, a product developed and marketed by Coca-Cola. Georgia is coffee in a can (see Figure 16.11).

Figure 16.11   Although Americans aren't keen on drinking coffee from a can, Japanese drink it up.

Coca-Cola promotes Georgia with advertisements featuring songs by local bands. These songs have often been so popular that they also sell extremely well in stores. In a recent press release, Etsuko Katsube, director and senior vice president in charge of strategic marketing at Coca-Cola Japan, put it clearly: "We are dedicated to being the best marketing and brand-building company in Japan, using local insights and creative talent to produce ads that truly connect with Japanese consumers." Georgia is just one of Coke's many local products. In Brazil and Chile, it markets a fruit beverage called Kapo (see Figure 16.12); in Central and Eastern Europe, it markets a fruit juice called Cappy.

Figure 16.12   The web site for Kapo, another of Coke's successful local products.

FYI

Diet Coke is known as "Coca-Cola Light" in most markets outside the United States.

When Localizing Is the Wrong Thing to Do

The Georgia phenomenon raises a crucial issue for companies expanding abroad: When is localizing *not* such a good thing? Felipe Korzenny, principal of Cheskin (**www.cheskin.com**), an international research firm, notes that Latin Americans are sometimes more attracted to Americanized promotions and products than localized promotions: "Localization presents interesting paradoxes particularly because of the behavior of the consuming classes in Latin America, which in many ways try to emulate the U.S."

Localized Promotions Within the U.S.

Within the U.S., marketing is no easier than abroad, particularly with more Americans speaking a language other than English. The largest non-English-speaking market is Spanish speakers. Yet referring to a group by their language can be dangerous. Spanish speakers come from many different countries, with many different cultures. Korzenny points out a few traits of U.S. Hispanics that marketers should be aware of:

- Tend to require much more product information

- Tend to be more concrete in decision making as opposed to abstract

- Tend to have a strong emotional attachment to products they got to know in their countries of origin

- Strongly lean toward giving children whatever they want because they are compensating for deprivation

---

Got Leche?

The famous "Got Milk?" slogan for the California Milk Processor Board is not so popular with U.S. Hispanics. Fortunately, the milk board hired an agency that specializes in advertising to U.S. Hispanics. Had the milk board translated the slogan literally, the ad would have read "Are you lactating?" The agency changed the slogan to "Have you given them enough milk lately?" and targeted the ads directly at mothers and grandmothers, the primary milk purchasers of the family. It was impossible to localize the "Got milk?" humor because Latino mothers didn't view the idea of not having enough milk in the home as humorous. Sometimes localization requires creating an entirely new marketing message.

Source: San Francisco Chronicle, *August 2001.*

EMAIL MARKETING

Don't underestimate the power of email and how it can help drive traffic to your web site. Perhaps your company already has a database of email addresses. You can segment out a target list simply by looking at country-specific domain names at the end of the email addresses. It's not a perfect solution, but it's a good start. Then translate a short introductory letter and email it with a link to the localized web site.

Technical Details

The process of sending emails in different languages may require adjusting your email client settings. The current versions of Microsoft Outlook and Eudora support a wide range of character sets. Just as web pages have **charset** tags to tell the browsers what encoding is used, emails rely on MIME headers, which can also include charset indicators. If you don't adjust your MIME charset to match the encoding of the text within the email, your email might be transcoded before it's reached its destination, as shown in Figures 16.13, 16.14, and 16.15.

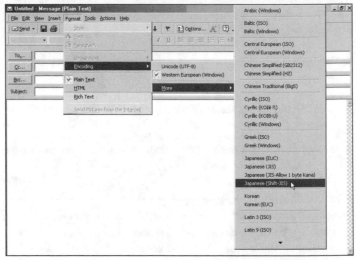

Figure 16.13   Microsoft Outlook supports email in a full range of encodings.

Figure 16.14   First, adjust your language preferences for outgoing and incoming mail under Tools, Options, Mail Format.

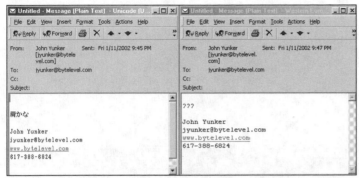

Figure 16.15 Same email, different encodings. The email on the left is encoded as Unicode; the one on the right, as Western Windows. The English text makes it through successfully, but the Japanese text does not.

Press Relations

PR is the least expensive form of advertising you can find. And, thanks to email, you don't have to spend a dime to tell the major news outlets in your target country that you have a localized web site. Once again, ask your translators or your foreign office to supply a list of media portals and contact names. For more information, the Public Relations Society of America (**www.prsa.org**) offers both international and multicultural special-interest groups.

439

THE LOCAL TOUCH

The days of "one size fits all" advertising are quickly being replaced by "one size fits one." The way you promote your French web site might be completely different from the way you promote your German web site, and so on. Just as web sites must be localized, so too must their promotions. Fortunately, you don't need the budget of General Motors to promote your web site globally; local search engines can provide significant traffic with little or no upfront expense.

Increasingly, the secret to succeeding globally isn't so much about having a global reach, but about having a local touch. In the next, and final, chapter, you'll look at where web globalization is headed and what you need to know to prepare for it.

Figure 1   The FIFA World Cup English-language home page.

FIFA WORLD CUP

Every four years, FIFA (Fédération Internationale de Football Association) holds the World Cup, arguably the most popular sporting event in the world. In June 2002, the World Cup was jointly hosted by Korea and Japan. It drew more than 2 million spectators, and more than a billion people watched the matches on television. The Internet also played a vital role in the World Cup. In December 2001, FIFA, in partnership with Yahoo!, launched the FIFA World Cup web site.

---

www.fifaworldcup.com

Localized web sites: The FIFA World Cup site is currently available in:

- English
- French
- German
- Japanese
- Korean
- Spanish

ANALYSIS

The FIFA web site illustrates the importance of thinking locally. Even though the World Cup is a global event, most people who visit the web site really care only about their home teams, so each language site is localized for fans of teams that share that language (see Figures 2 and 3). For the Japanese site, the choice is simple: Feature as much information as possible about the team from Japan. But the Spanish site is not so simple; more than half a dozen teams represent Spanish-speaking countries. Some teams do not have a language-specific site, such as Russia, Sweden, Brazil, and Italy, so FIFA is considering adding Italian and Portuguese sites for future World Cup events.

Figure 2   The FIFA languages sites provide localized content. The Korea site features the Korean team...

Figure 3   ...and the Spanish site features the Argentina team.

Many Sources, Many Targets

Many web sites rely on one source language, but the FIFA web site relies on many source languages. A sports article can be written in Japanese, French, or English and then localized for some or all of the other language web sites. As shown in Figure 4, this "many-to-many" model of content management can be much more challenging logistically to maintain than the "one-to-many" model. With the one-to-many model, one person can theoretically act as the gatekeeper for all source-language content; for a many-to-many model, however, multiple gatekeepers may be necessary. To further complicate matters, the FIFA site is highly time-sensitive; because much of the content is event driven, the workflow must be built for speed.

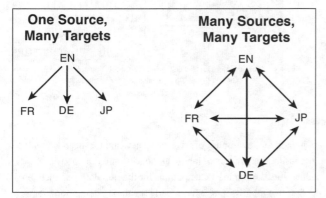

Figure 4   On the FIFA World Cup web site, there's no such thing as one source language.

Many organizations prefer the one-to-many model because it enables them to control the message across all locales. Yet some organizations prefer a more decentralized management structure, in which content can be produced by any locale and distributed to any of the other locales. The many-to-many model is much more fluid, so it might not be appropriate for all organizations. However, this model in many ways represents the model of the future, in which all locales are considered equal in creating and disseminating content. As you develop a global strategy, you'll need to decide whether you want each localized site to follow the parent site or exercise a degree of independence. The key to FIFA's success, says Charles-Henry Contamine, head of Internet operations for FIFA, is "localizing some content, while not alienating the global audience."

Global Event, Local Promotion

The FIFA/Yahoo! promotional alliance is an effective way to maximize global expo-sure one country at a time. Yahoo! promoted the FIFA World Cup sites on its many country-specific portals, as shown in Figure 5. For example, the Korea promotional button is placed on the Yahoo! Korea page; if you click on it, you are taken directly to the FIFA Korean web page.

Figure 5   These ads were located on the country-specific Yahoo! portals. When users click on the ad, they are taken to their language-specific web page.

Measuring Success

Many web sites are judged by the amount of traffic they get, and localized web sites are no exception. Assessing the success of language-specific sites can be tricky, however. Figure 6 illustrates Contamine's calculations for the popularity of each lan-guage site after the first two months. English is clearly the most popular language so far, although Contamine expected Spanish to increase in popularity, in relation to the other languages, as the event drew nearer.

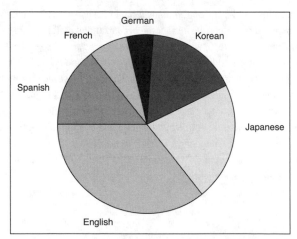

Figure 6   Which language is most popular?

By just glancing at the pie chart, you might assume that English is more popular than Korean, but success is relative. For example, there are considerably more English speakers online than Korean speakers, so you could argue that the Korean site is more popular with Korean speakers than the English site is with English speakers. However, the crucial detail is that many more teams in the World Cup are from English-speaking countries (such as South Africa, the U.S., and England), and only one team is from a Korean-speaking country. People don't visit language-specific web sites just for the language; they visit for the content. There's no perfect way to analyze web traffic, but it's important not to assume failure if a certain language draws fewer visitors than other languages.

Q&A WITH FIFA

Charles-Henry Contamine
Head of Internet Operations, FIFA

Is the translation managed in house or outsourced to a vendor? Does Yahoo! assist with the translation?

Translation is outsourced to vendors. Through the deal with Yahoo!, FIFA has carefully selected the vendors to ensure a very high level of quality. The translated content must appear as if it was written in the target language. When evaluating translation, several criteria must be considered:

- *Overall quality of translations*

- *Ability to translate from several languages into several others*

- *Excellent football knowledge—you don' t write about this sport the same way in French or German or Spanish*

- *Ability to handle extremely tight deadlines, especially for match reports and major announcements*

How did you determine what "flavor" of Spanish to use? And did anyone complain that you didn't offer any other variations?

We' ve gone for Castilian Spanish, which has the advantage of being universally recognized. So far, the Spanish-language traffic comes mainly from Mexico, the U.S., Argentina, and Spain, and no users have complained about it.

It appears that the content itself is localized for each language/country. How is this process managed? For example, are articles written specifically in the target languages, or are there articles translated into all six languages—or both?

Both, depending on the nature of the stories. Some are global; some are more relevant to a specific language. For example, an in-depth analysis of Argentina will appeal more to the Spanish and English versions of the site, while the others may be satisfied with a shorter version. Because each language channel is managed by a native-language editor, it allows more flexibility in the editorial selection.

How much traffic does the site currently get, and how much do you expect during the competition?

For its first month online, December 2001, FIFAworldcup.com generated 24 million page views and received 1.5 million unique visitors. Realistic projections are something of a hazardous science, but we expect to handle around 40 million page views a day during the event, with peaks depending on the matches. For instance, during FIFA World Cup France '98, the busiest day on the Internet was the day England played Argentina and lost to penalties. At that time, 7 million page views in a day was a staggering number.

How do you manage email in multiple languages?

Feedback email is dispatched to the relevant editors, depending on the language it's written in. For example, if an email is sent from the Japanese version of the site, it goes straight to the Japanese editor. However, we've placed a disclaimer telling people that due to the volume of email, FIFA cannot guarantee responding to each email individually.

Any advice for a company planning a web globalization project?

It really depends on the nature of the web site itself. Sports, and especially football, have a worldwide reach and a passionate local following. You want to strike the right balance between localized and global content. Increasing the number of languages will certainly broaden your global reach, but localized content will ensure that people keep coming back for more.

HANDS-ON: UNICODE

Overview ──

This is the final Hands-On chapter. By now, you have localized one web page into eight languages—the languages spoken by more than 80% of the world's population. This final Hands-On chapter focuses on a character encoding that promises to make web localization, into any language, a great deal easier: Unicode. All files used in this chapter are available for download; go to **www.bytelevel.com/beyondborders**.

FIRST THOUGHTS

Unicode is not a language, but it deserves a Hands-On chapter of its own because it is unlike any other character set you'll use. In fact, in a few years it may be the only character set you use. Unicode has been called the "mother of all character sets" because it includes most, if not all, of the characters in the world's major languages. Technically speaking, Unicode is both a character set and an encoding, or a "character encoding system," although most people simply call it a character set. To understand how Unicode works, in this chapter you'll convert the global gateway—now consisting of all graphics—back into text. As you'll recall from earlier Hands-On chapters, a web page can specify only one character encoding, yet the global gateway includes characters from several different, and conflicting, character encodings. This dilemma forced you to embed the global gateway within graphics. With Unicode, however, you can specify one encoding and still include the world's many characters on one web page.

TOOLS

All you really need is a text editor that handles Unicode, such as Word 2000. There is also a popular free Unicode text editor, UniPad, available at **www.unipad.org**. For this exercise, however, you will modify the gateway using the following tools, so you can get a feel for how a web editor handles Unicode:

Operating system:	Windows XP
HTML:	FrontPage 2000

ABOUT UNICODE

The evolution of Unicode began more than a decade ago when the Unicode Consortium and an ISO working group set out to create a universal character set. As Unicode evolved over the years, it expanded to include more and more characters. Unicode 3.1, the most current version available, includes 94,140 characters—a far cry from the days of ASCII (see Figure 1).

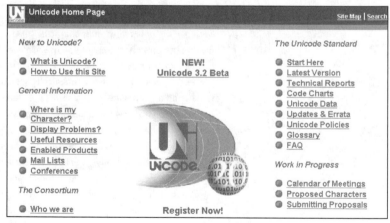

Figure 1   For more information, visit the Unicode Consortium web site at **www.unicode.org**.

Unicode was designed to be backward-compatible with as many major character sets as possible. For example, the first 256 characters of Unicode look strikingly similar to Latin 1, which was intentional. Unicode is a coded character set, which means that each character is assigned a number—and one number only. If everyone used Unicode, character set conflicts would be a thing of the past. What follows is a list of the major scripts included in Unicode:

The Primary Scripts Supported by Unicode 3.1

Arabic	Gujarati	Ogham
Armenian	Gurmukhi	Old Italic (Etruscan)
Bengali	Han	Oriya
Bopomofo	Hangul Hebrew	Runic
Canadian Syllabics	Hiragana	Sinhala
Cherokee	Kannada	Syriac
Cyrillic	Katakana	Tamil
Deseret	Khmer	Telugu
Devanagari	Latin	Thaana
Ethiopic	Lao	Thai
Georgian	Malayalam	Tibetan
Gothic	Mongolian	Yi
Greek	Myanmar	

The "Unification" of Unicode

The letter *A* is used in many languages, but Unicode includes it just once. Unicode prevents redundancy by not representing the same character multiple times just because multiple languages rely on it. This unification of scripts has met with some resistance from people who feel that some languages, such as Simplified and Traditional Chinese, should not have been unified, or should have been unified in a different manner. The reasons are too complex to go into detail here, but just keep in mind that even Unicode is not a universally loved character set.

Unicode includes an enormous range of characters, many of which are not associated with a language. These special characters and symbols include the following:

Numbers

Diacritics

Punctuation

Mathematical symbols

Musical symbols (Western and Byzantine)

Technical symbols

Dingbats

Arrows, blocks, box drawing forms, and geometric shapes

Braille patterns

Unicode doesn't concern itself with how the glyph actually appears on your computer screen. What Unicode is concerned with are the properties associated with that character, such as which direction it should flow (left to right, for example). Table 1 shows a few examples of character properties.

Table 1 Selected Unicode Characters

Code Point	Character Description
189B	Mongolian letter manchu ali gali nga
17A7	Khmer independent vowel qu
1E64	Latin capital letter *s* with acute accent and dot above
1F55	Greek small letter upsilon with dasia and oxia
FB1F	Hebrew ligature yiddish yod yod patah
2E96	CJK radical heart one
FCAA	Arabic ligature hah with meem initial form
0433	Cyrillic small letter ghe
057D	Armenian small letter seh

Note: Code points are shown in hexadecimal notation (see the sidebar "Hexadecimal").

Hexadecimal

Unicode notation is written in hexadecimal (hex), a base-16 numbering system. The decimal system is base-10, which means it relies on 10 digits: 0–9. Hexadecimal relies on 16 digits, 0–F, as follows: 0, 1, 2, 3, 4, 5, 6, 7, 8, 9, A, B, C, D, E, F. Hexadecimal notation is not always easy to grasp at first, but if you want to convert quickly from decimal to Unicode, most calculators support the conversion. The Windows calculator, when converted to scientific view, offers hex conversion and even binary conversion, as shown in Figure 2.

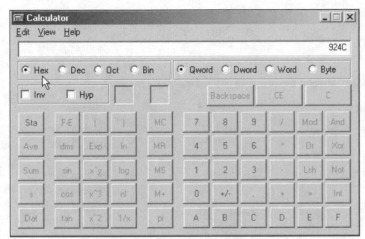

Figure 2   Using the Windows calculator, you can convert between different numbering systems: decimal, hexadecimal, even binary.

Code Chart Mappings

Although Unicode is designed to replace most of the world's character sets, the world's character sets aren't going to die out without a fight. As a result, Unicode was designed to peacefully coexist with the other major character sets, by supporting relatively straightforward mapping tables. Mapping tables work behind the scenes to help software convert text between encodings. When you use the Save as Encoded option in Word 2000, the software simply maps the code points to a new set of code points based on the selected character set. The following two mapping tables are excerpted from Unicode. In Table 2, notice that the code points stay the same when mapping between ISO 8859-1 and Unicode; in Table 3, however, the code points change with Shift_JIS.

Table 2 Mapping Between ISO 8859-1 and Unicode

ISO 8859-1	Unicode	Character
0x41	0x0041	Latin capital letter *A*
0x42	0x0042	Latin capital letter *B*
0x43	0x0043	Latin capital letter *C*
0x44	0x0044	Latin capital letter *D*
0x45	0x0045	Latin capital letter *E*
0x46	0x0046	Latin capital letter *F*
0x47	0x0047	Latin capital letter *G*

Table 3 Mapping Between Shift_JIS and Unicode

Shift_JIS	Unicode	Character
0x82BA	0x305C	Hiragana letter ZE
0x82BB	0x305D	Hiragana letter SO
0x82BC	0x305E	Hiragana letter ZO
0x82BD	0x305F	Hiragana letter TA
0x82BE	0x3060	Hiragana letter DA
0x82BF	0x3061	Hiragana letter TI
0x82C0	0x3062	Hiragana letter DI
0x82C1	0x3063	Hiragana letter small TU
0x82C2	0x3064	Hiragana letter TU

Unicode Encodings

Unicode is one character set, but it has more than one encoding, such as UTF-8, UTF-16, and UTF-32. The acronyms stand for Unicode Transformational Format, and the numbers indicate how many bits may be used to represent a character. UTF-8 is the standard encoding for web pages because it's backward-compatible with servers and routers that can accommodate only single-byte characters. UTF-8 is actually a multibyte encoding, in that a character can be one, two, or four bytes long, depending on its value. An important advantage of using UTF-8 is that it uses only as many bytes as are necessary. For example, any of the Latin 1 characters, because they occupy the first 256 spaces of Unicode, still require only a single byte in UTF-8. The greater the code point, the greater the odds that it will require more than one byte, as shown in Figure 3.

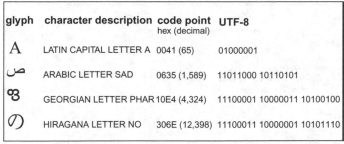

glyph	character description	code point hex (decimal)	UTF-8
A	LATIN CAPITAL LETTER A	0041 (65)	01000001
ص	ARABIC LETTER SAD	0635 (1,589)	11011000 10110101
ჳ	GEORGIAN LETTER PHAR	10E4 (4,324)	11100001 10000011 10100100
の	HIRAGANA LETTER NO	306E (12,398)	11100011 10000001 10101110

Figure 3 Selected characters and the number of bits required to represent them in UTF-8. Notice how the number of bits varies from one byte to three, hence the term "multibyte encoding."

─ Take the Unicode Test ─

To successfully display the entire Unicode character set, you need a current browser and a font with a very wide range of glyphs. In fact, few fonts include the full range of Unicode glyphs. To test your computer, there are two sites you can visit, shown in Figures 4 and 5.

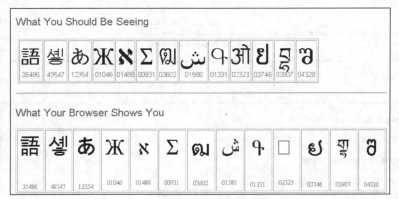

Figure 4 James Kass created a brief Unicode character test page at **http://home.att.net/~jameskass/SEEME.HTM**. In Internet Explorer 5.5, most, but not all, characters are displayed correctly.

continues

455

Take the Unicode Test   (continued)

Test pages for Unicode character ranges

The pages in the following list can be used to display the ranges of characters defined in the Unicode 3.0 Character Database, within the limitations imposed by your Web browser and the proportional font that you are using. There is also a page with a sample of Unicode characters from each range.

General Scripts

- Basic Latin
- Latin-1 Supplement
- Latin Extended-A
- Latin Extended-B
- Latin Extended Additional
- IPA Extensions
- Arabic
- Armenian
- Bengali
- Canadian Aboriginal Syllabics
- Cherokee
- Cyrillic
- Devanagari
- Ethiopic
- Kannada
- Khmer
- Lao
- Malayalam
- Mongolian
- Myanmar
- Ogham
- Old Italic
- Oriya
- Runic
- Sinhala
- Syriac
- Tamil
- Telugu

Figure 5   Alan Wood developed a site where you can test the full Unicode character set: www.hclrss.demon.co.uk/unicode.

FYI

Unicode Font Information and Resources

www.hclrss.demon.co.uk/unicode/fonts.html

www.geocities.com/i18nguy/unicode-example.html

www.bjondi.com/products/char_agent.db

GLOBAL GATEWAY: UNICODE STYLE

To illustrate how Unicode supports multiple scripts, you'll re-create the global gateway using plain text. First, open the source web page and remove the graphics from the gateway. Then copy and paste the text as shown in Figure 6.

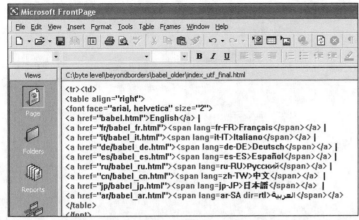

Figure 6 Insert the text links in their native scripts. Be sure to label the language of the text, such as **<SPAN lang="fr-FR">**. Also note that the direction tag is included for the Arabic text.

FrontPage automatically converts characters to fit within a specified default encoding. So if you have the web page configured for Latin 1, FrontPage converts any character that falls outside the range of character entities, as shown in Figure 7. The way to prevent this from happening is to change the default encoding beforehand to UTF-8 (see Figure 8).

457

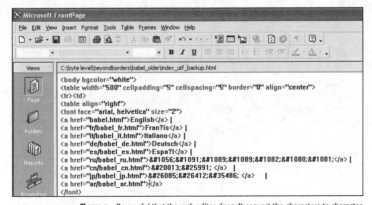

Figure 7 Be careful that the web editor doesn't convert the characters to character entities, as shown in this figure.

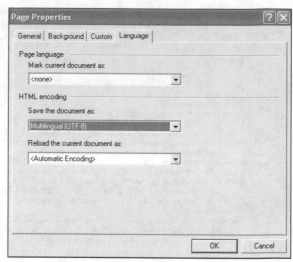

Figure 8   In FrontPage 2000, adjust the HTML encoding preference to Multilingual (UTF-8). This option prevents FrontPage from automatically converting text to character entities.

After you've inserted all the text, preview the web page in various browsers. Your gateway should look something like Figure 9. If some of the characters are missing, you are probably missing the necessary font on your system.

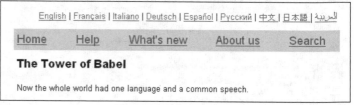

Figure 9   The finished gateway in plain text, using UTF-8 encoding.

Although I don't recommend using pull-down menus for global gateways, if you must use a pull-down, try to use Unicode for it, too. As shown in the Sun Microsystems web page (see Figure 10), Unicode allows the display of a wide range of characters. If, for example, this page had been encoded in Latin 1, the Asian text would have not been displayed at all.

Figure 10   When you use Unicode, even pull-down menus can feature text in multiple scripts, as shown here on the Sun Microsystems web page (**www.sun.com**).

UNICODE FONTS

To view the spectrum of characters included in Unicode, you'll need a font that supports a broad range of scripts. In fact, there are no fonts available to date that include every Unicode character. Of course, the odds of someone needing to view every character are slim. It's important to understand that you don't need a font that supports many scripts just because a web page is encoded as UTF-8. All you need is a font that includes the characters in that particular web page. The standard Latin 1 fonts that you already use to view English-language web pages will continue to work if the encoding switches to UTF-8. However, Microsoft does offer a Unicode font in XP, Arial Unicode MS, which includes a wide range of characters. Not surprisingly, it's also a large font: more than 23MB.

459

Want to Send Email in Unicode?

James Kass offers a tutorial at **http://home.att.net/~jameskass/interoutlook.html**.

FYI

To see how to convert between different Unicode encodings, Mark Davis, president of the Unicode Consortium, has made a text converter available at **http://www.macchiato.com/unicode/convert.html**.

THE FUTURE IS UNICODE

Because Unicode is language-neutral and as inclusive as possible, it promises a level of equality among languages never before seen. For web developers, Unicode will alleviate many of the character set conflicts that plague us today. Unicode is already the official character set of the Internet; it's just a matter of time before it becomes the default character set of the Internet.

17

THE FUTURE OF WEB GLOBALIZATION

Given that companies ranging from Microsoft to McDonald's now owe half their revenues to the world outside their native countries, globalization is showing little signs of slowing. As long as companies find success in new markets, they will need to localize their web sites (and other content) to serve these new markets. However, although web globalization for most companies is inevitable, it is anything but predictable. With this in mind, the following sections outline some likely trends in the areas of web development, commerce, and content.

WEB DEVELOPMENT

The Internet has largely been retrofitted to accommodate multiple languages, and it has done a reasonably good job. But for the web to effectively serve a growing, multilingual, multicountry audience, the underlying Internet standards and protocols need to be upgraded; fortunately, many of these upgrades are well under way.

<charset=UTF-8>

First there was **<charset=ascii>**, and then **<charset=8859-1>**. Soon you will see the Unicode encoding **<charset=UTF-8>** at the top of an increasing number of HTML pages. Unicode promises a level of linguistic inclusiveness never before seen on the Internet—or anywhere else, for that matter. The only major remaining obstacle to its success is getting everybody to use it. That may not be too far away, as more and more people upgrade to Unicode-friendly browsers and hardware. Many companies are already selectively using Unicode on their web sites (see Figure 17.1), and considerably more are using Unicode in their databases to manage multiple languages. Unicode won't solve all our problems, but it will free web developers from fretting over character sets and the many conflicts between them.

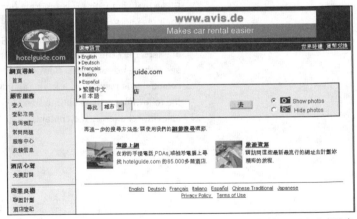

Figure 17.1 The HotelGuide web site uses Unicode (UTF-8).

XML Takes Content Global

XML, which stands for eXtensible Markup Language, is a markup language, like HTML, that functions as a sort of flexible "content wrapper." It is currently used in many content management systems and is ideal for internationalization because it's

Unicode-based and because it so strictly separates form from content. For a comprehensive resource on XML and its role in globalization, see *XML Internationalization and Localization*, by Yves Savourel (Sams Publishing, 2001).

FYI

For more information on XML and internationalization, go to:

www.xml.com

www.w3.org/TR/2000/REC-xml-20001006

www-106.ibm.com/developerworks/xml

http://people.netscape.com/ftang/paper/unicode18/abstract.html

---

Standardization (and Homogenization)

The shopping cart has become a global icon, thanks to the Internet in general and Amazon in particular. Many people are not so thankful, lamenting an increasingly homogenous Internet, in which web sites mimic one another in appearance and functionality. Yet some degree of standardization is essential; few people want to relearn how to purchase a product online from web site to web site, which they're often forced to do. This tug-of-war between standardization and innovation is not going to end anytime soon, nor should it. As you expand globally, it's important not to enforce standardization on countries and cultures that prefer a different way of doing things. We all need to be considerate as we push forward, keeping in mind that not all countries, cultures, and languages have been widely included in this great globalization movement.

Dreamweaver 12: The Globalization Edition

It's not hard to imagine a day when there will be a Macromedia Dreamweaver 12 or Microsoft FrontPage 2008 or GoLive 9 that supports web globalization, possibly with workflow management and budgeting tools built in. Currently, globalization tools are expensive and difficult to learn, but this will surely change. As smaller businesses build localized web sites, they will demand the same types of tools that the multinationals of the world are using, and vendors will eventually give them what they want.

In addition, companies aren't going to want to purchase separate products for content management and globalization management. Until recently, companies first had to install content management systems (CMSs) and then install globalization management systems (GMSs). We are already seeing the blurring of lines between these

463

two types of applications as vendors work together more closely. Before long, there will be no distinction between the two. As more companies build global web sites, globalization management will be just another feature of content management.

Webmasters Learn New Languages

It used to be that webmasters needed to understand only HTML. Today, they often need to know a few programming languages as well. In the future, they might also need to know a few human languages. Although bilingual and multilingual webmasters won't necessarily be expected to translate web pages, they will have an edge on webmasters who speak only one language. Even a basic understanding of the world's major languages—such as knowing the difference between Simplified and Traditional Chinese—will help you succeed in the new, multilingual future of web development.

COMMERCE

Wal-Mart, the largest company in America, has retail stores in China, Korea, Germany, and Mexico, among others, but you wouldn't know it by looking at its home page, which is in English only. With a little web searching, you can find the Wal-Mart Mexico and Wal-Mart Germany home pages, but there is no Wal-Mart China or Korea web site. In the future, customers will come to expect localized web sites, and companies, particularly service-based companies, will have to respond accordingly. Companies won't be the only ones who will change their attitudes toward web globalization—so too will the companies that provide web globalization services.

Services Over Software

Eventually, all the popular web development and design tools, such Photoshop, Illustrator, and Dreamweaver, will support Unicode. As a result, web developers and designers will be able to more easily develop web pages in any major language. Localization firms, because they'll no longer have a monopoly on localization software, will need to focus more on quality, customer service, and value-added services. Translation quality will become a key differentiator among translators and the firms that employ them. Value-added services will include search engine optimization, global brand naming and testing, market research, and regulatory consulting. Not all firms will make the leap, but those that do will transform themselves from single-service providers to globalization consultants—a role that is growing increasingly vital to a global economy.

Raised Customer Expectations

If your competitors offer localized web sites, it won't be long before your customers expect, or demand, that you do the same. Companies such as Amazon and Yahoo! have raised the standard for usability and speed; expect companies to raise standards for web localization. How well is your text translated? Do you offer multilingual phone support? Does your search engine return results in the user's language? Be prepared to answer more and more of these questions. As customers come to expect more from localized web sites, companies will face the challenges of meeting their expectations.

Tougher Competition

When you open yourself up to the world, you open yourself up to a world of competition. Today, a company may be able to gain a competitive advantage simply by translating a few of its web pages. In the years ahead, however, as more companies invest more resources into globalization, the bar will be raised. Localized façades will be seen as what they are—façades—and people will gravitate to the companies that understand their culture as well as their language. The true competitive advantage won't be just your web site, but your entire company. How globally aware are your colleagues? How sensitive are they to the world around them? The attitudes and perceptions of your colleagues will play a critical role in your eventual success—or lack thereof.

465

CONTENT

If there is any certainty about the future of web content, it's that there will be a lot more of it—and in more languages and formats. As content grows in size and complexity, so too will the costs of managing it. As a result, expect companies to keep a close eye on how content is created and managed, no matter what the language.

A Few Good Editors

Human translation isn't going to get any less expensive in the years ahead, so expect to see companies looking more closely at the words they choose to translate. Many larger companies will find that the savings generated by careful editing could pay for a full-time editor. In addition, expect to see companies not only editing down text, but also writing text with translation in mind. It won't be unusual to see marketers write in "global" English, knowing that the text will be localized for different markets, including the U.S. From a writer's standpoint, a universal approach to writing may indeed be easier in the long run, as it forces a focus on global themes and benefits, and limits localized humor and clichés. The universal text can then be more easily and quickly localized country by country.

The Future Is Less Graphic

The days of web designers embedding generous amounts of text within graphics are drawing to a close. Given the time and costs associated with editing and changing text within graphic language by language, companies will begin to scrutinize their use of graphics more closely than ever. Even graphics without text will be used more cautiously, as they must first be tested globally to ensure that they aren't offending or confusing the intended audience.

Multilingual and Mobile

People in the U.S. have a vastly different view of the Internet than do people in Japan. In Japan, more than 30 million people access the Internet through their mobile phones, primarily through a service known as i-Mode. Imagine viewing the Internet through a two-inch screen. Not only are the screens small, but the download speeds are quite slow. Yet i-Mode is enormously popular because most Japanese do not have home PCs and generally prefer mobile devices. The effect on how companies manage content is significant. Web developers must place an even higher priority on low-bandwidth, high-speed content delivery. On a cell phone, every word and graphic counts. Subscribers pay by the kilobit, so they won't patiently wait for needless graphics or text.

NTT DoCoMo, the company that launched i-Mode, is launching similar services in Europe and the U.S. Yahoo! now provides content for i-Mode delivery (see Figure 17.2). How people will respond to i-Mode remains to be seen, but most analysts say the future of mobile access in countries without extensive land-line connections is already bright.

Figure 17.2   A view of Yahoo! mobile—light on text and pictures.

Consider Latin America, where the majority of homes do not have phone lines, and more people have mobile phones than wire-line phones. This trend will only continue to accelerate because it's cheaper for companies to provide mobile service than to connect homes wire by wire.

Analysts also predict the coming of 3G, or third-generation mobile service. 3G promises very fast Internet connections, so fast that you could plug your computer into your mobile phone and surf the Internet just as you do at home—or your mobile phone becomes your primary computer. No matter how the future unfolds, companies need to prepare for mobile delivery of content, which means relying on databases, XML, and an economy of words and visuals. The way the world is developing, mobile will be the primary platform for most Internet users.

Machine Translation Gets the Respect It Deserves

Machine translation (MT) is far from perfect. At times, it's downright laughable, as translators are more than happy to point out. But in its defense, it's fast and it's free. You want to know what that German web site says? Just go to **http://world.altavista.com** and have it translated on the spot. There will always be situations in which machine translation is inappropriate—instructions, product descriptions, and legalese, for example—but machine translation will continue to play a vital role in global communication, particularly as its quality continues to improve. Companies will, in fact, find that machine translation, when used selectively, works efficiently and saves them a lot of money. Also expect to see real-time voice translation evolve to the point that people can get customer support by phone. Although high-quality translation is always your goal, you shouldn't let the lack of funds prevent you from offering no translation at all. Machine translation is here to stay.

The White House: Is That All There Is?

If the White House wanted to fully communicate to the world as well as the U.S., it would go much further than English- and Spanish-language web sites—the only two languages provided thus far (see Figure 17.3).

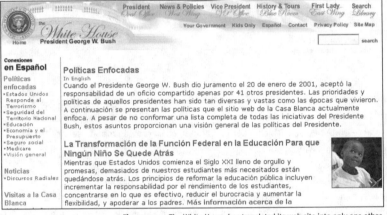

Figure 17.3 The White House has translated its web site into only one other language besides English.

The Future of Language

According to many experts, over the next 50 years, anywhere between 200 to 800 languages will cease to exist, their last living speakers gone forever. Lameen Souag is curator of the Rosetta Project (**www.rosettaproject.org**), a nonprofit organization developing the modern equivalent of the Rosetta Stone (see Figure 17.4). He says that more than 400 languages have just a few elderly speakers remaining, and many more that have a few hundred speakers, but are no longer being taught to children. "If nothing is done, these will probably survive for another 40 years or so," says Souag.

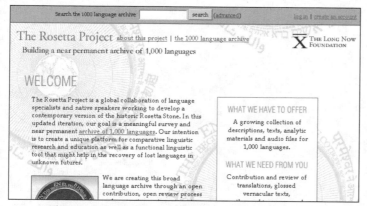

Figure 17.4   The Rosetta Project seeks volunteers to help preserve the world's languages.

The Rosetta Project has catalogued more than 1,000 languages and will eventually have the records transcribed on tiny, indestructible disks that will be spread around the world.

One Country; Many Languages

Papua New Guinea, a country roughly the size of the state of California, has 715 indigenous languages.

Source: CIA World Factbook; **http://www.cia.gov/cia/publications/factbook**

ONE INTERNET, ONE LANGUAGE AT A TIME

Web globalization isn't easy and it isn't always cheap, but you'll find it's a lot easier to adapt your web site to the world than it is to wait for the world to adapt to your web site. Fortunately, web globalization is still in its infancy. You don't need a dozen languages to begin; one to two languages is usually a good start. Most organizations are working on their first localized web sites, and many more have yet to begin. However, this field is growing quickly. It won't be long before organizations view localized web sites as a necessity rather than a luxury. And it won't be long before many of the trends mentioned in this chapter begin to take hold. By keeping these developments in mind, you'll be well positioned to meet the challenges of a growing, multilingual Internet.

A

GLOSSARY

ACE   *See* ASCII-compatible encoding.

alignment   The process of connecting the source and target segments into pairs for translation memory.

ASCII   Acronym for American Standard Code for Information Interchange. ASCII is a 7-bit coded character set and has since been widely replaced by ISO 8859-1.

ASCII-compatible encoding (ACE)   The result of converting internationalized domain names (IDNs) into an ASCII string that can be resolved by DNS servers.

back-translation   Hiring another translation agency or freelance translator (after your site has been translated) to tell you what your site is saying to him or her; functions as part of a quality audit.

bi-directional language (bidi)   Includes text that flows from right to left and left to right. Arabic and Hebrew text, for example, flows from right to left, but also includes text that flows from left to right, such as numbers and text from other languages.

bit   The smallest unit a computer can process is a bit, represented by a 1 or a 0. Computers think in numbers, represented in bits, which means every character and every web page is represented by a combination of 1s and 0s.

broadband   An Internet connection that is generally faster than a dial-up modem. Typical broadband connections include DSL (digital subscriber line), cable, or digital satellite.

byte   One byte is equal to eight bits.

CAT   *See* computer-aided translation.

ccTLD   Country code top-level domain; *see* domain name.

change order   When a translation or localization project expands beyond the quoted scope, the vendor typically creates a change order detailing the added charges and timetable, which must be approved by the client before work begins.

character   The smallest component of written language that has semantic value; refers to the abstract meaning and/or shape, rather than the specific shape (that is, its rendering in a specific typeface), which is referred to as a *glyph* (source: Unicode Consortium; **www.unicode.org**).

character entity (named and numeric)   The HTML protocol includes character entities as an alternative method of representing characters. An entity can be in the form of a named entity, such as **€**, or numeric entity, such as **¯**.

character set   A collection of characters typically grouped by script.

character set conflict   HTML allows for the use of only one character set per web page. Sometimes the web page specifies characters from more than one character set, thereby creating a conflict. The long-term solution to such conflicts is the use of the "super character set" Unicode.

CL   *See* controlled language.

client   Can refer to an organization that hires translators or a translation/localization agency. A *client* can also refer to a web browser or email application.

CMS   *See* content management system.

coded character set   When the characters of a character set are mapped to numbers, or code points, the character set is called a coded character set. The distinction between character set and coded character set is important as computers work only in numbers.

Codepage   Microsoft has developed its own coded character sets, called Codepages. Each Codepage is typically a modification of existing ISO character sets. For example, Codepage 1251 is a modification of ISO 8859-1 in which extra characters were added.

computer-aided translation (CAT)   A broad term that may include a wide range of software tools designed to help translators work more quickly and/or improve the quality of their work. CAT tools range from electronic bilingual dictionaries to translation memory software.

concatenation   Linking two or more objects. Concatenation is often used in software and web development to create text strings that are assembled dynamically in pieces. Concatenation can cause problems when text is translated, as the pieces might no longer fit together so neatly.

content audit   A comprehensive review of all web site content, typically conducted before redesigns, but also important before web globalization projects. A content audit helps an organization decide as early as possible what components of a site need to be localized and whether they will be localized.

content management system (CMS)   A CMS refers to software designed to help organizations manage the creation and dissemination of web content. CMS applications become increasingly important as web sites grow larger, more decentralized, and more sophisticated.

content negotiation   A still-evolving system of delivering language-specific content to web browsers based on the language preference of the web browser.

controlled language (CL)   In the field of translation, a controlled language imposes strict rules designed to result in text that is more easily, clearly, and consistently translated. Rules often apply to terminology, grammar, and length of sentences. Also referred to as *simplified language*.

cookie   Think of cookies as nametags for computers, stored on a web user's computer after visiting a web site. Many web sites rely on cookies to maintain a more personal relationship with visitors. Language and country preferences are increasingly being added to the list of data stored in cookies.

customer relationship management (CRM)   The process of developing a better understanding of and a closer relationship with an organization's customers. CRM software packages facilitate this process.

DBCS   *See* double-byte character set.

DHTML   *See* Dynamic Hypertext Markup Language.

DNS   *See* Domain Name System or Domain Name Service.

473

domain name A unique alphanumeric string that identifies a particular computer or domain, such as "amazon.com." The domain name consists of two parts: the top-level domain and the second-level domain. The top level is a generic top-level domain (gTLD) or country code top-level domain (ccTLD).

Domain Name System or Domain Name Service (DNS) A distributed system of translating domain names into their matching numeric Internet Protocol (IP) addresses. The DNS allows web users to locate a web site by its easy-to-remember domain name rather than the more cumbersome IP address, which is a string of numbers.

double-byte character set (DBCS) Some character sets contain more than 256 characters—the most that can be represented in a single-byte character set. Adding a second byte enables you to represent more than 65,000 characters. Double-byte character sets have been widely used for Chinese and Japanese.

Dynamic Hypertext Markup Language (DHTML) A combination of scripts and standards that have evolved to make web pages more animated and interactive. Put simply, DHTML allows a web page to interact with the user long after it has been fully downloaded.

encoding, encoding scheme A system of mapping characters to numbers so that computers can manipulate them. After a character set is encoded, it is called a coded character set. Encoding can be confusing because it also means the mapping of coded characters to actual byte values; for example, Unicode is a coded character set. Each character is assigned one number only, but each of these numbers can be assigned different byte values to accommodate computing systems, so there are several encodings: UTF-8, UTF-16, and UTF-32.

euro The official currency of 12 countries within the European Union.

exact match When translation memory software scans new text, it looks for sentences that match previously translated sentences. If it finds a perfect match, ignoring any formatting information, the two are considered an exact match.

eXtensible Markup Language (XML) XML, a markup language like HTML, acts as a flexible "content wrapper."

FIGS A common abbreviation for the European languages French, Italian, German, and Spanish.

font A collection of glyphs typically grouped by language or script.

fuzzy match When translation memory software scans new text, it looks for sentences that match previously translated sentences. When it encounters two sentences that are similar but not an exact match, it is called a fuzzy match. The degree of fuzziness is expressed as a percentage, such as "80% fuzzy match."

G11N, g11n   The abbreviation for globalization; *see* globalization. The number 11 refers to the number of letters between *g* and *n*.

gateway (international gateway, global gateway)   The web interface, and underlying functionality, used to direct users to their localized web pages.

generational strategy   A gradual approach to web globalization in which a company could, for example, begin with one localized site and limited functionality and then build from there, gradually adding languages and layers of sophistication.

gisting   A very rough form of translation in which only the "gist" of the text is translated. Machine translation tools are generally only capable of gisting.

globalization (g11n)   Globalization means vastly different things to different people, but for the purposes of this book, it is the process of expanding an organization beyond its native market. When applied to a web site, globalization encompasses the full range of actions required to adapt that web site for new markets, such as business strategy, internationalization, localization, translation, testing, support, and promotion. Although globalization generally applies to expanding an organization's geographic reach, it can apply to expanding an organization's linguistic or cultural reach, such as an American company that translates its web site for Americans who do not speak English.

globalization management system (GMS)   Software designed to help an organization manage ongoing web localization, particularly text translation. Globalization software can include many of the features of content management systems or may work in tandem with such a system. Features might include workflow management, translation memory integration, and vendor management tools.

globalization workflow   Basically a to-do list of all the tasks needed to internationalize and localize a web site.

global resource file   In web globalization, a resource file contains all translatable text strings. Centralizing all text strings saves time and often reduces room for error.

global template   A web design template that standardizes such elements as navigation, colors, and typefaces, but allows room for localized content and promotions.

glyph   An image used to visually represent a character. In other words, it's how a character is rendered in a particular typeface or font.

GMS   *See* globalization management system.

graceful degradation   The practice of building web pages so that they adapt themselves to the user's browser. This practice can also be applied to global gateways.

gTLD   Generic top-level domain; *see* domain name.

harmonization   Similar to standardization. The term has been traditionally used in the regulatory fields to describe the effort to standardize rules and regulations between countries. Harmonization seeks to minimize barriers to cross-border trade.

hexadecimal   A numbering system that uses 16 digits. The decimal system uses 10 digits: 0, 1, 2, 3, 4, 5, 6, 7, 8, and 9. Hexadecimal uses these digits: 0, 1, 2, 3, 4, 5, 6, 7, 8, 9, A, B, C, D, E, and F. Unicode characters are encoded by using hexadecimal notation.

Hypertext Markup Language (HTML)   A standard for publishing and viewing content on the Internet.

Hypertext Transfer Protocol (HTTP)   Defines how browsers and servers communicate with one another to effectively transmit and display HTML documents. A key component of this protocol in regards to the multilingual Internet is the communication of document encodings.

I18N, i18n   Abbreviation for internationalization. The number 18 refers to the number of letters between *i* and *n*.

ICANN   *See* Internet Corporation for Assigned Names and Numbers.

ideographic writing system   A writing system that relies on symbols that represent ideas, rather than sounds, to communicate meaning. Chinese began as an ideographic writing system.

IDN   *See* internationalized domain name.

IME   *See* input method editor.

input method editor (IME)   A software tool that enables a Latin keyboard to input non-Latin characters. IMEs are commonly used for Japanese, Chinese, and Korean characters.

International Organization for Standardization (ISO)   ISO is a voluntary, worldwide federation of national standards bodies founded in 1946. It promotes the development of standardization to facilitate the international exchange of goods and services and cooperation in the spheres of intellectual, scientific, technological, and economic activity. ISO includes one representative from the national standards organizations of about 100 member countries (source: ISO; **www.iso.ch**).

internationalization (i18n)   The process of designing and building a web site (or software application) so that it can be more easily localized. Internationalization entails isolating the elements of a site that will need to be changed during localization and making the necessary allowances for their modification. Internationalization can be more extensive for an application that requires Asian localization versus one that might need only Western European localization.

internationalized domain name (IDN)   A system for allowing non-ASCII characters into the domain name. Currently, many registrars offer multilingual registration, but there is no official standard. For more information, visit the IETF IDN Working Group at **www.ietf.org**.

Internet Corporation for Assigned Names and Numbers (ICANN)   ICANN (**www.icann.org**) manages IP address space allocation, protocol parameter assignment, domain name system management, and root server system management functions.

Internet Engineering Task Force (IETF)   A group that works to solve the technical challenges of the Internet, such as the internationalization of domain names (**www.ietf.org**).

L10N, L10n   Abbreviation for localization. The number 10 refers to the number of letters between *L* and *n*.

language pair   The combination of source language and target language, such as English → French. The arrow indicates the relationship between the two languages. Translators generally specialize in just one language pair—their native language and one other language.

locale   A combination of language and region or country, such as en-US or en-UK. A number of attributes are typically associated with each locale, such as language, number format, time and date formats, currency, and so forth.

localization (L10n)   The adaptation of a web site to a locale. The process can include a wide range of linguistic, cultural, and technical modifications, such as text translation; conversion of date, time, and measurement formats; and customization of the interface.

localization kit   Before web localization can begin, a localization kit is developed. It includes the necessary files, glossaries, guidelines, checklists, tracking sheets, and style guides to enable efficient and consistent translation. Also called a *translation kit*.

localization vendor   A localization vendor differentiates itself from a translation vendor by providing the technical expertise and tools necessary to localize HTML files, graphics, and databases, often in addition to translation.

localized façade   A site that translates only its first few pages.

MBCS   *See* multibyte character set.

mCommerce   Short for mobile commerce, the ability to access the Internet and conduct transactions by using a cellular phone or other mobile device.

machine translation (MT)   The process of translating from one human language to another using software. The term dates back to a time when computers were called machines. One of the most popular (and free) MT applications is Babel Fish (**http://world.altavista.com**).

masculinity (MAS) index   One of Geert Hofstede's five dimensions of culture; measures how traditional roles are assigned to gender in different cultures. A high MAS index emphasizes division of labor and roles between genders.

metadata   Data that defines or describes the data being managed. It may include context descriptions, technical details, and instructions.

MT   *See* machine translation.

multibyte character set (MBCS)   A Latin-based language uses a relatively short script of characters, but some languages, such as Japanese or Chinese, rely on several thousands of characters. To represent all these characters numerically so that computers can manage them, more than one byte is required. Unicode is a multibyte character set because it relies on encodings that vary in byte length, depending on the code point of the character being represented. For example, a Latin character remains as a single byte, but a Chinese character could require three bytes.

named character entity   *See* character entity.

numeric character entity   *See* character entity.

overweight web page   In broad terms, an overweight web page uses so many elements—text, graphics, functionality—that the page size negatively affects the download time for the end user. The weight of a page can be calculated in kilobytes (KB); the average web page weight is 89KB. If a web site is larger than 80KB, web users who rely on slower connections might not be patient enough to wait for the web page to display.

phonetic writing system   A writing system relying on symbols that represent sounds. The Latin alphabet is a phonetic system. There are two major phonetic systems: alphabetic (each character represents a vowel or consonant) and syllabic (each character represents a combination of consonants and/or vowels).

power-distance (PD)   One of Geert Hofstede's five dimensions of culture; reflects the extent to which people within a culture accept (or expect) unequal power distribution. High PD countries exhibited centralized power structures and clearly defined class distinctions.

RFP   Request for Proposal.

rich text format (RTF)   An encoding system for formatted text that allows the transfer of documents between operating systems and applications without loss of formatting. Translators and translation agencies rely heavily on this file format because it preserves files in their native encoding and is platform neutral.

rollover image   An effect created by using an "on" and "off" graphic image, one on top of the other. When the web user's mouse rolls over the off graphic, the on graphic appears. Also known as a *mouseover*. Rollover graphics are most frequently used on buttons.

RTF   *See* rich text format.

segment   In translation memory, the fundamental unit of text that can be stored into memory—typically a sentence.

source language   The language one translates from.

target language   The language one translates into.

terminology glossary   A collection of terminology, slogans, and navigational wording that must be consistently translated (or not translated) throughout the web site.

terminology manager   A software tool that aids in the translation process by storing source and target terms. Terminology managers are often included as part of a larger translation memory software product.

text contraction/text expansion   When text is translated into another language, the resulting target text might end up longer or shorter than the source text. For example, when English is translated into German, text can expand by as much as 40%; conversely, when English is translated into Chinese, the resulting text may be 20% shorter.

TM   *See* translation memory.

TMX   *See* Translation Memory eXchange.

translation   Process of transferring the meaning of the text from one language to another.

translation memory (TM)   The process of saving previous translations as source sentence/target sentence pairs so that they can be reused if a similar source sentence appears again. The larger a translation memory grows, the more valuable it generally becomes because it reduces the number of source sentences that require manual translation. Translation memory also aids in overall translation consistency.

479

Translation Memory eXchange (TMX)   A standard for enabling the exchange of translation memories between different software tools. It is managed by the Localization Industry Standards Association (LISA) and is designed to work with XML.

translation vendor   Translation vendors manage translators—in-house, freelance, or both. They might specialize in a few language pairs or could manage as many as 60 language pairs. A translation vendor manages, at a minimum, text translation. Some vendors also manage graphics localization and other technical aspects of web localization.

transliteration   Transferring the sound of the text in one language into the text of another language. Translation results in new words that convey the same meaning, but transliteration results in new words that sound like the old words, regardless of meaning. Transliteration is frequently used for creating "romanized" versions of text in Asian, Arabic, or Cyrillic languages.

Unicode   A universal coded character set, designed to include the characters from all the world's major languages. Unicode Version 3.1 contains 94,140 encoded characters. The Unicode Consortium (**www.unicode.org**) developed Unicode.

validation   An orderly process of checking files throughout the localization process to ensure that errors haven't been introduced by translators, editors, or web developers.

variable   Anything that changes from market to market, or even within a market, such as measurements and sizes or prices and currencies.

vendor   Can include individual translators, translation agencies (who manage multiple translators), localization agencies, or software vendors.

visual keyboard   A software tool available with the Microsoft Office suite that makes it easier for users to type languages not represented on the physical keyboard.

XML   *See* eXtensible Markup Language.

B

GLOBAL COLOR CHART

Colors mean different things to different people. Sometimes, colors mean different things to different cultures. Table B.1, compiled from many sources, will give you an idea of the range of meanings a color can have. It is by no means definitive, nor is it prescriptive.

The meaning of color is like the meaning of language: constantly evolving and usually open to interpretation. The meaning of a color can vary not only between cultures but also within cultures. A color might even have two contradictory meanings. For example, in the U.S., a person dressed in black may be going to a funeral or to a dance club. Context plays a critical role in defining color, as does the combination of colors. In France, the combination of blue, white, and red signify *liberté*, *égalité*, and *fraternité*, respectively, in the tricolor. In the U.S., the same three colors are also used in the flag, but the meanings are slightly different.

Table B.1 **What Colors Signify Around the World**

Red

Region	Significance	Example
U.S.	Excitement, warning, sex, passion, spicy, valor	Stop signs, fire trucks
Mexico	Religion, vibrancy, death	Aztec color for the north, national flag
Brazil	Visibility, vibrancy	Red cars illegal in Brazil and Ecuador because of the perception that they cause more accidents
Greece	Love, autumn, good luck	Wine, eggs dyed red for Easter for luck
U.K.	Authority, power, government, visibility	Mailboxes, buses, telephone booths
Africa	Death, bloodshed	Mourning clothing
China, Hong Kong, Taiwan	Communism, celebration, good luck, joy, fertility	Wedding dresses, lucky money envelopes, red ink used in obituaries
Japan	Blood, passion, self-sacrifice, strength	Public phones, color of flag (rising sun)
India	Birth, fertility	Wedding dress, henna color in hair
Scandinavia	Strength	Eric the Red

What Color Is a Mailbox?

It all depends on where you are. In the U.K., Morocco, and Egypt, mailboxes are red; in Sweden, they're yellow.

Blue

Region	Significance	Example
U.S.	Justice, perseverance, trust, official business	Uniforms, mailboxes, color of flag, color of the Chief Executive
Scandinavia	Cleanliness	Hospital supplies
India	Heavens, love, truth	Krishna's skin
Greece	National pride	Color of flag
Israel	Holiness	In ancient history, priestly garments were dyed with a blue ink obtained from a now-extinct sea creature known as the Chilazon
Germany	Loyalty, formality	Government letters traditionally are mailed in blue envelopes

White

Region	Significance	Example
U.S.	Purity, innocence, virginity	Bedding, hospital uniforms
U.K.	Leisure, sports	Sportswear
China, Hong Kong, Taiwan	Death, mourning, purity	Funeral clothing, packages
India	Death, rebirth, serenity	Brahman (highest caste)
Africa	Victory, purity	School uniforms of young girls

What Color Signifies Death?

It depends on where you are. Black signifies death in the West, but in most of Asia, white signifies death.

Black

Region	Significance	Example
U.S.	Death, sophistication, formality	Color of mourning, formal wear
U.K.	Death, formality	Formal wear, color of taxis
Brazil	Sophistication, mourning, formality	Formal clothing, mourning clothing, religious clothing
Mexico	Mourning, respect	Clerical robes
Germany	Death, grief, hopelessness, formality	Clergy attire, black automobiles of government ministers

Green

Region	Significance	Example
U.S.	Environmental, freshness, health, inexperience, envy	Money, nature, highway signs, being "green with envy"
Ireland	Catholicism, nationalism	National color
Germany	Hope, conservation	Police uniforms
Arab Middle East	Holiness	Holy color of Islam; the Prophet Muhammad wore a green turban, and green is believed to have been his favorite color. Mosques are frequently decorated with green tiles.

What Color Is a Police Uniform?

Once again, it all depends. Blue or black may be the standard colors in the U.S., but German police wear green.

Yellow

Region	Significance	Example
U.S.	Visibility, caution, faith	Police area, color of taxis, yellow ribbon as symbol for loved one to return home
Scandinavia	Warmth	Mailboxes in Sweden
India	Commerce	Taxis
Germany	Envy, jealousy	Germans use the phrase "yellow with envy"
Israel	Saintliness	Halo of God

Purple

Region	Significance	Example
U.S.	Nobility, law, bravery	Purple Heart, collegiate colors
Latin America	Death	Purple flowers sent to funerals
Italy	Color of the church, authority	Used by high-ranking officials and the Catholic church

Sources: Blunders in International Business, *David. A. Ricks, Cambridge, MA: Blackwell Business, 1997;* Global Graphics: Color, *L.K. Peterson, Rockport, MA: Rockport Publishers, 2000; Web of Culture (**www.webofculture.com/worldsmart**); interview with Joseph Braude, analyst, Pyramid Research, 2002; and interview with Richard Nangle, German translator, 2002.*

C

CHARACTER ENTITIES

Character entities allow you to display a character on a web page without actually inputting that character. The need for entities arose during the days when ASCII ruled the Internet. Because the ASCII character set was so limited (see Figure C.1), web developers needed a way to represent everything from accented characters to the copyright symbol. With character entities, you could instruct web browsers to display non-ASCII characters.

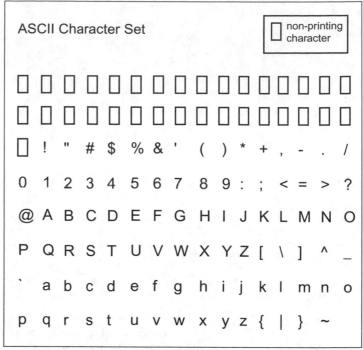

Figure C.1   Character entities helped accommodate the inherent limitations of ASCII.

NAMES AND NUMERIC ENTITIES

Character entities can be represented as *named entities* or *numeric entities*. For example, to display the copyright symbol on a web page, you can enter **©** or **#169;**. The ampersand instructs the browser that a named entity is being used, and the number sign indicates that a numeric entity is being used. The named system is more user friendly but quite limited because there are only a limited number of named entities from which to choose. The numeric system, although hardly user friendly, is virtually unlimited because all characters are represented by numeric code points. For instance, using the Unicode character set, you could represent all 91,000 characters using nothing but numeric entities. Tables C.1 through C.3 include the more frequently used named and numerical entities. For the complete list of entities, go to **http://www.w3c.org/TR/REC-html40/sgml/entities.html**.

Table C.1 ISO 8859-1 (Latin 1) Entities

Character	Named Entity	Numeric Entity	Description
			nonbreaking space
¡	&iexcl;	&#161;	inverted exclamation mark
¢	&cent;	&#162;	cent sign
£	&pound;	&#163;	pound sterling sign
¤	&curren;	&#164;	general currency sign
¥	&yen;	&#165;	yen sign
¦	&brvbar;	&#166;	broken (vertical) bar
§	&sect;	&#167;	section sign
¨	&uml;	&#168;	umlaut (dieresis)
©	&copy;	&#169;	copyright sign
ª	&ordf;	&#170;	ordinal indicator, feminine
«	&laquo;	&#171;	angle quotation mark, left
¬	&not;	&#172;	not sign
	&shy;	&#173;	soft hyphen
®	&reg;	&#174;	registered sign
¯	&macr;	&#175;	macron
°	&deg;	&#176;	degree sign
±	&plusmn;	&#177;	plus-or-minus sign
²	&sup2;	&#178;	superscript two
³	&sup3;	&#179;	superscript three
´	&acute;	&#180;	acute accent
µ	&micro;	&#181;	micro sign
¶	&para;	&#182;	pilcrow (paragraph sign)
·	&middot;	&#183;	middle dot
¸	&cedil;	&#184;	cedilla
¹	&sup1;	&#185;	superscript one
º	&ordm;	&#186;	ordinal indicator, masculine
»	&raquo;	&#187;	angle quotation mark, right
¼	&frac14;	&#188;	fraction (one-quarter)
½	&frac12;	&#189;	fraction (one-half)
¾	&frac34;	&#190;	fraction (three-quarters)
¿	&iquest;	&#191;	inverted question mark
À	&Agrave;	&#192;	capital A, grave accent
Á	&Aacute;	&#193;	capital A, acute accent
Â	&Acirc;	&#194;	capital A, circumflex accent
Ã	&Atilde;	&#195;	capital A, tilde
Ä	&Auml;	&#196;	capital A, with dieresis or umlaut mark

491

continues

Table C.1 ISO 8859-1 (Latin 1) Entities   continued

Å	Å	Å	capital A, ring
Æ	&Aelig;	Æ	capital AE diphthong (ligature)
Ç	Ç	Ç	capital C, cedilla
È	È	È	capital E, grave accent
É	É	É	capital E, acute accent
Ê	Ê	Ê	capital E, circumflex accent
Ë	Ë	Ë	capital E, dieresis or umlaut mark
Ì	Ì	Ì	capital I, grave accent
Í	Í	Í	capital I, acute accent
Î	Î	Î	capital I, circumflex accent
Ï	Ï	Ï	capital I, dieresis or umlaut mark
Ð	Ð	Ð	capital Eth, Icelandic
Ñ	Ñ	Ñ	capital N, tilde
Ò	Ò	Ò	capital O, grave accent
Ó	Ó	Ó	capital O, acute accent
Ô	Ô	Ô	capital O, circumflex accent
Õ	Õ	Õ	capital O, tilde
Ö	Ö	Ö	capital O, dieresis or umlaut mark
×	×	×	multiply sign
Ø	Ø	Ø	capital O, slash
Ù	Ù	Ù	capital U, grave accent
Ú	Ú	Ú	capital U, acute accent
Û	Û	Û	capital U, circumflex accent
Ü	Ü	Ü	capital U, with dieresis or umlaut mark
Ý	Ý	Ý	capital Y, acute accent
Þ	Þ	Þ	capital THORN, Icelandic
ß	ß	ß	small sharp s, German (sz ligature)
à	à	à	small a, grave accent
á	á	á	small a, acute accent
â	â	â	small a, circumflex accent
ã	ã	ã	small a, tilde
ä	ä	ä	small a, with dieresis or umlaut mark
å	å	å	small a, ring
æ	æ	æ	small ae diphthong (ligature)
ç	ç	ç	small c, cedilla

è	&egrave;	&#232;	small e, grave accent
é	&eacute;	&#233;	small e, acute accent
ê	&ecirc;	&#234;	small e, circumflex accent
ë	&euml;	&#235;	small e, with dieresis or umlaut mark
ì	&igrave;	&#236;	small i, grave accent
í	&iacute;	&#237;	small i, acute accent
î	&icirc;	&#238;	small i, circumflex accent
ï	&iuml;	&#239;	small i, with dieresis or umlaut mark
ð	&eth;	&#240;	small eth, Icelandic
ñ	&ntilde;	&#241;	small n, tilde
ò	&ograve;	&#242;	small o, grave accent
ó	&oacute;	&#243;	small o, acute accent
ô	&ocirc;	&#244;	small o, circumflex accent
õ	&otilde;	&#245;	small o, tilde
ö	&ouml;	&#246;	small o, with dieresis or umlaut mark
÷	&divide;	&#247;	divide sign
ø	&oslash;	&#248;	small o, slash
ù	&ugrave;	&#249;	small u, grave accent
ú	&uacute;	&#250;	small u, acute accent
û	&ucirc;	&#251;	small u, circumflex accent
ü	&uuml;	&#252;	small u, with dieresis or umlaut mark
ý	&yacute;	&#253;	small y, acute accent
þ	&thorn;	&#254;	small thorn, Icelandic
ÿ	&yuml;	&#255;	small y, with dieresis or umlaut mark

493

Table C.2 **Selected Greek Character Entities**

Character	Named Entity	Numeric Entity	Description
A	&alpha;	&#913;	Greek capital letter alpha
β	&beta;	&#914;	Greek capital letter beta
Γ	&gamma;	&#915;	Greek capital letter gamma
Δ	&delta;	&#916;	Greek capital letter delta
E	&epsilon;	&#917;	Greek capital letter epsilon
Z	&zeta;	&#918;	Greek capital letter zeta
H	&eta;	&#919;	Greek capital letter eta

continues

Table C.2 **Selected Greek Character Entities**   continued

Θ	&theta;	&#920;	Greek capital letter theta
Ι	&iota;	&#921;	Greek capital letter iota
Κ	&kappa;	&#922;	Greek capital letter kappa
Λ	&lambda;	&#923;	Greek capital letter lambda
Μ	&mu;	&#924;	Greek capital letter mu
Ν	&nu;	&#925;	Greek capital letter nu
Ξ	&xi;	&#926;	Greek capital letter xi
Ο	&omicron;	&#927;	Greek capital letter omicron
Π	&pi;	&#928;	Greek capital letter pi
Ρ	&rho;	&#929;	Greek capital letter rho
Σ	&sigma;	&#931;	Greek capital letter sigma
Τ	&tau;	&#932;	Greek capital letter tau
Υ	&upsilon;	&#933;	Greek capital letter upsilon
Φ	&phi;	&#934;	Greek capital letter phi
Χ	&chi;	&#935;	Greek capital letter chi
Ψ	&psi;	&#936;	Greek capital letter psi
Ω	&omega;	&#937;	Greek capital letter omega

Table C.3 **Selected Symbol Entities**

Character	Named Entity	Numeric Entity	Description
™	&trade;	&#8482;	trademark sign
←	&larr;	&#2190;	leftward arrow
↑	&uarr;	&#2191;	upward arrow
→	&rarr;	&#2192;	rightward arrow
↓	&darr;	&#2193;	downward arrow
↔	&harr;	&#2194;	left-right arrow
♠	&spades;	&#9824;	black spade suit
♣	&clubs;	&#9827;	black club suit (shamrock)
♥	&hearts;	&#9829;	black heart suit (valentine)
♦	&diams;	&#9830;	black diamond suit

UNICODE, MICROSOFT, AND "SMART QUOTES"

Although Unicode is now the official HTML character set, there are still legacy issues
to be aware of, such as the mismatch between Unicode and Codepage 1252.
Microsoft created Codepage 1252 as an alternative to Latin 1. In doing so, it added
characters that included, among other things, the curly quotes popularly referred to
as "smart quotes." The full list of characters that Microsoft added in the 128–159
code point range are shown in Table C.4.

Table C.4 **The "Special Characters" of Codepage 1252**

Character	Numeric Entity	Character	Numeric Entity
€	&#128;	'	&#145;
'	&#130;	'	&#146;
ƒ	&#131;	"	&#147;
"	&#132;	"	&#148;
…	&#133;	•	&#149;
†	&#134;	—	&#150;
‡	&#135;	~	&#151;
ˆ	&#136;	™	&#152;
‰	&#137;	š	&#153;
Š	&#138;	›	&#154;
‹	&#139;	œ	&#155;
Œ	&#140;	ž	&#158;
Ž	&#142;	Ÿ	&#159;

495

Unicode, which is the official HTML character set, is aligned with Latin 1, not
Codepage 1252. Web developers who want to insert smart quotes into web pages
are faced with a dilemma. Using Codepage 1252, the open and closed double quotation marks are located at code points 147 and 148. In Unicode, however, they're at
code points 8220 and 8221. If you want to use the "special characters" of Codepage
1252 in a web page, you should use Unicode numeric entities, as shown in Table C.5,
instead of referring to Codepage 1252 code points. Better yet, avoid numeric entities
altogether in this situation and use named entities, also shown in this table.

Table C.5 **Selected Unicode Entities**

Character	Named Entity	Numeric Entity	Description
–	&ndash;	&#8211;	en dash
--	&mdash;	&#8212;	em dash

continues

Table C.5 **Selected Unicode Entities   continued**

'	&lsquo;	&#8216;	left single quotation mark
'	&rsquo;	&#8217;	right single quotation mark
‚	&sbquo;	&#8218;	single low-9 quotation mark
"	&ldquo;	&#8220;	left double quotation mark
"	&rdquo;	&#8221;	right double quotation mark
„	&bdquo;	&#8222;	double low-9 quotation mark
‡	&dagger;	&#8225;	double dagger
‰	&permil;	&#8240;	per mille sign
‹	&lsaquo;	&#8249;	single left-pointing angle quotation mark*
›	&rsaquo;	&#8250;	single right-pointing angle quotation mark*
€	&euro;	&#8364;	euro sign
™	&trade;	&#8482;	trademark symbol

*Proposed but not yet ISO standardized.

Source: World Wide Web Consortium (**www.w3c.org**).

D

LANGUAGE AND COUNTRY CODES

Language and country codes play many vital roles on the Internet:

- **Language tags.** Language and country codes are used in HTML documents in the **LANG** tag to identify the content language.

- **ccTLDs.** Country codes are used in country code top-level domains (ccTLDs), as explained in Chapter 14, "Mastering Your (Country) Domain."

- **Content negotiation.** Language and country codes are used in the HTTP protocol to enable content negotiation between servers and browsers, as explained in Chapter 11, "World Wide Design."

- **Organization.** Language and country codes are used by web developers to efficiently organize and manage web content.

LANGUAGE CODES, COUNTRY CODES, AND LOCALES

Language and country codes were created by the Organization for International Standardization (ISO). ISO 639, *Codes for the representation of names of languages*, includes two parts: 639-1 and 639-2. Part 1 defines two-letter codes for 136 languages and Part 2 expands the number of languages included to 460, using three-letter codes. Because most companies use well under 50 languages on their web sites, 639-1 works perfectly well, but keep in mind that there are more than 6,000 spoken languages in the world. The SIL International (**www.sil.org**) has proposed a comprehensive list of language codes that effectively includes everything. For the time being, however, stick with the two-digit codes.

For countries, ISO 3166, *Codes for the representation of names of countries*, includes two-digit, three-digit, and numerical codes. In all, approximately 240 countries are represented; the total number is rarely static because countries are often merging or splitting. The most visible use of country codes are in top-level domains, such as **www.amazon.fr** or **www.novell.de**; the Internet Assigned Numbers Authority (IANA) manages the country codes as they apply to top-level domains.

Language and country codes are often used together to more accurately describe a language (such as fr-CA for the French spoken in Canada). They are also used to describe locales. The combination of language and country codes is an imperfect method of describing a language because languages are rarely located in just one region. For now, though, it's the best system we have. What follows are some of the more popular language/country pairs:

FYI

By convention, in language/country pairs, the language is written in lowercase, and the country in uppercase, with a hyphen or an underscore in between. Although an underscore is fine in HTML, be aware that XML requires that you use a hyphen separator.

Selected Language Codes/Locales

fr-FR	French France
fr-CA	French Canada
en-UK	English U.K.
en-US	English U.S.
de-DE	German Germany

ja-JP   Japanese Japan

ru-RU   Russian Russia

zh-CN   Chinese China (Simplified)

zh-TW   Chinese Taiwan (Traditional)

kr-KR   Korean Korea

it-IT   Italian Italy

pt-BR   Portuguese Brazil

pt-PT   Portuguese Portugal

es-MX   Spanish Mexico

es-ES   Spanish Spain

es-EC   Spanish Ecuador

fr-CH   French Switzerland

de-CH   German Switzerland

it-CH   Italian Switzerland

fr-BE   French Belgium

sv-SE   Swedish Sweden

fi-FI   Finnish Finland

en-ZA   English South Africa

he-IL   Hebrew Israel

501

FYI

HTML 4 defines the rules for language codes at **www.w3c.org/International/O-HTML-tags.html**.

Tables D.1 and D.2 include all current language and country codes. Please keep an eye on ISO for updates.

Table D.1 **Language Codes**

Language	ISO 639-1	ISO 639-2	Language	ISO 639-1	ISO 639-2
Afar	aa	aar	Balinese		ban
Abkhazian	ab	abk	Basque	eu	baq/eus
Achinese		ace	Basa		bas
Acoli		ach	Baltic (Other)		bat
Adangme		ada	Beja		bej
Afro-Asiatic (Other)		afa	Belarusian	be	bel
Afrihili		afh	Bemba		bem
Afrikaans	af	afr	Bengali	bn	ben
Akan		aka	Berber (Other)		ber
Akkadian		akk	Bhojpuri		bho
Albanian	sq	alb/sqi	Bihari	bh	bih
Aleut		ale	Bikol		bik
Algonquian languages		alg	Bini		bin
Amharic	am	amh	Bislama	bi	bis
English, Old (ca. 450–1100)		ang	Siksika		bla
Apache languages		apa	Bantu (Other)		bnt
Arabic	ar	ara	Tibetan	bo	bod/tib
Aramaic		arc	Bosnian	bs	bos
Armenian	hy	arm/hye	Braj		bra
Araucanian		arn	Breton	br	bre
Arapaho		arp	Batak (Indonesia)		btk
Artificial (Other)		art	Buriat		bua
Arawak		arw	Buginese		bug
Assamese	as	asm	Bulgarian	bg	bul
Athapascan languages		ath	Burmese	my	bur/mya
Australian languages		aus	Caddo		cad
Avaric		ava	Central American Indian (Other)		cai
Avestan	ae	ave	Carib		car
Awadhi		awa	Catalan	ca	cat
Aymara	ay	aym	Caucasian (Other)		cau
Azerbaijani	az	aze	Cebuano		ceb
Banda		bad	Celtic (Other)		cel
Bamileke languages		bai	Czech	cs	ces/cze
Bashkir	ba	bak	Chamorro	ch	cha
Baluchi		bal	Chibcha		chb
Bambara		bam	Chechen	ce	che

Language	ISO 639-1	ISO 639-2	Language	ISO 639-1	ISO 639-2
Chagatai		chg	Dutch	nl	dut/nld
Chinese	zh	chi/zho	Dyula		dyu
Chuukese		chk	Dzongkha	dz	dzo
Mari		chm	Efik		efi
Chinook jargon		chn	Egyptian (Ancient)		egy
Choctaw		cho	Ekajuk		eka
Chipewyan		chp	Greek, Modern	el	ell/gre
Cherokee		chr	(1453–present)		
Church Slavic	cu	chu	Elamite		elx
Chuvash	cv	chv	English	en	eng
Cheyenne		chy	English, Middle		enm
Chamic languages		cmc	(1100–1500)		
Coptic		cop	Esperanto	eo	epo
Cornish	kw	cor	Estonian	et	est
Corsican	co	cos	Basque	eu	eus/baq
Creoles and pidgins,		cpe	Ewe		ewe
English-based (Other)			Ewondo		ewo
Creoles and pidgins,		cpf	Fang		fan
French-based (Other)			Faroese	fo	fao
Creoles and pidgins,		cpp	Persian	fa	fas/per
Portuguese-based (Other)			Fanti		fat
Cree		cre	Fijian	fj	fij
Creoles and pidgins (Other)		crp	Finnish	fi	fin
Cushitic (Other)		cus	Finno-Ugrian (Other)		fiu
Welsh	cy	cym/wel	Fon		fon
Czech	cs	cze/ces	French	fr	fra/fre
Dakota		dak	French	fr	fre/fra
Danish	da	dan	French, Middle		frm
Dayak		day	(ca. 1400–1800)		
Delaware		del	French, Old		fro
Slave (Athapascan)		den	(842–ca. 1400)		
German	de	deu/ger	Frisian	fy	fry
Dogrib		dgr	Fulah		ful
Dinka		din	Friulian		fur
Divehi		div	Ga		gaa
Dogri		doi	Gayo		gay
Dravidian (Other)		dra	Gbaya		gba
Duala		dua	Germanic (Other)		gem
Dutch, Middle		dum	Georgian	ka	geo/kat
(ca.1050-1350)			German	de	ger/deu

503

continues

Table D.1 **Language Codes** **(Continued)**

Language	ISO 639-1	ISO 639-2	Language	ISO 639-1	ISO 639-2
Geez		gez	Interlingue	ie	ile
Gilbertese		gil	Iloko		ilo
Gaelic; Scottish Gaelic	gd	gla	Indic (Other)		inc
Irish	ga	gle	Indonesian	id	ind
Gallegan	gl	glg	Indo-European (Other)		ine
Manx	gv	glv	Inupiaq	ik	ipk
German, Middle High (ca. 1050–1500)		gmh	Iranian (Other)		ira
			Iroquoian languages		iro
German, Old High (ca. 750–1050)		goh	Icelandic	is	isl/ice
			Italian	it	ita
Gondi		gon	Javanese	jv	jav
Gorontalo		gor	Japanese	ja	jpn
Gothic		got	Judeo-Persian		jpr
Grebo		grb	Judeo-Arabic		jrb
Greek, Ancient (to 1453)		grc	Kara-Kalpak		kaa
Greek, Modern (1453–present)	el	gre/ell	Kabyle		kab
			Kachin		kac
Guarani	gn	grn	Kalaallisut	kl	kal
Gujarati	gu	guj	Kamba		kam
Gwich´in		gwi	Kannada	kn	kan
Haida		hai	Karen		kar
Hausa	ha	hau	Kashmiri	ks	kas
Hawaiian		haw	Georgian	ka	kat/geo
Hebrew	he	heb	Kanuri		kau
Herero	hz	her	Kawi		kaw
Hiligaynon		hil	Kazakh	kk	kaz
Himachali		him	Khasi		kha
Hindi	hi	hin	Khoisan (Other)		khi
Hittite		hit	Khmer	km	khm
Hmong		hmn	Khotanese		kho
Hiri Motu	ho	hmo	Kikuyu; Gikuyu	ki	kik
Croatian	hr	hrv/scr	Kinyarwanda	rw	kin
Hungarian	hu	hun	Kirghiz	ky	kir
Hupa		hup	Kimbundu		kmb
Armenian	hy	hye/arm	Konkani		kok
Iban		iba	Komi	kv	kom
Igbo		ibo	Kongo		kon
Icelandic	is	ice/isl	Korean	ko	kor
Ijo		ijo	Kosraean		kos
Inuktitut	iu	iku	Kpelle		kpe

Language	ISO 639-1	ISO 639-2	Language	ISO 639-1	ISO 639-2
Kru		kro	Irish, Middle (900–1200)		mga
Kurukh		kru			
Kuanyama	kj	kua	Micmac		mic
Kumyk		kum	Minangkabau		min
Kurdish	ku	kur	Miscellaneous languages		mis
Kutenai		kut	Macedonian	mk	mkd/mac
Ladino		lad	Mon-Khmer (Other)		mkh
Lahnda		lah	Malagasy	mg	mlg
Lamba		lam	Maltese	mt	mlt
Lao	lo	lao	Manchu		mnc
Latin	la	lat	Manipuri		mni
Latvian	lv	lav	Manobo languages		mno
Lezghian		lez	Mohawk		moh
Lingala	ln	lin	Moldavian	mo	mol
Lithuanian	lt	lit	Mongolian	mn	mon
Mongo		lol	Mossi		mos
Lozi		loz	Maori	mi	mri/mao
Letzeburgesch	lb	ltz	Malay	ms	msa/may
Luba-Lulua		lua	Multiple languages		mul
Luba-Katanga		lub	Munda languages		mun
Ganda		lug	Creek		mus
Luiseno		lui	Marwari		mwr
Lunda		lun	Burmese	my	mya/bur
Luo (Kenya and Tanzania)		luo	Mayan languages		myn
			Nahuatl		nah
Lushai		lus	North American Indian		nai
Macedonian	mk	mac/mkd	Nauru	na	nau
Madurese		mad	Navajo	nv	nav
Magahi		mag	Ndebele, South	nr	nbl
Marshall	mh	mah	Ndebele, North	nd	nde
Maithili		mai	Ndonga	ng	ndo
Makasar		mak	Low German; Low Saxon; German, Low; Saxon, Low		nds
Malayalam	ml	mal			
Mandingo		man			
Maori	mi	mao/mri	Nepali	ne	nep
Austronesian (Other)		map	Newari		new
Marathi	mr	mar	Nias		nia
Masai		mas	Niger-Kordofanian (Other)		nic
Malay	ms	may/msa	Niuean		niu
Mandar		mdr	Dutch	nl	nld/dut
Mende		men			

505

continues

Table D.1 **Language Codes** **(Continued)**

Language	ISO 639-1	ISO 639-2	Language	ISO 639-1	ISO 639-2
Norse, Old		non	Provençal, Old (to 1500)		pro
Norwegian	no	nor			
Norwegian Nynorsk; Nynorsk, Norwegian	nn	nno	Pushto	ps	pus
			Reserved for local use		qaa-qtz
Norwegian Bokmål; Bokmål, Norwegian	nb	nob	Quechua	qu	que
			Rajasthani		raj
Sotho, Northern		nso	Rapanui		rap
Nubian languages		nub	Rarotongan		rar
Chichewa; Nyanja	ny	nya	Romance (Other)		roa
Nyamwezi		nym	Racto-Romance	rm	roh
Nyankole		nyn	Romany		rom
Nyoro		nyo	Romanian	ro	ron/rum
Nzima		nzi	Romanian	ro	rum/ron
Occitan (post-1500); Provençal	oc	oci	Rundi	rn	run
			Russian	ru	rus
Ojibwa		oji	Sandawe		sad
Oriya	or	ori	Sango	sg	sag
Oromo	om	orm	Yakut		sah
Osage		osa	South American Indian (Other)		sai
Ossetian; Ossetic	os	oss			
Turkish, Ottoman (1500–1928)		ota	Salishan languages		sal
			Samaritan Aramaic		sam
Otomian languages		oto	Sanskrit	sa	san
Papuan (Other)		paa	Sasak		sas
Pangasinan		pag	Santali		sat
Pahlavi		pal	Serbian	sr	scc/srp
Pampanga		pam	Scots		sco
Panjabi	pa	pan	Croatian	hr	scr/hrv
Papiamento		pap	Selkup		sel
Palauan		pau	Semitic (Other)		sem
Persian, Old (ca. 600–400 B.C.)		peo	Irish, Old (to 900)		sga
			Sign languages		sgn
Persian	fa	per/fas	Shan		shn
Philippine (Other)		phi	Sidamo		sid
Phoenician		phn	Sinhalese	si	sin
Pali	pi	pli	Siouan languages		sio
Polish	pl	pol	Sino-Tibetan (Other)		sit
Pohnpeian		pon	Slavic (Other)		sla
Portuguese	pt	por	Slovak	sk	slk/slo
Prakrit languages		pra	Slovak	sk	slo/slk

Language	ISO 639-1	ISO 639-2	Language	ISO 639-1	ISO 639-2
Slovenian	sl	slv	Tlingit		tli
Northern Sami	se	sme	Tamashek		tmh
Sami languages (Other)		smi	Tonga (Nyasa)		tog
Samoan	sm	smo	Tonga (Tonga Islands)	to	ton
Shona	sn	sna	Tok Pisin		tpi
Sindhi	sd	snd	Tsimshian		tsi
Soninke		snk	Tswana	tn	tsn
Sogdian		sog	Tsonga	ts	tso
Somali	so	som	Turkmen	tk	tuk
Songhai		son	Tumbuka		tum
Sotho, Southern	st	sot	Turkish	tr	tur
Spanish; Castilian	es	spa	Altaic (Other)		tut
Albanian	sq	sqi/alb	Tuvalu		tvl
Sardinian	sc	srd	Twi	tw	twi
Serbian	sr	srp/scc	Tuvinian		tyv
Serer		srr	Ugaritic		uga
Nilo-Saharan (Other)		ssa	Uighur	ug	uig
Swati	ss	ssw	Ukrainian	uk	ukr
Sukuma		suk	Umbundu		umb
Sundanese	su	sun	Undetermined		und
Susu		sus	Urdu	ur	urd
Sumerian		sux	Uzbek	uz	uzb
Swahili	sw	swa	Vai		vai
Swedish	sv	swe	Venda		ven
Syriac		syr	Vietnamese	vi	vie
Tahitian	ty	tah	Volapük	vo	vol
Tai (Other)		tai	Votic		vot
Tamil	ta	tam	Wakashan languages		wak
Tatar	tt	tat	Walamo		wal
Telugu	te	tel	Waray		war
Timne		tem	Washo		was
Tereno		ter	Welsh	cy	wel/cym
Tetum		tet	Sorbian languages		wen
Tajik	tg	tgk	Wolof	wo	wol
Tagalog	tl	tgl	Xhosa	xh	xho
Thai	th	tha	Yao		yao
Tibetan	bo	tib/bod	Yapese		yap
Tigre		tig	Yiddish	yi	yid
Tigrinya	ti	tir	Yoruba	yo	yor
Tiv		tiv	Yupik languages		ypk
Tokelau		tkl			

507

continues

Table D.1 Language Codes (Continued)

Zapotec		zap
Zenaga		zen
Zhuang; Chuang	za	zha
Chinese	zh	zho/chi
Zande		znd
Zulu	zu	zul
Zuni		zun

Source: Organization for International Standardization (ISO). Please note ISO does not make its list freely available. To view ISO 639-1 and 639-2, go to **http://lcweb.loc.gov/standards/iso639-2/langcodes.html**.

Table D.2 Country Codes

Country	Code	Country	Code
Ascension Island	ac	Bolivia	bo
Andorra	ad	Brazil	br
United Arab Emirates	ae	Bahamas	bs
Afghanistan	af	Bhutan	bt
Antigua and Barbuda	ag	Bouvet Island	bv
Anguilla	ai	Botswana	bw
Albania	al	Belarus	by
Armenia	am	Belize	bz
Netherlands Antilles	an	Canada	ca
Angola	ao	Cocos (Keeling) Islands	cc
Antarctica	aq	Congo, Democratic Republic of the	cd
Argentina	ar	Central African Republic	cf
American Samoa	as	Congo, Republic of	cg
Austria	at	Switzerland	ch
Australia	au	Cote d'Ivoire	ci
Aruba	aw	Cook Islands	ck
Azerbaijan	az	Chile	cl
Bosnia and Herzegovina	ba	Cameroon	cm
Barbados	bb	China	cn
Bangladesh	bd	Colombia	co
Belgium	be	Costa Rica	cr
Burkina Faso	bf	Cuba	cu
Bulgaria	bg	Cap Verde	cv
Bahrain	bh	Christmas Island	cx
Burundi	bi	Cyprus	cy
Benin	bj	Czech Republic	cz
Bermuda	bm	Germany	de
Brunei Darussalam	bn	Djibouti	dj

Country	Code	Country	Code
Denmark	dk	Hungary	hu
Dominica	dm	Indonesia	id
Dominican Republic	do	Ireland	ie
Algeria	dz	Israel	il
Ecuador	ec	Isle of Man	im
Estonia	ee	India	in
Egypt	eg	British Indian Ocean Territory	io
Western Sahara	eh	Iraq	iq
Eritrea	er	Iran (Islamic Republic of)	ir
Spain	es	Iceland	is
Ethiopia	et	Italy	it
Finland	fi	Jersey	je
Fiji	fj	Jamaica	jm
Falkland Islands (Malvina)	fk	Jordan	jo
Micronesia, Federal State of	fm	Japan	jp
Faroe Islands	fo	Kenya	ke
France	fr	Kyrgyzstan	kg
Gabon	ga	Cambodia	kh
Grenada	gd	Kiribati	ki
Georgia	ge	Comoros	km
French Guiana	gf	Saint Kitts and Nevis	kn
Guernsey	gg	Korea, Democratic People's Republic of	kp
Ghana	gh		
Gibraltar	gi	Korea, Republic of	kr
Greenland	gl	Kuwait	kw
Gambia	gm	Cayman Islands	ky
Guinea	gn	Kazakhstan	kz
Guadeloupe	gp	Lao People's Democratic Republic	la
Equatorial Guinea	gq	Lebanon	lb
Greece	gr	Saint Lucia	lc
South Georgia and the South Sandwich Islands	gs	Liechtenstein	li
		Sri Lanka	lk
Guatemala	gt	Liberia	lr
Guam	gu	Lesotho	ls
Guinea-Bissau	gw	Lithuania	lt
Guyana	gy	Luxembourg	lu
Hong Kong	hk	Latvia	lv
Heard and McDonald Islands	hm	Libyan Arab Jamahiriya	ly
Honduras	hn	Morocco	ma
Croatia/Hrvatska	hr		
Haiti	ht		

continues

Table D.2 Country Codes (Continued)

Country	Code	Country	Code
Monaco	mc	Poland	pl
Moldova, Republic of	md	St. Pierre and Miquelon	pm
Madagascar	mg	Pitcairn Island	pn
Marshall Islands	mh	Puerto Rico	pr
Macedonia, Former Yugoslav Republic	mk	Palestinian Territories	ps
		Portugal	pt
Mali	ml	Palau	pw
Myanmar	mm	Paraguay	py
Mongolia	mn	Qatar	qa
Macau	mo	Reunion Island	re
Northern Mariana Islands	mp	Romania	ro
Martinique	mq	Russian Federation	ru
Mauritania	mr	Rwanda	rw
Montserrat	ms	Saudi Arabia	sa
Malta	mt	Solomon Islands	sb
Mauritius	mu	Seychelles	sc
Maldives	mv	Sudan	sd
Malawi	mw	Sweden	se
Mexico	mx	Singapore	sg
Malaysia	my	St. Helena	sh
Mozambique	mz	Slovenia	si
Namibia	na	Svalbard and Jan Mayen Islands	sj
New Caledonia	nc	Slovak Republic	sk
Niger	ne	Sierra Leone	sl
Norfolk Island	nf	San Marino	sm
Nigeria	ng	Senegal	sn
Nicaragua	ni	Somalia	so
Netherlands	nl	Suriname	sr
Norway	no	Sao Tome and Principe	st
Nepal	np	El Salvador	sv
Nauru	nr	Syrian Arab Republic	sy
Niue	nu	Swaziland	sz
New Zealand	nz	Turks and Caicos Islands	tc
Oman	om	Chad	td
Panama	pa	French Southern Territories	tf
Peru	pe	Togo	tg
French Polynesia	pf	Thailand	th
Papua New Guinea	pg	Tajikistan	tj
Philippines	ph	Tokelau	tk
Pakistan	pk	Turkmenistan	tm

Country	Code
Tunisia	tn
Tonga	to
East Timor	tp
Turkey	tr
Trinidad and Tobago	tt
Tuvalu	tv
Taiwan	tw
Tanzania	tz
Ukraine	ua
Uganda	ug
United Kingdom	uk
U.S. Minor Outlying Islands	um
United States	us
Uruguay	uy
Uzbekistan	uz
Holy See (City of Vatican State)	va
Saint Vincent and the Grenadines	vc
Venezuela	ve
Virgin Islands (British)	vg
Virgin Islands (USA)	vi
Vietnam	vn
Vanuatu	vu
Wallis and Futuna Islands	wf
Western Samoa	ws
Yemen	ye
Mayotte	yt
Yugoslavia	yu
South Africa	za
Zambia	zm
Zimbabwe	zw

Source: Organization for International Standardization (ISO),
http://www.iso.org/iso/en/prods-services/iso3166ma.

511

E

ENCODINGS

The chart in this appendix includes some of the more common encodings, or "charsets," used to represent languages. Charsets are included in <META> tags within HTML documents, as well as in header files sent between servers, web browsers, and email clients. The purpose of the charset is to ensure that all software applications understand the encoding of the text so that they can properly manipulate and display it.

In an HTML file, the **charset** declaration should appear in a **<META>** tag, as close to the top of the page as possible. Most English-language web developers should be accustomed to the following **<META>** tag:

`<meta http-equiv="content-type" content="text/html; charset=iso-8859-1">`

To represent a different language or script, such as Japanese, the **iso-8859-1** would be replaced by **shift-jis**. Note that the declarations are not case sensitive, but are conventionally entered in lowercase characters. No spaces are allowed.

Technically, the **charset** declaration is an encoding, not a character set. This distinction becomes an issue with scripts that have one character set but many encodings. Unicode, for example, is a character set with more than one encoding: UTF-8, UTF-16, UTF-32. The **charset** declaration would be not be **unicode** but rather **utf-8**. For the most part, however, a character set and encoding are one and the same, and referred to as a "coded character set."

When using the chart in Table E.1, you'll notice that often more than one charset is available. In most cases, you'll want to use the ISO charset, but not always. In the future, web sites will rely more on the Unicode character set, effectively replacing this entire list with the following encoding:

`<meta http-equiv="content-type" content="text/html; charset=utf-8">`

Table E.1   Languages and Corresponding Charsets

Language	Charset
Afrikaans	iso-8859-1, windows-1252
Albanian	iso-8859-1, windows-1252
Arabic	iso-8859-6, windows-1256
Basque	iso-8859-1, windows-1252
Bulgarian	iso-8859-5
Catalan	iso-8859-1, windows-1252
Celtic	iso-8859-14
Chinese (Simplified)	gb2312, euc-cn, hz-gb-2312, gbk, gb18030
Chinese (Traditional)	big5, euc-tw
Czech	iso-8859-2
Danish	iso-8859-1, windows-1252

Language	Charset
Dutch	iso-8859-1, windows-1252
English	iso-8859-1, windows-1252
Estonian	iso-8859-15
Finnish	iso-8859-1, windows-1252
French	iso-8859-1, windows-1252
German	iso-8859-1, windows-1252
Greek	iso-8859-7, windows-1253
Hebrew	iso-8859-8
Hungarian	iso-8859-2
Icelandic	iso-8859-1
Italian	iso-8859-1, windows-1252
Japanese	shift-jis, iso-2022-jp, euc-jp
Latvian	iso-8859-13, windows-1257
Lithuanian	iso-8859-13, windows-1257
Macedonian	iso-8859-5
Norwegian	iso-8859-1, windows-1252
Polish	iso-8859-2
Portuguese	iso-8859-1, windows-1252
Romanian	iso-8859-2
Russian	iso-8859-5, koi8-r
Scottish	iso-8859-1, windows-1252
Serbian	iso-8859-5
Slovak	iso-8859-2
Slovenian	iso-8859-2
Spanish	iso-8859-1, windows-1252
Swedish	iso-8859-1, windows-1252
Thai	windows-874, tis-620
Turkish	iso-8859-9, windows-1254
Ukrainian	iso-8859-5, koi8-u
Vietnamese	windows-1258
All major languages	utf-8, utf-16, utf-32 (Unicode)

Source: World Wide Web Consortium (**www.w3c.org**).

FYI

HTML encoding names are maintained by the Internet Assigned Numbers Authority (IANA). To view the complete list, go to **http://www.iana.org/assignments/character-sets**.

F

INTERNATIONAL NOTATION STANDARDS

Different countries and cultures have different ways of displaying numbers, times, and dates; some have different calendars altogether. This appendix highlights some of the differences in notation standards around the world as well as the movement to standardize date and time notation.

2/6/02 OR 6/2/02?

In the U.K., 2/6/02 means June 2, 2002, but in the U.S., it means February 6, 2002—the source of immeasurable international confusion over the years. What makes notation particularly confusing is that a country can have more than one acceptable standard. In the U.S., you might see a date represented as 2/6/02; February 6, 2002; or even 2-6-2002. Fortunately, operating systems have grown increasingly sophisticated at dealing with notation issues. To see how Office XP tackles notation, go to Control Panel, Regions and Languages. Figure F.1 illustrates how notation is changed based on different locales.

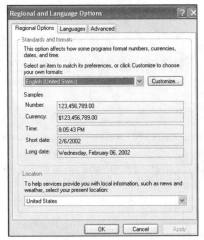

Figure F.1   Adjusting regional preferences in Microsoft Office XP.

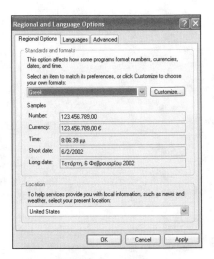

Table F.1 includes a selection of locales from Microsoft Office XP. Note how inconsistent even the display of currencies is between European countries such as Germany and Italy. Even though they now share the same currency (the euro), they have a different way of displaying it.

Table F.1 **Selected Notation Standards**

Country	Number	Currency	Date	Time
English (U.S.)	123,456,789.00	$123,456,789.00	2/6/2002	8:10:00 PM
English (U.K.)	123,456,789.00	£123,456,789.00	6/2/2002	20:10:00
English (New Zealand)	123,456,789.00	$123,456,789.00	6/2/2002	8:10:00 p.m.
English (South Africa)	123,456,789.00	R 123,456,789.00	2/6/2002	8:10:00 PM
Spanish (Spain)	123.456.789,00	123.456.789,00 €	6/2/2002	20:10:00
Spanish (Chile)	123.456.789,00	$ 123.456.789,00	6/2/2002	20:10:00
Spanish (Uruguay)	123.456.789,00	$U 123.456.789,00	6/2/2002	08:10:00 p.m.
Spanish (Mexico)	123,456,789.00	$123,456,789.00	6/2/2002	08:10:00 p.m.
German	123.456.789,00	123.456.789,00 €	06.02.2002	20:10:00
Italy	123.456.789,00	€ 123.456.789,00	6/2/2002	20.10.00
French (France)	123 456 789,00	123 456 789,00 €	6/2/2002	20:10:00
French (Canada)	123 456 789,00	123 456 789,00 $	2/6/2002	20:10:00
Norwegian	123 456 789,00	kr 123 456 789,00	06.02.2002	20:10:00
Russian	123 456 789,00	123 456 789,00R.	06.02.2002	20:10:00
Romanian	123.456.789,00	123.456.789,00 lei	06.02.2002	20:10:00
Swedish	123 456 789,00	123.456.789,00 kr	2/6/2002	20:10:00
Poland	123 456 789,00	123 456 789,00 zl	2/6/2002	20:10:00
Japanese	123,456,789.00	¥123,456,789	2/6/2002	20:10:00
China (PRC)	123,456,789.00	¥123,456,789.00	2/6/2002	20:10:00
Slovak	123 456 789,00	123 456 789,00 Sk	6.2.2002	20:10:00
Thai	123,456,789.00	฿123,456,789.00	6/2/2545*	20:10:00
Turkish	123.456.789,00	123.456.789,00 TL	06.02.2002	20:10:00
Urdu	123,456,789.00	Rs123,456,789.00	06/2/2002	8:10:00 PM
Belarusian	123 456 789,00	123 456 789,00 p.	06.02.2002	20:10:00
Bulgarian	123 456 789,00	123 456 789,00 ЛВ	06.2.2002 г	20:10:00
English (South Africa)	123,456,789.00	R 123,456,789.00	2/6/2002	8:10:00 PM
Hebrew	123,456,789.00	₪ 123,456,789.00	06/2/2002	20:10:00
Albanian	123.456.789,00	123.456.789,00Lek	2/6/2002	8:10:00.MD
Icelandic	123.456.789,00	123.456.789,00 kr.	6.2.2002	20:10:00

519

Source: Microsoft Office XP

*The Thai calendar is calculated from the beginning of the Buddhist Era (BE) in 543 B.C.

STANDARDIZING TIME AND DATE NOTATION

The International Organization for Standardization (ISO) has created a standard method of representing dates and times (ISO 8601). The standard relies on a simple philosophy: Keep the larger units of measure to the left. In other words, the years and the hours stay to the left; the days and the seconds stay to the right. Here are the templates:

Date: **YYYY-MM-DD**

Example: 2002-02-08 to indicate February 8, 2002.

Time: **hh:mm:ss**

Example: 20:10:00 to indicate 8:10 p.m.

The ISO standard is an important step toward global usability, but as you can see in Table F.1, it hasn't gained worldwide acceptance yet. Time notation is clearly getting more consistent, but dates still have a long way to go.

FYI

For more information on international time and date notation, go to:

http://www.cl.cam.ac.uk/~mgk25/iso-time.html

http://www.twinsun.com/tz/tz-link.htm

INDEX

B

527

537

J

M

543

T

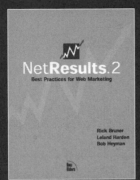

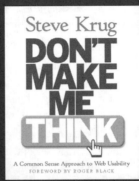

VOICES THAT MATTER

HOW TO CONTACT US

VISIT OUR WEB SITE

WWW.NEWRIDERS.COM

On our web site, you'll find information about our other books, authors, tables of contents, and book errata. You will also find information about book registration and how to purchase our books, both domestically and internationally.

EMAIL US

Contact us at: **nrfeedback@newriders.com**

- If you have comments or questions about this book
- To report errors that you have found in this book
- If you have a book proposal to submit or are interested in writing for New Riders
- If you are an expert in a computer topic or technology and are interested in being a technical editor who reviews manuscripts for technical accuracy

Contact us at: **nreducation@newriders.com**

- If you are an instructor from an educational institution who wants to preview New Riders books for classroom use. Email should include your name, title, school, department, address, phone number, office days/hours, text in use, and enrollment, along with your request for desk/examination copies and/or additional information.

Contact us at: **nrmedia@newriders.com**

- If you are a member of the media who is interested in reviewing copies of New Riders books. Send your name, mailing address, and email address, along with the name of the publication or web site you work for.

BULK PURCHASES/CORPORATE SALES

The publisher offers discounts on this book when ordered in quantity for bulk purchases and special sales. For sales within the U.S., please contact: Corporate and Government Sales (800) 382-3419 or **corpsales@pearsontechgroup.com**. Outside of the U.S., please contact: International Sales (317) 581-3793 or **international@pearsontechgroup.com**.

WRITE TO US

New Riders Publishing
201 W. 103rd St.
Indianapolis, IN 46290-1097

CALL/FAX US

Toll-free (800) 571-5840
If outside U.S. (317) 581-3500
Ask for New Riders
FAX: (317) 581-4663

New Riders

WWW.NEWRIDERS.COM

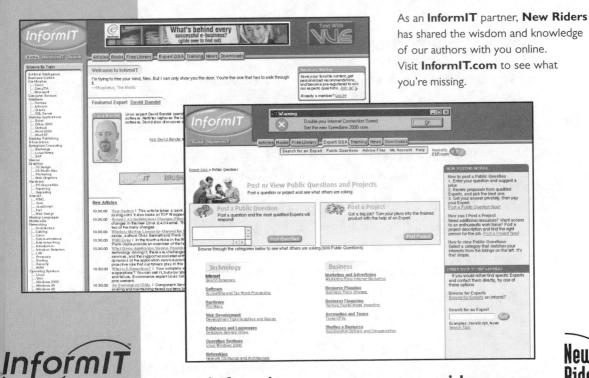

Publishing the Voices that Matter

OUR AUTHORS

PRESS ROOM

| web development | design | photoshop | new media | 3-D | server technologies |

EDUCATORS

ABOUT US

CONTACT US

You already know that New Riders brings you the **Voices that Matter**.

But what does that mean? It means that New Riders brings you the

Voices that challenge your assumptions, take your talents to the next

level, or simply help you better understand the complex technical world

we're all navigating.

Visit **www.newriders.com** to find:

- ▸ **10% discount** and **free shipping** on all book purchases
- ▸ Never before published chapters
- ▸ Sample chapters and excerpts
- ▸ Author bios and interviews
- ▸ Contests and enter-to-wins
- ▸ Up-to-date industry event information
- ▸ Book reviews
- ▸ Special offers from our friends and partners
- ▸ Info on how to join our User Group program
- ▸ Ways to have your Voice heard

New Riders

WWW.NEWRIDERS.COM